COMPLEXITIES

COMPLEXITIES

Beyond Nature & Nurture

Edited by Susan McKinnon *&* Sydel Silverman

THE UNIVERSITY OF CHICAGO PRESS · CHICAGO AND LONDON

Susan McKinnon is associate professor of anthropology at the University
of Virgina and the author of *Shattered Sun: Hierarchy, Gender, and Alliance
in the Tanimbar Islands* and co-editor of *Relative Values: Reconfiguring
Kinship Studies.*

Sydel Silverman is president emerita of the Wenner-Gren Foundation
for Anthropological Research and professor emerita of anthropology at
the City University of New York. She is the author or editor of several
books, including *The Beast on the Table: Conferencing with Anthropologists*
and *Totems and Teachers: Key Figures in the History of Anthropology.*

The University of Chicago Press, Chicago 60637
The University of Chicago Press, Ltd., London
© 2005 by The University of Chicago
All rights reserved. Published 2005
Printed in the United States of America

14 13 12 11 10 09 08 07 06 05   5 4 3 2 1

ISBN (cloth): 0-226-50023-3
ISBN (paper): 0-226-50024-1

Library of Congress Cataloging-in-Publication Data

Complexities : beyond nature and nurture / edited by Susan McKinnon
and Sydel Silverman.
      p.   cm.
   Includes bibliographical references and index.
   ISBN 0-226-50023-3 (cloth : alk. paper) — ISBN 0-226-50024-1
(pbk. : alk. paper)
   1. Anthropology.   2. Physical anthropology.   3. Anthropological
linguistics.   4. Anthropology, Prehistoric.   I. McKinnon, Susan,
1949–   II. Silverman, Sydel.
   GN27.C648   2005
   301—dc22   2004020978

♾ The paper used in this publication meets the minimum requirements
of the American National Standard for Information Sciences—
Permanence of Paper for Printed Library Materials, ANSI Z39.48-1992.

CONTENTS

PREFACE

THE IDEA FOR THIS BOOK had its origin in a Wenner-Gren Foundation conference that took place in November 1999 in Cabo San Lucas, Mexico. The conference—"Anthropology at the End of the Century"—was intended to be a means of reflecting upon anthropology at the millennial transition.[1] One of us (Silverman) was about to retire as president of the foundation and conceived the notion of bringing together the organizers of the twenty-five or so symposia she had overseen during the thirteen years just past. Because the symposia were designed to identify cutting-edge issues or problems, assess the state of knowledge, and chart future courses of research, and because they ranged over the four subfields of anthropology, it seemed that they could be used as a window on anthropology at the turn of the millennium.

The group that came together was diverse, in terms of the subfields and specialties that were included: ten cultural anthropologists, three archaeologists, two linguists, and seven biological anthropologists (two primatologists, three evolutionary morphologists, and two human biologists). Many of the participants were skeptical about whether they would have anything to talk about beyond the shared frustrations of their experiences as symposium organizers. Others thought that, at best, we would have a parade of presentations on each of the areas or topics included. All of us were wrong.

Over and over, lines of common interest emerged concerning issues that

1. Participants in the conference were Timothy Bromage, Linda Fedigan, William Foley, Kathleen Gibson, Nina Glick Schiller, Alan Goodman, John Gumperz, Gilbert Herdt, Thomas Leatherman, Shirley Lindenbaum, Margaret Lock, William McGrew, Susan McKinnon, Barbara Miller, James A. Moore, John H. Moore, Mary Ellen Morbeck, Nancy Parezo, Anna Roosevelt, Sydel Silverman, Carla Sinopoli, and Donald Tuzin.

resonated in different fields, cut across specialties, and exposed shared assumptions and problems. Even those who were the least persuaded that the traditional four-field organization of American anthropology was still viable (if ever it was) came away with a strong sense that the subfields had a great deal to say to one another and indeed needed one another.

As the sessions unfolded, several themes emerged, but it immediately became clear that the one theme that resonated most strongly with all of us was that of complexity—the need to incorporate complexity into our accounts and the struggle to find ways of problematizing, analyzing, and writing about complexity. William Foley, for instance, described his symposium's goal of refashioning linguistics away from hegemonic models that invoked a language instinct and toward an approach that takes account of linguistic diversity, structured variation in language use, and the complexities of language as social practice. Over the course of the conference, the complexity theme was articulated in contrast to reductionism—those theories and explanatory accounts that reduce phenomena to some presumably more "basic" level. Whether the discussions were of human biological variation or sexuality, of genes or transnationalism, participants from one subfield after another spoke of the challenges posed by reductionisms of different kinds. For the most part, these reductionist trends originated from outside anthropology, but all our conferees were alarmed at how firm a hold they had taken in both academic and public life and at how feeble the response had been from anthropologists.

The conference exposed the urgent need for anthropology as a discipline to address reductive accounts of social life, both critically and publicly. As a first step, Susan McKinnon, Alan Goodman, and William Foley together conceived the idea of a panel—"Anthropology United: Challenging Biosocial Reductivisms in the Academy, Popular Media, and Public Policy"—which convened at the November 2000 meeting of the American Anthropological Association, whose theme was, coincidentally, "The Public Face of Anthropology." In addition to the three organizers, four other participants in the original Wenner-Gren conference (Gilbert Herdt, Margaret Lock, John Gumperz, and Nina Glick Schiller) gave presentations; three other papers were added (by Jonathan Marks, by Thomas Patterson, and a joint paper by Mary Orgel, Jacqueline Urla, and Alan Swedlund); and Sydel Silverman served as discussant. Buoyed by the evident interest in the topic addressed by the panel, several of us agreed that it was worth pursuing publication, and two of us took on the task of editing a volume. To balance the representation of the subfields and bring in related issues, we solicited additional contributions from Eve Danziger, Kathleen Gibson, Katherine MacKinnon and Agustín Fuentes, Lynn Meskell, Mary Moran, and Karen-Sue Taussig.

Complexities unites scholars from the four subfields of anthropology to articulate a concerted challenge to the range of reductionisms prevalent today not only in the academy but also in the contemporary media and in policy debates. It is our belief that, given its distinctive disciplinary configuration, American anthropology is uniquely positioned for this kind of critical engagement with one of the most controversial questions of our time: how we are to understand human diversity and complexity and use that understanding in the social worlds within which we live.

Introduction

Susan McKinnon & Sydel Silverman

*C*OMPLEXITIES BRINGS TOGETHER a united and multifaceted argument from the four fields of anthropology to challenge the current resurgence of reductive theories of human biological and social life and to offer accessible alternatives to them. Numerous reductive accounts of biosocial life have ricocheted through the academy, the media, and public discourse in recent years. Daily we read assertions that everything from disease to intelligence—not to mention the presumed characteristics of gender, race, and sexuality—can be explained mainly by reference to biology and, more specifically, genetics. We are told that our human nature was fixed forever in the Pleistocene. We are asked to believe that utilitarian principles of individual self-maximization are sufficient to explain the multiplicity of human cultural forms. And we repeatedly witness the political economy of averages, ideals, and standardizations that stigmatize biological, cultural, and linguistic diversity.

We do not argue against all reductionism. On the contrary, we believe that reductionist strategies have their uses in the sciences, and that the search for universal and shared qualities of human existence is a valuable scientific goal. We do, however, question some of the ways in which reductive and universalizing accounts of human biological and social life have been constructed. First, we see as problematic those constructions that begin from the presupposition that what is essential, and therefore true, is to be found through the isolation and study of the smallest or most fundamental units. In the case of humans, those units are increasingly understood to be genes. It is thus assumed that the major features of human biosocial life must be biologically—or genetically—determined. This assumption has two consequences: it fails to contextualize human existence within the larger and variable cultural and political-economic forces that shape it; and it reduces to genetics many characteristics and processes that have social origins.

Another difficulty stems from the fact that specific Euro-American ideas about the world are often presumed to be universal, simply a reflection of "the way things work." This occurs when one particular (Euro-American) manifestation of what is known by anthropologists to be culturally vari-able—for instance, notions of gender difference—is raised to the level of a universal. This ethnocentrism derives from limited knowledge about the historical and contemporary diversity of human societies, cultures, and languages.

Such supposed universals, moreover, are often naturalized[1] through the claim that they are part of a human biological repertoire rooted in deep evo-lutionary time. Contemporary Euro-American understandings of social categories and processes are treated as given in nature, by reference to our presumed similarities to other species and to mythologized notions of hu-man evolution. Culturally specific understandings are thus projected back into human prehistory and, having thereby assumed the authority of time-lessness, are subsequently used to validate contemporary relations.

Complexities mobilizes anthropological knowledge of human diversity and biosocial complexity in order to challenge both the reductionism of these accounts and their implications for public life. In doing so, we do not intend merely to rehearse the long-standing debate over nature versus nur-ture. The issues in that debate have by no means been resolved, and it con-tinues to be necessary to bring anthropological understandings of cultural variation and contingency to bear on the recurrent claims that "biology is destiny." However, we believe that the contrast is, in fact, a false one. Nei-ther nature nor nurture exists without the other. On the one hand, what we understand as "nature" is culturally defined, and the so-called givens of na-ture come into being only through developmental processes that unfold within environments—from the intrauterine to the culturally created en-vironments in which humans live out their life cycles. On the other hand, "nurture" operates on an array of organic entities, from genes and mole-cules to whole organisms and ecosystems, which have evolved throughout the history of our species. That nature and nurture are inextricably linked, constituting a continually interactive set of processes, is now widely ac-cepted in principle. What we know too little about is what is involved in that interaction. The task before us—and the larger goal of this book—is to probe the complexities in the nature/nurture linkage.

It is our contention that the most productive way of proceeding with this task is to bring the four subdisciplines of anthropology—social or cultural anthropology, linguistic anthropology, archaeology, and biological anthropology—into dialogue with one another. Essentializing arguments tend to interweave analogies of biology, language, psychology, political economy, and history into mutually reinforcing narratives, which can best be teased apart by analyses that draw on the expertise of all four fields. We are particularly interested in tracing the ways in which the varieties of reductionism are read into and through one another and mutually authorize one another, so as to create seamless and seemingly objective accounts of the nature of the world, human experience, and social life.

Any claim to universality rests upon cross-cultural validation. However, many of the reductive accounts that are challenged in this volume were produced by people with little cross-cultural or historical expertise: they are linguists who have never studied a language other than English; they are social scientists who assert universals about gender and kinship without knowledge of any system of gender or kinship except their own; they are animal behaviorists who impute cultural traits to insects and birds but have never grappled with the intricacies of a human culture; they are psychologists who construct evolutionary myths of origin without having worked on a prehistoric site or confronted the difficulties of historical interpretation.

Anthropologists approach the study of human universals and diversity in a fundamentally different way. For one thing, they spend a lot of time in the "field." They learn to speak and use other languages; they live for extended periods of time in other cultures to comprehend their workings; they excavate prehistoric sites to see what can and cannot be said about evolution and the human past; and they study nonhuman primates in natural habitats to learn about the behavior of our nearest evolutionary relatives. This does not mean that anthropologists have unmediated access to truth, but it gives them a head start on appreciating and analyzing the complexities of social phenomena. Most importantly, encounters with the variable structures of human social life have compelled anthropologists to develop an idea of culture that is not reducible to human biology and psychology. Rather, anthropologists think of culture as the result of a creative process that yields diverse understandings about the nature of the world that both shape and are shaped by the ongoing negotiations of people's lives. In what follows, we develop these arguments as they unfold over the four parts of the book.

Sociobiology and Evolutionary Psychology

Recent years have seen a rash of proposed models of human evolution in the writings of scientists and in the popular media that reduce evolutionary processes to a few simple principles and attempt to explain contemporary behavior and social patterns by assuming their universality and then locating them in this presumed evolutionary past. The most prominent of these models have come from sociobiology and its offspring, evolutionary psychology. Because these approaches receive a great deal of attention in the present collection, it is worth a closer look at their premises and proposals.

The reductive accounts of sociobiology and evolutionary psychology are popular not because they have discovered the true foundation of human behavior but because they validate culturally specific Euro-American understandings about human nature and social life. These accounts do indeed provide a "new synthesis," as Edward O. Wilson (1975) called it, one that draws different strands of reductionism—biogenetic, economic, and evolutionary—into a single thread. Human behavior and mental capabilities are understood to be directed by the action of genes; genes are seen to operate in accordance with utilitarian economic principles; and the economic logic of genetic determinism is understood to have been fixed in an original environment of evolutionary adaptation and to have remained virtually unchanged over time and across cultures. This multistranded reductionism is given form in the presumption that there are certain universals of the human mind (language, perception, etc.), of human characteristics (e.g., gender), and of social forms (e.g., kinship and marriage). The totality is a myth of origin that is compelling precisely because it resonates strongly with Euro-American presuppositions about the nature of the world.

In the landmark book that ushered in sociobiology, Wilson (1975) proposed that social behavior in all species was a product of natural selection governed by Darwinian principles of reproductive competition. The book had only a single, final chapter devoted to humans, but Wilson's approach was picked up by many—both in a range of academic disciplines and in public discourse—and taken as explanatory of human behavior. In anthropology it was especially influential in primatology (where it was transformed into behavioral ecology), in human evolutionary studies, and among a subset of "neo-Darwinian" cultural anthropologists and archaeologists. Other anthropologists, while acknowledging the evolutionary basis of human behavioral patterns, took strong issue with the erasure of cultural variability and of social and historical context in the application of this approach to humans (see, e.g., Sahlins 1976).

Evolutionary psychology took hold about a decade later than its forerunner. Broadly speaking, "evolutionary psychology" has referred to the study of the evolution of mental capacities and mental processes (and the social behaviors that manifest them), but the term has come to be associated with a particular approach to that study.[2] This new evolutionary psychology builds on the older sociobiology in its view that the mind (like social behavior) is as much a material phenomenon as are anatomical and physiological features and is subject to the same evolutionary forces. The mind (with its psychological characteristics), no less than the brain where it resides, is an evolved "organ." Evolutionary psychology shares with sociobiology the presumption that discrete items of contemporary human behavior can be matched with counterparts in prehistoric humans and in other species. As in sociobiology, it is assumed that each such item can be assigned a function that made it adaptive in some past evolutionary stage. The explosion of genetic and neuroscience research added a further twist: the idea that each item is represented by a particular gene (or genetic complex) and a specific neurological structure, or "module," in the brain.

The project of evolutionary psychology, in the end, is an attempt to find a thumbnail biological-evolutionary explanation for every conceivable feature of modern life: from divorce rates to ethnic cleansing in the former Yugoslavia to why powerful men dump their first wives for younger models. It is the subject of frequent media features with titles like "Infidelity: It's in Your Genes," "Is There a Gene for Compassion?" and "The Biology of Violence." Although some anthropologists have been part of this project—either as researchers and advocates or through the (selective) citations of their work— most anthropologists are highly critical of its assumptions and implications.

This volume addresses several of the central tenets of evolutionary psychology: the idea that humans have fixed, genetically determined mental structures; the notion that these mental structures developed as adaptations to a particular environment in which our species is presumed to have evolved; the assumption that one can unproblematically draw analogies between human and animal behavior; and the presupposition that it is possible to explain human nature without reference to culture and, conversely, that culture can be explained by reference to genetically determined mental modules developed in the evolutionary past.

Challenging Reductive Theories of Mind

Part 1 of the book considers the presumptions of evolutionary psychologists concerning the mind. While sociobiologists limited their scope to behavior and did not claim to penetrate the mind, evolutionary psychologists consider themselves experts not only on the behavior of humans but also— drawing on cognitive psychology and linguistics—on their minds. In the work of John Tooby and Leda Cosmides, "the adapted mind" is construed as made up of a series of modules or design features in the brain (Tooby and Cosmides 1992; see also Buss 1991, 1999). Each of these was selected for, they surmise, because it solved a specific problem in the evolutionary past (an undifferentiated "Pleistocene"). Their method is to start by proposing cognitive items they think constitute modules, such as social exchange, sexual jealousy, kin recognition, cheating detection, and self-esteem. Each item is assigned a function and an adaptive value that it "must" have had during the Pleistocene. Since the modules are assumed to be lodged in the modern brain, the psychologist can study them by devising cognitive-performance tests using contemporary samples (usually their undergraduate students) as subjects. If the results of tests purporting to reflect one or another module match expectations, then the whole theoretical apparatus is declared to be supported. The neuroscience of the brain and the genetic underpinnings (the "hardwiring") are imputed; they are not studied directly. (For a critique of evolutionary psychology, see the essays in Rose and Rose 2000.)

In chapter 1, Kathleen Gibson uses evidence from paleoanthropology, contemporary research on human and other mammalian brains, and developmental psychology to examine two assumptions of this approach to mind: that there are genetically determined, functionally specific modules that evolved to solve particular adaptive problems; and that these adaptations were responses to features of an "environment of evolutionary adaptation." Gibson demonstrates, following Richard Potts and others (Potts 1996, 1998; see also Fausto-Sterling 2000a; Gould 2000), that the actual environments in which human ancestors evolved were highly variable, dynamic, and fluctuating. The neural mechanisms that evolved in humans put a premium on versatility and on the capacity to respond to diverse contexts and novel conditions. In other words, selection favored open programs of behavior and cognition, the very opposite of the discrete function-specific modules of evolutionary psychology. Gibson goes on to connect the evidence for the evolutionary plasticity of the human brain with recent findings in brain research. These findings indicate that the human brain can best be conceptualized as a generalized learning and problem-solving device, whose creative potential and functional specializations are developed over a lifetime through continual environment-gene interactions.

Evolutionary psychology rests upon an argument for innate mental structures that draws upon a particular development within the discipline of linguistics. Under the influence of Noam Chomsky during the 1960s, mainstream linguistics came to be dominated by a deductive formalism aimed at a universalizing theory of mind (Chomsky 1965, 1971). This model stood in contrast to those of the linguistic subdiscipline of anthropology, which was concerned with natural language seen as communicative activity occurring within and shaped by sociocultural contexts (Hymes 1964, 1974; Gumperz and Hymes 1972; Gumperz 1982a, 1982b; Duranti and Goodwin 1992). The distinction between formalist linguistics and linguistic anthropology ran along several lines. First, the two had different objectives: formal linguistics aimed to understand the mental structures underlying the competence for language, whereas linguistic anthropology sought to comprehend the way human beings use language to construct, and act within, meaningful socio-cultural worlds. Second, their databases were radically different: formal linguistics narrowed its scope to a few well-known languages, especially English, which it took to be paradigmatic of all languages; linguistic anthropologists, in contrast, sought the widest possible range of natural languages, particularly non-Western ones, whose structures they found not to be universally reducible to those of English. Third, formal linguistics moved ever closer to the cognitive sciences, which shared a commitment to seeking universals of mind and cognition, whereas linguistic anthropologists explored a range of culturally specific understandings of mind and cognition. (For discussion of these trends, see Gumperz 1965; Durbin 1967; Foley 1993, 1997.)

Linguistic anthropology has a long history of attending to the linguistic diversity of the world, the social construction and use of language, and the cultural specificity of perception and cognition. Building upon the work of earlier anthropologists such as Franz Boas ([1911] 1966, 1940), Bronislaw Malinowski (1923, [1935] 1965), Edward Sapir (1921, 1949), and Benjamin Whorf (1956), linguistic anthropologists have produced a wealth of materials that document the variety of language structures and the complexities in the social uses of language. In recent years, these anthropologists have been joined by a number of linguists and psychologists in seeking alternatives to formal approaches through attention to linguistic practices and to the social construction of language and cognition (e.g., Gumperz and Levinson 1996). Taken together, the long history of linguistic anthropology and the new studies of language practice and cognition pose significant challenges to the universalistic presuppositions of formal linguistics.

William Foley (chapter 2) and Eve Danziger (chapter 3) powerfully articulate this challenge in relation to language structure and the intersection of language and cognition. Foley argues against the Universal Grammar of formal linguistics and the manner in which it is used by evolutionary psychologists in their claims for innate mental structures. The claim for an innate Universal Grammar depends, of course, upon a demonstration that language universals exist. Examining a range of Austronesian and Native American languages, Foley shows that one commonly presupposed linguistic universal—the distinction between nouns and verbs—is, in fact, not universal at all. In attending to a wide array of extant languages, Foley exposes the poverty of linguistic theories that generalize from a few Western languages. By undermining the validity of a Universal Grammar and therefore of fixed, genetically determined, and universal mental structures, Foley makes a persuasive case for the considerable plasticity of human linguistic and mental capabilities.

Danziger extends the discussion of linguistic universals to categorization and sensory perception. Cognitive linguists have argued that linguistic categories do not simply name objective and preexisting units of reality but rather derive from human experience with the world. However, Danziger suggests that this argument relies upon a particular idea of "experience," one that presupposes that human sensory and perceptual experience is natural and universal—both outside of and underlying cultural categorization. Thus, for cognitive linguists, it is sufficient for researchers to rely upon their intuitions about sensory perception, since these are presumed to be precultural and universal. Drawing on linguistic studies of the Mopan Maya, Danziger demonstrates how both linguistic categorizations and sensory perceptions come to feel, for their users, like an objective reflection of preexisting reality. Her material makes it evident that even the perceptual intuitions we have about physical orientation in space are neither natural nor universal but instead are culturally acquired, and therefore culturally variable. Danziger's chapter, like Foley's, shows that close attention to actual languages and cultures—both methodologically and theoretically—is crucial if we are to understand human cognitive capabilities.

The Limits of Universal Models: Gender and Kinship

Part 2 of the book focuses on the manner in which particular Euro-American understandings have been elevated to the status of universals, which are presumed to underlie and explain the varieties of human experience. These so-called universals are reductive because they assume that a set of culturally specific ideas are actually objective descriptions of fundamental categories that apply to all times and all cultures, thereby erasing the distinctiveness of other historical and cultural understandings of the world.

The chapters in this part explore how such universals have been invoked in certain scenarios of human evolution and prehistory, focusing, in particular, on gender and kinship.[3] The authors use knowledge gained by several subdisciplines of anthropology: primatology, which points to both productive uses and misuses of comparisons between human and nonhuman primates; cultural anthropology, which demonstrates the diversity of gender and kinship across societies; biological anthropology, which offers perspectives on reproductive strategies; and archaeology, which expands the database of cultural variability into the prehistoric past.

We begin with the issue of generalization from animal to human behavior. Both sociobiologists and evolutionary psychologists refer extensively to studies of animal behavior, but their approaches are somewhat different. Sociobiologists generally begin with lower species and only later attempt to extend their findings to humans, while evolutionary psychologists start with the presumption that human nature can be deduced intuitively, or inferred from study of a few humans, and then explained by analogy with other animals. However, both approaches phrase analogies in similar ways, using the categories of human sociality (promiscuity, altruism, and the like) to describe the behavior of other species such as birds and insects.

In chapter 4, Katherine MacKinnon and Agustín Fuentes call into question facile generalizations from animal behavior to humans by considering the evidence on nonhuman primates—the animals most likely to be relevant to humans. They examine two themes—male aggression and dominance—that have been prominent in primate studies and have been used to argue for the innate, universal nature of specific characteristics of human gender, sexuality, and kinship. Their review of recent field research reveals, however, that the wide array of primate species displays a high degree of variability and flexibility. There are diverse primate behavioral patterns, not a single one, even among our nearest cousins, the chimpanzees. Evidence from primatology does not, therefore, support either the innateness or the universality of features of gender, sexuality, or kinship among primates, let alone among humans (see also Marks 2002). If analogies from our closest evolutionary kin are problematic, then those from more distant species are much more so.

Observations of nonhuman primates demonstrate behavioral variability; in humans, such variability is magnified enormously by the operation of culture, which endows all social relationships with symbolic meaning. The accounts of evolutionary psychologists erase not only the distinctive features of the human brain—its flexibility and creativity—but also the results of its symbolic capacity, namely human culture. In chapter 5, Susan McKinnon considers one area of human activity that lies at the core of evolutionary psychology: kinship and marriage. In light of extensive cross-cultural evidence, McKinnon demonstrates that the diversity and complexity of human systems of kinship and marriage can be neither comprehended nor predicted by the genetic calculus and ethnocentric presuppositions about gender that are central to evolutionary psychologists' arguments. Indeed, categories of kinship and marriage are shaped by cultural understandings that everywhere transcend the genetic logic and the gendered preference mechanisms that evolutionary psychologists presume are universal. McKinnon goes on to use the evidence of kinship and marriage to make a case for a theory of mind and of culture that accounts for, rather than explains away, the facts of human creativity.

One of the key pieces of "evidence" that evolutionary psychologists use to argue for gender asymmetries in reproductive strategies is the waist-to-hip ratio (WHR). Evolutionary psychologists assume that differential parental investment results in divergent "mating" strategies: males seek reproductively fit females, while females seek financially fit males. Given these differential reproductive strategies, males supposedly evolved psychological "preference mechanisms" (which ultimately became genetically encoded) for those traits in females—including a low WHR—that signal health, fertility, and reproductive availability. In chapter 6, Mary Orgel, Jacqueline Urla, and Alan Swedlund challenge the universality of the WHR argument on the grounds that it does not hold up cross-culturally: it is contradicted by the diversity both of ideas of attractiveness and of existing body types. Moreover, in conflating preference with actual body types, the WHR hypothesis assumes rather than proves the evolutionary link between them. The authors make the point that by positing hardwired, "evolved" traits such as the WHR, evolutionary psychologists naturalize contemporary understandings of sex and gender, which are made to seem as if they have been fixed for all time, independent of cultural differences or historical transformations.

In chapter 7, Lynn Meskell takes up a similar theme of idealized womanhood but in an archaeological context, which impels her to confront the problems inherent in reading the evidence for ideas about gender in prehistory. Meskell demonstrates how particular Euro-American notions about gender—as well as ideological commitments to a theory of an original matriarchy—have shaped and skewed the conclusions that classical archaeologists and certain feminists have drawn from the prehistoric site of Çatalhöyük in present-day Turkey. To the extent that particular gender characteristics are taken to be natural—and therefore extended uncritically across epochs—it will be impossible, Meskell argues, to construct an archaeology of gender that is sensitive to cultural difference and historical variability. To demonstrate her point, Meskell contrasts the accounts of gender at Çatalhöyük given by earlier archaeologists and by New Age feminists with those of contemporary archaeologists who have studied the site.

Once evidence from the various branches of anthropology is examined, it becomes clear that historical narratives such as those created by evolutionary psychologists have not uncovered the universal foundations of gender and kinship but have assembled myths of origins out of the specificities of Euro-American understandings. Such myths serve to validate the normativity of those understandings, but they are not supported by what we know about nonhuman-primate and human social life.

Putting Genes in Context

Nowhere has reductionism been more prominent, both in scientific analyses and in public discourse, than in the use of genetics as the primary principle of explanation of all that is human. This is most striking in contemporary biomedical approaches to the causes and treatment of disease.

Genetics has been a factor in our understanding of human characteristics ever since Gregor Mendel's principles of inheritance, which were rediscovered at the beginning of the twentieth century, were seen as applying to humans as well as to other species. With the discovery of the structure of DNA in the 1950s, genetic research advanced rapidly. Its progress culminated in the inauguration of the Human Genome Project around 1990, a massive investment of public resources (joined by private entrepreneurs) in an effort to sequence the entire genome of the human species. The project did not invent biological determinism—which has been with us from the hereditarian and racial theories that had their origins before the twentieth century to more recent versions—but it gave impetus to a trend already under way. As genetics became more sophisticated, and especially with the mapping of the human genome, biological determinism increasingly became genetic determinism (Lewontin, Rose, and Kamin 1984; Lewontin 1991, 2000; Marks 1995).

The use of genetics is not necessarily genetic determinism. Indeed, anthropology has made highly productive use of the revolution in genetics. Genetic analysis was first employed by anthropologists to trace population affinities and histories using specific inherited traits (such as the ABO blood types). With the evolutionary synthesis of the 1940s, the "old" (typological) physical anthropology gave way to a "new" approach, which included population genetics as an integral part of the study of evolutionary change (see Washburn 1951). In this approach, genes were understood to be in dynamic interplay with external factors shaping natural selection—as, for example, in Frank Livingstone's study (1958) of the selective advantage of the gene for sickle-cell anemia in malarial environments. The actual genes that were considered in such analyses were limited to those few that seemed to conform to simple patterns of Mendelian inheritance.

Advances in genetics from the 1980s on opened up enormous new possibilities for research in many areas of anthropology. In primatology, the new technology for amplifying DNA made it possible to pursue a number of problems that heretofore had to be approached through indirect strategies. In paleoanthropology, the "molecular clock" provided an independent time scale against which the fossil record could be interpreted. In archaeology and human biology, genetic methodologies have been especially valuable in the study of population histories and relationships. Cultural anthropologists have begun to examine the social impact of genetics in such areas as disease etiology, new reproductive technologies, and transgenic organisms; their studies are leading to the reconfiguration of much of the subject matter of this subdiscipline—for example, in approaches to kinship and in medical anthropology. At the same time, each of these research endeavors has encountered difficult issues—theoretical, methodological, and ethical—and has raised as many problems of interpretation and practice as it has solved.

This work has highlighted the extent to which genetic "information" is shaped by and interwoven with social practices and cultural interpretations. Thus, anthropologists and other social scientists have become troubled by the growing tendency to treat genetics as an all-purpose explanation (Nelkin and Lindee 1995; Hubbard and Wald 1999; Goodman, Heath, and Lindee 2003). It is this genetic determinism that is addressed by a number of the authors in this book. They argue that, where humans are concerned, the action and significance of genes cannot be understood in isolation but only in relation to social and cultural contexts.

In part 3, the focus is on how genetics enters into and is modulated by the interplay of multiple factors in health and disease. Thomas Leatherman and Alan Goodman (chapter 8) begin by reviewing the kinds of reductionism that have dominated biological anthropology in the past. They make the case that a more adequate biocultural approach must place human biology in relation to wider political-economic and cultural forces. They challenge the persistence of the idea of race-as-biology in the study of disease, which reduces complex processes to a few genetically determined factors. They then offer a case study of nutrition, health, and the growing incidence of obesity and diabetes in Maya communities in the Yucatan that have been impacted by tourism-led development, and they suggest a different way of grasping the interconnection between human biology and the physical and social environment. The example argues for situating human genetics and biology not only within familial and epidemiological histories but also within the political economy of national and global flows of culture and capital.

In chapter 9, Margaret Lock takes up the theme of reductionism and holism in the study of illness by looking at the complex "tangle" that constitutes what we now term Alzheimer's disease. She examines what she calls the "internalizing" and "externalizing" discourses that surround the efforts of scientists and clinicians to understand this condition. On the one hand, internalizing discourses, at their most extreme, see genes as independent and self-replicating entities; in Alzheimer's disease, faulty gene replication is internal to the individual body, and the cure is some sort of gene therapy. On the other hand, externalizing discourses emphasize the need to contextualize any genetic component of the disease within patterns of social behavior and in relation to the larger social, political, economic, and environmental factors that contribute to ill health. Such externalizing discourses focus on prevention and on causal pathways as well as on therapies. Lock argues that despite representations in the popular media, geneticists themselves recognize the complex causality of Alzheimer's disease, and they shy away from reductive, internalizing discourses. Indeed, both Lock and the geneticists she interviewed stress that, particularly in this era following the mapping of the human genome, genetic determinism cannot be sustained: only through the careful analysis of the interactions among genes, proteins, social behavior, and social and environmental factors will it be possible to comprehend a disease like Alzheimer's.

Karen-Sue Taussig develops this point in chapter 10 by exploring the struggles over genetic materials, knowledge, and clinical practice that are taking place at the intersection of scientific research agendas, corporate interests, medical activism, and people's embodied experiences of disease. In the discourses of genetic medicine, there is a tension between the assumption that genetic knowledge, in itself, will lead directly to successful medical interventions and the reality that translating genetic knowledge into effective clinical interventions will depend upon linking genes to persons, families, and medical and epidemiological histories. Using examples from contemporary research on the human genome and genetic medicine, Taussig considers a range of strategies that are being developed to make genetic materials scientifically meaningful and clinically useful. In addition, Taussig claims, the social relations that are constructed through these strategies—relations among researchers, corporations, and human subjects—will be critical not only for the agency of human subjects but also for our very ideas about what counts as an acceptable human being.

The Politics of Reductionism

Reductive accounts of human nature and social life have become a part of the political discourse in our society. Such accounts are regularly invoked in talk about issues ranging from welfare, marriage, child care, and the family to nutrition, disease, mental illness, health care, insurance, and business ethics. They are at the center of contemporary discussions of contraception, birth, abortion, and the new reproductive technologies and of the uses of innovations in biotechnology. They are pervasive in debates about the rights of various categories of social persons and cultural groups and about policies concerning immigration, migration, and international relations, as well as labor, language, and education. On the one hand, these reductive accounts naturalize certain human qualities and present a fixed and unchanging human nature, which then is taken as a guidepost to the right and proper organization of society. On the other hand, by erasing the variability among human groups or ascribing that variability to underlying natural essences, they deflect any attempt at analysis of cultural and historical processes. In these ways, they readily become the justification for political beliefs and policies that support social inequalities, exclude certain categories of people or practices from full recognition in public life, or treat "others" (both within our society and in the world outside it) according to their place in a presumed order of nature.

Several of the chapters in parts 1–3 of this book touch on the implications of reductionist accounts for such issues of public life. The chapters in part 4 focus specifically on some of the ways that reductionist notions enter into contemporary politics. These chapters select three different themes from the array of relevant issues to illustrate how anthropological analysis attempts to confront the complexity of social life as it is played out in the contemporary world.

In chapter 11, Mary Moran takes up the crucial matter of how Americans think about foreign affairs—specifically, how they are encouraged to understand violence and warfare in the non-Western world. She considers, in particular, the naturalizing assumptions about so-called tribal and ethnic warfare in the "New Barbarism" hypothesis promoted by some contemporary political analysts and much favored by policy makers. This hypothesis holds that cultural identity is stable and unchanging and that the clash of identities ("ancient tribal hatreds") inevitably leads to conflict. Reviewing the history of recent violence in Africa, especially Liberia, and citing anthropological studies of warfare in a range of cases from Guatemala to Sri Lanka, Moran comes to a different conclusion: local rivalries and lines of stratification—which rarely conformed to "ethnic" divisions and were not "relics of the past"—were transformed into "tribal" or "clan" warfare in recent historical contexts, often as a result of changes initiated from outside. She criticizes the misrepresentation of the anthropological concept of culture and argues that all human beings, not only supposedly prerational peoples, are "rooted in culture." She shows that the New Barbarism hypothesis and similar notions are based on a systematic misunderstanding of both culture and history.

Language policies, no less than those governing other areas of social and political life, have often been shaped by reductionist assumptions. In chapter 12, John Gumperz and Jenny Cook-Gumperz examine the process whereby certain languages were declared to be "national languages" or the standard of correct speech at the expense of all other language varieties in the society. This process, which was part of historical nation-building projects, continues in the present—for instance, in the English-only movement in the United States. The chapter traces the relationship between language standardization and the dominance of certain traditions in linguistics, which imposed a form of reductionism by treating language as an innate mental structure and as an abstract system of grammar divorced from any social context. New approaches in linguistic anthropology, however, are looking at language as communicative practices situated in real-life contexts. Thus, they are able to address issues of power and ideology in language use and to throw light on current debates over governmental and educational policy.

Finally, in chapter 13, Nina Glick Schiller considers how people in the contemporary world themselves use naturalizing ideas about biological ancestry and biological connectedness—the very ideas that have had such destructive effects in many times and places in history and at present and that anthropologists have repeatedly argued against. In looking at this phenomenon among Haitians who are using metaphors of "blood" to construct a new form of nationalism, Glick Schiller faces a central conundrum in anthropology: the reductionism that we reject on analytic grounds is often employed as a strategic tool by the people we study. It behooves the anthropologist to understand people's uses of such ideologies even while criticizing the assumptions inherent in them. Glick Schiller takes a historical view of the link between biological ideologies (originally "race") and nationalisms of different kinds. In the nineteenth century, myths of peoplehood— referring to those united by "blood"—were invoked in nation-building projects, in much the same way as standard languages were employed. After World War II, the language of race disappeared from most nationalist rhetoric, but as globalization advanced, "blood" reappeared as a means of creating identity among populations dispersed from their homelands. She examines such "long-distance nationalisms" and analyzes several sets of actors who use metaphors of biological belonging for their diverse political agendas. Glick Schiller concludes that we cannot just dismiss such ideologies as erroneous but must come to grips with the conditions that lead the disempowered to embrace them in their struggles.

This collection does not claim to represent the whole of anthropological opinion, nor—we reiterate—is it critical of all theories that employ reductionism. We recognize that there are legitimate theoretical differences among anthropologists about what constitutes productive reductionism, whether as ultimate explanation or as methodological strategy. What we wish to challenge are reductionisms of various kinds that neglect all that we have learned about the complexities of human cultural and biological processes—complexities that are severely violated by their reduction to some supposedly more basic level.

As we wrote this introduction, a new book by Steven Pinker, *The Blank Slate: The Modern Denial of Human Nature* (2002), was released to considerable media fanfare. And we listened as metaphors that combine genetic and evolutionary reductionism continued to reverberate in public discourse, surfacing in the most unlikely places. A television network executive who was discussing his programming strategy noted that the pattern of "people watching together . . . goes back to the early DNA encoding of humans who gathered around the campfire to tell stories" (*New York Times,* September 22, 2002). A nature writer observing the power-lunch crowd at an upscale Manhattan restaurant explained why he was doing it: "We're genetically programmed to be interested in what the rich do." And he added, "I thought about trying to . . . pretend to be one of them, but it wasn't going to work. . . . The built-in system we have for detecting cheaters would have showed me up pretty quickly" (*New York Times,* October 13, 2002). In *Complexities,* we contest such cartoon representations of human nature and the so-called scientific claims of works such as *The Blank Slate.*

In waging their battle against those they claim deny human nature and those who challenge certain reductionisms, genetic determinism, and innatism, Pinker and his colleagues (among them most of the evolutionary psychologists cited in this book) offer their own ideas as to what the innate traits of the mind might be. Pinker pays lip service to the notion of cultural variability, stating that "familiar categories of behavior—marriage customs, food taboos, folk superstitions, and so on—certainly do vary across cultures and have to be learned." But he goes on to claim that "the deeper mechanisms of mental computation that generate them may be universal and innate" (Pinker 2002: 39). Apart from the hypothetical assertion ("may be"), there are two problems with this formulation. First, no "deeper mechanisms" have ever been demonstrated to underlie variable cultural behavior, nor have any "generative" mechanisms been discovered. Second, those whom Pinker cites with approval often treat particular "marriage customs, food taboos, folk superstitions, and so on" as if they were universal, not variable. There is a slipperiness in the way such claims are made. When asked for specifics of "innate social behavior," Pinker lists such items as the primacy of family ties and a propensity to share—qualities that, when expressed in these general terms, no anthropologist would dispute. Innate abilities, for Pinker, include undeniable human capacities such as language and a sense of space and number (*New York Times,* September 17, 2002). As generalities, these are all true enough but unsurprising. However, as soon as they are translated into specifics—for instance, specific features of language as opposed to "language," or particular exchange or marriage systems as opposed to the "propensity to share" or "to mate"—they become more novel but also highly dubious. As in many efforts to depict human universals, the items are either true but vacuous, or interesting but wrong.

Complexities questions not only the reductionisms of Pinker and his colleagues but also their distorted representations of the anthropological view of human nature as a "sacred doctrine" that "the mind has no innate traits" but exists as a "blank slate." Far from a denial of human nature, *Complexities* is an affirmation of human nature as the product of our species' evolutionary trajectory and as rooted in a continual interplay of biological and cultural processes. In our view, the essence of human nature is a brain that has been selected for adaptability and plasticity. It is also in the nature of humans to be fundamentally and intensely social and to exist—always and everywhere—within networks of social relations and webs of cultural meanings that they both shape and are shaped by.

Such a view of human capabilities requires that we go beyond any simple opposition between nature and nurture. In working toward this kind of understanding of our species, the authors of this volume contest unwarranted reductionisms and affirm what anthropology has learned—through a century of research—about the complexity and diversity of human life.

Notes

1. For a discussion of the process of naturalization, see Yanagisako and Delaney 1995.

2. Among the more prominent proponents of this particular brand of evolutionary psychology are David Buss, Leda Cosmides, Martin Daly, Richard Dawkins, Steven Pinker, Harvey Plotkin, Donald Symons, John Tooby, and Margo Wilson. See Barkow, Cosmides, and Tooby 1992; Buss 1991, 1992, 1994, 1999, 2000; Cosmides and Tooby 1992; Daly and Wilson 1988, 1999; Dawkins 1976; Jones 1999; Pinker 1994, 1997, 2002; Plotkin 1998; Symons 1979, 1995; Tooby and Cosmides 1989, 1992; Wilson and Daley 1992; and Wright 1994.

3. Researchers in anthropology and other disciplines have long questioned the presumption that categories such as gender are natural and universal, as cross-cultural and historical studies have demonstrated that such categories are highly variable in different cultures. A long series of feminist works in anthropology questioned the seemingly universal subordination of women (Rosaldo and Lamphere 1974; Reiter 1975; Schlegel 1977) and, subsequently, the presupposition that there are universal characteristics of gender (MacCormack and Strathern 1980; Ortner and Whitehead 1981). This work demonstrated that characteristics of gender that had been assumed to be natural and universal were, in the end, Euro-American understandings writ large (Collier and Yanagisako 1987; Yanagisako and Delaney 1995). The field of sci-

ence studies further revealed how science has played a key role in validating the naturalization of gender (Fausto-Sterling 1985, 2000b), and similar deconstructive work has exposed the assumptions underlying categories of race (Harding 1993), sexuality (Herdt 1984, 1994, 1997, 1999; LeVay 1996), and kinship (Schneider 1980; Collier and Yanagisako 1987; Franklin and McKinnon 2001).

References

Barkow, Jerome H., Leda Cosmides, and John Tooby, eds. 1992. *The Adapted Mind: Evolutionary Psychology and the Generation of Culture.* New York: Oxford University Press.

Boas, Franz. [1911] 1966. *Introduction to the Handbook of American Indian Languages.* Lincoln: University of Nebraska Press. (Published with J. W. Powell, *Indian Linguistic Families of America North of Mexico,* ed. Preston Holder.)

———. 1940. *Race, Language, and Culture.* New York: Free Press.

Buss, David M. 1991. Evolutionary Personality Psychology. *Annual Review of Psychology* 42: 459–91.

———. 1992. Mate Preference Mechanisms: Consequences for Partner Choice and Intrasexual Competition. In Barkow, Cosmides, and Tooby 1992: 249–66.

———. 1994. *The Evolution of Desire: Strategies of Human Mating.* New York: Basic Books.

———. 1999. *Evolutionary Psychology: The New Science of the Mind.* Boston: Allyn and Bacon.

———. 2000. *The Dangerous Passion: Why Jealousy Is as Necessary as Love and Sex.* New York: Free Press.

Chomsky, Noam. *Aspects of a Theory of Syntax.* Cambridge: MIT Press.

———. 1971. *Syntactic Structures.* The Hague: Mouton.

Collier, Jane Fishburne, and Sylvia Junko Yanagisako, eds. 1987. *Gender and Kinship: Essays toward a Unified Analysis.* Stanford: Stanford University Press.

Cosmides, Leda, and John Tooby. 1992. Cognitive Adaptations for Social Exchange. In Barkow, Cosmides, and Tooby 1992: 163–228.

Daly, Martin, and Margo Wilson. 1988. *Homicide.* Hawthorn, NY: Aldine de Gruyter.

———. 1999. *The Truth about Cinderella: A Darwinian View of Parental Love.* New Haven: Yale University Press.

Dawkins, Richard. 1976. *The Selfish Gene.* New York: Oxford University Press.

Duranti, Alessandro, and Charles Goodwin. 1992. *Rethinking Context: Language as an Interaction Phenomenon.* Cambridge: Cambridge University Press.

Durbin, Marshall. 1967. Language. In *Biennial Review of Anthropology,* ed. Bernard J. Siegel and Alan R. Beals, pp. 209–57. Stanford: Stanford University Press.

Fausto-Sterling, Anne. 1985. *Myths of Gender: Biological Theories about Women and Men.* New York: Basic Books.

———. 2000a. Beyond Difference: Feminism and Evolutionary Psychology. In Rose and Rose 2000: 209–28.

———. 2000b. *Sexing the Body: Gender Politics and the Construction of Sexuality.* New York: Basic Books.

Foley, William. 1997. *Anthropological Linguistics: An Introduction.* Oxford: Blackwell.

Foley, William, ed. 1993. *The Role of Theory in Language Description.* Berlin: Mouton de Gruyter.

Franklin, Sarah, and Susan McKinnon, eds. 2001. *Relative Values: Reconfiguring Kinship Studies.* Durham, NC: Duke University Press.

Goodman, Alan, Deborah Heath, and Susan Lindee, eds. 2003. *Genetic Nature/Culture: Anthropology and Science beyond the Two Culture Divide.* Berkeley and Los Angeles: University of California Press.

Gould, Stephen Jay. 2000. More Things in Heaven and Earth. In Rose and Rose 2000: 101–26.

Gumperz, John J. 1965. Language. In *Biennial Review of Anthropology,* ed. Bernard J. Siegel, pp. 84–120. Stanford: Stanford University Press.

———. 1982a. *Discourse Strategies.* Cambridge: Cambridge University Press.

———, ed. 1982b. *Language and Social Identity.* Cambridge: Cambridge University Press.

Gumperz, John J., and Dell H. Hymes, eds. 1972. *Directions in Sociolinguistics: The Ethnography of Communication.* New York: Holt, Rinehart, and Winston.

Gumperz, John J., and Stephen Levinson, eds. 1996. *Linguistic Relativity.* Cambridge: Cambridge University Press.

Harding, Sandra, ed. 1993. *The "Racial" Economy of Science: Toward a Democratic Future.* Bloomington: Indiana University Press.

Herdt, Gilbert. 1984. *Ritualized Homosexuality in Melanesia.* Berkeley and Los Angeles: University of California Press.

———. 1997. *Same Sex, Different Cultures: Perspectives on Gay and Lesbian Lives.* New York: Westview Press.

———. 1999. *Sambia Sexual Culture: Essays from the Field.* Chicago: University of Chicago Press.

Herdt, Gilbert, ed. 1994. *Third Sex, Third Gender: Beyond Sexual Dimorphism in Culture and History.* New York: Zone Books.

Hubbard, Ruth, and Elijah Wald. 1999. *Exploding the Gene Myth.* Boston: Beacon Press.

Hymes, Dell H. 1974. *Foundations in Sociolinguistics: An Ethnographic Approach.* Philadelphia: University of Pennsylvania Press.

Hymes, Dell H., ed. 1964. *Language in Culture and Society: A Reader in Linguistics and Anthropology.* New York: Harper Row.

Jones, Doug. 1999. Evolutionary Psychology. *Annual Review of Anthropology* 28: 553–75.

LeVay, Simon. 1996. *Queer Science: The Use and Abuse of Research into Homosexuality.* Cambridge: MIT Press.

Lewontin, Richard C. 1991. *Biology as Ideology: The Doctrine of DNA.* New York: Harper-Perennial.

———. 2000. *It Ain't Necessarily So: The Dream of the Human Genome and Other Illusions.* New York: New York Review of Books.

Lewontin, Richard C., Steven Rose, and Leon J. Kamin. 1984. *Not in Our Genes: Biology, Ideology, and Human Nature.* New York: Pantheon.

Livingstone, Frank B. 1958. Anthropological Implications of Sickle Cell Gene Distribution in West Africa. *American Anthropologist* 60: 533–62.

MacCormack, Carol, and Marilyn Strathern, eds. 1980. *Nature, Culture and Gender.* Cambridge: Cambridge University Press.

Malinowski, Bronislaw. 1923. The Problem of Meaning in Primitive Languages. In *The Meaning of Meaning,* ed. C. K. Ogden and I. A. Richards, pp. 451–510. London: K. Paul, Trench, Trubner.

———. [1935] 1965. *Coral Gardens and Their Magic.* Vol. 2, *The Language of Magic and Gardening.* Bloomington: Indiana University Press.

Marks, Jonathan. 1995. *Human Biodiversity: Genes, Race, and History.* New York: Aldine de Gruyter.

———. 2002. *What It Means to Be 98% Chimpanzee.* Berkeley and Los Angeles: University of California Press.

Nelkin, Dorothy, and M. Susan Lindee. 1995. *The DNA Mystique: The Gene as a Cultural Icon.* New York: W. H. Freeman.

Ortner, Sherry B., and Harriet Whitehead, eds. 1981. *Sexual Meanings: The Cultural Construction of Gender and Sexuality.* Cambridge: Cambridge University Press.

Pinker, Steven. 1994. *The Language Instinct.* New York: HarperCollins.

———. 1997. *How the Mind Works.* New York: Norton.

———. 2002. *The Blank Slate: The Modern Denial of Human Nature.* New York: Viking.

Plotkin, Harvey. 1998. *Evolution in Mind: An Introduction to Evolutionary Psychology.* Cambridge: Harvard University Press.

Potts, Richard. 1996. *Humanity's Descent: The Consequences of Ecological Instability.* New York: William Morrow and Co.

———. 1998. Variability Selection in Hominid Evolution. *Evolutionary Anthropology* 7: 81–96.

Reiter, Rayna. 1975. *Toward an Anthropology of Women.* New York: Monthly Review Press.

Rosaldo, Michelle Zimbalist, and Louise Lamphere, eds. 1974. *Women, Culture, and Society.* Stanford: Stanford University Press.

Rose, Hilary, and Steven Rose, eds. 2000. *Alas, Poor Darwin: Arguments against Evolutionary Psychology.* New York: Harmony Books.

Sahlins, Marshall. 1976. *The Use and Abuse of Biology.* Ann Arbor: University of Michigan Press.

Sapir, Edward. 1921. *Language.* New York: Harcourt, Brace and World.

———. 1949. *Selected Writings of Edward* Sapir. Edited by David Mandelbaum. Berkeley and Los Angeles: University of California Press.

Schlegel, Alice, ed. 1977. *Sexual Stratification: A Cross-cultural View.* New York: Columbia University Press.

Schneider, David M. 1980. *A Critique of the Study of Kinship.* Ann Arbor: University of Michigan Press.

Symons, Donald. 1979. *The Evolution of Human Sexuality.* New York: Oxford University Press.

———. 1995. Beauty Is in the Adaptations of the Beholder: The Evolutionary Psychology of Human Female Sexual Attractiveness. In *Sexual Nature, Sexual Culture,* ed. Paul R. Abramson and Steven D. Pinkerton, pp. 80–118. Chicago: University of Chicago Press.

Tooby, John, and Leda Cosmides. 1989. The Innate versus the Manifest: How Universal Does Universal Have to Be? *Behavioral and Brain Sciences* 12: 36–37.

———. 1992. The Psychological Foundations of Culture. In Barkow, Cosmides, and Tooby 1992: 19–136.

Washburn, Sherwood L. 1951. The New Physical Anthropology. *Transactions of the New York Academy of Sciences* 13(2): 261–63.

Whorf, Benjamin Lee. 1956. *Language, Thought, and Reality: Selected Writings of Benjamin Lee Whorf,* ed. John B. Carroll. Cambridge: MIT Press.

Wilson, Edward O. 1975. *Sociobiology: The New Synthesis.* Cambridge: Harvard University Press.

Wilson, Margo, and Martin Daly. 1992. The Man Who Mistook His Wife for a Chattel. In Barkow, Cosmides, and Tooby 1992: 289–326.

Wright, Robert. 1994. *The Moral Animal: Evolutionary Psychology and Everyday Life.* New York: Vintage Books.

Yanagisako, Sylvia Junko, and Carol Delaney, eds. 1995. *Naturalizing Power: Essays in Feminist Cultural Analysis.* New York: Routledge.

PART I

---

*Challenging
Reductive Theories
of Mind*

CHAPTER 1

Epigenesis, Brain Plasticity, and Behavioral Versatility: Alternatives to Standard Evolutionary Psychology Models

Kathleen R. Gibson

CREATIVITY, VERSATILITY, and advanced learning capacities are primary hallmarks of the human mind. Our species inhabits six continents that encompass environments as diverse as the Arctic, the tropical rain forest, and the Australian outback. Individual humans routinely move between different climatic zones and cultures, and they readily adapt to the dramatic technological and social changes that now occur within individual life spans. Moreover, in less than ten thousand years, a mere blink of the eye in evolutionary terms, much of the human world has moved from a hunter-gatherer to a postindustrial lifestyle, all the while exhibiting such extraordinary reproductive success that our very numbers now threaten the planet. These accomplishments reflect the ability of humans, working individually or in groups, to devise novel solutions to new environmental challenges and to transmit these solutions to others through social learning processes.

This human behavioral versatility stands in contrast to prominent evolutionary psychology models that posit that the human brain is neither a generalized learning device nor a generalized problem-solving device. Rather, it is assumed to consist of numerous domain-specific, genetically determined neural processing modules designed to solve highly specific problems encountered during human evolution (Fodor 1983; Irons 1998) or, more specifically, during the Pleistocene hunter-gatherer environment of evolutionary adaptation (the EEA) (Barkow, Cosmides, and Tooby 1992). Cosmides and Tooby, for example, hypothesize that the human brain has numerous distinct mental modules related to social intelligence, including probable innate "cheater detector," "theory of mind" (the ability to infer others' intentions and thoughts), and "reciprocal altruism" modules (Cosmides and Tooby 1992; Tooby and Cosmides 1992). Similarly, Pinker (1994) and

Chomsky (1972) inform us that our brains possess innate syntactic capacities that are unrelated to other cognitive and intellectual skills, that indeed there may be a specific language gene (cf. Foley, chapter 2, this volume).

Evolutionary psychology models have distinct strengths, especially the recognition that humans are biological beings whose behavioral capacities evolved under natural selection and are mediated by neurological, genetic, and other biological mechanisms. Standard evolutionary psychology models (SEPMs), however, ignore the well-established genetic and developmental principles of pleiotropy (individual genes have multiple phenotypic effects) and epigenesis (phenotypic traits reflect genetic and environmental interactions during development). Thus, they often inappropriately generalize from phenotype to genotype and are inherently flawed in the scientific sense. This chapter summarizes evidence that, rather than being a collection of highly specific, genetically determined mental modules, the human brain is a highly plastic organ that develops functional specialization over the course of a lifetime through interactions between environmental and genetic effects. It also examines evidence that the human brain was designed via natural selection to provide the mental flexibility and creativity needed to confront varied, often novel, environmental conditions. The functionally plastic nature of the human brain and its inherent creativity render suspect all arguments that complex behaviors are controlled by innate, highly localized, behaviorally specific neural modules.

The Highly Variable Environments of Evolutionary Adaptation

As summarized by Irons (1998), the concept of an environment of evolutionary adaptation was first proposed by the psychologist John Bowlby (1969, 1973), who considered the natural human environment to be the one inhabited by humans for the two million years prior to the last few thousand years—although he did not specify much about the nature of that environment. This concept is reiterated with minor modification in *The Adapted Mind* (Barkow, Cosmides, and Tooby 1992), whose contributors propose that the human mind is adapted to the Pleistocene hunter-gatherer environment occupied by humans for two million years prior to the invention of agriculture, again without specifying much about that environment. They claim that too little time has elapsed since the invention of agriculture for natural selection to have changed human behavioral adaptations.

This concept that our hunter-gatherer ancestors encountered relatively uniform challenges for two million years stands as a central tenet of the SEPMs, although not one that has gone unchallenged even in the evolutionary psychology community. Irons (1998), for instance, notes that during the approximately two-million-year period prior to the emergence of agriculture, several new hominid species evolved. This suggests considerable behavioral and genetic change during this time frame. In the last few thousand years, as Irons notes, humans in some populations have also evolved adaptations to milk drinking and to malaria that are not present in all human populations. This indicates that contrary to SEPMs, sufficient time has elapsed since the invention of agriculture for new genetic adaptations to have arisen.

Moreover, there is no single hunter-gatherer environment and probably never has been. Modern hunter-gatherers encounter diverse environmental challenges with respect to climate, terrain, and resource availability. True, all hunter-gatherers must have means of predicting the time and place of food availability, of traveling to and from foraging sites, of procuring, processing, and transporting foods, of finding mates, of rearing children, and of protecting themselves from environmental hazards. Although all modern hunter-gatherers must meet these common challenges, they do so by highly varied means. Depending on the population and the season, hunter-gatherer staple foods may include nuts, tubers, beans, fruits, fish, sea lions, fowl, shellfish, ungulates, rodents, kangaroos, or invertebrate prey—a diversity of foods that require a diversity of foraging and processing techniques. Populations that forage on similar foods may also use very different techniques. Animal prey, for instance, can be driven over cliffs or into corrals, cornered in mountain passes, stalked by individuals armed with spears, bows, bolas, or boomerangs, ensnared in traps or lured with bait and mating calls. Diverse hunting strategies demand varied forms of social interaction and social sharing. Similarly, travel and protection from climatic, predator, and other environmental hazards demand different strategies depending on location.

Comparative behavioral evidence and paleontological data suggest that versatile human behavior patterns have a long evolutionary history. Our closest phylogenetic relatives, the chimpanzees, display population variations in foraging, tool-using, and communicative techniques that indicate a capacity to invent and socially disseminate novel behaviors (Boesch 2000; McGrew 1992; McGrew et al. 2001; Russon 2000; Whiten et al. 1999; Wrangham et al. 1994). Some chimpanzee populations, for example, use sticks to "fish" for termites. That is, they insert sticks into openings in termite mounds and allow termites to crawl up the sticks. Others use sticks to dig into the termite mound. Similarly, some chimpanzee populations use tools to crack nuts; others simply choose not to eat the same nuts, even when they are present in their environment. Population variations in social behavior also exist. For example, chimpanzees in the Mahale Mountains, when grooming each other, extend their nongrooming hands above their heads and clasp them (McGrew et al. 2001). Chimpanzees at the Gombe Stream do not exhibit this behavioral pattern. Chimpanzees and other great apes also manifest a certain amount of developmental plasticity, as is evident from the behaviors of apes reared by humans. Human-reared apes, for instance, may comprehend much spoken English and communicate symbolically using gestures similar to those used in the American Sign Language of the deaf or by using visual pictograms. Those reared in the wild fail to master these skills even after being captured and trained (Savage-Rumbaugh et al. 1993). Human-reared apes also appear to exceed apes reared in the wild in their imitative and mirror self-recognition capacities (Parker, Mitchell, and Boccia 1994). Comparable levels of developmental plasticity, creativity, and social learning skills would have been present in the last common ancestors of chimpanzees and humans.

It was once thought that hominids evolved in a savanna habitat and that some hominid characteristics, such as bipedalism and tool use, were specific adaptations to savanna life. We now know, however, that forest-living chimpanzees use tools (Boesch 1993). The fossil record also indicates that the earliest hominids, in the period from about 2 to 4 million years ago, rather than living in the savanna, lived in highly "mosaic" environments containing wet woodlands and lakeside environments as well as more open habitats (Potts 1996, 1998). These hominids were already bipedal, but they also retained tree-climbing adaptations. Thus, they appear to have exploited both arboreal and terrestrial habitats. By about 2.4 million years ago, savanna habitats were expanding, and by about 1.8 million years ago, fully bipedal hominids had appeared. During this period, however, and throughout the subsequent Pleistocene, evidence indicates that mean global temperatures and sea levels fluctuated frequently, leading to periodic changes in terrestrial climates. For example, at one fossil site, Olduvai Gorge, the habitat was at times a relatively moist, humid, lakeside environment and at other times dry and semiarid. These climatic fluctuations resulted in repeated, major changes in the fauna and flora available for human consumption and, thus, favored the survival of versatile hominids capable of exploiting generalist behavioral strategies (Potts 1996, 1998). Selection would also have favored hominids capable of devising novel solutions to novel problems and of transmitting successful solutions to kin or mates.

Indeed, paleontological evidence indicates that by 2.5 million years ago hominids had responded to these environmental conditions by expanding their diets to incorporate foods not found in the diets of great apes—including the meat of big game, bone marrow, and, possibly, deeply buried tubers (Blumenschine and Cavallo 1992; Foley 1995–96; Potts 1998; Tattersall and Schwarz 2000). Archaeological evidence also indicates that by 2.5 million years ago hominids may have been caching tools and foods at specific sites for future use—a new behavioral pattern not found among the apes (Potts 1998). By 1.8 million years ago, or about the time evolutionary psychologists assume our ancestors had adopted the EEA, behavioral versatility had allowed hominids to leave Africa and to occupy distinctly non-apelike environments in Asia and Georgia (Tattersall and Schwarz 2000).

Hence, even prior to the emergence of our species, hominid predecessors had demonstrated a behavioral versatility that enabled them to survive in a diversity of climatic and geographical conditions. This suggests that natural selection favored those hominids with the neural and mental capacities to solve novel problems rather than those able to solve only those problems encountered by their ancestors.

By the time of the emergence of anatomically modern humans, the evidence for behavioral flexibility and creativity in response to varying environmental challenges is incontrovertible. Even prior to the development of the European Upper Paleolithic, human populations in the Levant evidenced seasonal migration cycles possibly as complex as those exploited by any modern human group (Lieberman and Shea 1994). Evidently, they had learned to exploit seasonal feeding "bonanzas," such as seasonal crops and seasonally migrating animal prey (Gibson 1996a). Europeans began hunting large herd animals and learned to predict and exploit the seasonal migrations of herds of caribou and the seasonal spawning of salmon (Mellars 1973; Stiner 1994); populations in South Africa timed seasonal migrations to coincide with the beaching of sea lions (Klein 1989); East African populations developed complex fishing gear (Brooks et al. 1995; Yellen et al. 1995); and other groups reached Australia, where they flourished in environments whose fauna and flora bore little resemblance to anything previously encountered by hominids (Roberts, Jones, and Smith 1990).

In sum, at no period of human evolution did our ancestors exploit a single EEA. The geographical distances and evolutionary time frames are sufficient that given genetic or reproductive isolation, individual populations might have evolved dedicated neural processing modules to meet the specific needs of their own environments (Irons 1998). That this did not happen, however, is evident from the ability of peoples from all parts of the world to interbreed and to readily adopt each other's cultural practices, as well as from the abilities of peoples throughout the world to adapt to the modern postindustrial world. The behavioral and paleontological evidence, thus, suggests that the human brain has been designed for behavioral versatility rather than for the solving of a relatively few frequently encountered ancestral problems.

Epigenesis and Neural Plasticity:
Partial Foundations of Human Versatility

The SEPMs assume that many identified mental or linguistic capacities of modern human adults reflect the functioning of domain-specific neural modules (i.e., functionally encapsulated areas of the brain), that these modules are innate, and that they evolved subject to specific selective pressures. Genetic and developmental evidence, however, sheds doubt on these assumptions.

Most genes influencing complex traits have multiple phenotypic effects (pleiotropy). This well-established principle should caution all behavioral scientists against assuming that each identifiable human behavioral capacity is controlled by a specific, dedicated gene. Indeed, it mandates a search for genes with multiple effects. A further mandate for such searches derives from our current knowledge that humans possess approximately 30,000 genes and that humans and chimpanzees differ in only 1.6 percent of their DNA (Paabo 2001). This minimal genetic difference must account for all of the genetically based physical and behavioral differences between humans and chimpanzees.

In fact, a gene has now been identified that is sometimes referred to as a language gene (Lai et al. 2001). Predictably, it follows the principle of pleiotropy in that a mutated form of this gene has multiple effects involving syntax, dysarthria, facial dyspraxia, and IQ. That any theory postulating individual genetic control of multiple small neuronal populations must be faulty is also evident from the fact that although there are approximately 30,000 human genes, there are 1 trillion neurons and between 100 and 1000 trillion synapses (Ehrlich 2000). What is needed is not a theory that one gene = one mental module = one complex behavior but a theory of how a small number of genes can construct a complex brain and enable a diversity of behaviors.

Anatomical and functional studies of normal and diseased human brains, however, often appear to lend support to concepts of multiple, domain-specific neural modules. All normal human brains, for instance, contain dedicated sensory and motor processing areas that are predictably located in the same neuroanatomical areas in most people. In some species, species-typical facial, spatial, and object recognition cortical areas have also been identified (Haxby et al. 1996; Movshon et al. 1985; Tanaka 1996).

Broca's and Wernicke's areas of the left human neocortex have long been thought to be dedicated linguistic processors, and some scholars have postulated that separate cortical areas mediate recognition of differing word classes such as those for animate versus inanimate objects (Grabowski and Damasio 2000).

Much recent work, however, questions these assumptions. It is possible, for example, that facial recognition areas may actually function primarily for the detection of fine visual details and visual novelty (Gauthier et al. 1999). Similarly, concepts of the functions of Broca's area have changed with time. Broca's area was once thought to control speech, then thought to control syntax, and later postulated to function in the hierarchical organization of both speech and manual behaviors (Greenfield 1991). Moreover, modern imaging studies of functioning human brains clearly demonstrate that language processing, far from being controlled by a few isolated neural areas, involves widespread activity of much of the neocortex, the cerebellum, the basal ganglia, and the thalamus (Grabowski and Damasio 2000). These findings raise important issues about precisely what is localized in the brain. Are behaviors and cognitive capacities, as we define them, localized to specific neural regions? Alternatively, perhaps, different neural areas possess distinct neural processing mechanisms that may contribute to varied behavioral and cognitive domains.

Studies of adult brains, moreover, can shed no light on developmental processes that lead to neural functional specialization. All complex phenotypic traits develop via epigenetic processes—that is, through interactions of genetic and environmental inputs. When evolutionary psychologists generalize from adult behaviors to genotype, they fail to explore these complex interactions or the possibility that those dedicated neural processing areas that appear to exist in adult brains may be products of epigenetic processes. In other words, adult domain-specific neural processing areas may reflect developmental inputs and specializations rather than being under strict genetic determination (Greenfield 1991; Karmiloff and Karmiloff-Smith 2001; Karmiloff-Smith 1992). If so, the brain may be a far more versatile organ than SEPMs suggest. The only way to determine if this is so is to study development.

In fact, epigenesis and the neural plasticity that makes it possible have long been evident even to those with no training in science or medicine. It is, for example, common knowledge that people born without hands can develop the ability to tie shoes, paint, and use simple tools with their feet and that blind individuals often seem to have unusually acute hearing. Serious scientific investigations of neural and behavioral plasticity began in the late 1950s and early 1960s with demonstrations that rats reared in environments enriched with other rats and with objects, such as exercise wheels, outperformed those reared in isolation or without environmental objects when asked to solve maze-learning tasks (Diamond, Krech, and Rosensweig 1964). The "enriched" rats also had larger brains, decreased neuronal density, and increased numbers of glial cells, dendritic spines, and synapses. Subsequent studies indicated that nutritional deprivation early in life can mimic the effects of social deprivation and that "enriched" environments continue to have positive effects on the brains of rats equivalent in age to seventy- or eighty-year-old humans (Diamond 1988).

Ethical considerations prevent deliberate human experimentation. Natural experiments sometimes occur, however, such as famines or social deprivation induced by warfare. Studies of childhood victims of such events indicate that children seriously deprived of nutrients or social input during fetal or early childhood ages have lower average IQs than others (Morgan and Gibson 1991). Similarly, modern research indicates that people who are well educated and continue to be intellectually active throughout their lives are less likely to suffer from Alzheimer's disease (Lock, chapter 9, this volume). These findings of neural and intellectual plasticity in response to environmental input are often cited in support of Head Start programs, but curiously they tend to be overlooked by those who assume strict genetic determination of intellectual processes and/or who assume that social class or ethnic differences in brain size and IQ are primarily genetically determined (Herrnstein and Murray 1994).

That appropriate environmental inputs during periods of maturation play a mandatory role in the development of some neural systems also indicates the epigenetic nature of brain development. In both cats and monkeys, for example, normal maturation of neural visual areas requires visual input during the first few months of postnatal life (Hubel, Wiesel, and LeVay 1977). Similarly, in humans, muscular problems that prevent coordinated movements of both eyes must be corrected in early childhood if normal depth perception is to develop (von Noorden and Crawford 1992).

Neural plasticity also manifests itself when some neural areas assume new neural functions in response to unusual inputs during growth and maturation. Blind individuals trained in Braille from childhood, for instance, develop heightened tactile sense in their "reading" finger (Sadato et al. 1996). This increased tactile sensation is mediated by the neocortical area that, in most humans, serves as primary visual cortex (Greenough, Black, and Wallace 1987). Visual deprivation in laboratory animals can lead to increased size of the auditory cortex. Similarly, in humans born congenitally deaf and trained in sign language from childhood, "auditory" regions of the temporal lobe assume visual functions (Neville 1991). The assumption by one hemisphere of functions normally controlled by the other also serves as an example of functional plasticity. In normal human adults, the left hemisphere controls movements of the right arm and leg and is linguistically dominant. If the left hemisphere is damaged in childhood, however, the right hemisphere can assume many of its motor and linguistic functions (Hallett 2000). Given that sensory-specific neural processing areas and language areas are sometimes considered prime examples of innate neural modules, the now well-demonstrated plasticity of these areas would seem sufficient evidence to negate theories of innate neural modules. Certainly, these developmental findings indicate that, in a functional sense, maturing mammalian and human brains are classic epigenetic systems that acquire species-typical neural processing mechanisms and behavioral capacities through interactions between genes and environmental inputs (Brauth, Hall, and Dooling 1991).

Brains are also epigenetic organs in the anatomical sense. During early development, mammalian brains greatly overproduce neurons, axons, and synapses, and neuronal connections develop that are not normally found in adult brains. Only those neurons and connections that achieve functionality survive (Greenough, Black, and Wallace 1987; Rakic and Kornack 2001). For example, while the optic nerve of the adult rhesus monkey contains about 1.2 million fibers, that of the embryo contains about twice as many; and there are four times as many fibers in the corpus callosum of the newborn monkey as in the adult (Rakic 1991). This process of neuronal/synaptic overproduction followed by the pruning of inactive neurons and connections is a genetically economical means of producing a complex brain. Rather than strict genetic control of each individual functional neuronal pool, genes would appear to code for massive overproduction of neurons and synapses that are then fine-tuned by environmental input. Most mammals, of course, not only possess species-typical genes but mature in species-typical environments. Hence, most naturally acquire species-typical brains and behaviors through epigenetic processes rather than through strict genetic determinism. When environmental inputs are unusual, however, the neural results may also sometimes be unusual.

Although neural plasticity is primarily evident during the maturational period, some plasticity remains in adulthood (Greenough, Black, and Wallace 1987) and, thus, permits continued learning as well as adaptive responses to injuries. For example, amputations or paralyses of fingers, hands, or limbs in monkeys and humans are routinely followed by decreased amounts of neural tissue representing the amputated/paralyzed structures and increased amounts of neural tissue representing the remaining and normally functioning anatomical structures (Merzenich and Kaas 1982; Pons,

Garraghty, and Mishkin 1988; Pons et al. 1991). Cortical reorganizations in adult humans and primates can also follow small behavioral changes or small environmental insults. For example, in monkeys, temporary immobilization of the hand or arm may lead to functional reorganization of the motor cortex within days (Nudo et al. 1996), and in humans several days of practicing the piano can lead to enlargement of the pertinent cortical regions (Grabowki and Damasio 2000).

Adult neural plasticity reflects different anatomical processes than the selective pruning of neurons and connections evident during maturation. Adult mammals remain capable of forming new cortical synapses in response to learning, and they can generate new neurons in a subcortical neural structure, the hippocampus (Gould et al. 1999). Also, some synapses and neurons are thought to survive the early pruning but to exhibit minimal activity until unmasked by an environmental insult that inhibits or destroys other, more dominant pathways or until stimulated by new behaviors and experiences (Greenough, Black, and Wallace 1987; Hallett 2000). Phantom limb pain may provide an example of this latter phenomenon. Subsequent to amputation, humans often experience pain in the nonexistent limb. In these instances, lightly brushing other body parts can result in sensation perceived to originate in the amputated limb. This pain can sometimes be relieved by a form of visual therapy in which the patient is supplied with a mirror box that reflects the image of the nonamputated limb, thereby creating the illusion that the amputated limb is in the box and moving in coordination with the normal limb (Ramachandran, Rogers-Ramachandran, and Cobb 1995). Phantom limb pain is thought to reflect an unmasking of neural connections that already exist in the brain (Ramachandran, Stewart, and Rogers-Ramachandran 1992; Ramachandran, Rogers-Ramachandran, and Cobb 1995).

The findings that normal brain development is a functionally plastic epigenetic process and that some functional plasticity remains throughout life have significant implications for modern human behavior. Just as epigenetic processes allow apes reared with humans to acquire language facilities not normally manifest in the wild, they allow humans to acquire functional modifications of their brains that permit the acquisition of skills, such as reading, writing, typing, and playing computer games, that are not part of our evolutionary heritage. If, in contrast, our cognitive and behavioral capacities were primarily controlled by innate, predetermined "neural modules" designed to solve specific problems encountered during the Pleistocene, we would lack this behavioral flexibility. Our brains may look the same as those of our Pleistocene hunter-gatherer ancestors, but in some re-spects they may be functionally quite different, because environmental inputs during the developmental process are now quite different.

We can only speculate about what epigenesis may mean with regard to social behavior, morality, and other complex behavioral systems of specific interest to evolutionary psychologists such as theory of mind, reciprocal altruism, and the detection of cheaters. In contrast to neuroscientists, SEPM theorists rarely attempt actually to identify the neural regions that subserve the behaviors and cognitive capacities of interest to them, and some of them explicitly deny the potential relevance of developmental studies (Fodor 1983; Cosmides and Tooby 1992). Rather, they assume that if a potentially adaptive mental capacity can be identified in adult humans, it must be controlled by an innate neural module dedicated to that capacity. For example, SEPM theorists use the ability of human adults to detect cheaters as evidence for the existence of a specific, genetically determined, neural cheater detector module. However, they never actually identify any area in the brain that functions specifically to detect cheating and have never found any part of the genome that appears to relate in any way to detecting cheaters. They justify this methodology by calling it reverse engineering and likening it to the dismantling of mechanical equipment in order to determine its function and means of manufacture. In actuality, this methodology amounts to inappropriate generalization from behavioral phenotype to genotype. The clear evidence of the epigenetic nature of brain development invalidates this methodology. Even if at some future date adult brains were found to contain regions dedicated to cheater detection or reciprocal altruism, that would be insufficient evidence to draw sweeping conclusions about their genetic or developmental determination.

Mental Constructional Processes:
Additional Components of Human Versatility

Epigenesis and neural plasticity are fundamental processes of both mammalian and human brain development. They contribute to human behavioral flexibility and creativity, but they cannot account for why human accomplishments in a variety of creative realms have greatly exceeded those of other animals. Comparative data suggest that in varied behavioral domains, the main features distinguishing great ape and human behaviors reflect quantitative increases in information-processing capacities (Gibson 1990, 1996a, 1996b, 2002). In other words, in contrast to evolutionary psychology models that postulate specific genetic and domain-specific neural control of many individual behaviors and cognitive capacities, the comparative evidence suggests that one process—mental construction—underlies a wide range of behaviors. Theoretical evidence suggests that the increased mental constructional capacity of humans as compared to great apes emerges from increased brain size (Gibson 1990, 1996a, 1996b, 2002). Hence, increased mental construction requires only an amount of genetic change needed to account for our brain expansion. Developmental considerations suggest that very few genetic differences need be postulated to account for brain expansion, because the increased size of the human brain appears to result from one simple change—a few extra cell divisions during the period of embryonic and fetal brain development (Rakic and Kornack 2001).

Specifically, the increased information-processing capacity of the human brain allows humans to combine and recombine greater numbers of actions, perceptions, and concepts together to create higher-order conceptual or behavioral constructs than do apes. These constructions are often hierarchical in that new constructs are subordinated into still higher-order constructs. The recombinatory and hierarchical nature of human mental constructions, as well as the human ability to incorporate large amounts of information into varied constructs, appears to account for human creative abilities. In humans, information-processing capacity and mental constructional skills steadily increase from infancy to adolescence, thereby helping to account for the increased cognitive capacities of older children and adults in comparison to infants (Case 1985).

Hierarchical mental construction underlies human creativity in a variety of realms, including athletics, dance, mime, art, music, toolmaking, language, and social intelligence (Gibson 1996a, 1996b, 2002). In the technical domain, for example, apes make simple tools. They do not construct tools composed of separate components. Humans construct tools, shelters, artworks, musical instruments, and other objects of multiple components by first manufacturing subcomponents such as wooden shafts, spear points, hides, and cordage and then joining these manufactured items together to make varied objects such as spears, digging sticks, tents, and rafts. Each step in the construction of the final object is subordinated to and embedded within the overall constructional plan. Subcomponents of many tools can also serve as subcomponents of a seemingly infinite variety of different tools, thus accounting for human creativity in the realms of art and architecture.

Chomsky has claimed that human syntax is unique and unrelated to any other cognitive capacity (Chomsky 1972, 1980). Sentence construction, however, is just that—a mental construction that in many ways resembles tool construction (Gibson 1996b; Gibson and Jessee 1999). It always involves combinations of words and phrases that are subordinated to and embedded within higher-order expressions, and each word or phrase can be used as a component of a seemingly infinite variety of different sentences.

Mental constructional processes also underlie complex socially related cognitive functions, such as the ability to infer others' intentions and thoughts (sometimes called theory of mind), because these abilities involve taking multiple concepts and embedding them into higher-order concepts. Consider, for example, the following series of concepts that could be held by two people, Jane and Susan. Jane believes that Susan is smart. Susan wants Jane to believe that she is smart. Jane doesn't want Susan to know that she believes Susan is smart. Susan knows that Jane really believes she (Susan) is smart but that Jane is pretending to believe that Susan is dumb because she wants to intimidate her. Each subsequent thought process is progressively more complex and information rich in that it contains a greater number of concepts that are subordinated to and embedded within the overall mental construction. Such processes correspond to what the philosopher Daniel Dennett has delineated as levels of intentionality. According to Dennett (1988: 185), the statements "x believes that p" and "y wants that q" correspond to first-order intentional systems. "X wants y to believe that x is hungry" is a second-order system, while "x wants y to believe that x believes he is all alone" is a third-order system. In summary, the capacity to comprehend others' intentions and thoughts is a mental constructional process involving subordination and layers of embeddedness just as can be seen in linguistic and technical behaviors.

Analyses of monkey and ape behaviors provide some evidence for second-order intentionality in monkeys and for third-order intentionality in great apes (Whiten and Byrne 1988). Most human adults can keep track of, at most, five or six orders of intentionality (Dennett 1988). Human children do less well, and older children have more sophisticated understandings of intentionality than do younger ones. Within the first year of life, babies can infer what others are attending to (Butterworth 1992), and they attempt to annoy and amuse others (Reddy 1992). By the second year, they exhibit comforting and helping behaviors (Dunn 1992). During the second year, they also incorporate the word "want" into their vocabularies (Dunn 1992) and can predict what others will do based on their understandings of others' desires (Bennett 1992). The words "think" and "know" generally enter a child's vocabulary during the third year, and by three years of age, children can predict others' behaviors based on what they think others believe (Bennett 1992; Dunn 1992). It is not until about four years of age, however, that they can pass tests that indicate an understanding that others may have false or erroneous beliefs (Wellman 1992) and not until six to eight years of age that they exhibit second-order embedding of belief concepts—that is, "Susan thinks that Bob thinks" (Leekham 1992).

Some animal behaviorists and developmental psychologists consider the abilities to lie and to detect others' lies to be manifestations of animal and human capacities to understand others' intentions and mental states (Leekham 1992; Whiten and Byrne 1988; Byrne and Whiten 1992). Again, monkeys and apes exhibit some capacities in these domains, but they fall far short of humans. Distinguishing truth from falsehood also manifests itself in a variety of behavioral contexts other than lying and cheating, such as pretend play, storytelling, joking, understatement, and sarcasm (Leekham 1992). Abilities to understand, engage in, and detect various forms of falsity, like theory of mind, expand during child development. By the second year of life, human children engage in pretend play and may tell simple lies (Dunn 1992; Leekham 1992). By four years, they can distinguish mistakes from lies, and by six they can distinguish lies intended as jokes from lies intended to deceive and mislead. It is not, however, until age thirteen that most children can distinguish intended deception from sarcasm (Leekham 1992).

Fodor (1983), Cosmides and Tooby (1992), Irons (1998), and others—who eschew comparative and developmental analyses in favor of focusing on only adult human behaviors—propose separate, innate, dedicated neural modules for theory of mind, cheater detection, and other behavioral capacities that depend on understanding others' intentions and beliefs, such as reciprocal altruism (e.g., if I do a favor for you today, I think you will be willing to do a favor for me tomorrow). The common cognitive processes that underpin each of these capacities and their complex evolutionary and developmental roots suggest, however, that such propositions are overly facile. If, for example, the ability to distinguish truth from falsity is a manifestation of the ability to infer others' intentions and beliefs, as suggested by animal behaviorists and developmental psychologists (Whiten and Byrne 1988; Leekham 1992), why would we need separate genes and separate innate neural modules for theory of mind and cheater detection? If nonhuman primates and young children have more rudimentary theories of mind than do human adults, must we postulate several theory of mind genes and neural modules, some of which code for animal or infantile mental capacities and others for adult human capacities? Should we postulate five separate innate neural modules for distinguishing lies, jokes, irony, sarcasm, and pretense? Genetic economy suggests that such approaches will lead to blind alleys. Too few genes distinguish humans and chimpanzees for each identifiable behavioral distinction to be controlled by a separate gene or group of genes.

Indeed, some psychologists have provided developmental models that suggest that no innate theory of mind neural modules need be postulated at all. One of the first manifestations of understanding others' viewpoints is the phenomenon of joint attention, whereby infants learn to focus attention jointly on another individual and on an object of interest to that individual. This, itself, is a mental construction, because it requires combining the separate perceptions of an object and of another person into one larger concept: the person is interested in the object. Butterworth (1992) has demonstrated that joint attention directly develops from the infant's perceptual experiences and is not innate. Case (1985) has suggested that the further maturation of children's understanding of others' thought processes follows classic mental constructional paths in that older children take more information into account when trying to understand what others are thinking and subordinate some items of information to others in an attempt to develop a comprehensive understanding of and reaction to a given social situation. Other psychologists also dismiss concepts of an innate theory of mind by suggesting that there is no such thing as a theory of mind (Harris 1992). Children's abilities to understand others' beliefs develop in parallel with their own self-understanding (Astington and Gopnik 1992). Three-year-olds, for instance, not only lack understanding that others may have false beliefs but may also fail to understand that they themselves may have false beliefs. These findings of parallel development between understanding one's own mind and understanding others' minds imply to Harris (1992) that children learn to infer others' feelings, thoughts, and intentions by analogical reasoning processes based on their own behaviors in relationship to their own internal mental states: for example, I cry when I am sad; Sue is crying; she must be sad. It is evident from such work that the maturation of children's concepts of others' intentions and thoughts can be explained by mental constructional processes.

A mental constructional model also accords with the principles of pleiotropy, genetic economy, and epigenesis, and it explains our abilities to devise creative solutions to novel problems. In contrast, models that postulate genetically controlled, functionally dedicated neural modules for each problem encountered during our evolutionary history are genetically expensive, violate principles of pleiotropy, and cannot explain why we can solve problems and adapt to environments not encountered by our ancestors.

Summary

Over the last decades, some evolutionary psychologists and linguists have argued that the human mind consists of numerous, specialized, innate neural modules designed to meet specific problems encountered in the Pleistocene hunter-gatherer environment. This chapter argues, in contrast, that there has never been a single environment of evolutionary adaptation. Rather, modern humans and their earlier hominid ancestors encounter(ed) and successfully adapt(ed) to highly varied environments. This human adaptability reflects the neural plasticity and epigenetic processes that shape the maturing human brain. It also reflects a basic intellectual process— mental construction—that allows humans to combine and recombine actions and concepts to create novel solutions to novel problems. This model has distinct advantages over SEPMs in that it is compatible with our understandings of minimal genetic change between humans and apes and with our understandings that most genes affect multiple traits and exert their effects through epigenetic processes.

The existence of mental constructional processes indicates that the human brain is not only an epigenetic and functionally plastic organ. The brain also endows our species with mental capacities that allow humans to create a seemingly infinite number of linguistic, technical, artistic, social, musical, and motor constructs and, hence, to adapt to changing and novel environments. Given that humans have exploited variable environments for millennia, it is likely that the major selective pressures throughout all of hominid evolution up to the present day have acted in favor of the mental creativity and flexibility that the human mental constructional process provides rather than in favor of functionally dedicated neural modules to meet the very specific environmental demands of a given time and place.

References

Astington, Janet W., and Alison Gopnik. 1992. Developing Understanding of Desire and Intention. In Whiten 1992: 39–50.

Barkow, Jerome H., Leda Cosmides, and John Tooby, eds. 1992. *The Adapted Mind: Evolutionary Psychology and the Generation of Culture*. New York: Oxford University Press.

Bennett, Jonathan. 1992. How to Read Minds in Behaviour: A Suggestion from a Philosopher. In Whiten 1992: 97–108.

Blumenschine, Robert J., and John A. Cavallo. 1992. Scavenging and Human Evolution. *Scientific American* 276: 90–96.

Boesch, Christophe. 1993.Aspects of Transmission of Tool-Use in Wild Chimpanzees. In *Tools, Language and Cognition in Human Evolution*, ed. Kathleen R. Gibson and Tim Ingold, pp. 171–84. Cambridge: Cambridge University Press.

———. 2000. Culture Behaviour in Chimpanzees. Paper presented at the Wenner-Gren Foundation Symposium 127, "Culture and the Cultural: New Tasks for an Old Concept," Morelia, Mexico, September 8–15.

Bowlby, John. 1969. *Attachment and Loss*. Vol. 1, *Attachment*. New York: Basic Books.

———. 1973. *Attachment and Loss*. Vol. 2, *Separation, Anxiety, and Anger*. New York: Basic Books.

Brauth, Steven E., William S. Hall, and Robert J. Dooling, eds. 1991. *Plasticity of Development.* Cambridge: MIT Press.

Brooks, Alison S., David M. Helgren, Jon S. Cramer, Alan Franklin, William Hornyak, Jody M. Keating, Richard G. Klein, William J. Rink, Henry Schwarcz, J. N. Leith Smith, Kathlyn Stewart, Nancy E. Todd, Jacques Verniers, and John E. Yellen. 1995. Dating and Context of Three Middle Stone Age Sites with Bone Points in the Upper Semliki Valley, Zaire. *Science* 268: 548–53.

Butterworth, George. 1992. The Ontogeny and Phylogeny of Joint Visual Attention. In Whiten 1992: 233–52.

Byrne, Richard, and Andrew Whiten. 1992. Computation and Mindreading in Primate Tactical Deception. In Whiten 1992: 127–42.

Case, Robbie. 1985. *Intellectual Development: Birth to Adulthood.* New York: Academic Press.

Chomsky, Noam. 1972. *Language and Mind.* New York: Harcourt Brace Jovanovitch.

———. 1980. Rules and Representations. *Behavior and Brain Science* 3: 1–61.

Cosmides, Leda, and John Tooby. 1992. Cognitive Adaptations for Social Exchange. In Barkow, Cosmides, and Tooby 1992: 163–228.

Dennett, Daniel C. 1988. The Intentional Stance in Theory and Practice. In *Machiavellian Intelligence: Social Expertise and the Evolution of Intellect in Monkeys, Apes, and Humans,* ed. Richard W. Byrne and Andrew Whiten, pp. 180–202. Oxford: Clarendon Press.

Diamond, Marian C. 1988. *Enriching Heredity.* New York: Free Press.

Diamond, Marian C., David Krech, and Mark R. Rosensweig. 1964. The Effects of an Enriched Environment on the Histology of the Rat Cerebral Cortex. *Journal of Comparative Neurology* 123: 111–20.

Dunn, Judy. 1992. The Work of the Imagination. In Whiten 1992: 51–62.

Ehrlich, Paul. 2000. *Human Natures: Genes, Cultures, and the Human Prospect.* Washington, DC: Island Press.

Fodor, Jerry A. 1983. *The Modularity of Mind: An Essay on Faculty Psychology.* Cambridge: MIT Press.

Foley, Robert. 1995–96. The Adaptive Legacy of Human Evolution: A Search for the Environment of Evolutionary Adaptedness. *Evolutionary Anthropology* 4: 194–203.

Gauthier, Isabel, Michael Tarr, Adam W. Anderson, Pawel Skudlarski, and John C. Gore. 1999. Activation of the Middle Fusiform "Face Area" Increases with Expertise in Recognizing Novel Objects. *Nature Neuroscience* 2: 568–73.

Gibson, Kathleen R. 1990. New Perspectives on Instincts and Intelligence: Brain Size and the Emergence of Hierarchical Mental Constructional Skills. In *"Language" and Intelligence in Monkeys and Apes: Comparative Developmental Perspectives,* ed. Sue T. Parker and Kathleen R. Gibson, pp. 97–128. Cambridge: Cambridge University Press.

———. 1996a. The Biocultural Human Brain, Seasonal Migrations, and the Emergence of the European Upper Paleolithic. In *Modelling the Early Human Mind,* ed. Paul Mellars and Kathleen R. Gibson, pp. 33–47. Cambridge: McDonald Institute for Archaeological Research.

———. 1996b. The Ontogeny and Evolution of the Brain, Cognition, and Language. In *Handbook of Symbolic Evolution,* ed. Andrew Lock and Charles R. Peters, pp. 407–30. Oxford: Clarendon Press.

———. 2002. Evolution of Human Intelligence: The Roles of Brain Size and Mental Construction. *Brain, Behavior, and Evolution* 59: 10–20.

Gibson, Kathleen R., and Stephen Jessee. 1999. Language Evolution and the Expansion of Multiple Neurological Processing Areas. In *The Origins of Language: What Non-human Pri-*

mates Can Tell Us, ed. Barbara King, pp. 189–228. Santa Fe, NM: School of American Research Press.

Gould, Elizabeth, Alison J. Reeves, Mazyzar Fallah, Patima Tanapat, Charles G. Gross, and Eberhard Fuchs. 1999. Hippocampal Neurogenesis in Adult Old World Primates. *Proceedings of the National Academy of Sciences* 96: 5263–67.

Grabowski, Thomas J., and Antonio R. Damasio. 2000. Investigating Language with Neuroimaging. In *Brain Mapping: The Systems,* ed. Arthur W. Toga and John C. Mazziotta, pp. 425–61. New York: Academic Press.

Greenfield, Patricia M. 1991. Language, Tools, and the Brain. *Behavior and Brain Sciences* 14: 531–95.

Greenough, William T., James E. Black, and Christopher Wallace. 1987. Experience and Brain Development. *Child Development* 58: 539–59.

Hallett, Mark. 2000. Plasticity. In *Brain Mapping: The Disorders,* ed. John C. Mazziotta, Arthur W. Toga, and Richard S. J. Frackowiak, pp. 569–86. New York: Academic Press.

Harris, Paul. 1992. The Work of the Imagination. In Whiten 1992: 283–304.

Haxby, James V., Leslie G. Ungerleider, Barry Horwitz, Jose M. Maisog, Stanley I. Rapoport, and Cheryl L. Grady. 1996. Face Encoding and Recognition in the Human Brain. *Proceedings of the National Academy of Sciences* 93: 922–27.

Herrnstein, Robert J., and Charles Murray. 1994. *The Bell Curve: Intelligence and Class Structure in American Life.* New York: Free Press.

Hubel, David, Torsten N. Wiesel, and Simon LeVay. 1977. Plasticity of Ocular Dominance Columns in Monkey Striate Cortex. *Philosophical Transactions of the Royal Society of London* B278: 377–409.

Irons, William. 1998. Adaptively Relevant Environments versus the Environment of Evolutionary Adaptedness. *Evolutionary Anthropology* 6: 194–204.

Karmiloff, Kyra, and Annette Karmiloff-Smith. 2001. *Pathways to Language from Fetus to Adolescent.* Cambridge: Harvard University Press.

Karmiloff-Smith, Annette. 1992. *Beyond Modularity: A Developmental Perspective.* Cambridge: MIT Press.

Klein, Richard. 1989. Biological and Behavioural Perspectives on Modern Human Origins in Southern Africa. In *The Human Revolution: Behavioural and Biological Perspectives on the Origins of Modern Humans,* ed. Paul Mellars and Christopher Stringer, pp. 529–46. Edinburgh: Edinburgh University Press.

Lai, Cecilia S. L., Simon E. Fisher, Jane A. Hurst, Faraneh Vargha-Khadem, and Anthony P. Monaco. 2001. A Forkhead-Domain Gene Is Mutated in a Severe Speech and Language Disorder. *Nature* 413: 519–23.

Leekham, Susan R. 1992. Jokes and Lies: Children's Understanding of Intentional Falsehood. In Whiten 1992: 159–74.

Lieberman, Daniel E., and John J. Shea. 1994. Behavioral Differences between Archaic and Modern Humans in the Levantine Mousterian. *American Anthropologist* 96: 300–332.

McGrew, William C. 1992. *Chimpanzee Material Culture: Implications for Human Evolution.* Cambridge: Cambridge University Press.

McGrew, William C., Linda F. Marchant, S. E. Scott, and C. E. Tutin. 2001. Intergroup Differences in a Social Custom of Wild Chimpanzees: The Grooming Hand Clasp of the Mahale Mountains. *Current Anthropology* 42: 148–53.

Mellars, Paul. 1973. The Character of the Middle–Upper Palaeolithic Transition in Southwest France. In *The Explanation of Culture Change,* ed. Colin Renfrew, pp. 255–76. London: Duckworth.

Merzenich, Michael, and Jon H. Kaas. 1982. Reorganization of Mammalian Somatosensory Cortex Following Peripheral Nerve Injury. *Trends in Neurosciences* 5: 434–36.

Morgan, Brian, and Kathleen R. Gibson. 1991. Nutritional and Environmental Interactions during Brain Development. In *Brain Maturation and Cognitive Development: Comparative and Cross-Cultural Perspectives,* ed. Kathleen R. Gibson and Anne C. Petersen, pp. 91–106. Hawthorne, NY: Aldine de Gruyter.

Movshon, J. Anthony, Edward H. Adelson, Martin S. Gizzi, and William T. Newsome. 1985. The Analysis of Moving Visual Patterns. In *Pattern Recognition Mechanisms,* ed. Carlos Chagas, Ricardo Gattass, and Charles Gross, pp. 117–51. Pontificiae Academiae Scientiarum Scripta Varia 54. Rome: Vatican Press. (Reprinted in *Experimental Brain Research,* Supplementum 11: 117–51, 1986.)

Neville, Helen J. 1991 Neurobiology of Cognitive and Language Processing: Effects of Early Experience. In *Brain Maturation and Cognitive Development,* ed. Kathleen R. Gibson and Anne C. Petersen, pp. 355–80. Hawthorne, NY: Aldine de Gruyter.

Nudo, Randolph J., Birute M. Wise, Frank SiFuentes, and Garrett W. Milliken. 1996. Neural Substrate for the Effects of Rehabilitation Training on Motor Recovery after Ischemic Infarct. *Science* 272: 1791–94.

Paabo, Svante. 2001. The Human Genome and Our View of Ourselves. *Science* 291: 1219–20.

Parker, Sue T., Robert W. Mitchell, and Maria L. Boccia, eds. 1994. *Self-Awareness in Animals and Humans: Developmental Perspectives.* Cambridge: Cambridge University Press.

Pinker, Steven. 1994. *The Language Instinct.* New York: W. J. Morrow and Co.

Pons, Tim P., Preston E. Garraghty, and Mortimer Mishkin. 1988. Lesion Induced Plasticity in the Second Somatosensory Cortex of Adult Macaques. *Proceedings of the National Academy of Sciences* 83: 5279–81.

Pons, Tim P., Preston E. Garraghty, Alexander K. Ommaya, Jon H. Kaas, Edward Taub, and Mortimer Mishkin. 1991. Massive Cortical Reorganization after Sensory Deafferentiation in Adult Macaques. *Science* 252: 1857–60.

Potts, Richard. 1996. *Humanity's Descent: The Consequences of Ecological Instability.* New York: William Morrow and Co.

———. 1998. Variability Selection in Hominid Evolution. *Evolutionary Anthropology* 7: 81–96.

Rakic, Pasko. 1991. Plasticity of Cortical Development. In Brauth, Hall, and Dooling 1991: 127–61.

Rakic, Pasko, and David R. Kornack. 2001. Neocortical Expansion and Elaboration during Primate Evolution: A View from Neuroembryology. In *Evolutionary Anatomy of the Primate Cerebral Cortex,* ed. Dean Falk and Kathleen R. Gibson, pp. 30–56. Cambridge: Cambridge University Press.

Ramachandran, Vilayanur S., Diane Rogers-Ramachandran, and S. Cobb. 1995. Touching the Phantom Limb. *Nature* 377: 489–90.

Ramachandran, V. S., M. S. Stewart, and D. C. Rogers-Ramachandran. 1992. Perceptual correlates of massive cortical reorganization. *Neuroreport* 3(7): 583–86.

Reddy, Vasudevi. 1992. Playing with Others Expectations: Teasing and Mucking About in the First Year. In Whiten 1992: 143–58.

Roberts, Richard G., Rys Jones, and M. A. Smith. 1990. Thermoluminescence Dating of a 50,000-Year-Old Human Occupation Site in Northern Australia. *Nature* 345: 153–56.

Russon, Anne E. 2000. How Great Apes Create Their Cultures. Paper presented at the Wenner-Gren Foundation Symposium 127, "Culture and the Cultural: New Tasks for an Old Concept," Morelia, Mexico, September 8–15.

Sadato, Norihiro, Alvaro Pascual-Leone, Jordan Grafman, Vicente Ibanez, Marie-Pierre Der-
ber, George Dold, and Mark Hallett. 1996. Activation of the Primary Visual Cortex by
Braille Reading in Blind Subjects. *Nature* 380: 526–28.

Savage-Rumbaugh, E. Sue, Jeannine Murphy, Rose A. Sevcik, Karen E. Brakke, Shelly L.
Williams, and Duane M. Rumbaugh. 1993. Language Comprehension in Ape and Child.
Monographs in Child Development 58: 1–220.

Stiner, Mary. 1994. *Honor among Thieves.* Princeton: Princeton University Press.

Tanaka, Kunihito. 1996. Inferotemporal Cortex and Object Vision. *Annual Reviews of Neuroscience* 16: 109.

Tattersall, Ian, and Jeffrey Schwarz. 2000. *Extinct Humans.* Boulder, CO: Westview Press.

Tooby, John, and Leda Cosmides. 1992. The Psychological Foundations of Culture. In Barkow,
Cosmides, and Tooby 1992: 19–135.

von Noorden, Gunter K., and Morris L. Crawford. 1992. The Lateral Geniculate Nucleus in
Human Strabismic Amblyopia. *Investigative Ophthalmology* 33(9): 2729–32.

Wellman, Henry M. 1992. From Desires to Beliefs: Acquisition of a Theory of Mind. In Whiten
1992: 19–38.

Whiten, Andrew, ed. 1992. *Natural Theories of Mind: Evolution, Development, and Simulation
of Everyday Mindreading.* Oxford: Blackwell.

Whiten, Andrew, and Richard Byrne. 1988. The Manipulation of Attention in Primate Tactical Deception. In *Machiavellian Intelligence: Social Expertise and the Evolution of Intellect
in Monkeys, Apes, and Humans,* ed. Richard W. Byrne and Andrew Whiten, pp. 211–23.
Oxford: Clarendon Press.

Whiten, Andrew, Jane Goodall, William C. McGrew, Toshiyukai Nishida, Vernon Reynolds,
Yukimaru Sugiyama, Caroline E. Tutin, Richard W. Wrangham, and Christophe Boesch.
1999. Cultures in Chimpanzees. *Nature* 399: 682–85.

Wrangham, Richard W., William C. McGrew, Franz R. M. de Waal, and Paul G. Heltne, eds.
1994. *Chimpanzee Cultures.* Cambridge: Harvard University Press.

Yellen, John E., Alison S. Brooks, Els Cornelissen, Michael J. Mehlman, and Kathlyn Stewart.
1995. A Middle Stone Age Worked Bone Industry from Katanda, Upper Semliki Valley,
Zaire. *Science* 268: 553–56.

CHAPTER 2

Do Humans Have Innate Mental Structures?
Some Arguments from Linguistics

William A. Foley

THE CHAPTERS IN THIS VOLUME argue for fundamental properties of variation and complexity in human cultural categories and social institutions. Much current theorizing in the social and behavioral sciences is, by contrast, dominated by reductive approaches, which invoke innate (often genetic) and hence universal bases for human behavior. Evolutionary psychology (Jones 1999; Pinker 1997; Plotkin 1998) is one such reductive school, which appeals to neo-Darwinian tenets to account for human cognitive and social behavior; it asserts that human behavior is generated by innate mental structures that have been selected for during the hunter-gatherer epoch and localized in the species-wide genome.

Much of the argument presented for evolutionary psychology's general understanding of the human mind and its development is adapted from contemporary theoretical linguistics and psycholinguistics and their assertions of language universals and modularity in language structure. The core claim is the "Poverty of the Stimulus Argument" from language acquisition studies, which claims that because the kind of language behavior that a child witnesses is too nonspecific and degraded and the amount too limited to account for the wonderfully rich and complex language that she acquires, a richly endowed, innate language "organ" must be posited. Evolutionary psychologists regularly invoke parallel arguments in other fields of mental activity, buoyed by the seeming success of such arguments in linguistics.

It is worth clarifying here what is meant by "innate" in this context. Obviously, all humans belong to the same species and would be expected to share certain characteristics due to inherited species-wide features, just as snakes lack legs, and some of these must surely be mental faculties. But the claim is much stronger than this: it is precisely that the mental faculties will unfold in a set, specified way regardless of any input from learning or the environment (in currently popular jargon they are "hardwired"). Indeed, it is the view that such mental structures are set at birth and, excepting any serious anatomical pathology, can be actualized only in universal behavioral outcomes (for further discussion, see Elman et al. 1996: 20–34).

But how robust are these claims of a richly endowed, innate language faculty? In linguistics these claims are articulated in terms of an array of postulated language universals, which are determined through research on language acquisition and language variation. These proposed language universals—the realization of innate mental structures in the language "organ"—must by definition constrain the form of all languages. Obviously, the argument for innate mental structures for language holds up only to the extent that the specific claims for robust language universals do. I will argue in this chapter that one very commonly asserted language universal—the contrast between nouns and verbs—is not a true language universal. I will demonstrate that, although there may be systems of universal constraints in language acquisition, innate or otherwise, they underdetermine the final result: a range of possibilities remains open, and indeed we can witness shifts among them.

Innateness and Universals in Language

While living our lives in navigating the world, a recurring contrast of similarity and difference seems readily apparent to us. The world seems to present us with cats and dogs, and we know that cats belong to one category and dogs to another—that all cats are similar in some features and, in this, they contrast with, are different from, dogs. Whether this categorial difference is in the world or in the language in which we make such distinctions is the old philosophical problem of universals. For example, when we attribute the property of being 'red' to two objects, does this 'redness' really exist in the objects themselves, independent of our description of them (an "essentialist" view), or only in our linguistic description of these things as being 'red' (a position traditionally known as "nominalist")? Is the property given in nature or established by convention?

Contemporary essentialist positions typically cast themselves as accounts of the relationship between commonality and variation—in anthropological terms, fundamentally a particular construal of the Boasian notion of the "psychic unity of humankind," an assertion of a fundamental panhuman unity of cognitive functioning. Clearly, even a cursory glance at the world reveals diversity, not unity, at all levels of human cultural, social, and linguistic behavior. So contemporary essentialists, following an age-old tradition that stretches back to Plato, appeal to a primary distinction between appearance and reality. Behind the apparent surface diversity lies a deeper and more real unity, from which the surface diversity—in a word, variation—is generated. Further, there are broad algorithmic principles that can be explicitly stated and by which the surface diversity is generated from the underlying unity. Faced with a contrast between commonality and variation, essentialists come down on the side of commonality as elementary truth. The problem for them then becomes accounting for variation. The current popular solution in the cognitive sciences, as we shall see, is simply to define it away—as mere superficial appearance, as performance rather than competence, as "noise." [1]

Currently, the strongest essentialist positions articulated in the social and behavioral sciences are various versions of what I will call "strong nativism." Stated simply, "strong nativism" is the view that human behavior of various types is simply the articulation of basic, universal, and innate mental structures. In the currently most popular version of this view, evolutionary psychology, this often boils down to an assertion that the grounds of these innate mental structures are genetically determined, having been built into the human genome as a result of evolutionary selectional pressures in the long human hunter-gatherer epoch (Cosmides and Tooby 1992; Pinker 1997). Over the last two decades, a number of developmental psychologists have presented evidence (summarized in Wellman and Gelman 1992; Spelke and Newport 1998; Bloom 2000) that human infants are endowed with a rich understanding of the way the physical world works and the types of natural biological objects (e.g., plants, animals, and humans) within that world. Adapting an argument from what linguistics called the "Poverty of the Stimulus Argument"—to be discussed in detail below—these psychologists have maintained that the early, prelinguistic, and often subtle and detailed nature of this knowledge strongly points to its innateness and hence universality for the human species. Evolutionary psychologists (e.g., Pinker 1997) have gone a stage further and stated flatly that such innate knowledge must be the result of adaptive selectional pressures and localized in the species-wide genome.

Clearly, the ideas of Chomsky (1980) and Fodor (1975, 1983) and much of the work in theoretical linguistics are paradigmatic for evolutionary psychology (see Plotkin 1998: 125–38 for a good example) and hence require a more detailed look. First, it is observed that language is a panhuman skill and that the structures of all individual languages are extremely complex, with elaborate recursive structures and many complex and obscure categories.[2] Second, it is noted that children acquire this skill effortlessly and nearly completely by five to six years of age, and even by three years they have quite an exceptional facility, especially when compared with often rudimentary abilities in other cognitive domains like arithmetic. Third, and this is the crucial Poverty of the Stimulus Argument, children are not explicitly tutored much—and in some cultures not at all—in the structures of their language. The complexity of all languages is such that no amount of tutoring could teach more than a tiny fraction of the necessary knowledge, and, furthermore, much of the knowledge they acquire is actualized in the absence of any possible evidence. For example, give a five-year-old child a made-up word like 'groob' and prompt him for the past tense, and he will unhesitatingly say 'groobed', which, of course, he could never have heard, because it is not an English word. On the basis of arguments like these, Chomsky and cohort (see, e.g., Pinker 1994) conclude that the knowledge of language must be innate and, further, that languages are not really learned but are the realizations of an innate (and, for Pinker 1994, genetically endowed) "language instinct," which is only actualized by the trigger of a spoken language in the child's cultural environment. Similarly, Fodor (1975, 1983) reviews the arguments for innate conceptual knowledge: given our rich system of semantic and conceptual knowledge and the poverty of the evidence provided to learn it, a uniform "language of thought" must be innate, a claim that nicely dovetails with the arguments of the developmental psychologists mentioned above. Note that Jones, in an overview of evolutionary psychology for the *Annual Review of Anthropology* (1999), provides a list of some fifty innate and universal conceptual primitives for this "language of thought."

But if the knowledge of language is innate, simply the flowering of a panhuman "language instinct," how do we account for the obvious significant variation in the structure of human languages? Not atypically, Chomsky and cohort appeal to the Platonic legacy and an abstract and idealized Universal Grammar, which is the endowment of all humans and which is actualized as fundamental and thoroughgoing constraints on the structure of any possible human language. Variation is seriously devalued and commonality valorized, to the extent that variation is simply performance or the "noise" of realization in the material external world.[3] Variation is so minimized and Platonic essentialism upheld that the claim is often made that all languages are really just varieties of one language. The rhetorical force of this view has been well encapsulated in the statement that Martian explorers of Earth on their return home would report that the species *Homo sapiens* has just one language with very superficial variations.

All of these assertions are very congenial to positions of strong nativism and its congener, genetic determinism (of course, not the same, but related views, and in the public—and not so public—mind, confused). Chomsky's views and the field of theoretical linguistics have become paradigmatic for many of the other subdisciplines of cognitive science, and especially for the new development of evolutionary psychology. How well do these claims of the innateness of the knowledge of language stand up? Unfortunately, many of the fundamentals for this position have not been developed empirically. Proponents of innatist views of language typically talk about the "logical problem" of language acquisition—how can children learn a language in the face of such degraded input?—but strong empirical evidence for robust innateness in language acquisition has sadly not been forthcoming (beyond the work on conceptual understanding noted above). Actual language acquisition data seem to demonstrate much greater variation in the development of language structures cross-linguistically than strong nativism might lead us to imagine (Slobin 1997). If a robust innate Universal Grammar really underlies all languages, it must substantially constrain the structure of any individual language, so that all must conform to certain characteristics. This is the domain of language universals, the set of typological features that must be realized in all languages, the surface manifestation of the deep abstract Universal Grammar.

Grammatical Categories: Nouns and Verbs

Perhaps the single most commonly claimed substantive language universal is the distinction between two of the major word classes: noun and verb. Pinker states that "in all languages words for objects and people are nouns ... words for actions and changes of state are verbs" (1994: 284). Hence the contrast between noun and verb is a feature of Universal Grammar and innate, thereby constraining the structure of all languages. Clearly, children do not need to learn the contrast between noun and verb, because it is innate. But note that Pinker's statement is a correlational one: a relationship between a formal, syntactic contrast, noun versus verb, and a meaning-based one, objects and people versus actions and happenings. The syntactic contrast may be innate, but how is the semantic one established, and, further, how is the semantic opposition tied to the syntactic one?

Before proceeding to address these questions, I need first to provide more detail on the semantics of the major word classes: noun, verb, and adjective. Nouns denote an act of categorization (Wierzbicka 1986). Those things that most transparently and perceptibly constitute categories in the world will most amenably be labeled by words belonging to the noun class. Those things demonstrating clear and definite categoriality, with sharp boundaries, well-formed shapes (in a word, distinctly embodied), are the meanings of prototypical nouns—for example, Pinker's objects (or Bloom's

[2000] Spelke-objects) and persons. Words denoting natural kinds like animals (Atran 1998) or artifacts (Bloom 2000) are all excellent exemplars of nouns because these things stand out in our dealings with the world as obvious categories (see also Berlin 1992). Adjectives denote acts of description, the attribution of properties. Words that describe properties of objects or animate beings like size (big, small), dimension (tall, narrow, long), age (old, new), color (black, red), value (good, bad), or traits (wise, clever, silly) (Dixon 1977) are all good exemplars of the word class adjective. When words denoting properties are used not in attribution to a category but as the basis for an act of categorization, they then become nouns, as in the deaf (a category of people wholly constituted on the basis of sharing the property of being deaf) or blacks and whites (two categories of human beings constituted on the basis of the color of their skin). So while 'black' may be prototypically assigned to the class of adjective on the semantic basis of its being an act of description in terms of the property of a color, it may also secondarily be a noun when that property is the grounds for categorization. Unlike the word classes noun and verb, the class of adjectives is not typically claimed to be universal. It is commonly noted that there are languages that lack this class. Of course, they do not lack words denoting properties, but these are assigned to or split between the formal syntactic classes of noun and verb.

Verbs are words that denote acts of predication. While 'categorization' and 'attribution' are terms and concepts that may be understood in familiar, everyday terms, 'predication' is a term in the formal jargon of linguistics and logic and not intelligible outside that context. Ultimately, 'predicate' is a term from logic and has two different uses, drawn from the traditional and the modern systems of logic respectively. In the traditional logic of Aristotle, sentences and propositions are analyzed into a predicate, which says something newsworthy about something, and a subject, about which something is said—for example, the dogs (subject) are hungry (predicate). What makes something newsworthy or at least notable is change or being unexpected, so that acts of predication will prototypically be associated with words that describe non-time-stable situations (Givon 1984), for example, actions, events, or processes, the usual semantics of members of the word class verb. On the other hand, the Aristotelian subject is what is held constant across various predications, that is, across any newsworthy descriptions we might make of it. This constancy favors descriptive stability and is thereby linked to words that describe well-defined and sharp categories, prototypically entities with bodies, the defining properties of which are taken to be largely unchanged through time; in short, subjects should be nouns, just as predicates should be verbs. We can predicate of a subject something other than an action, event, or process. We can predicate that it has a property (John is tall) or that it belongs to a category (dogs are carnivores) but, at least in English, this requires a predicating verb—'be' or a substitute—which then takes the property denoting adjective or category denoting noun. This requirement for a predicating verb like 'be' is undoubtedly a language-specific fact; many languages allow adjectives or nouns to function directly as predicating words, but even in such cases, good arguments can be presented to demonstrate that they are poorer predicators then verbs. So the following Aristotelian schema can be said to hold:

(1)

One of the strong objections to this Aristotelian schema is that it confuses a logical structure that may be quite serviceable for the analysis of logical propositions with a rhetorical structure that is needed for the analysis of sentences. Sentences occur, not in isolation, but as part of a sequence in a discourse. Real sentences are often not neatly divisible into a subject-predicate bifurcation. Sometimes what is newsworthy or predicated is the entire sentence, not just the verb: "What happened? A TREE just fell on the house" versus "Why did you cut it down? Well actually, we didn't; the tree FELL ON THE HOUSE"—where high pitch indicated by capitals shows the onset of the act of predication (Sasse 1987). Work on the rhetorical structure of sentences in text over the last century has strongly indicated the need for text-based concepts like topics (what is being talked about) and focus (the newsworthy information being provided about them in the text)—a distinction that rather crosscuts the old Aristotelian subject-predicate structure. Perhaps in the prototypical European language case they conflate as in (2):

(2)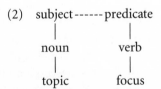

But an alignment like (2) is neither universal nor true of every sentence in any language, suggesting that the subject-predicate structure is in fact a Eurocentric idealized projection of the rhetorical structure of topic-focus in sentences. We might also query whether the opposition of predicate against subject is the only or even the best way to define an act of predication.

Considerations like these lead to an examination of the modern notion of predication, derived from the work of the German philosopher Gottlob

Frege. Here predication is understood in terms of the formal mathematical notions of a predicate calculus, where a predicate is an operation that holds over a set of one or more variables: $F(x)$, fall(x) [someone falls], hit(x, y) [someone hits something], give (x, y, z) [someone gives someone something]. This approach avoids the Aristotelian problem by obviating the link to newsworthiness for any act of predication (and hence conflation with focus); predication is simply an operation over variables. The weakness of this view is that it also removes any necessary association with non-time-stable situations, actions, events, and processes—in a word, verbs—as prototypical predicates, because any term can be a possible operation: tall(x) [someone is tall], carnivore (x) [something is a carnivore], etc. As a system of logic and the representation of logical structure this may well be desirable; but as an account of the structure of all natural languages it cannot be complete. Note that this Fregean notion of predicate is what is constant across contexts, the unit of the event, while the associated arguments are variables, for example, give (x, y, z). Every act of giving implies someone giving something to someone/something else, but what is given is unimportant for the type of event ('giving'), as is who gives (me, the Buddha, Nelson Mandela) or what is given (a dollar, a mustard seed, a peace prize). We have a contrast now between what is essential (the predicate, the act of giving) and what are possible realizations (the argument variables, the participants). Focusing on the noun-verb distinction, the words that denote events (verbs) are the variables (newsworthy predicates) in the Aristotelian subject-predicate analysis but the constants of the Fregean predicate calculus viewpoint, while the words that denote objects (nouns) are the constants in the Aristotelian system (subjects about which predications are made) but the variable arguments in the Fregean one.

How Children Acquire Language: Nouns and Verbs

While the semantic contrast of categorization linked to objects versus predication (of either the Aristotelian or the Fregean type) associated with actions, events, and processes may be the core of the putative universal noun-verb distinction, it is obvious that in any language many words formally assigned to the noun or verb classes fail to conform to these norms. Clearly, there are words describing events like meeting or appraisal that are syntactically nouns. And, as we have seen, words denoting categories can be predicates: dogs are carnivores; John is a fool. Indeed, words for objects can be transparently predicating verbs as well: a hammer, he hammered the nail; a book, he booked the criminals. This leads to a serious learning problem for the child: how is she to determine which words are nouns and which verbs?

The noun-verb contrast may be innate, but the assignment of individual words is not. How does the child do this?

Many strong nativists appeal to the argument for the poverty of the stimulus here. Again the claim is that the data available to children to learn the meaning of words are so incomplete, degraded, and susceptible to multiple interpretations that simple associationist learning is ruled out. The argument is a logical one, adapted from Quine (1960; for further discussion, see Foley 1997). Presented with an animate, hopping, furry object with long ears and a bobbed tail, how does the child learn to denote this by the word 'rabbit'? Any number of hypotheses can be entertained for the meaning of this word when presented with this stimulus: it means 'soft fur', 'long ears', 'rabbit stuff', 'furry animal', 'my pet', 'rabbit-y', or even 'a stage of rabbit becoming or rabbit-ing'. The proper meaning is radically undetermined by the stimulus input and cannot be acquired by normal associationist learning mechanisms. Therefore, it is argued, any learning must be supplemented by some innate knowledge that guides the acquisition—Fodor's (1975) "language of thought" in another guise. In other words, to make acquisition possible, something must restrict the search domain for possible meanings. Developmental psychologists (see summary in Bloom 2000) have proposed a number of principles, involving innate knowledge of folk physics, folk biology, etc., that guide the delimitation of word meanings. Two of these— termed the "whole-object bias constraint" and the "generic-level naming constraint"—are operative in the above example and cause the child to zero in on 'rabbit' as denoting the creature in front of her: (1) the whole-object bias constraint leads her to take it as a label for the whole object and not a part of it; and (2) the generic-level naming constraint causes her to take it as a name for this particular natural kind of object, not, say, furry animals in general (Atran 1998).

Principles like these may indeed play a role in allowing the child to get a toehold in the acquisition of nouns. But concepts labeled by verbs do not have the time-stable, material-world constancy that is so vital in permitting these principles to give the child an edge in acquiring the meanings of nouns, contrary to the assertions of Golinkoff et al. (1995). While the contrast between rabbit and kookaburra is highly salient in their time-stable divergent embodiments, that between hit and touch is not, but depends on the speaker's perspective. While the notion of perspective is relevant in both the object/noun and event/verb domains, it is quite different in the two domains. Perspective in the object/noun domain is mainly taxonomic (X is a kind of Y): kookaburra, bird, creature (Clark 1987, 1993). But in the event/ verb domain it is mainly syntagmatic, and not exclusive; "John sold the book to Fred," "Fred bought the book from John," and "Fred paid John for the book" can all describe the same perceptible event (see also Clark 1997). While the nature of the world with its salient perceptible distinctions between kookaburras and rabbits may aid the child in working out the meanings of the words describing these animals, perceptible world differences are not as useful in distinguishing between buying and paying. The semantics of verbs is clearly conceptually more difficult than that of nouns, and there are at present no convincing proposals for verbal-meaning acquisition principles similar to those suggested for the acquisition of the meanings of nouns. For example, consider the problem of learning the meaning of 'bark' in 'dog barks'. Clearly, the act of barking and the dog are not separable in the perceptible stimuli. While the meaning of 'dog' can be learned by comparison with other contexts involving dogs because dogs are time-stable, coherent, movable, and animate objects, this is not the case for 'bark': it is never isolatable from the dog. How the child learns its meaning probably depends much more on the contextual principles highlighted by Tomasello and Akhtar (1995) than on any innate, domain-specific cognitive guides like the whole-object bias constraint. Given that the child already knows 'dog' and the adult is saying the dog barks, the child uses her ability to ascribe an intentional state to the adult—namely, the adult is describing something newsworthy in the environment related to the dog. Tomasello and Akhtar's (1995) principle of "attending to what is new" then leads to an association of 'bark' with the salient sound produced by the dog.

Most studies of word acquisition show an early preponderance of nouns in children's vocabularies, although Gopnik and Choi (1995) argue this weighting of nouns over verbs is not universal. Tomasello and Olguin, in an intriguing pair of studies (Tomasello and Olguin 1993; Olguin and Tomasello 1993), demonstrate convincingly that twenty-five-month-old children acquiring English already have a robust grammatical category of noun but do not yet have an equivalent category of verb. Tomasello (1992) develops his "verb island hypothesis": children have words denoting actions and processes, but these fail to cohere into a single class of verb. There is no evidence of verb general grammatical properties: the indication of associated nouns is inconsistent and often particular to each verb, and the children never productively add the -ed past inflection to any of the newly learned words for actions and processes. Event-denoting words seem to behave idiosyncratically, with no overarching grammatical unity—hence, the "verb island hypothesis." All this is in very marked contrast to the knowledge of nouns at this age, which productively take -s for marking plural and are used creatively in a range of roles. Why the difference? Olguin and Tomasello (1993) postulate that verbs are the main organizing pivot of early (and adult) grammatical constructions and consequently are not easily amenable to being treated as mental objects for analysis. Note that the prototypical correlation between physical objecthood and the meaning of nouns should increase the ease with which nouns themselves could become mental objects for manipulation—that is, for analysis. Karmiloff-Smith (1992) argues that some systematic properties of complex domains only reveal themselves when the child reflects on them, analyzes them, and notes commonalities, and then redescribes them on a more comprehensive abstracted level. It is plausibly easier to do this redescription with nouns than verbs because verbs are not as readily isolatable from context (see Silverstein 1981 on limits to linguistic awareness) and are the pivots of the linguistic structures children utter.

But a fundamental process of higher-level redescription as discussed by Karmiloff-Smith (1992) is clearly also necessary for the learning of the meanings of nouns, no matter how pervasively guided this learning might be by putative innate constraints like the whole-object bias. Consider the meaning of 'dog'. The child hears the sound sequence d-o-g and, guided by the whole-object bias constraint and the generic-level naming constraint, learns that 'dog' is a sign for that particular type of animate object. But the child has not learned the meaning of 'dog'. She has simply learned the reference of 'dog'—that is, the object in the material world that 'dog' points to is the animal dog. But this is simply an indexical relationship, a space-time contiguity of sign and referent, not a true symbolic one, which must be a conventionalized, non-space-time-bound relationship between sign and concept. This is dog's reference, but not its sense. How does the child move from the index to the symbol? This requires fleshing out her understanding of dog with its properties, a redescription of what a dog is—in a word, the sense of dog. As Deacon (1997) points out, this requires a semantic field of dogs and cats, rabbits and bears, in which the child can redescribe the indexical relationship she has learned between dog and the animate real-world object as a symbolic one in which dogs implicate cats in shared features such as animal and pet, and in contrasting ones such as barking versus meowing and bones versus birds. Although domain-specific cognitive principles like the whole-object bias, generic-level naming, and mutual exclusivity (Golinkoff, Mervis, and Hirsh-Pasek 1994) may all play important roles in forging the indexical relationship sign to referent, they do not account for the crucial redescription from index to symbol. What is relevant for this move is Clark's (1997) and Tomasello's (1999) idea of perspective: recognizing the intentional (Searle 1998) choice of speakers to highlight different aspects of an object or scene: for example, general versus specific (dog versus kelpie), functional variability (father, man, teacher), or initiation (give versus get). Children must learn perspective by reading the intentions of speakers and following the principle of "attend to what is new" to override mutual exclusivity of terms. If the child knows 'dog' and, on meeting a new dog, hears her father say 'kelpie', a principle of mutual exclusivity of terms would lead her to try to find something new in the environment to attach the label 'kelpie' to. But given a reading of the adult's intention to talk about the dog and no other salient feature, the child concludes that 'dog' and 'kelpie' are perspectively different labels for dogs. A kelpie is a kind of dog; this realization leads to a description of features of kinds of dogs and how they might differ from cats and rabbits, ultimately building up the conceptual bedrock for the meaning of the symbol 'dog'.

This account tells us how children might ultimately learn the meanings of words, but it fails to explain how they learn that some of these are nouns and some are verbs. Essentially, there are two views here: semantic and syntactic bootstrapping. Semantic bootstrapping starts from a universal (presumably innate, but not necessarily in all variants of this approach), prototypical association between objects (time-stable entities) and nouns and between events (non-time-stable situations) and verbs. Children learn that words labeling each of these prototypes are nouns and verbs respectively. Children then extend these categories out to words labeling things more or less diverging from these prototypes—for instance, nouns like 'meeting' or 'appraisal' or verbs like 'afford' or 'fit'. How this extension is accomplished is never spelled out in much detail, but it must entail some role for syntactic bootstrapping; for example, there is common grammatical behavior for each type of word, so each type must belong to one class, noun or verb. Syntactic bootstrapping goes back to an early classic paper by Brown (1957) in which he demonstrated that three- to four-year-old children, when asked to identify 'another picture of sibbing' (verb frame), would construe 'sib' as a verb denoting an action of 'sibbing' but, when asked for 'another picture of a sib' (noun frame), would take 'sib' as a count noun referring to an object 'sib'. Syntactic bootstrapping thus works on distributional properties, the differential grammatical behavior of types of words, to induce word class membership. But how to know which grammatical behavior to attend to? For example, both nouns and verbs take a suffix -s in English: nouns, for pluralization, kookaburra-s; verbs, for present tense, laugh-s. How does the child ignore this in favor of the fact that verbs also take -ing, laugh-ing, but nouns do not, *kookaburra-ing? And what about the fact that many nouns do not take plural -s: *rice-s? Clearly, something has to guide the child in her inductions from syntactic bootstrapping, and this must be semantic bootstrapping: focus on the prototypes, discover their grammatical behavior, and induce from there. Note that the fascination of psychologists and linguists with morphologically simple English grossly underestimates this problem for syntactic bootstrapping: many highly complex languages have such elaborate systems of inflection that it may be a very onerous task indeed to disentangle the distinct word classes. Yimas, a Papuan language of New Guinea (Foley 1991), has more than a dozen different types of nouns, with several dozen distinct endings to indicate noun plurality. The difficulty for the child in working out a clear unified class of noun from this salad should not be underrated. Or in the case of a language like Choctaw (Davies 1986), with verb classes, in which the members of each verb class take distinct systems of inflection, how does a uniform class of verb emerge? Or even consider the problem of dual-category words (Nelson 1995) in English. A word like 'drink' is both a noun and a verb: three drink-s, he drink-s wine. How does the child work this out? A number of researchers have pointed out that dual-category words are a significant percentage of children's early lexicon (Dromi 1987; Nelson 1995; Tomasello 1992).

This last problem is potentially much more serious than it first appears. Consider a language in which virtually all the words behave like English 'drink'. How could a child ever work out classes of noun and verb in such cases, and further is there any reason to postulate distinct classes of noun and verb in such languages? Note that both semantic and syntactic bootstrapping would fail here: syntactic bootstrapping because there is no unique behavior to identify nouns and verbs; and semantic bootstrapping because words denoting prototypical objects would behave like those denoting prototypical events, and vice versa, making a mockery of any attempt to link either to a distinct word class. We must conclude that such languages would not present distinct classes of noun and verb, and I will now proceed to argue that there are indeed such languages. Such a claim directly challenges the assertion of the universality of the classes noun and verb, one of the most robustly held of all putative language universals, and thereby versions of strong nativism which mandate such universals. Any rebuttal of cherished putative linguistic universals directly questions the role of a deep abstract Universal Grammar in guiding language acquisition and ultimately constraining tightly the possible structures of human languages. To the extent that these linguistic universals fail to be validated, the case for innatism is undermined, and in turn, the rhetorical force of evolutionary psychology's own adaptation of argumentation following the lead of linguistics impaired.

The Contrast between Nouns and Verbs Is Not Universal

To get a feel of what the semantics of languages without a noun-verb distinction might be like, consider the English word 'rain'. As a native speaker of English, I have no clear intuitions as to whether 'rain' is a noun or a verb.

Obviously, per its grammatical behavior, it is both: heavy rain-s (noun), it's rain-ing heavily (verb). Furthermore, ontologically, rain has the properties of both a *thing* (it touches me; I feel it on my skin; I do see the water which is rain) and an *event* (it happens: rain is a weather event; it has relatively fleeting time stability; it has an incremental unfolding progression, including a beginning, duration, and end, and heavy versus light stages). Rain in the material world has the properties of both an object and an event, and in the world of the English language, 'rain' may be a noun or a verb. While 'rain' may be peripheral in the structure of English, there are languages in which this pattern is central to their lexical organization. Starting with a simple case, consider the Tongan word *tu'i* 'lead' (Broschart 1997):

(3a) ko   e   tu'i o   Tonga
     PROPER ART lead POSS Tonga
     'the king of Tonga'

(3b) 'oku kei tu'i 'a   Sione
     PRES still lead SUBJ John
     'John still rules'

Note that the same word tu'i is used as part of an act of categorization (like a noun) in (3a) and as part of an act of predication (like a verb) in (3b), but in neither case is there any change in its form. The acts of categorization and predication inhere, not in the word tu'i (i.e., it is neither a noun or a verb), but in the associated particles, e ARTicle and 'oku PREsent tense. The article e 'the' signals that an object is being referred to and tu'i 'lead' provides a search domain over which the reference may be applied, so that the act of categorization is only accomplished by setting up a potential domain for reference. Similarly, the AUXiliary 'oku PRES performs an act of predication and provides a time frame within which the predication is to hold; the complement tu'i simply supplies the domain of predication. In neither (3a) nor (3b) does tu'i 'lead' function as a noun or verb, categorizing or predicating; these functions belong to the associated particles. The word tu'i is therefore neither noun nor verb but precategorial; the functions served by nouns and verbs in more familiar languages are accomplished by the article and auxiliary particles:

(4)   reference-categorizing   predicating

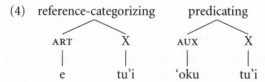

Note that this pattern is pervasive for Tongan roots, whether they denote prototypical objects (fefine 'woman') or events (lele 'run') (Broschart 1997):

(5a) 'oku fefine   e   kau lelé
    PRES woman ART PL run
    'the runners are female'

(5b) 'oku lele e   kau fefiné
    PRES run ART PL woman
    'the women are running'

In (5a) fefine 'woman' following 'oku PRES is used predicatively and like a verb, while lele 'run' co-occurs with the ARTicle e 'the' and functions in the referential-categorizing manner of a noun. In (5b) the roles are reversed, but with no alterations to the words, just a change in governing particle. The event word lele 'run' occurs with 'oku PRES and predicates like a verb, while fefine 'woman' is governed by the ARTicle e 'the' and behaves like a typical noun in categorizing. For English speakers, (5b) may seem more "natural" in that it conforms with our expectations of the behavior of event-denoting words as verbs and hence predicating and of object-denoting words as nouns and therefore categorizing. However, this judgment is in no way supported by the Tongan data. The example in (5a) is every bit as basic grammatically as (5b), and this should counsel us to be wary of elevating specific traits of English and familiar European languages to claims of substantive language universals and building these into the very structure of theorizing about the nature of language.

Nor are these patterns of Tongan in (3) and (5) rare cross-linguistically: they are attested in many other Austronesian languages, such as Tagalog, and in the Native languages of the Northwest Coast of North America, such as those of the Wakashan and Salishan families (Boas 1911; Sapir 1921; Swadesh 1939; Kinkade 1983; Jelinek and Demers 1994):

Nootka (Wakashan) (Swadesh 1939)
(6a) mamu·k-ma   qu·ʔas-ʔi
    work-AUX:PRES man-ART:DEF
        PRED   REF-CAT
    'the man is working'

(6b) qu·ʔas-ma   mamu·k-ʔi
    man-AUX:PRES work-ART:DEF
    PRED   REF-CAT
    'the worker is a man'

Upper Chehalis (Salishan) (Kinkade 1983)

(7a) ʔac-táw-ɬ   tit   ʔac-mə́lkʼʷ-ɬ
      STATE-be big-INTR   ART   STATE-be wrapped up-INTR
              PRED   REF-CAT
      'the package is big'

(7b) ʔac-mə́lkʼʷ-ɬ   tit   ʔac-táw-ɬ
      STATE-be wrapped up-INTR   ART   STATE-be big-INTR
              PRED   REF-CAT
      'the big one is wrapped up'

Tagalog (Austronesian)

(8a) nag-ta-trabaho ang abogado
      AUX:PRES-work   ART   lawyer
              PRED   REF-CAT
      'the lawyer is working'

(8b) nag-a-abogado   ang   nag-ta-trabaho
      AUX:PRES-lawyer   ART   AUX:PRES-work
              PRED   REF-CAT
      'the one working is becoming a lawyer'

Note that for all these languages there are transparently object-denoting words (Nootka quʼʔas 'man' and Tagalog abogado 'lawyer') that function as predicates—that is, verbally, with exactly the same formal realization as event-denoting words. There are also event-denoting words (Nootka mamuʼk- 'work' and Tagalog trabaho 'work') that function referentially-categorizingly, as nouns do, with the same grammatical indication, an ARTicle, as prototypical object-denoting words. There is neither need nor motivation for postulating distinct noun and verb syntactic classes, and further, there is no obvious way by either semantic or syntactic bootstrapping that a child learner could discover such a grammatical distinction in these languages. We must conclude that, contrary to received wisdom in this area, the noun-verb distinction is not universal.

Language Variation as Complexity

In wider typological terms, what are we to make of this contrast between familiar noun-verb European languages like German, French, and probably English and the more exotic precategorial Tongan, Tagalog, and Nootka? In noun-verb languages, the contrast of predication versus reference-categorization is inherent in the meanings of the words and is tied to lack of time stability versus constancy and hence ultimately to the prototypes of nouns and verbs, events and objects respectively (Broschart 1997). On the other hand, in precategorial languages there is no inherent tie between predication and lack of time stability and categorization and constancy, or ultimately prototypes of events and objects.[4] This is undoubtedly a fundamental break in the typology of human language: there are noun-verb languages and there are precategorial languages (and probably still more types waiting to be discovered). This typological contrast cannot be subsumed under a parsimonious Universal Grammar built in the image of English. Whatever is innate or "instinctual" (Pinker 1994)—and therefore fixed—in humans acquiring language, it can be neither the noun-verb distinction nor any necessary connection between nouns, objecthood, and categorization and verbs, eventhood, and predication. These connections are learned, not preset, because, as we have seen, the lexicon and grammatical patterns can be built otherwise. Whatever innate endowment for language we may have, it does not predetermine the division of words into the classes of nouns and verbs. The argument for innate mental structures in the human language "organ," advanced on the basis of linguistic universals, holds up only to the extent that the argument for the universality of specific linguistic features does. Given that the distinction between nouns and verbs is not universal, any argument for mental structures proposed on the basis of this putative linguistic universal is flawed.

What are the implications of these findings for strong nativist schools like evolutionary psychology? Evolutionary psychology takes much of its argumentation from linguistics (see, e.g., Plotkin 1998), but from linguistics of a highly denuded and theoretically overly abstracted kind, in which logical argument takes precedence over careful, empirical, and phenomenological studies of actual languages, and idealized universals projected from English are valorized over real linguistic diversity. Evolutionary psychology's indebtedness to linguistics is undoubtedly because such a priori focused linguistics is highly congenial to evolutionary psychology's a priori arguments from a variant of neo-Darwinian evolutionary theory.

In my view no real progress can be made in either linguistics or psychology until the question of human variation is faced head on. Evidence from a number of fields now strongly supports the contention that human cognitive endowments, however innate or domain specific, radically underdetermine the possibilities of human cognitive functions. The role of culture-based learning cannot be removed. The hackneyed old dichotomy of nature versus nurture should be retired: human cognition requires both, interacting in complex ways. This is to be expected. Human beings are organisms, with a genetic blueprint like any other, but our nervous system exhibits enormous plasticity, a property that continually has increased in the vertebrate line, and one that favors learning over instinct (see Gibson, chap. 1, this volume). As Elman et al. (1996) argue, what is innate is highly unlikely to be representable information—for instance, a syntactic category distinction between nouns and verbs—but architectural constraints on how things can be learned and represented. Thus, what is innate in this view are the ways connections can be formed rather than any mental structures or "organs" in which information as mental representations is stored. Information is an emergent property from the interaction of the organism (its biological endowment) with its environment and is not inherent in either (Maturana and Varela 1987); it is certainly not fixed in a structure of the human genome set down in the hunter-gatherer period. All evidence points to a central role of plasticity in human learning, now and in the past; this, if anything, is the lesson we can draw from evolutionary developments over the eons. And plasticity implies complexity, a place for humans where psyche and ethnos mutually unfold each other.

Pedagogical Postscript

It is important to point to the significance of these conclusions for pedagogical theory and practice. The Western grammatical and lexicographic tradition, derived as it is from languages with a strong noun-verb distinction like Greek and Latin, are unlikely to be completely adequate for precategorial languages like Tongan and Tagalog. Enriched linguistic tools are required to describe the semantic and grammatical systems of these languages well. Producing pedagogical materials for these languages with techniques derived from the Greco-Latinate linguistic tradition is not likely to provide students with the most insightful framework for learning. Indeed, one could probably justifiably characterize the efforts of much of scientific (and not so scientific) linguistics in these languages over the last few centuries as a kind of linguistic imperialism (killing off indigenous languages being another, more pernicious kind). It should be the goal of linguistics as a branch of anthropology to be free of such linguacentrism.

Notes

1. Such an approach, of course, has an ancient pedigree. For Plato, only the abstract, timeless universal "Ideas" existed; all else is contingent and imperfect. The other alternative, taking variation and change as fundamental, is more typical of Asian philosophical traditions like Buddhism (Dreyfus 1997) but is sporadically found in the West (e.g., Whitehead 1985) or in American pragmatism (Dewey 1977; James 1978, 1996; Rorty 1979, 1989, 1991). Here the question of commonality and constancy is problematic, and again often it is defined away, oc-

casionally by taking an idealist position. Most commonly, in contemporary social science, the primacy of variation is articulated in various constructivist theories.

2. Recursion is the ability to nest structures within each other, in Chinese-box-like fashion, theoretically without limit. English possessive phrases are a good example: the king, the king of England, the king of England's brother, the king of England's brother's wife, the king of England's brother's wife's sister, and so on.

3. See Chomsky's (1986) contrast between internal language, the true innate knowledge of language, and external language, the spoken/signed forms of language that one performs and perceives.

4. Whatever the basic meanings of the words themselves (an area poorly understood in these languages), predication/lack of time stability and categorization/constancy are in the associated particles and inflections, ARTicles and AUXiliaries. Although these languages might be Aristotelian in their binary sentence structure of predicate + referent/category, they clearly are Fregean in that the words themselves are just TYPE-variables whose specific instantiations are stipulated by functors, referential/categorizing ARTicles and predicating AUXiliaries or inflections; for example, Tongan fefine 'woman' can be referential/categorizing (e fefine ART woman 'the woman') or predicating ('oku fefine AUX:PRES woman 'be female'). Noun-verb languages are more consistently Aristotelian: the predicating word ties to lack of time stability, which ties to eventhood and hence to verb, whereas the subject ties to constancy, to objecthood, and finally to noun. All this isomorphism facilitates the acquisition of the noun-verb distinction through a combination of semantic and syntactic bootstrapping.

References

Atran, Scott. 1998. Folk Biology and the Anthropology of Science: Cognitive Universals and Cultural Particulars. *Behavioral and Brain Sciences* 21: 547–609.

Berlin, Brent. 1992. *Ethnobiological Classification.* Princeton: Princeton University Press.

Bloom, Paul. 2000. *How Children Learn the Meanings of Words.* Cambridge: MIT Press.

Boas, Franz. 1911. Kwakiutl. In *Handbook of American Indian Languages,* vol. 1, ed. Franz Boas, pp. 423–557. Bulletin of the Bureau of American Ethnology. Washington, DC: Smithsonian Institute.

Broschart, Jürgen. 1997. Why Tongan Does It Differently: Categorical Distinctions in a Language without Nouns and Verbs. *Linguistic Typology* 1: 125–65.

Brown, Roger. 1957. Linguistic Determinism and the Part of Speech. *Journal of Abnormal and Social Psychology* 55: 1–5.

Chomsky, Noam. 1980. *Rules and Representations.* New York: Columbia University Press.

———. 1986. *Knowledge of Language: Its Nature, Origin, and Use.* New York: Praeger.

Clark, Eve. 1987. The Principle of Contrast: A Constraint on Language Acquisition. In *Mechanisms of Language Acquisition: The Twentieth Annual Carnegie Symposium on Cognition,* ed. Brian McWhinney, pp. 1–33. Hillsdale, NJ: Erlbaum.

———. 1993. *The Lexicon in Acquisition.* Cambridge: Cambridge University Press.

———. 1997. Conceptual Perspective and Lexical Choice in Acquisition. *Cognition* 64: 1–37.

Cosmides, Leda, and John Tooby. 1992. Cognitive Adaptations for Social Exchange. In *The Adapted Mind: Evolutionary Psychology and the Generation of Culture,* ed. Jerome Barkow, Leda Cosmides, and John Tooby, pp. 163–228. New York: Oxford University Press.

Davies, William. 1986. *Choctaw Verb Agreement and Universal Grammar.* Dordrecht, Netherlands: Reidel.

Deacon, Terrence. 1997. *The Symbolic Species: The Co-evolution of Language and the Brain.* New York: Norton.

Dewey, John. 1977. *Experience and Nature.* Chicago: Open Court.

Dixon, Robert. 1977. Where Have All the Adjectives Gone? *Studies in Language* 1: 19–80.

Dreyfus, Georges. 1997. *Recognizing Reality.* Albany: State University of New York Press.

Dromi, Esther. 1987. *Early Lexical Development.* Cambridge: Cambridge University Press.

Elman, Jeffrey, Elizabeth Bates, Mark Johnson, Annette Karmiloff-Smith, Domenico Parisi, and Kim Plunkett. 1996. *Rethinking Innateness.* Cambridge: MIT Press.

Fodor, Jerry. 1975. *The Language of Thought.* New York: Crowell.

———. 1983. *The Modularity of Mind.* Cambridge: MIT Press.

Foley, William. 1991. *The Yimas Language of New Guinea.* Stanford: Stanford University Press.

———. 1997. *Anthropological Linguistics: An Introduction.* Oxford: Blackwell.

Givon, Talmy. 1984. *Syntax: A Functional-Typological Introduction.* Vol. 1. Amsterdam: Benjamins.

Golinkoff, Roberta, Kathy Hirsh-Pasek, Carolyn Mervis, William Frawley, and Maria Parillo. 1995. Lexical Principles Can Be Extended to the Acquisition of Verbs. In *Beyond Names for Things: Young Children's Acquisition of Verbs,* ed. Michael Tomasello and William Merriman, pp. 185–222. Hillsdale, NJ: Erlbaum.

Golinkoff, Roberta, Carolyn Mervis, and Kathy Hirsh-Pasek. 1994. Early Object Labels: The Case for a Developmental Lexical Principles Framework. *Journal of Child Language* 21: 125–55.

Gopnik, Alison, and Soonja Choi. 1995. Names, Relational Words, and Cognitive Development in English and Korean Speakers: Nouns Are Not Always Learned before Verbs. In *Beyond Names for Things: Young Children's Acquisition of Verbs,* ed. Michael Tomasello and William Merriman, pp. 63–80. Hillsdale, NJ: Erlbaum.

James, William. 1978. *Pragmatism and the Meaning of Truth.* Cambridge: Harvard University Press.

———. 1996. *Essays in Radical Empiricism.* Lincoln: University of Nebraska Press.

Jelinek, Eloise, and Richard Demers. 1994. Predicates and Pronominal Arguments in Straits Salish. *Language* 70: 697–736.

Jones, Doug. 1999. Evolutionary Psychology. *Annual Review of Anthropology* 28: 553–75.

Karmiloff-Smith, Annette. 1992. *Beyond Modularity.* Cambridge: MIT Press.

Kinkade, Dale. 1983. Salish Evidence against the Universality of "Noun" and "Verb." *Lingua* 60: 25–40.

Maturana, Humberto, and Francisco Varela. 1987. *The Tree of Knowledge: The Biological Roots of Human Understanding.* Boston: New Science Library.

Nelson, Katherine. 1995. The Dual Category Problem in the Acquisition of Action Words. In *Beyond Names for Things: Young Children's Acquisition of Verbs,* ed. Michael Tomasello and William Merriman, pp. 223–50. Hillsdale, NJ: Erlbaum.

Olguin, Raquel, and Michael Tomasello. 1993. Twenty Five Month Old Children Do Not Have a Category of Verb. *Cognitive Development* 8: 245–72.

Pinker, Steven. 1994. *The Language Instinct.* New York: Harper-Collins.

———. 1997. *How the Mind Works.* New York: Norton.

Plotkin, Harvey. 1998. *Evolution in Mind: An Introduction to Evolutionary Psychology.* Cambridge: Harvard University Press.

Quine, Willard. 1960. *Word and Object.* Cambridge: MIT Press.

Rorty, Richard. 1979. *Philosophy and the Mirror of Nature.* Princeton: Princeton University Press.

———. 1989. *Contingency, Irony and Solidarity.* Cambridge: Cambridge University Press.

———. 1991. *Objectivism, Relativism and Truth.* Cambridge: Cambridge University Press.

Sapir, Edward. 1921. *Language.* New York: Harcourt, Brace and World.

Sasse, Hans-Jürgen. 1987. The Thetic/Categorical Distinction Revisited. *Linguistics* 25: 511–80.

Searle, John R. 1998. *Mind, Language, and Society.* New York: Basic Books.

Silverstein, Michael. 1981. The Limits of Awareness. Working Papers in Sociolinguistics, 84. Austin, TX: Southwest Education Laboratory.

Slobin, Dan. 1997. *The Crosslinguistic Study of Language Acquisition.* 5 vols. Hillsdale, NJ: Erlbaum.

Spelke, Elizabeth, and Elissa Newport. 1998. Nativism, Empiricism and the Development of Knowledge. In *Handbook of Child Psychology,* vol. 1, ed. Richard Lerner, pp. 275–340. New York: Wiley.

Swadesh, Morris. 1939. Nootka Internal Syntax. *International Journal of American Linguistics* 9: 77–102.

Tomasello, Michael. 1992. *First Verbs: A Case Study of Early Grammatical Development.* Cambridge: Cambridge University Press.

———. 1999. *The Cultural Origins of Human Cognition.* Cambridge: Harvard University Press.

Tomasello, Michael, and Nameera Akhtar. 1995. Two Year Olds Use Pragmatic Cues to Differentiate Reference to Objects and Actions. *Cognitive Development* 10: 201–24.

Tomasello, Michael, and Raquel Olguin. 1993. Twenty Three Month Old Children Have a Category of Noun. *Cognitive Development* 8: 451–64.

Wellman, Henry, and Susan Gelman. 1992. Cognitive Development: Foundational Theories of Core Domains. *Annual Review of Psychology* 43: 337–75.

Whitehead, Alfred. 1985. *Process and Reality.* New York: Free Press.

Wierzbicka, Anna. 1986. What's in a Noun? (Or: How Do Nouns Differ in Meaning from Adjectives?) *Studies in Language* 10: 353–89.

CHAPTER 3

The Eye of the Beholder: How Linguistic Categorization Affects "Natural" Experience

Eve Danziger

> QUESTION: What do you call a guy who graduates at the bottom of his medical school class?
> ANSWER: Doctor.

This joke illustrates how human categorization imposes artificial discontinuities onto continuous phenomena. The categories thus created serve a variety of social, symbolic, and practical purposes. Anthropologists have found that the more socially and symbolically useful a particular category is in a society—innocent or guilty? friend or foe?—the more necessary it is to impose a strict conceptual discontinuity at the point where an appropriate reference must be distinguished from an inappropriate one (Durkheim and Mauss [1901] 1963; Lévi-Strauss [1962] 1966; Douglas 1966).

Much more interesting than the mere fact that humans categorize in this way is the fact that, once imposed, the arbitrary discontinuities of human classification can take on a conceptual life of their own and apparently have the power—to different degrees in different cases—to foster in their users the persuasive illusion that the reality that is classified is actually objectively discontinuous. Why else indeed, but for the realization that one may have entertained such an illusion about the concept "doctor," is the exchange above perceived as a joke and not simply as a statement of fact?

The tendency to believe that the categories conventionally imposed by one's particular cultural and linguistic tradition actually label preexisting and natural units of reality is widespread across human societies. Recognition of this phenomenon has underpinned the anthropological enterprise for most of its history. Recently, a powerful critique of the entire Western philosophical tradition along the same lines (Lakoff and Johnson 1999; see also Lakoff and Johnson 1980) has also emerged in the new interdisciplinary field of cognitive linguistics. The critique put forward by cognitive linguistics is that classic philosophical approaches are in error wherever they claim that putatively objective and essential categories transcend the perspective of their human users. It traces the origins of such doctrines to the intellectual illusion that linguistic categories simply name or label independently existing units of reality, a view of human linguistic categorization that has been dubbed the "classical categorization" view (Lakoff and Johnson 1980) because of its origins in the philosophy of Aristotle.

The "classical" approach proposes that linguistic categorization is a matter of identifying the common feature or features intrinsically possessed by all of the entities that belong in the named set. There is no room in this view for half measures; if an entity is perceived to possess the feature that licenses membership in the category, it is granted conceptual status as a full member of the category, regardless of other attributes that might makes its membership questionable. This is illustrated in the *doctor* exchange, which shows how little room there is in the conceptual category corresponding to English *doctor* for gradations of membership. I will refer to this type of categorization as the "all-or-nothing" type, and to the corresponding view of reality (entities exist in reality as discrete units that are readily distinguishable from one another; reality is not a continuum) as the "discontinuity illusion."

In unmasking the discontinuity illusion, a large proportion of the effort within cognitive linguistics has gone into exploring the graded nature of the realities to which words actually refer and into defending the role played by human experience, rather than by preexisting states of "objective" reality, in linguistic categorization (Lakoff 1987; Langacker 1986, 1987; Jackendoff 1987). The reopening of such familiar anthropological lines of argument from within cognitive science, and directed at the Western intellectual tradition, is welcome indeed. In particular, cognitive linguistics has taken aim squarely at the geneticized version of objectivism that has dominated linguistics for the last half century. In the view of Noam Chomsky (1975) and his followers, all significant linguistic categories exist independently of the situation of their users—including the particular language learned. The categories are present from birth, encoded in human DNA in a form that is autonomous of any subsequent experience.

Yet, even while effectively reestablishing human experience as foundational in the study of language, cognitive linguistics has been increasingly inclined to restrict the kinds of experience it is willing to consider to purely sensorimotor forms. It focuses on the kinds of experience that owe their existence to the physiology of the human organism, and it neglects those that come with belonging to a particular social or cultural group. This tendency has culminated in the announcement of an entirely new paradigm in the study of human affairs. The self-styled "embodied mind" approach (Lakoff and Johnson 1999) places individual sensorimotor experience at the heart of human categorization, and therefore at the heart of all of the human sciences. This paradigm assumes that there exists a fundamental and readily intuited distinction between "natural" firsthand physiological experience and experiences originating in social life or cultural convention. In this view, not only are all individual physiological experiences alike cross-culturally, but they are also thought to underlie and inform those experiences deemed to originate in social and cultural conventions.

In what follows I will use two case studies from my own research to underscore the point that, in fact, the reverse is often true. Both social scientists and perceptual psychologists know full well that "all-or-nothing" categorization, and the accompanying illusion that words function to name the units of an objective and discontinuous reality, are not confined to the tomes of Western philosophy but are also a widespread fact of everyday human life, even in non-Western societies. As such, our everyday intuitions about what is "natural" in human experience—including sensory experience—are often the products of the very categorization processes that cognitive linguistics invokes these intuitions to explain. Cognitive linguistics misses this essential point by continuing, in the Chomskyan vein, to treat language as purely an individual phenomenon to be reinvented by each individual in every generation. But linguistic and other cultural categories are collective conventions that themselves can inspire and construct, as well as reflect, aspects of the individual's experience.

Classical Categorization and the Discontinuity Illusion in Everyday Life: Two Case Studies

In its emphasis on experience rather than on innate structures in accounting for linguistic meaning, the cognitive linguistics approach represents a significant advance over its immediate predecessor: the hyperrationalism of the Chomskyan view. The positive contribution of cognitive linguistics has been to promote the role of the human subject in understanding the making of meaning. The categories in which humans think do not preexist them in some transcendental fashion, and they have no "objective" reality beyond the confines of human experience (see also Sapir [1933] 1949). However, the kind of experience that is imagined to underlie human cognition in the cognitive linguistics paradigm is that of the purely sensorimotor, not understood to be significantly modified by the intrusion of particular cultural or linguistic practices. In reverting to a notion of experience that thus appeals to sensory universals at the expense of cultural particulars, this valuable advance is in danger of degenerating to become yet another reductionist and universalizing model of human life and human meaning.

The problem resides in a view of language that cognitive linguistics appears to have inherited from the Chomskyan paradigm—that language is a phenomenon properly studied at the level of the individual organism alone. But individual human experience always very saliently includes experience with preexisting linguistic and cultural categories. The protestations of cognitive linguists to the contrary, these categories indeed often show "classical," all-or-nothing structure and may project their conventional divisions of reality onto the experience of the physiological individual. Therefore, our own intuitions about what is universal and natural, even in sensorimotor experience, may well themselves be the products of cultural classification.

To reinforce these points, I now discuss two different cases from my own work. I show, first, that all-or-nothing categorization, involving feature-based definitions, indeed occurs in everyday human life and, second, that the structure of such categories imposes itself upon the individual experience of their users, giving the users the intuition of self-evident "naturalness" (the discontinuity illusion). The first example describes some of the ideas, practices, and intuitions surrounding family relationships among the Mopan Maya, a group of subsistence farmers located in Central America. The second concerns the difference between the perceptual intuitions of literate and nonliterate people in several language communities when confronted by two-dimensional mirror-image reflections.

CASE STUDY 1: CLASSICAL CATEGORIES AND EVERYDAY LIFE

Cognitive linguistics made its reputation on the discovery (Berlin and Kay 1969) that speakers often agree in their intuitions that certain of the referents denoted by a linguistic term can be considered "better examples" of the term than others. For example, American English-speaking college students overwhelmingly agree that *robin* is a better example of *bird* than is *penguin* (Rosch 1978). This general finding has led to the proposal that linguistic categories are internally structured in cognition, with "best-example" (focal) referent concepts at the psychological center and other referent concepts at the psychological periphery. Peripheral referents are understood to be linked to the central one(s) through associative chains called semantic extensions (see Lounsbury 1964, 1969, for early theoretical statements of the idea). So, for example (Lakoff 1987), if we ascertain by asking a number of English speakers that a woman who conceives, bears, and rears her child is the best-example referent of the English linguistic category *mother,* then we propose a cognitive structure for that category in which this referent is at the center, and other possible referents (surrogate mothers, adoptive mothers, classificatory mothers, reverend mothers) occupy the conceptual periphery and are attached to the best example by various and different associative links. It is also proposed that the best-example (focal) referent is such by virtue of "natural" and directly physiological experience with such referents around the world (see also Malinowski 1930).

It is further often noted that the center-and-periphery structure collocates with "fuzzy edges" in a category. That is, categories are often not strictly bounded in human reflective intuition; if we get sufficiently far from the center of our category, we may discover that native speakers are without certainty when asked whether a given referent should count as a member of the category at all (e.g., *pterodactyl* for *bird? ovum donor* for *mother?*). The view that the clear-center-and-fuzzy-periphery kind of conceptual structure is pervasive—not only in speakers' reflective judgments about word meanings but also in everyday linguistic practice—is widely proclaimed today, and analyses in this vein proliferate (Lakoff 1987; Langacker 1986, 1987; Kronenfeld 1996; G. Palmer 1996).

Clearly, this is a very different view of categorization from the all-or-nothing view described above. In classical categorization, recall, referents are believed to cohere into categories by virtue of their possession of some common defining feature. In that model, all legitimate referents are equally good examples of the category, and there can be no uncertainty about category membership: a referent either does or does not possess the characteristic (often an essential quality) that licenses membership in the category. Cognitive linguistics has done an excellent job of pointing out how the very notion that referents inherently "possess" certain attributes—rather than that humans experience them in certain ways—has been the gateway to all sorts of fallaciously objectivizing or transcendentalizing scholarly accounts of the universe (Lakoff and Johnson 1999).

The power of the critique is marred, however, by the fact that cognitive linguistics tends to dismiss all-or-nothing categorization as the preserve of dusty and mistaken philosophers, the absentminded descendants of Aristotle, who are out of touch with the realities of linguistic categorization in the lives of everyday folk. Cognitive linguistics discerns correctly the power of classical, all-or-nothing categorization to create the discontinuity illusion—the illusion that reality matches up neatly with the units of language. But in its enthusiasm to celebrate its discovery of clear-center-and-fuzzy-periphery categorization, cognitive linguistics ignores the actual pervasiveness of feature-based categorization—complete with discontinuity illusion—in all societies (irrespective of Aristotelian influence) and at the most everyday level.

The Mopan Maya are an indigenous group of farmers located in eastern Central America, descendants of the famous ancient Maya of the same region.[1] Among these people today, much respect is paid to age and experience. The members of your family are terminologically distinguished by whether they belong to your own or to your parents' age-grade, rather than by what English speakers would consider their exact genealogical relationship. For example, a parent's sibling who is close to yourself in age is classified with your own siblings, but a parent's sibling who is much older than yourself is classified with your grandparents (see Danziger 2001b for details). Of course, age is a continuum, but in Mopan it is culturally important to determine exactly to which age-grade category each of your relatives belongs so that you can offer to each of them the correct degree of respect by using the correct age-grade term in greeting him or her. If you do not address a relative with the appropriate relationship term, you will be considered very rude and are likely to be told that you are behaving "like a dog" or "like an animal." If your relative is of the opposite sex from yourself, failure to greet him or her with the right age-grade term provokes especial horror, of the kind associated with incest taboo violations.

As well as monitoring their own speech, Mopan speakers judge others' use of age-graded respect greeting terms and they scrutinize it for impropriety. If speakers are to avoid scandal and sacrilege, they must know whether or not a kinship term applies to their own relationship with every other individual in the community. If such a term is applicable, they must know what term it should be. And Mopan people *do* know. Parents inform their children about respect relationships and instruct them from childhood. All those who are considered relatives belong to one or another of the age-graded terminological categories, and there is never uncertainty as to which category is correct for a given individual. Most importantly for our purposes, Mopan speakers do not believe that these terminological categories are matters of convenience or arbitrary labeling. They believe (as we do) that their kinship terms label actual statuses that preexist their labels.

An interesting situation arises when a young Mopan person gets married. All of one's new spouse's siblings will become one's in-laws, and it is suddenly necessary to decide which terminological category is the right one for each. Once again, age-grade is the determining factor. A spouse's eldest sister, for example, is as likely to be classified with the mother-in-law as with the younger sisters (fig. 1). At engagement parties, time is set aside for elders to debate and ultimately to declare in public exactly what the new spouse will henceforth call each of the new in-laws. Since this requires that discontinuous categories be created over what is actually a continuous field (age), this is no simple matter. Foreseeably, there is often difficulty in agreeing on

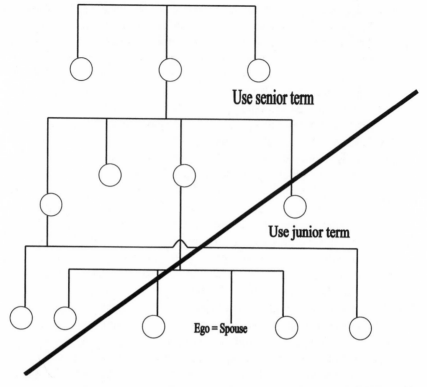

Figure 1. Mopan relationships acquired through marriage. Relatives in the same generation are ordered left to right in order of decreasing chronological age.

the term to apply to a particular relationship. But even where there is explicit difference of opinion, every candidate is, by the end of the gathering, firmly placed by public fiat squarely into one category or another—there are no "fuzzy" cases allowed.

Certain aspects of the whole procedure appear clearly arbitrary to the outside observer. But from the discussions that occur, it is equally clear that the participants believe that their decision about which term to apply, although a thorny one, should be guided by the effort to discover the "true" nature of the referent. To them the issue is to decide whether this person is "objectively" in the new spouse's age-grade or not.[2]

This is a case of classical categorization engaged in by unlikely Aristotelians—and for the purposes of everyday life. Clear judgments about category membership across what is actually a continuous referential field (relative age) are culturally required. This means that, just as in our *doctor* example, some assignments of referents to terminological category are not clear or best-example cases. But—again as illustrated in the *doctor* exchange—the participants entertain the strong intuition that all cases are clear once decided. They maintain that the terminology follows reality, and not vice versa. Most important of all, this is not by any means a special situation. Anthropologists have determined that social categorization of this classical, all-or-nothing sort occurs very frequently around the world. And intuitions as to the naturalness of the realities so classified are often very strong indeed.

CASE STUDY 2: PHYSICAL PERCEPTION AND CULTURAL CATEGORIZATION

Cognitive linguistics has made a distinct contribution in pointing out that linguistic categories owe their existence to human experience with referents and not to the properties of the referents themselves. But as work in this paradigm has progressed, the kind of experience that is invoked to play the crucial role of best-example referent in most cases of linguistic categorization has increasingly been drawn from an imagined, so-called natural realm of individual sensory perception and physical movement, shared by all humans, and now explicitly understood to be located in human neurology (although not necessarily in genetics). The cognitive primacy of this unproblematically noncultural realm of "human-sized experience" (Lakoff 1987) in cognitive linguistics is no longer a hypothesis to be tested but a basic assumption of the approach. Indeed, it is the major thesis on which its latest incarnation, the embodied mind approach, makes its claim to importance.

Following the pattern of the earlier research which, recall, simply asked speakers to consult their reflective intuitions about the best-example referents of a word, the new paradigm continues to allow conscious intuition to decide exactly which aspects of experience are most natural and therefore most likely to be instantiated in the neurology of every member of our species. These reductionist assumptions are all the more troubling in that even the original method for establishing the existence and nature of focal referents (demonstrating many speakers' intuitive agreement on the identity of best examples) has degenerated to the point where the analyst's own intuitions alone virtually always suffice to license the claim that a given referent is the best example for most speakers, and that the requisite cognitive architecture of focal referent, motivated extensional chains, and fuzzy boundaries indeed exists in these speakers' minds. Despite the explicit and repeated claim that these analyses represent the "cognitive" state of affairs for actual speakers, rather than reified philosophical accounts, the proposed analyses are almost never subjected to empirical verification or scrutiny.

The programmatic assertion that the physical and sensory are the universal and "natural" sources of focal referents in human conceptualization renders the analyst's solitary task of intuiting which are the focal referents in any given case ever less demanding, and the hypothesis of physiological primacy ever more self-fulfilling.[3] In fact, we know that human sensory perception is not sealed off from penetration and modification by cultural learning. And we know this in part precisely because we can document that our conscious intuition about what is "natural" in perceived reality is at times clearly the product of penetration of this kind. The anthropologist Edward Sapir was among the first to explore this territory. He made several brilliant demonstrations of the fact that speech sounds have a psychological, rather than a purely physical, existence for speakers (Sapir 1925, [1933] 1949). In one well-known example, Sapir (1925) pointed out that the sounds represented by the letter *k* in the English words *kill* and *skill* do not have the same physical properties. This can be ascertained by holding the palm of the hand close to the face when pronouncing the two words. In *kill*, the *k* is accompanied by a puff of air; in *skill*, it is not. The fact that English speakers do not hear this physical difference is significant, since in some of the world's languages (e.g., Hindi) it is actually exploited to distinguish among different words. The physical difference is therefore clearly within the range of human perception. The fact that English speakers nevertheless perceive it as inaudible is clear testimony to the fact that the phenomenology of our sensory experience is open to modification by the use of sensory stimuli in culturally organized systems for the making of meaning.[4]

Sapir's observations can today be fitted into a robust corpus of more recent findings that goes by the name of "categorical perception" in cognitive psychology (Harnard 1987).[5] That corpus tends rather resoundingly to refute the thesis that human perception is immune to and independent of cultural learning. On the contrary, it shows that very often, when apparently imperceptible sensory contrasts are useful in discriminating between all-or-nothing categories that have cultural significance, their ready discrimination is acquired by the experts charged with making the relevant decisions—and the perceptions involved come to seem "natural" and obvious to them. Likewise, humans may lose sensitivity to small but perceptible sensory distinctions that have no cultural function for them, as in the *kill/skill* example.

This happens, exactly as Sapir proposed, in the speech sounds of language (Jusczyk 1996) as well as when language is embedded in the visual/spatial modality (Emmorey 1993).[6] Such effects are also to be observed beyond language—for example, when certain professionals have to decide on the basis of visual inspection whether a particular baby chick, about to be sold for egg production, is in fact female (Biederman and Shiffrar 1987), or when others must say whether a certain blurry shadow in an X-ray photograph means remission or radical surgery (Norman et al. 1992). Uniting such disparate cases is the common finding that human perceptual intuitions are susceptible to modification in response to the fact of cultural categorization. Taken together, these findings show beyond any doubt that human perceptual understandings are sensitive to the conventions of cultural and linguistic categorization. Any particular speaker's conscious intuitions about what is natural in physical reality cannot be taken at face value for a simple view of the world of culture-free universals.

In another case study from my own work, I now briefly show that a certain strong intuition of perceptual naturalness, shared by most of my readers, is almost certainly culturally and linguistically acquired.[7] Schoolchildren at about the age of four or five often encounter a particular difficulty as they learn to read and write (Casey 1984). They tend sometimes to reverse their letters, suggesting that the conventional right-left orientation of the letters of the Roman alphabet (e.g., the letter [b] versus the letter [d]) is as yet a matter of indifference to them. They even sometimes adopt a style of writing in which, when the end of one line of left-to-right writing is reached, they continue writing right-to-left on the next line, with all the letters right-left reversed.

However, as time goes by, these children mature, and most of them acquire the orientational conventions necessary to writing and reading English. They come to share the intuition of the adults around them that the inverted forms that they had formerly produced are mistakes. In fact, they come to feel that right-facing and left-facing two-dimensional forms are fundamentally perceptually distinct and that to base critical functional contrasts on them, as we do in the Roman alphabet, is a perfectly natural thing to do.

And they are quite wrong. In fact, it's the other way around. Basing functional contrasts on the difference between right-facing and left-facing two-dimensional figures itself creates the intuition of the "natural" perceptual distinctness of such figures. In learning to read and write in the Roman alphabet, children learn, quite literally, to see the world in a way that they had not done before, and in a way that many adults who do not happen to be literate in the Roman alphabet do not see it.

In work conducted by the Cognitive Anthropology Research Group of the Max Planck Institute for Psycholinguistics, a formal tool for eliciting intuitions about left-right contrasts across language and literacy contexts was designed (see fig. 2). Participants in the study were shown two different plastic cards with simple abstract line drawings printed on them. They were asked to judge whether or not the simpler figure on one card could be found as part of (or "inside") the more complex figure drawn on the other. There were five complex-figure cards (only one is illustrated, in the left column of

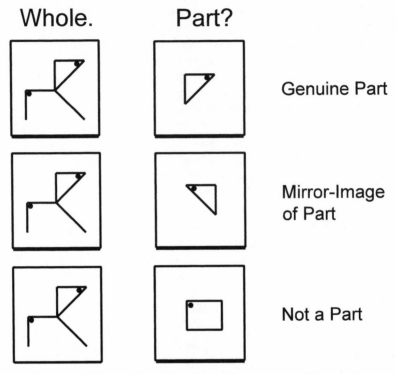

Whole.   Part?

Genuine Part

Mirror-Image
of Part

Not a Part

Figure 2. A formal tool for eliciting intuitions about left-right contrasts across language and literacy contexts. (Cognitive Anthropology Research Group, reprinted with permission of Max Planck Institute for Psycholinguistics)

fig. 2), and each was shown three different times, once in conjunction with a genuine part (top pair in fig. 2), once with a clear non-part (bottom pair in fig. 2), and once with a figure that is the left-right mirror image of the true part (middle pair in fig. 2).

Participants were instructed to accept the genuine part and to reject both the clear non-part and the mirror-image part. Note that what is requested is an intuitive perceptual judgment as to the sameness or differentness of mirror-image reflections. Adults in ten different language communities and representing six different language families were asked to complete an expanded version of this formal task.[8] Both literate and nonliterate adults were represented. Roman-alphabet literates from many cultural backgrounds readily saw mirror-image reflections as distinct from one another, rejecting the mirror-image matches across multiple trials, as per the study's instructions. But if adults were not literate in the Roman alphabet, this sense of the naturalness of the right-left mirror-image distinction was far from universally present. That is, many nonliterate adults around the world preferred to accept rather than to reject the mirror-image part, even with explicit instructions to the contrary (Levinson and Brown 1994; Danziger and Pederson 1998; Danziger 1999; Pederson 2003).[9]

In short, the perceptual intuition that two-dimensional right-left rotated figures are readily distinguishable—natural as it appears to those of us who hold it—is culturally acquired. In learning to read and write the Roman alphabet, countless children undergo a process of perceptual socialization in which their sensory intuitions come to conform to certain perceptual conventions which have a cultural function in their own—but not in all—societies.[10]

Findings such as these make all of our perceptual intuitions highly suspect. They need not augur against the existence of any experiential, conceptual, or linguistic universals at all (see Danziger 2001a for extended discussion), but they do show that first-pass intuitions as to what is "natural" in experience across cultures must be examined very carefully before they are enshrined as such. It is a grave mistake to assume that any given speaker's intuitions about what is natural in perception represent a transparent reflection of universal and noncultural experience. We cannot assume that our perceptual intuitions, no matter how persuasive, are sealed off from cultural penetration, or that they are available as universal inputs to putatively more cultural domains of conceptualization.

The Problem of the Stratigraphic Metaphor

Cognitive linguistics has been instrumental in showing how everyday metaphors inform scientific thinking. The embodied mind paradigm, now emerging from the field of cognitive linguistics, itself shows signs of becoming a prime example. From economic history to child development, reductionism can be found reposing in a recurrent "stratigraphic" metaphor (Geertz 1973: 37). In this metaphor, human life is divided up into a series of qualitatively different units, each consisting of independently organized material and each susceptible to the different modes of analysis characterizing the distinct academic disciplines of the Western tradition (sociology, psychology, or biology, to name but a few). We can see this operating across the intellectual spectrum—from materialist economic models of social life (Marx) to theories of child development that view growth as a matter of biological "unfolding" (Piaget). The model is stratigraphic because the units are conceptualized, like sealed soil strata, as vertical layers, each of which underlies another. With the right tools and techniques, the more "superficial" layers may be successfully stripped off in sequence to reveal the intact lower layers beneath. This metaphor incorporates the assumption that while the lower layers are sealed off from and invulnerable to penetration by the material contained in the layers above them, influence can and does pass upward from underlying to more superficial layers.

A strongly stratigraphic architecture is to be found in the proposals of the embodied mind paradigm. The continuing move toward situating focal referents in universal sensory experience adds the usual stratigraphic content (physical and sensory reality underlies social and conceptual reality) to what was already a clearly stratigraphic form (one sense of any given word conceptually "underlies" the others). Faith in a sealed stratigraphic architecture is also what allows the cognitive linguist to appeal with confidence to his or her own intuitions as to what constitutes "natural" sensory experience. If the lower layers are firmly sealed off from the upper ones, the analyst need have no fear that such intuitions might themselves be the products of local cultural and linguistic practice. A key omission in the embodied mind initiative, then, is its neglect of the effect that linguistic categorization can have on individuals' intuitions about their own experiences, including sensory experiences. This omission arises from a failure to incorporate into the theory the fact that human individuals always encounter languages as social facts which predate the individuals' own existence. As part of this encounter, individuals must sometimes deal with all-or-nothing categorizations—a form of cognitive ordering found in all cultural traditions and not unique to classical philosophy. All language users are therefore vulnerable to the discontinuity illusion, one that can affect even the most-forceful-seeming intuitions about perceptual experience. This makes it impossible to trust individual reflective intuitions for reliable data about the boundary between the natural and the cultural.

Conclusion

In arguing that students of language should not succumb in their analyses to essentialist illusions about a discontinuous reality, and indeed in pointing out the relationship of these illusions to all-or-nothing types of linguistic categorization (classical categorization), cognitive linguistics reopens and advances some of the best ideas in the linguistic anthropology tradition. However, in suggesting that all-or-nothing categorization is merely a scholarly invention and is not actually used by real speakers in everyday life, cognitive linguistics is simply empirically mistaken. Worse, in denying the role played by all-or-nothing categorization in actual speech and in everyday life, cognitive linguistics denies the significant contribution of linguistic convention itself to the intuitions and experience of any human individual.

As social and symbolic anthropologists have amply documented, and as the Maya kinship example here illustrates, all-or-nothing categorization, complete with accompanying discontinuity illusion, is alive and thriving, far beyond the reach of Aristotelian philosophy. And, as the findings of cognitive psychologists demonstrate, and the mirror-image study exemplifies, cultural and linguistic categories readily impose their structure onto individuals' experience. By relying heavily on analysts' and others' intuitions both about the primacy of physiological experience and about the nature of such experience, the embodied mind paradigm makes itself vulnerable in its own analyses to the very discontinuity illusion that it seeks to deconstruct. As always (Whorf [1940] 1956), it rests with those of us who wish to know more about the nature of our common humanity to proceed by being skeptical of, rather than by relying on, our intuitions of what it is that constitutes the "natural."

Notes

1. My work with the Mopan Maya was supported by the Wenner-Gren Foundation for Anthropological Research and by the Social Sciences and Humanities Research Council of Canada. See Danziger 2001b and Gregory 1984 for more ethnographic detail about the Mopan.

2. The difference in chronological age between the two parties is ostensibly the issue. But decisions are influenced by other questions. Is the new in-law already married? If so, count as "older." Or is he or she still attending school? If so, count as "younger."

3. This empirical slippage has not gone completely unnoticed within the paradigm itself, which does acknowledge in principle the distinction between "phenomenological" (i.e., consciously intuited) and other cognitive levels of embodiment (Lakoff and Johnson 1999: 102–3). But the practical application of such a distinction would require a more skeptical attitude toward the use of intuition in analysis than is actually to be observed. Even those few cognitive linguists (e.g., Sandra and Rice 1995) who valiantly endeavor to reintroduce empirical accountability into the paradigm do not leave the domain of conscious intuition. Instead, their response takes the form of a return to asking large numbers of speakers for their intuitions about best-example referents (see also Lyons 1986 for critical discussion of introspection as a method in cognitive research).

4. For an example of the opposite effect (illusion of physical difference where there is none), read the following two phrases out loud, as they are written, to a native speaker of English. Does your listener feel that the middle word in phrase *a* rhymes with the middle word in phrase *b*?

(*a*) The firs' example

(*b*) The verse example

Despite the fact that the words *firs'* and *verse* end with the same physical sound, many English speakers have a strong feeling that the words do not rhyme, since *firs'* is actually an abbreviated form of *first*. This is an auditory illusion, revealing that *firs'* and *first* are perceived by English speakers as members of a single meaningful category and not merely as brute sensory stimuli (this example is calqued from example II, Sarcee, in Sapir [1933] 1949: 52–54).

5. I am grateful to Robert Goldstone for drawing my attention to this body of scholarship.

6. Notably, categorical perception effects have also been documented as a function of language-particular color classifications (Kay and Kempton 1984; see also Goldstone 1995).

7. The research was supported by the Cognitive Anthropology Research Group of the Max Planck Institute for Psycholinguistics. It was inspired by the work of Arlette Verhaeghe and Régine Kolinsky (1991) and informed by that of Stephen Palmer (1977). The experimental design was finalized by Stephen Levinson and Bernadette Schmidt. The Max Planck Institute for Psycholinguistics holds the copyright for figure 2, which is reprinted here with permission.

8. Data were collected by Penelope Brown (Tzeltal Maya), Eve Danziger (Mopan Maya), Deborah Hill (Longgu), Kyoko Inoue (Japanese), Elizabeth Keating (Pohnpeian), Steven Levinson (Tzeltal Maya), Paulette Levy (Totonac), Ester Messing (Dutch), Eric Pederson (Tamil), Gunter Senft (Kilivila), and Christel Stolz (Yucatec Maya). For fuller details see Danziger and Pederson 1998.

9. Intriguing findings by Kolinsky, Morais, and Verhaeghe (1994) show that the neurology involved in the brute perception of this sort of figure is similar across literate and nonliterate individuals; this is irrelevant to the same individuals' intuitions about what they are "naturally" perceiving.

10. Other research has also shown that even among those who participate in the intuition that lateral rotation of arrangements in space makes a difference, the experience of that intuition is culturally variable. In many cultures such rotation is neither described nor experienced as "right-left" inversion but as inversion in the relationship of figures to the surrounding landscape (something like "north-south" or "inland-seaward" inversion). See Pederson et al. 1998 for details.

References

Berlin, Brent, and Paul Kay. 1969. *Basic Color Terms: Their Universality and Growth.* Berkeley and Los Angeles: University of California Press.

Biederman, Irving, and Margaret M. Shiffrar. 1987. Sexing Day-Old Chicks: A Case Study and Expert Systems Analysis of a Difficult Perceptual Learning Task. *Journal of Experimental Psychology: Learning, Memory, and Cognition* 13(4): 640–45.

Casey, M. Beth. 1984. Individual Differences in Use of Left-Right Visual Cues: A Reexamination of Mirror-Image Confusions in Preschoolers. *Developmental Psychology* 20(4): 551–59.

Chomsky, Noam. 1975. *Reflections on Language.* New York: Random House.

Danziger, Eve. 1999. Language, Space and Sociolect: Cognitive Correlates of Gendered Speech in Mopan Maya. In *Language Diversity and Cognitive Representations*, ed. Catherine Fuchs and Stéphane Robert, pp. 85–106. Amsterdam: Benjamins.

———. 2001a. Cross-Cultural Studies in Language and Thought: Is There a Metalanguage? In *The Psychology of Cultural Experience*, ed. Carmella C. Moore and Holly F. Mathews, pp. 199–222. Publications for the Society of Psychological Anthropology. Cambridge: Cambridge University Press.

———. 2001b. *Relatively Speaking: Language, Thought, and Kinship among the Mopan Maya.* New York: Oxford University Press.

Danziger, Eve, and Eric Pederson. 1998. Through the Looking-Glass: Literacy, Writing Systems, and Mirror-Image Discrimination. *Written Language and Literacy* 1(2): 153–64.

Douglas, Mary. 1966. *Purity and Danger.* New York: Frederick A. Praeger.

Durkheim, Emile, and Marcel Mauss. [1901] 1963. *Primitive Classification.* Translated by Rodney Needham. Chicago: University of Chicago Press.

Emmorey, Karen. 1993. Processing a Dynamic Visual-Spatial Language: Psycholinguistic Studies of American Sign Language. *Journal of Psycholinguistic Research* 22(2): 153–87.

Geertz, Clifford. 1973. The Impact of the Concept of Culture on the Concept of Man. In *The Interpretation of Cultures: Selected Essays,* by Clifford Geertz, pp. 33–54. New York: Basic Books.

Goldstone, Robert L. 1995. Effects of Categorization in Color Perception. *Psychological Science* 6(5): 298–304.

Gregory, James R. 1984. *The Mopan: Culture and Ethnicity in a Changing Belizean Community.* University of Missouri Monographs in Anthropology, no. 7. Columbia: Museum of Anthropology, University of Missouri—Columbia.

Harnard, Stevan. 1987. *Categorical Perception: The Groundwork of Cognition.* Cambridge: Cambridge University Press.

Jackendoff, Ray. 1987. On beyond Zebra: The Relation of Linguistic and Visual Information. *Cognition* 26: 89–114.

Jusczyk, Peter W. 1996. Developmental Speech Perception. In *Principles of Experimental Phonetics,* ed. Norman J. Lass, pp. 328–61. New York: Musby.

Kay, Paul, and Willett Kempton. 1984. What Is the Sapir-Whorf Hypothesis? *American Anthropologist* 86: 65–79.

Kolinsky, Régine, José Morais, and Arlette Verhaeghe. 1994. Visual Separability: A Study on Unschooled Adults. *Perception* 23: 471–86.

Kronenfeld, David B. 1996. *Plastic Glasses and Church Fathers.* New York: Oxford University Press.

Lakoff, George. 1987. *Women, Fire, and Dangerous Things: What Categories Reveal about the Mind.* Chicago: University of Chicago Press.

Lakoff, George, and Mark Johnson. 1980. *Metaphors We Live By.* Chicago: University of Chicago Press.

———. 1999. *Philosophy in the Flesh: The Embodied Mind and Its Challenge to Western Thought.* New York: Basic Books.

Langacker, Ronald W. 1986. An Introduction to Cognitive Grammar. *Cognitive Science* 10: 1–40.

———1987. *Foundations of Cognitive Grammar.* Vol. 1, *Theoretical Prerequisites.* Stanford: Stanford University Press.

Levinson, Stephen C., and Penelope Brown. 1994. Immanuel Kant among the Tenejapans: Anthropology as Empirical Philosophy. *Ethos* 22(1): 3–41.

Lévi-Strauss, Claude. [1962] 1966. The Logic of Totemic Classifications. In *The Savage Mind,* pp. 35–74. London: Weidenfeld and Nicolson; Chicago: University of Chicago Press.

Lounsbury, Floyd G. 1964. A Formal Account of the Crow and Omaha Type Kinship Terminologies. In *Explorations in Cultural Anthropology,* ed. Ward H. Goodenough, pp. 351–93. New York: McGraw-Hill.

———. 1969. Language and Culture. In *Language and Philosophy,* ed. Sidney Hook, pp. 3–29. New York: New York University Press.

Lyons, William E. 1986. *The Disappearance of Introspection.* Cambridge: MIT Press.

Malinowski, Bronislaw. 1930. Kinship. *Man,* item 17: 19–29.

Norman, Geoffrey R., Lee R. Brooks, Craig L. Coblentz, and Catherine J. Babcook. 1992. The Correlation of Feature Identification and Category Judgments in Diagnostic Radiology. *Memory and Cognition* 20(4): 344–55.

Palmer, Gary. 1996. *Toward a Theory of Cultural Linguistics*. Austin: University of Texas Press.

Palmer, Stephen E. 1977. Hierarchical Structure in Perceptual Representation. *Cognitive Psychology* 9: 441–74.

Pederson, Eric. 2003. Mirror-Image Discrimination among Nonliterate, Monoliterate, and Biliterate Tamil Speakers. *Written Language and Literacy* 6(1): 71–91.

Pederson, Eric, Eve Danziger, Stephen Levinson, Sotaro Kita, Gunter Senft, and David Wilkins. 1998. Semantic Typology and Spatial Conceptualization. *Language* 74(3): 557–89.

Rosch, Eleanor. 1978. Principles of Categorization. In *Cognition and Categorization*, ed. Eleanor Rosch and Barbara Lloyd, pp. 27–48. Hillsdale, NJ: Lawrence Erlbaum.

Sandra, Dominiek, and Sally Rice. 1995. Network Analyses of Prepositional Meaning: Mirroring Whose Mind—The Linguist's or the Language User's? *Cognitive Linguistics* 6(1): 89–130.

Sapir, Edward. 1925. Sound Patterns in Language. *Language* 1: 37–51.

———. [1933] 1949. The Psychological Reality of Phonemes. In *Selected Writings of Edward Sapir in Language, Culture, and Personality*, ed. David G. Mandelbaum, pp. 46–60. Los Angeles: University of California Press.

Verhaeghe, Arlette, and Régine Kolinsky. 1991. Discriminação entre figuras orientadas em espelho em função do modo de apresentação em adultos escolarizados e adultos iletrados. In *Actas das I Jornadas de Estudo dos Processos Cognitivos*, pp. 51–67. Lisbon: Sociedade Portuguesa de Psicologia.

Whorf, Benjamin Lee. [1940] 1956. Science and Linguistics. In *Language, Thought, and Reality: Selected Writings of Benjamin Lee Whorf*, ed. John B. Carroll, pp. 207–19. New York: MIT Press.

PART II

---

*The Limits
of Universal Models*

CHAPTER 4

Reassessing Male Aggression and Dominance: The Evidence from Primatology

Katherine C. MacKinnon and Agustín Fuentes

> We are primates, products of the evolutionary process, and the promise of primatology is a better understanding of the peculiar creature we call man.—*Sherwood Washburn,* "The Promise of Primatology"

IDEAS ABOUT nonhuman primates have long been used to talk about human gender and aggression. Due to phylogenetic relatedness and popular conceptions of similarities, behavioral studies of nonhuman primates have a much greater impact on ideas about human behavior than studies of other groups of organisms. Because of our biological basis for shared traits resulting from a common evolutionary heritage, nonhuman primate behavior is often put forward as evidence of an underlying natural condition or of normative roles in human behavior.

In recent years, the evidence for the diversity and complexity of nonhuman primate behavior has complicated the process of generalizing from primate to human behavior. Yet, at the same time, certain reductionist accounts—stemming primarily from sociobiology and evolutionary psychology—have found their way into popularized narratives that rely on analogies between primate and human behavior that have little basis in the evidence of primatology. This chapter focuses on the tension between these two trends in the uses of primatology, particularly as they relate to discussions of male aggression and male dominance. We will examine the representation of sex roles in nonhuman primate species and consider how the resulting constructs intersect with notions of gender behavior in human primates.

As our concern lies with the impact that nonhuman primate studies have on the conception of human evolution, and then by extension the popular notions surrounding the biological "roots" of human behavior, our focus is on the effect of sociobiological approaches and their recent offshoot, the field of evolutionary psychology. These orientations frequently assume a specific set of evolutionarily patterned differences between the sexes that underlie, and seemingly clarify, behavioral patterns in human genders. These include male aggression as a primary means of reproductive success, the male urge to mate with as many females as possible, female nonaggressive responses, and the female quest for a single protector mate with resources. Our main goal is to investigate bioreductionist views of male roles in the context of data from primate studies. We will discuss claims about the evolution of certain types of gendered behavior—in particular that relating to male aggression and male dominance.

Seeing Ourselves in Primates: Early Primate Studies

Prior to even the earliest field studies of the nonhuman primates, humans saw great similarities between themselves and the monkeys and apes. Charles Darwin (1871) used reports of the "sociability" of vervet and baboon monkeys to illustrate his discussion of the continuum of sociality across the animal kingdom and to emphasize the place of humans within it. Darwin specifically grouped humans with the apes and concluded that humans are "but one of several exceptional forms of Primates" and, moreover, that "we may infer that some ancient member of the anthropomorphous subgroup gave birth to man" (1871: 130).

Since the publication of *The Descent of Man and Selection in Relation to Sex* in 1871, we have continued to look to the nonhuman primates in our attempts to understand contemporary humans. Indeed, the relevance of nonhuman primates to questions of human evolution and behavior is one of the foundations of primate studies. Robert Yerkes, Clarence Carpenter, Solly Zuckerman, and Kinji Imanishi initiated the investigations into the social behavior of the nonhuman primates and essentially facilitated the creation of the current patterns and processes in primatology (Strier 1994; Strum and Fedigan 1999). Sherwood Washburn's "New Physical Anthropology" (1951) and his call for a comparative primatology—which would augment studies of anatomy and human behavioral evolution with comparative information from primates living in the wild—stimulated a whole generation of field primatologists. Louis Leakey, realizing the importance of the human-ape connection, fostered the long-term ape research projects of Dian Fossey, Jane Goodall, and Birute Galdikas, which laid the groundwork for the explosion in ape research over the past three decades. Throughout this time, behaviors that appear to have evolutionary importance took center stage: dominance relations, aggression, mating patterns, and the like. As the number of primate species studied increased, the data began to point to substantial variability in behavior within the primate order.

The Legacy of Sociobiology

Edward O. Wilson's publication of his book *Sociobiology: The New Synthesis* in 1975 marked a turning point in behavioral biology and was a landmark for a new paradigm in the study of the evolution of animal behavior. Wilson's theory attempted to explain behavior in terms of an organism's reproductive success, and by highlighting the role of natural selection, it shifted the focus away from other evolutionary processes such as gene flow and genetic drift. Researchers started to analyze social behavior within the framework of a general neo-Darwinian concept of natural selection. This resulted in the view that any form of behavior that might enhance an animal's ability to gain access to mates, engage in successful copulation, and produce viable offspring is functionally beneficial and, if it has a genetic basis, will be passed along and, thus, selected for.

This focus on reproductive success, combined with renewed interest in Bateman's (1948) anisogamy argument (see Tang-Martinez 2000; Randerson and Hurst 2001) and Trivers's (1972) ideas about parental investment, led to an array of ideas about the separate, distinct roles of males and females. Bateman's principle of anisogamy distinguishes between male and female "fitness," or reproductive success. Because males produce more, smaller, and cheaper gametes (sperm), their reproductive success is presumed to be maximized by many indiscriminate matings. Females, who produce fewer, larger, more costly gametes (eggs), are thought to maximize their reproductive success by fewer, more discriminate matings. Males are viewed as having greater potential fertility than females, and females are seen as the limiting resource. It is because of this difference that conflict arises. Trivers's (1972) theory of differential parental investment explained why males court females in some species. Females have a higher initial investment, so they should choose the best mate for their offspring. Females in some species also provide more parental care than males. This differential investment leads to a divergence in the reproductive success of males and females. In this theory, then, males are selected to compete for access to females (for a summary of subsequent changes and revisions to this theory, see Kokko and Jennions 2003).

Sociobiology influenced the field of primatology, as well as other fields of animal behavior, in a number of ways, but the primary effect was to shift the focus from populations to the individual as the target of natural selection. The current dominant paradigm in primatology, behavioral ecology, takes many (but not all) of the initial premises of Wilson's (1975) book as a significant component of its core. Moreover, since many of the leading primatologists today were trained during the 1970s and 1980s, they have been heavily influenced by the Wilsonian (sociobiological) thesis. The shift in thinking about the level of selection was striking, and it put primatology in the domain of "hard science," a science that would develop ostensibly testable hypotheses about individuals and group behavior. Not only did sociobiology stimulate new questions about behavior, but it also transformed many existing questions and, in doing so, redirected theoretical models away from social-science interpretations toward more biological ones. Reproductive strategies, in particular, became the main focus, and the differential costs of reproduction for males and females were viewed as a "battle of the sexes." Also, behavior that had previously been seen as anomalous or aberrant—but as potentially costly in evolutionary terms—now generally acquired strict selectionist explanations. Thus, over the last twenty-five years among those researchers influenced by sociobiology, there has been a shift from descriptive approaches to behavior (which focused on the proximate mechanisms involved) to more ultimate causational approaches. This changed the way research questions were formulated and hypotheses were constructed, and it directed the interpretation of data and subsequent results. In extreme cases, instead of first collecting the data and then figuring out what the animals were doing based on patterns in those data, some researchers initiated field research with specific preconceived notions of the way behavior should work. In such cases, "I wouldn't have believed it if I hadn't seen it" risks becoming "I wouldn't have seen it if I hadn't believed it." As Phyllis Dolhinow observes, "how you study behavior, your questions, your assumptions, and methods, will guide your definition of evidence and thereby shape your interpretations of why animals act the way they do" (1999: 120).

Evolutionary psychology (so called because it is a combination of evolutionary biology and cognitive psychology) is the contemporary heir to 1970s sociobiology, and it, too, invokes aspects of Darwinian theory to give evolutionary weight to notions of why humans act the way they do.[1] Evolutionary psychology is founded on the premise that the human brain contains cognitive structures that originally evolved to solve the reproductive problems encountered by our hunter-gatherer ancestors. In this context, neo-Darwinian theory is invoked to explain questions of human morality and emotion, and there is a focus on the "inherent nature" of everything from human aggression to personality to self-esteem.[2]

Advances in Comparative Primatology

At the same time that sociobiology and evolutionary psychology were gaining prominence, there was, as Karen Strier illustrates in "Myth of the Typical Primate" (1994), a steady expansion in the primate species studied. The diversity of species and ecotypes currently in the primatological database has altered our views of primates. We no longer focus exclusively on the savanna dwellers or even the apes as the "best" exemplars for human origins, and indeed we have begun to move away from strict categorizing of species' social organization in simplistic terms. As it turns out, there is not one generalized "primate pattern" found in nature but a variety of patterns with some common themes (Strier 1994).

Complexity in behavior and grouping patterns has been observed within primate species across a wide range of habitats (e.g., Fuentes 1999; Kirkpatrick 1998; Kirkpatrick et al. 1998; Rylands 1993; Strier 1994; Treves and Chapman 1996). Ecological pressures, social interactions, and aspects of an individual's life history elicit specific responses within the parameters set by physiology, environment, and experience. These biological parameters may allow for a wide range of potential expression, leading to variable and/or flexible behavior in individuals. As data sets increase, and flexibility becomes more visible at the level of the individual and the group—and therefore in social organization—it becomes abundantly evident that social organization is an *emergent property* (Allen and Starr 1982) that has characteristics not readily reducible to the context-specific interactions between individual animals.

Despite the reductive influence of sociobiology, primatology has taken great leaps in its knowledge of the morphological evolution of the primates over the past decades. The ability to assess and analyze genetic and physiological systems has revolutionized the way we go about asking and answering questions regarding our phylogenetic position and its relationship to the evolution of human society. With more than half a century of primatological data in hand, we are now in a position to make greater strides than ever before into the mysteries of primate social life, both nonhuman and human.

Primate Studies: What Do They Tell Us?

To fully understand modern humans we have to examine our place in the natural world. Since all primates share some morphological and behavioral characteristics (based on our common evolutionary history), comparative primate studies can help us reconstruct how early hominines (members of the human lineage that split from the African apes) might have adapted to different environments. By gaining insight into how early hominines lived, we can better understand ourselves today. We can investigate questions such as "Why are most primates social?" and "What factors may, or may not, influence social structures and mating patterns?" Comparative primatology is thus important and can contribute to our knowledge of human behavior, if done carefully (see Dolhinow 2002). This requires keeping certain precautions in mind: (*a*) variability among primate species means that generalizations referring to "primates" will be limited to the most broadly defined patterns; (*b*) phylogenetic relationships mean that not all primates are equally relevant to humans; and (*c*) phylogenetic similarity does not always mean homologous adaptations.

In what follows, we will take up two pivotal topics—male aggression and male dominance—as examples of the way in which complex human behaviors have been explained by extrapolation from hypothesized nonhuman-primate behaviors. These topics are important for our understanding of human gender roles and aggression, and they have recently taken center stage in the popular-scientific literature to exemplify the biological basis of certain human behaviors. We will review some of the representations in that literature, discuss how they contrast with the actual complexity of the phenomenon, and then examine the primate data and compare those findings with popular conceptions. We will show that the diversity and complexity of the primate data are in tension with and ultimately challenge reductionist theories in sociobiology and evolutionary psychology.

Male Aggression

Several recent books propose that humans are adapted to hate and kill their enemies and that heightened aggression often resulting in murder is a viable evolutionary strategy, especially for males (R. Wright 1994; Wrangham and Peterson 1996; Ghiglieri 1999). Such works argue that male violence is an important adaptive trait, a product of millions of years of specific evolutionary trends resulting in adaptations favoring violent aggression.

Male aggression and sexual coercion have become primary elements in the construction of hypotheses regarding the evolution of male primate behavior, especially in the apes, humans' closest relatives, and Old World monkeys. Arguments positing primate males' innate aggression toward females and their propensity to abuse sexual partners and murder nonbiological offspring have become cornerstones in attempts to understand both nonhuman-primate and human behavior (see Daly and Wilson 1999; Smuts and Smuts 1993; van Schaik and Janson 2000; Wrangham and Peterson 1996). The benefits that primate males can derive from exhibiting these behaviors are argued to be, in the long term, evolutionarily adaptive strategies: that is, by employing sexual coercion and infanticide under certain environmental conditions, some males derive higher overall reproductive success (on average) compared with males who do not follow these patterns.

Therefore, it is assumed that if primate males in many environments do exhibit these aggressive patterns, this behavioral profile is most likely a primate-wide trend, and so humans should have it too. In other words, it is assumed that these behavioral patterns have, over time, come to dominate male human behavior. Do the data support these assertions? Of the various hypotheses regarding male aggression toward females and infants that have been set forth, none is fully supported across most primate taxa, and there remains much contention about the data that have been offered to support such hypotheses (see Sussman 1999; Sussman and Garber 2004).

[margin note: rebudle]

Nonhuman-primate studies can indeed help to shed light on the biological basis for behaviors and our shared primatological heritage. Yet, as many authors (e.g., Dolhinow 2002; Ehrlich 2000; McKenna 1983; Sussman 1999) point out, biological roles for certain behavioral traits—such as aggression—in the evolutionary past do not directly dictate how humans today use such behaviors. For instance, certain aggressive behaviors were likely favored in our evolutionary heritage because of functions such as protection of one's life and the lives of offspring and/or group members, access to or protection of territory, access to mates and food, and as a component in the establishment of dominance relationships in the gregarious, social living that characterizes our taxonomic order. At the same time, we know that much of the causation for human aggression—the sociopolitical and economic contexts of war, for example—lies firmly in the domain of modern human existence. *[margin note: strength]* — product of culture + societal structure

The concept of aggression in the nonhuman primates can be elusive, and there are important aspects of this trait that we need to keep in mind when looking at its relevance to humans. First, there are diverse types of aggression that can achieve similar ends. Aggression is neither simply defined nor easily quantified. For example, primate aggression can range from simple threats to contact fighting and even to vocal contests between opponents who cannot see each other. These types of aggression can have similar outcomes depending on the interactive history of the individuals and their species, as well as on the specific environment in which the behaviors are exhibited. Among the primates there are many aggression-response repertoires, and context is important in how an individual will respond (Sussman and Garber 2004).

[margin note: historical enemies + antagonistic behavior due to environment + human encroachment]

Second, it is an open question whether more aggressive males are reproductively most successful, that is, whether being more aggressive gives those individuals more successful mating opportunities than they would otherwise have. Since we are concerned with adaptations, the relationship between male aggression and access to mating opportunities is an important variable.

There are other questions relevant to an examination of aggression: Is the situation in which nonhuman primates were observed directly relevant to humans? Do we have quantitative data for any of the apes—our closest relatives—or, for that matter, for humans? Do individuals within a population practice multiple, variable strategies? These questions must be answered before one can attempt to construct theories and models regarding the evolutionary value of aggressive behavior in humans.

SHIFTING VIEW ON MALE AGGRESSION

Early primate field studies centered on savanna-living baboons, and these studies set the precedent for viewing male dominance through aggression as the defining element of male control over females and of stable group living. Even as primate studies began to illuminate the variability of social patterns in nonhuman primates (see Fedigan 1992; Fuentes 1999; Strier 1994), the notion that aggressive males controlling females is a central tendency in primate social life continued to predominate. Ideas about the biological bases of gender roles in humans seemed to flow nicely from the "baboon model" that characterized much of primatology from the 1950s into the 1970s (Strier 1994; Strum and Fedigan 1999). The large baboon males (nearly twice the size of females) were seen as the anchors of the society, keeping control of wayward females and scattered offspring through aggression and power imbalance. This view persisted even in light of a growing body of conflicting data (see, e.g., Rowell 1972, 1984, 1988).

It is only relatively recently that we have begun to see what characterizes most primate species: a core group of females who remain in the group into which they were born and who determine many of the daily operations in the group such as group movement, finding food, and choosing sleeping trees at night. Thus, a "division of labor" in primate groups, with males as aggressive controllers and females as recipients of aggression, was shortsighted and limiting in its application to human gender roles (see Fedigan 1992).

Recently, our attempts to understand aggression have gone beyond behavioral observations, as such, to include more complex (and reciprocal) interactions between hormones and behavior. Previously, testosterone and other androgens were associated with both aggression and reproductive success in a direct causal relationship: that is, it was thought that higher testosterone equals more aggression, which in turn leads to greater reproductive success. Conveniently for pop theorists, males tend to have higher levels of testosterone than females (in primates). However, recent research has clarified that "the arrow linking testosterone with aggression and sex does not point only in one direction. It is bi-directional: hormones and behavior influence one another" (Berkovitch 1999: 238; see also Berkovitch

1999 and Sapolsky 1993 for summaries). These studies conclude that aggression sometimes plays a role in access to females and that testosterone is related to aggression, but social factors probably propel hormones at least as much as, if not more than, hormones trigger specific behaviors. This means that social complexities—the ebb and flow of interactions, life histories, and interindividual relationships (affiliative and aggressive)—probably exert more influence on overall reproductive success than does aggression alone. In fact, one can argue that aggression does not occur by itself and may be only a portion of the relevant behavioral patterns that males, and females, engage in over the course of their lives as they eat, sleep, associate with others, copulate, and occasionally fight. The relationships between androgens (testosterone and others) and aggression, mating, and other social interactions are complex and nonlinear (Berkovitch 1997, 1999; Sapolsky 1993, 1996).

So how has this renaissance in primatological investigations regarding the complexities of male aggression impacted the popular-science literature? We would say, not very much. A quick search of the Lexis-Nexis database or a perusal of the *New York Times* book reviews immediately leads one to assume that aggression was a primary driving factor in our evolutionary past, characterizes our primate relatives, and continues to be the major player in our evolutionary patterns today.

THE APE EVIDENCE

We are particularly concerned with the evidence on chimpanzees, and to a lesser extent gorillas, in view of their close phylogenetic relationship to humans. Male chimpanzees are reported to exhibit border-defense patrolling and murderous territorial confrontations (that is, "warfare") with neighboring troops, and gorilla males are purported to rely on the killing of infants as a prime reproductive strategy. However, in interpreting these observations, two points need to be kept in mind. First, there are variable interpretations of the data on chimpanzee and gorilla aggressive behavior and a general underestimation of the strong (possibly primary) role that cooperation plays in these ape societies (Aureli and de Waal 2000; de Waal 1989). Second, chimpanzees and gorillas have been evolving on their own for the same length of time as humans, so that any correlation we find in modern human and chimpanzee or gorilla behavior does not necessarily reflect an ancestral condition for any of these species (Sussman 1997).

over-emphasize aggression in reprod.

What do the data on our ape cousins suggest? The data show that violent, lethal behavior is not a common phenomenon in chimpanzees across the board, but that in the eastern subspecies it is relatively common. Dyadic violence (one-on-one conflict) has not been observed to lead to deaths in chimpanzees (Wrangham 1999). However, intra- and intercommunity coalitionary attacks (attacks by multiple individuals) have resulted in deaths. In eight studies of common chimpanzees spanning over 40 years (more than 180 study years) there have been fourteen adult and adolescent deaths directly related to intercommunity lethal violence, although as many as twenty deaths are assumed to be the result of violence from coalitionary attacks (M. Wilson and Wrangham 2003; Wrangham 1999). All of the observed and assumed instances of lethal aggression come from studies of the subspecies *Pan troglodytes schweinfurthii* at three sites in the eastern portion of the chimpanzee range. At Gombe, in studies conducted over a 40-year period, there have been six observed and three strongly inferred instances of lethal aggression. At Mahale, in 35 years there have been six inferred instances. At Kibale, across thirteen years of observation, three instances of lethal aggression were observed and two inferred. At the other main chimpanzee study sites, Bossou (24 years), Taï (21 years), Wamba (26 years), and Lemako (17 years), no deaths resulting from intercommunity or other lethal aggression have been observed or inferred (M. Wilson and Wrangham 2003; Wrangham 1999). However, instances of coalitionary violence have been observed at Taï, including one that resulted in serious injury (Boesch and Boesch-Achermann 2000).

Researchers have reported infanticide by both male and female *Pan troglodytes schweinfurthii*. From the four sites of Gombe, Mahale, Kibale, and Budongo, there are eleven observed and four inferred instances of adults killing infants in intercommunity conflicts and twelve in intragroup conflicts, but the majority of these attacks were carried out by adult females, not males (Arcadi and Wrangham 1999; M. Wilson and Wrangham 2003; Wrangham 1999). One possible case of infanticide also occurred in the West African site of Taï (*P. t. verus*) (M. Wilson and Wrangham 2003).

Most of our behavioral information on gorillas comes from a small population of the subspecies *Gorilla gorilla berengei* in the Virunga region of eastern central Africa. Watts (1996) reports that both male-male and male-female aggression are fairly common but wounding is rare. Robbins (1995) suggests that male gorillas tend to avoid close proximity to one another in order to avoid aggressive conflict. Sicotte (2002) believes that male displays toward females are probably not related to sexual coercion or other forms of short-term mating intimidation. Harcourt and Greenberg (2001) report that infanticide may be responsible for up to 14 percent of infant deaths in the Virunga population.

The current data indicate that lethal intragroup aggressive violence is relatively rare in both the chimpanzees and gorillas, but that severe lethal aggression has been observed in some chimpanzee populations and not in others. This lethal intercommunity aggression in *P. t. schweinfurthii* may indeed reflect behavioral adaptations to territorial conflict (the imbalance-of-power hypothesis; see M. Wilson and Wrangham 2003; Wrangham 1999). Gorilla males do not characteristically exhibit lethal aggression toward females or other males, although they may toward infants. However, current gorilla databases are limited and the best long-term data come from only one subspecies.

What can we conclude from these comparative data? A *capacity* for aggressive behavior in humans was probably present in the common ancestor of humans, chimpanzees, and gorillas. However, the *incidence* of such behavior is not evenly distributed in ape populations and must be understood in terms of the contingencies and contexts in which it is exhibited. Moreover, chimpanzees and gorillas, like humans, have responded and adapted to their respective environments and morphological trajectories for at least five to six million years, so that what we see today is a direct reflection of that process of adaptation, not a static snapshot of what we have all been like since the time of our derivation from a common ancestor.

An important body of evidence comes from studies of the bonobos (*Pan paniscus* or gracile chimpanzee). The bonobos are at least as phylogenetically close to us as robust (or common) chimpanzees (*Pan troglodytes*) but are generally sidelined in the construction of human norms through comparative ape data. The bonobos have different behavioral patterns from other chimpanzees. Bonobos ease their tensions through sexual encounters, the majority of which are nonreproductive. Some anthropologists have suggested the use of bonobos as an alternative model for hominid origins (see Zihlman 1996; Zihlman et al. 1978), based on a number of traits: bonobos are less sexually dimorphic in canine size; they are more generalized in their anatomy and limb proportions; and behaviorally they exhibit less aggression, more food sharing, more social bonding, and female dominance. The proposal of a bonobo model as an alternative to the robust-chimpanzee model with its "pervasive emphasis on male dominance and aggression" (Zihlman 1996: 297) has not, however, made substantial headway in the popular media or popular-scientific reports on the biological basis of human behavior.

It is likely that examining the apes and other primates will continue to inform our quest for insight into human nature. One emerging complexity is the high variability of aggression across populations of apes and humans, suggesting that further inquiry into the specifics of environmental, historical, and physiological parameters is urgently needed. In this context, reducing the complex primate data sets to straightforward analogies for ancestral human states restricts rather than expands our understanding of the human past and present.

Male Dominance

Closely related to the question of male aggression is that of male dominance. In 2000, during the heat of the presidential race, Vice President Albert Gore hired the "feminist" journalist and writer Naomi Wolf to help reshape his public image into that of an "alpha male." Why? The notion of "alpha"—or exclusive dominant status in a group—is derived from early assumptions about linear dominance hierarchies and the role of high-ranking males relative to other members of primate groups. These assumptions include the higher reproductive success of high-ranking males, their control over group social interactions and group movement, and preferred attraction by females to high-ranking males. We associate high dominance rank with positive social standing, as Gore realized. However, primatologists' understanding of dominance relations has altered dramatically over the last thirty years (Ray 1999).

The dominant, or alpha, animal in a group is often portrayed as the "king," the master of his harem, and the supreme leader of his group (Ray 1999). "Dominance" is a statement about a type of relationship between two individuals; "dominant" is an adjective that describes an individual who consistently prevails over another in dyadic contests. Dominance can also be a description of a ranked hierarchy among individuals within a social group (Ray 1999). But how do we measure dominance? Aggression, sex differences, life history, mating patterns, reproductive success, physiology, social inheritance, and group structure all impact the interindividual relationships we call dominance within a primate social group (Fedigan 1983, 1992; Ray 1999; Sapolsky 1993).

In about 40 percent of primate species, females are equal to, or dominant over, males. Six out of ten primate taxonomic families have females equal to, or dominant over, males; and females in many species are aggressive, competitive, "promiscuous," and transfer out of their natal groups (P. Wright 1993). Thus, a general portrayal of primate males as dominant over females (and as achieving that dominance status by way of aggressive interactions with other males) is not fully accurate and ignores the complexities in social structures and behaviors found across the primate taxa.

In many primate species, dominant males achieve their position by agonism, either through aggressive encounters with established males in the group during "takeovers" or "raids" or by slowly and systematically moving up through the ranks within a group. Therefore, dominant males are usually assumed to be better fighters, and it is often suggested that better fighters are more attractive to females and thus have more offspring. In other words, dominance in nonhuman primates is commonly believed to be positively correlated with greater reproductive advantages. This assessment, however, is called into question by the information we have on the complexities (behavioral and physiological) of dominance relationships in primates and their effect on reproductive success (Fedigan 1983; Ray 1999; Sapolsky 1993, 2000). A fundamental characteristic of dominance that is often overlooked is that it is a state, not a trait, and most males may in fact move through a range of ranks through their lifespan (for a general overview on this characteristic, see Ray 1999; and for more specific discussions of dominance in Japanese macaque monkeys, see Sprague 1998; Sprague, Suzuki, and Tsukahara 1996; Sprague and Suzuki 2000).

With the increase of paternity testing in field studies of nonhuman primates, we have seen evidence that the dominant, or alpha, male does not necessarily father the most offspring (see Bercovitch 1999). In fact, nearly half of recent studies in nonhuman primates report the lack of a strong correlation between high rank and reproductive success. The link is greater in some species than in others. Some studies report a stronger correlation between dominance and mating success in seasonal-breeding species, in which females are sexually receptive for only a limited time during the year (e.g., Colinshaw and Dunbar 1991), and one study attributes the correlation among seasonality, male dominance, and mating success to the ability of high-ranking males to put on more body fat than lower-ranking males (Bercovitch and Nurnberg 1996).

Thus, there seems to be a strong (but not universal) association between mating success and male dominance in seasonal breeders. However, humans are not seasonal breeders (nor are many other primate species). This distinction is critical because if the association between dominance, reproductive success, and life history is not a clear, linear one, then our assumptions about the meaning and substance of the alpha male must change. If being the alpha does not necessarily confer either the specific mating benefits or the evolutionary advantage previously assumed, then our explanations of why animals compete for status, and what they attain when they achieve it, cannot rely on such simplistic assumptions (see Sapolsky 2000). Current primatological studies no longer represent swaggering males dominating females; instead, they paint a much more complex picture of social relationships. However, in popular-science writings, there is continued reliance on past assumptions about and representation of male behavior (see, e.g., Buss 1994; Ghiglieri 1999; Low 2000; R. Wright 1994).

Why is the concept of gender roles in which males are portrayed as aggressive and dominant, and females as passive caregivers, so pervasive (see Buss 1994; Gray 1992; Low 2000; E. O. Wilson 1975)? The reductionist perspective of Trivers (1972) and E. O. Wilson (1975)—which places males and females as opponents in a battle of the sexes due to differential investment of energy in mating and reproduction—permeates mainstream investigations. A growing body of data, however, demonstrates that primate males' mating costs are much higher than previously assumed (see Berkovitch 1999) and that male and female reproductive divergence may not be as great as had been thought (Palombit 1999). Despite the possibilities that both males and females practice variable mating strategies, the presumption remains strong that males have a drive toward polygamy and females have a drive toward monogamy. That is, males are assumed to put as much effort as possible into mating with multiple females, as their costs are primarily in mating and are less than females' costs. Females, on the other hand, try to find the "best" male and mate with him, monogamously if possible (thus constraining the male).

While a number of primatologists have broken away from these assumptions (e.g., Fedigan 1992; Hrdy 1981), the debate and changes in primatologists' views remain relatively isolated in academic circles, only recently emerging in the media. The long-standing assumption that males attempt to mate with as many females as possible and that females try to find the best male and keep him monogamous therefore continues to color popular representations (and see, e.g., Buss 1994; Low 2000; Pinker 1997; R. Wright 1994). For instance, columnist Melissa Stoeltje summarizes the main points of David Buss's thesis in his book *The Evolution of Desire* (1994) in the following way. "Men (by and large) are hard-wired to want sexual variety. Women (by and large) are hard-wired to want commitment. Men are drawn to sweet, young things. Women want the promise of stability. Honed over time by the hard Darwinian realities of sexual selection, these urges are as old as the hills and as ingrained as the human taste for fat or fear of snakes" (*Houston Chronicle,* June 20, 1999).

Contrasting gender roles have also been invoked in attempts to reconstruct the evolution of human morphology. Thus, Owen Lovejoy (1981, 1993) has proposed that bipedality in our australopithecine ancestors resulted from a mixed provisioning and child-rearing strategy. Males were able to cover long distances and retrieve significant sustenance to support females and their offspring. Females were tied to local places by the energetic constraints of large and helpless offspring while the males were required to venture out, risking dangers, to gather food for the family. Although most biological anthropologists no longer subscribe to this hypothesis and view it as limiting our understanding of past behavior (e.g., Conroy 1998; Park 2002; Sussman 1999), it has retained significant currency in the popular literature. Again, the assumptions of extremely divergent male and female energetic costs and reproductive strategies and of widespread monogamy among primates reaffirm societal norms concerning kinship and gender through the misrepresentation of the available primatological and paleoanthropological data.

Modeling the Evolution of Human Behavior

Behavioral data on nonhuman primates clearly enhance our ability to model and assess the evolution of human behavioral patterns, and by continuing to expand our data sets, we arm ourselves with a rich source for inquiry. The living primates are our closest relatives, and understanding their behavior informs our investigations into our own. However, to apply a strict adaptationist strategy to all behavior—especially social behavior in humans—is to deny the wide range of evolutionary and cultural pathways that can lead to the expression of certain behaviors. We see three major problems with the way in which evolutionary theory is often used in reductionist thinking.

First, it is not usually acknowledged that natural selection (i.e., genetic changes in the frequencies of certain traits in populations due to differential reproductive success between individuals) is only one of many mechanisms for evolutionary change. Genetic drift, stochastic chance events, and selection with multiple peaks (Bateson 1982; Lewontin 1979; Oyama 1989) are all forces of evolution, but they get short shrift when natural selection is the primary focus. The idea that evolutionary forces other than natural selection play an important role is certainly not a new one. Recent reviews suggest that even when natural selection is correctly the focus of investigations, the strength of its impact on a particular trait may be overestimated due to environmentally induced covariances between phenotypes and fitness (Kruuk, Merilä, and Sheldon 2003). Evolutionary biologists have long incorporated other modes of genetic transmission between generations in their theories, and some point to the limits of an overemphasis on natural selection (see, e.g., Bateson 1982, 1986, 1988; Gould 1980; Gould and Lloyd 1999; Ho and Saunders 1984; Lewontin 1979; Oyama 1989; Vrba 1983).

Second, most genetically based traits are expressed through epigenetic and developmental processes, and these effects play crucial roles in the expression and maintenance of behavior. Epigenetic factors refer to facets of the complex interaction of genotype and environment in determining the characteristics and development of an organism. Such factors are often de-emphasized in the construction of generalized behavioral evolutionary models.

Third, a primarily Mendelian view of natural selection distorts the evo-lutionary process. While Mendelian genetics provides some clear-cut ex-amples of the mechanisms involved in the transmission of genetic informa-tion for many monogenic traits (i.e., traits that are influenced by one gene), it has not proven useful in understanding the transmission of complex be-havioral phenomena from one generation to the next. Many traits are poly-genic—that is, they are influenced by many genes at different loci (the gene's location on a chromosome)—and many are pleiotropic, meaning that one gene (or locus) influences many different traits. There is, therefore, no one-to-one relation between genes and most behaviors: there is no "gene for" adultery, aggression, or promiscuity, nor are there clear genetic corre-lates for primate behavioral strategies.

If we were to see aggressive behavior in male primates primarily as a product of natural selection, we would state that in many instances aggres-sive males are more dominant over others, have access to more females, and thus father more offspring. However, this simplistic view fails to take into account the fact that aggression itself is not selected for. There is no gene or other single selective agent for aggression (i.e., it does not operate in a Mendelian fashion), and it is a behavioral phenomenon that is neither sim-ply defined nor easily quantified. Furthermore, in humans, much of the causation for aggression lies distinctly in the realm of modern human cul-ture, so that past biological roles for aggression cannot directly dictate how humans currently use aggression.

The predilection for reducing complex behavioral patterns to relatively simple traits or strategies that are assumed to be inherited is widespread and is likely to ignore or misrepresent the complex patterns of transmission of genomic elements related to behavior. Many evolutionary theorists have not missed this point, indeed have made it the subject of numerous discussions in biology, particularly in the years after *Sociobiology* was published (see Bar-low 1980; Gould 1980; Silverberg 1980; E. O. Wilson 1976; but also see Bar-low 1989, 1991; Kitcher 1986). A nonreductionist evolutionary approach to behavior considers alternative evolutionary pathways that can lead to the ex-pression of certain behaviors, takes into account epigenetic and develop-mental effects on those behaviors, and views complex behavioral patterns as irreducible to simple traits that are inherited in a Mendelian fashion. Op-ponents of a strict reductionist approach are often categorized as "anti-evo-lution," or "anti-Darwin." This is not accurate. The antireductionist cri-tique does not question whether evolution by natural selection occurs (it does). Rather, it questions the way in which scientific results have been mis-directed and misconstrued in attempts to explain behavior.

Reductionist versus Nonreductionist Explanations: What Is at Stake?

As theoretical possibilities, one can envisage that man might be genetically deter-mined as aggressive or submissive, warlike or peaceful, territorial or wanderer, selfish or generous, mean or good. Are any of these possibilities likely to be realized? Would the fixation of any of these dispositions, so that they become uncontrollable urges or drives, increase the adaptiveness of a species which relies on culture for its survival? I believe that the answers to these questions are in the negative.
—*Theodosius Dobzhansky*, Evolutionary Biology

Cultural ideas of human gender and aggression have influenced the kinds of research questions asked and our interpretations of nonhuman primates. In some cases contemporary cultural understandings of gender have been read into nonhuman primate behavior and thereby "naturalized"—that is, made to appear as if they are part of our innate species history and thus universal for all humans across time. In this way, the reductive theories of sociobiol-ogy and evolutionary psychology give us a picture of males as competitive, aggressive, and motivated solely by a desire for high reproductive success. Females are portrayed as coy, choosy, and more interested in monogamous relationships. In contrast, the evidence from primatology paints a very dif-ferent picture—one in which the behavior of both males and females is var-ied and diverse across a wide range of habitats.

What is at stake in one view or the other? In one view, we end up with ideas about gender and aggression firmly embedded in notions of adaptive strategies and supported by reductionist scenarios. In the other, we see vari-able behavior among primates, which allows inferences about humans but certainly does not provide evidence of primordial "roots" for specific kinds of gendered behavior.

We must be cautious about assigning evolutionary significance to certain patterns of human gender and aggression. The primate record can indeed inform and broaden our interpretations of human behavior, but it does so only if we resist explanations based on small primate data sets and insist on examining the full range of primate behavioral repertoires. When we do so, it becomes clear that the hallmark of primates—and particularly those most closely related to humans—is behavioral and adaptive flexibility and variability.

Everything humans do has both genetic and cultural components. We are biocultural organisms. A danger in reductionist approaches is the po-tential for ignoring the complexity of biocultural interconnections and creating, instead, artificially simple linkages between cultural behavior (e.g., the form, style, and context of human aggression) and biological components (e.g., human physiology, morphology, and endocrinology). Even as we learn more about the interaction of genetic regulatory information, the external environment, and chance variations in development (see Fausto-Sterling 1992), the assumption persists of a genetically controlled, yet unspecified, mechanism for the expression of such behaviors, with environment and variability relegated to explanatory afterthoughts.

We know that evolution occurs and that natural selection is one of the major mechanisms of change. However, "just-so" stories based on selective invocation of primate examples will not serve us. Attention to the diverse array of data from comparative primate studies and to the complex interplay of culture and biology in human behavior is essential if we are to understand how human behavior has evolved.

Notes

1. Relevant evolutionary psychology texts include Barkow, Cosmides, and Tooby 1992; Caporael 2001; Cartwright 2000; Daly and Wilson 1988, 1999; Ridley 1993, 1997; Rossi 1995; R. Wright 1994. For assessments and critiques of evolutionary psychology, see Ehrlich and Feldman 2003; Jones 1999; Lloyd 1999; Oyama 2000; Rose and Rose 2000; Stanford 2001.

2. See, e.g., Chisholm 1999 and R. Wright 1994 on morality; Eagly and Wood 1999 on evolved male and female "dispositions"; Neubauer 1996 and Zimmerman 2000 on personality and self-esteem; Ridley 1993 on "human nature"; and Barkow, Cosmides, and Tooby 1992 on culture.

References

Allen, T. F. H., and Thomas B. Starr. 1982. *Hierarchy: Perspectives for Ecological Complexity.* Chicago: University of Chicago Press.

Arcadi, A. C., and Richard W. Wrangham. 1999. Infanticide in Chimpanzees: Review of Cases and a New Within-Group Observation from Kanyawara Study Group in Kibale National Park. *Primates* 40: 337–51.

Aureli, Filippo, and Frans B. M. de Waal, eds. 2000. *Natural Conflict Resolution.* Berkeley and Los Angeles: University of California Press.

Barkow, Jerome, Leda Cosmides, and John Tooby, eds. 1992. *The Adapted Mind: Evolutionary Psychology and the Generation of Culture.* New York: Oxford University Press.

Barlow, George W. 1980. The Development of Sociobiology: A Biologist's Perspective. In *Sociobiology: Beyond Nature/Nurture?* ed. George W. Barlow and James Silverberg, pp. 3–24. Boulder, CO: Westview Press.

———. 1989. Has Sociobiology Killed Ethology or Revitalized It? In *Perspectives in Ethology,* vol. 8, *Whither Ethology?* ed. Patrick P. G. Bateson and Peter H. Klopfer, pp. 1–45. New York: Plenum Press.

————. 1991. Nature-Nurture and the Debates Surrounding Ethology and Sociobiology. *American Zoologist* 31: 286–96.

Bateman, A. J. 1948. Intra-sexual Selection in *Drosophila melanogaster. Behaviour* 2(3): 349–68.

Bateson, Patrick P. G. 1982. Behavioural Development and Evolutionary Processes. In *Current Problems in Sociobiology,* ed. King's College Sociobiology Group, pp. 133–51. Cambridge: Cambridge University Press.

————1986. Sociobiology and Human Politics. In *Science and Beyond,* ed. S. Rose and L. Appignanesi, pp. 79–99. Oxford: Blackwell.

————. 1988. The Active Role of Behaviour in Evolution. In *Evolutionary Processes and Metaphors,* ed. Mae-Wan Ho and Sidney W. Fox, pp. 191–207. Chichester, UK: Wiley and Sons.

Bercovitch, Fred B. 1997. Reproductive Strategies of Rhesus Macaques. *Primates* 38: 247–63.

————. 1999. The Physiology of Male Reproductive Strategies. In *The Nonhuman Primates,* ed. Phyllis Dolhinow and Agustín Fuentes, pp. 237–44. Mountain View, CA: Mayfield Publishing Co.

Berkovitch, Fred B., and P. Nurnberg. 1996. Socioendocrine and Morphological Correlates of Paternity in Rhesus Macaques (*Macaca mulatta*). *Journal of Reproduction and Fertility* 107: 59–68.

Boesch, Christophe, and Hedwige Boesch-Achermann. 2000. *The Chimpanzees of the Taï Forest: Behavioural Ecology and Evolution.* Oxford: Oxford University Press.

Buss, David. 1994. *The Evolution of Desire: Strategies of Human Mating.* New York: Basic Books.

Caporael, L. R. 2001. Evolutionary Psychology: Toward a Unifying Theory and a Hybrid Science. *Annual Review of Psychology* 52: 607–28.

Cartwright, John. 2000. *Evolution and Human Behavior: Darwinian Perspectives on Human Nature.* Cambridge: MIT Press.

Chisholm, James S. 1999. *Death, Hope, and Sex: Steps to an Evolutionary Ecology of Mind and Morality.* Cambridge: Cambridge University Press.

Colinshaw, G., and Robin I. M. Dunbar. 1991. Dominance Rank and Mating Success in Male Primates. *Animal Behavior* 41: 1045–56.

Conroy, Glenn C. 1998. Paleoanthropology Today. *Evolutionary Anthropology* 6(5): 155–56.

Daly, Martin, and Margo Wilson. 1988. *Homicide.* Hawthorne, NY: Aldine de Gruyter.

————. 1999. Human Evolutionary Psychology and Animal Behaviour. *Animal Behaviour* 57: 509–19.

Darwin, Charles. 1871. *The Descent of Man and Selection in Relation to Sex.* London: John Murray.

de Waal, Frans B. M. 1989. *Peacemaking among Primates.* Cambridge: Harvard University Press.

Dobzhansky, Theodosius. 1972. On the Evolutionary Uniqueness of Man. In *Evolutionary Biology,* Vol. 6, ed. Theodosius Dobzhansky, Max K. Hecht, and William C. Steere, pp. 415–30. New York: Appleton-Century-Crofts.

Dolhinow, Phyllis. 1999. A Mystery: Explaining Behavior. In *The New Physical Anthropology: Science, Humanism, and Critical Reflection,* ed. Shirley C. Strum and Donald G. Lindburg, pp. 119–32. Upper Saddle River, NJ: Prentice Hall.

————. 2002. Anthropology and Primatology. In *Primates Face to Face: The Conservation Implications of Human-Nonhuman Primate Interconnections,* ed. Agustín Fuentes and Linda D. Wolfe, pp. 7–24. Cambridge: Cambridge University Press.

Eagly, A. H., and W. Wood. 1999. The Origins of Sex Differences in Human Behavior: Evolved Dispositions versus Social Roles. *American Psychologist* 54(6): 408–23.

Ehrlich, Paul. 2000. *Human Natures: Gene, Cultures, and the Human Prospect.* Washington, DC: Island Press.

Ehrlich, Paul, and Marcus Feldman. 2003. Genes and Cultures: What Creates Our Behavioral Phenome? *Current Anthropology* 44(1): 87–107.

Fausto-Sterling, Anne. 1992. Building Two-Way Streets: The Case of Feminism and Science. *National Women's Studies Association Journal* 4: 336–49.

Fedigan, Linda M. 1983. Dominance and Reproductive Success in Primates. *Yearbook of Physical Anthropology* 26: 91–129.

———. 1992. *Primate Paradigms: Sex Roles and Social Bonds.* 2nd ed. Chicago: University of Chicago Press.

Fuentes, Agustín. 1999. Variable Social Organizations: What Can Looking at Primate Groups Tell Us about the Evolution of Plasticity in Primate Societies? In *The Nonhuman Primates,* ed. Phyllis Dolhinow and Agustín Fuentes, pp. 183–88. Mountain View, CA: Mayfield Publishing Co.

Ghiglieri, Michael P. 1999. *The Dark Side of Man: Tracing the Origins of Male Violence.* Reading, MA: Perseus Press.

Gould, Stephen Jay. 1980. Sociobiology and the Theory of Natural Selection. In *Sociobiology: Beyond Nature/Nurture,* ed. George W. Barlow and James Silverberg, pp. 257–69. Boulder, CO: Westview Press.

Gould, Stephen Jay, and Elizabeth A. Lloyd. 1999. Individuality and Adaptation across Levels of Selection: How Shall We Name and Generalize the Unit of Darwinism? *Proceedings of the National Academy of Sciences* [USA] 96(21): 11,904–9.

Gray, John. 1992. *Men Are from Mars, Women Are from Venus: A Practical Guide for Improving Communication and Getting What You Want in Your Relationships.* New York: Harper-Collins Press.

Harcourt, Alexander H., and J. Greenberg. 2001. Do Gorilla Females Join Males to Avoid Infanticide? A Quantitative Model. *Animal Behavior* 62: 905–15.

Ho, Mae-Wan, and Peter T. Saunders, eds. 1984. *Beyond Neo-Darwinism: An Introduction to the New Evolutionary Paradigm.* London: Academic Press.

Hrdy, Sarah B. 1981. *The Woman That Never Evolved.* Cambridge: Harvard University Press.

Jones, Doug. 1999. Evolutionary Psychology. *Annual Review of Anthropology* 28: 553–75.

Kirkpatrick, R. Craig. 1998. Ecology and Behavior in Snub-Nosed and Douc Langurs. In *The Natural History of the Doucs and Snub-Nosed Monkeys,* ed. Nina G. Jablonski, pp. 155–90. Singapore: World Scientific.

Kirkpatrick, R. Craig, Y. C. Long, T. Zhong, and L. Xiao. 1998. Social Organization and Range Use in the Yunnan Snub-Nosed Monkey *Rhinopithecus bieti. International Journal of Primatology* 19(1): 13–51.

Kitcher, Phillip. 1986. The Trouble with Human Sociobiology is . . . *Behavioral and Brain Sciences* 9(1): 201–2.

Kokko, Hanna, and Michael Jennions. 2003. It Takes Two to Tango. *Trends in Ecology and Evolution* 18(3): 103–4.

Kruuk, Loeske E. B., Juha Merilä, and Ben C. Sheldon. 2003. When Environmental Variation Short-Circuits Natural Selection. *Trends in Ecology and Evolution* 18(5): 207–9.

Lewontin, Richard C. 1979. Sociobiology as an Adaptationist Program. *Behavioral Sciences* 24: 5–14.

Lloyd, Elizabeth A. 1999. Evolutionary Psychology: The Burdens of Proof. *Biology and Philosophy* 14: 211–33.

Lovejoy, C. Owen. 1981. The Origins of Man. *Science* 211: 341–50.

———. 1993. Modeling Human Origins: Are We Sexy because We Are Smart, or Smart because We Are Sexy? In *The Origin and Evolution of Humans and Humanness,* ed. D. Tab Rasmussen, pp. 1–26. Sudbury, MA: Jones and Bartlett.

Low, Bobbi S. 2000. *Why Sex Matters: A Darwinian Look at Human Behavior.* Princeton, NJ: Princeton University Press.

McKenna, James J. 1983. Primate Aggression and Evolution: An Overview of Sociobiological and Anthropological Perspectives. *Bulletin of the American Academy of Psychiatry and the Law* 2(2): 105–30.

Neubauer, Peter B. 1996. *Nature's Thumbprint: The New Genetics of Personality.* New York: Columbia University Press.

Oyama, Susan. 1989. Ontogeny and the Central Dogma: Do We Need the Concept of Genetic Programming in Order to Have an Evolutionary Perspective? In *Systems and Development: The Minnesota Symposium on Child Psychology,* vol. 22, ed. M. R. Gunnar and E. Thelen, pp. 1–34. Hillsdale, NJ: Lawrence Erlbaum.

———. 2000. *Evolution's Eye: A Systems View of the Biology-Culture Divide.* Durham, NC: Duke University Press.

Palombit, Ryan A. 1999. Infanticide and the Evolution of Pair Bonds in Nonhuman Primates. *Evolutionary Anthropology* 7(4): 117–29.

Park, Michael Alan. 2002. *Biological Anthropology.* 3rd ed. New York: McGraw Hill/Mayfield Publishing Co.

Pinker, Steven. 1997. *How the Mind Works.* New York: Norton.

Randerson, J. P., and L. D. Hurst. 2001. A Comparative Test of a Theory for the Evolution of Anisogamy. *Proceedings of the Royal Society of London* 268(1469): 879–84.

Ray, Elsworth. 1999. Social Dominance in Nonhuman Primates. In *The Nonhuman Primates,* ed. Phyllis Dolhinow and Agustín Fuentes, pp. 206–10. Mountain View, CA: Mayfield Publishing Co.

Ridley, Matt. 1993. *The Red Queen: Sex and the Evolution of Human Nature.* New York: Macmillan Publishing Co.

———. 1997. *The Origins of Virtue: Human Instincts and the Evolution of Cooperation.* New York: Viking Press.

Robbins, M. M. 1995. A Demographic Analysis of Male Life History and Social Structure of Mountain Gorillas. *Behaviour* 132: 21–47.

Rose, Hilary, and Steven Rose, eds. 2000. *Alas, Poor Darwin: Arguments against Evolutionary Psychology.* New York: Harmony Books.

Rossi, A. S. 1995. A Plea for Less Attention to Monkeys and Apes, and More to Human Biology and Evolutionary Psychology. *Politics and the Life Sciences* 14(2): 185–87.

Rowell, Thelma E. 1972. *The Social Behaviour of Monkeys.* Middlesex, UK: Penguin Press.

———. 1984. What Do Male Monkeys Do Besides Competing? In *Behavioral Evolution and Integrative Levels,* ed. Gary Greenburg and Ethel Tobach, pp. 205–12. Hillsdale, NJ: Lawrence Erlbaum.

———. 1988. Beyond the One-Male Group. *Behaviour* 104(3–4): 189–201.

Rylands, Anthony B., ed. 1993. *Marmosets and Tamarins: Systematics, Behavior, and Ecology.* Oxford: Oxford Scientific Publications.

Sapolsky, Robert M. 1993. The Physiology of Dominance in Stable versus Unstable Hierarchies. In *Primate Social Conflict,* ed. William A. Mason and Sarah P. Mendoza, pp. 171–204. Albany: State University of New York Press.

———. 1996. Why Should an Aged Male Baboon Ever Transfer Troops? *American Journal of Primatology* 39(3): 149–57.

———. 2000. Stress Hormones: Good and Bad. *Neurobiology of Disease* 7: 540–42.

Sicotte, Pascale. 2002. The Function of Male Aggressive Displays towards Females in Mountain Gorillas. *Primates* 43(4): 277–89.

Silverberg, James. 1980. Sociobiology, the New Synthesis? An Anthropologist's Perspective. In *Sociobiology: Beyond Nature/Nurture?* ed. George W. Barlow and James Silverberg, pp. 25–74. Boulder, CO: Westview Press.

Smuts, Barbara B., and R. W. Smuts. 1993. Male Aggression and Sexual Coercion of Females in Nonhuman Primates and Other Mammals: Evidence and Theoretical Implications. *Advances in the Study of Behavior* 22: 1–63.

Sprague, David S. 1998. Age, Dominance Rank, Natal Status, and Tenure among Male Macaques. *American Journal of Physical Anthropology* 105(4): 511–21.

Sprague, David S., and S. Suzuki. 2000. Lifetime Likelihood of Becoming an Alpha Male for Japanese Macaque Males. *American Journal of Physical Anthropology* (Supplement) 30: 288–89.

Sprague, David S., S. Suzuki, and T. Tsukahara. 1996. Variation in Social Mechanisms by Which Males Attained the Alpha Rank among Japanese Macaques. In *Evolution and Ecology of Macaque Societies,* ed. James E. Fa and Donald G. Lindburg, pp. 444–58. New York: Cambridge University Press.

Stanford, Craig B. 2001. *Significant Others: The Ape-Human Continuum and the Quest for Human Nature.* New York: Basic Books.

Strier, Karen B. 1994. Myth of the Typical Primate. *Yearbook of Physical Anthropology* 37: 233–71.

Strum, Shirley C., and Linda M. Fedigan. 1999. Theory, Method, Gender, and Culture: What Changed Our Views of Primate Society? In *The New Physical Anthropology: Science, Humanism, and Critical Reflection,* ed. Shirley C. Strum and Donald G. Lindburg, pp. 67–105. Upper Saddle River, NJ: Prentice Hall.

Sussman, Robert Wald. 1997. Exploring Our Basic Human Nature: Are Humans Inherently Violent? *AnthroNotes, Smithsonian National Museum of Natural History Bulletin for Teachers* 19(3): 1–6.

Sussman, Robert Wald, ed. 1999. *The Biological Basis of Human Behavior: A Critical Review.* 2nd ed. Upper Saddle River, NJ: Prentice Hall.

Sussman, Robert Wald, and Paul Garber. 2004. Rethinking the Role of Affiliation and Aggression among Primates. In *The Origin and Evolution of Sociality,* ed. Robert Wald Sussman and A. R. Chapman, pp. 161–90. New York: Aldine de Gruyter.

Tang-Martinez, Zuleyma. 2000. Paradigms and Primates: Bateman's Principle, Passive Females, and Perspectives from Other Taxa. In *Primate Encounters: Models of Science, Gender, and Society,* ed. Shirley C. Strum and Linda M. Fedigan, pp. 261–74. Chicago: University of Chicago Press.

Treves, A., and Colin A. Chapman. 1996. Conspecific Threat, Predation Avoidance, and Resource Defense: Implications for Grouping in Langurs. *Behavioral Ecology and Sociobiology* 39(1): 43–53.

Trivers, Robert L. 1972. Parental Investment and Sexual Selection. In *Sexual Selection and the Descent of Man, 1871–1971,* ed. Bernard Campbell, pp. 136–79. Chicago: Aldine.

van Schaik, Carel P., and Charles H. Janson. 2000. *Infanticide by Males and Its Implications.* Cambridge: Cambridge University Press.

Vrba, Elizabeth S. 1983. Macroevolutionary Trends: New Perspectives on the Roles of Adaptation and Incidental Effect. *Science* 221: 387–89.

Washburn, Sherwood L. 1951. The New Physical Anthropology. *Transactions of the New York Academy of Sciences* (Series II) 13: 298–304.

————. 1973. The Promise of Primatology. *American Journal of Physical Anthropology* 38: 177–82.

Watts, David P. 1996. Comparative Socio-ecology of Gorillas. In *Great Ape Societies,* ed. William C. McGrew, Linda F. Marchant, and Toshida Nishida, pp. 16–28. Cambridge: Cambridge University Press.

Wilson, Edward O. 1975. *Sociobiology: The New Synthesis.* Cambridge: Harvard University Press.

————. 1976. Academic Vigilantism and the Political Significance of Sociobiology. *BioScience* 26(3): 183, 187–90.

Wilson, Michael L., and Richard W. Wrangham. 2003. Intergroup Relations in Chimpanzees. *Annual Reviews in Anthropology* 32: 363–92.

Wrangham, Richard W. 1999. Evolution of Coalitionary Killing. *Yearbook of Physical Anthropology* 42: 1–30.

Wrangham, Richard W., and Dale Peterson. 1996. *Demonic Males: Apes and the Origins of Human Violence.* New York: Houghton Mifflin.

Wright, Patricia Chapple. 1993. Variations in Male-Female Dominance and Offspring Care in Non-human Primates. In *Sex and Gender Hierarchies,* ed. Barbara D. Miller, pp. 127–45. Cambridge: Cambridge University Press.

Wright, Robert. 1994. *The Moral Animal: Evolutionary Psychology and Everyday Life.* New York: Pantheon Books.

Zihlman, Adrienne L. 1996. Reconstructions Considered: Chimpanzee Models and Human Evolution. In *Great Ape Societies,* ed. William C. McGrew, Linda F. Marchant, and Toshida Nishida, pp. 293–304. Cambridge: Cambridge University Press.

Zihlman, Adrienne L., J. E. Cronin, D. L. Cramer, and Vincent Sarich. 1978. Pygmy Chimpanzee as a Possible Prototype for the Common Ancestor of Humans, Chimpanzees, and Gorillas. *Nature* 275: 744–46.

Zimmerman, L. A. 2000. *The SE Switch: Evolution and Our Self Esteem.* Orlando: Rivercross.

CHAPTER 5

On Kinship and Marriage: A Critique of the Genetic and Gender Calculus of Evolutionary Psychology

Susan McKinnon

OVER THE PAST DECADE or so, evolutionary psychologists have articulated accounts of human psychology that purport to explain both the origins and the contemporary forms of kinship and marriage across all cultures. They have based their accounts on a calculus of genetic self-maximization and gender differentiation that they presume to be universal and seek to establish less by reference to the behavior of humans than to the behavior of birds, insects, and nonhuman mammals. Evolutionary psychologists have tended to ignore or explain away the rich historical and anthropological record of the varieties of human systems of kinship and marriage, and they have disregarded anthropological descriptions of cultural diversity and their implications for theories of the mind. The goal of this chapter, therefore, is to enlist anthropology's expertise on the cross-cultural varieties of kinship and marriage in order to challenge both the presuppositions about genetics and gender that underlie the narratives of evolutionary psychologists and the theories of mind and culture that inform these presuppositions.

The Basic Scenario: The Genetic and Gender Calculus of Kinship and Marriage

For evolutionary psychologists, complex social worlds are ultimately defined by the ongoing logic of natural selection and driven by individual self-interest, ruthless competition, and single-minded efforts to maximize reproductive success. The competitive struggle of individuals on the battlefield of natural selection is seen to be mitigated in one sense only. In contrast to this larger domain of competition, evolutionary psychologists distinguish another domain, that of kinship, which is modified by a potential for altruism that supposedly derives from the calculation of genetic closeness and self-interest (Pinker 1997: 426–30).[1]

Indeed, for evolutionary psychologists, kinship is defined in terms of genetic relatedness, which is seen to have several specific characteristics. As Steven Pinker notes, kinship relationships are assumed to be "digital. You're either someone's mother or you aren't" (1997: 430). The idea, here, is that there is a one-to-one relationship between genetic and social relation that makes kinship categories clear-cut and self-evident. There is, in addition, a calculus of genetic closeness that is read as a measure of kinship proximity. For instance, one shares more genes and is therefore closer to one's own biological children than to one's siblings' biological children. One can thus plot degrees of genetic closeness and distance—and hence degrees of kinship—as one moves out from any individual to more and more distant relations. Most importantly, evolutionary psychologists assert that kinship behavior (such as solidarity, nurturance, and altruism) follows directly from the degree of genetic relatedness: the higher the degree of genetic relatedness, the higher the degree of altruistic kinship behavior. Driven to maximize their own reproductive success, people wish to "invest" only in their own genetic children (or closely related kin) and do not want to "waste" resources on children that are not genetically their own (Daly and Wilson 1998: 17, 38–39; see also, e.g., Buss 1994: 67, 125–26).

Within this genetic calculus of kinship, as argued by evolutionary psychologists, there is a gendered calculus of kinship and marriage (or, as they prefer to call it, "mating"). They claim that sexual reproductive difference mandates distinct gendered characteristics, psychologies, and strategies for men and women that came into being and were fixed forever in what they call the "environment of evolutionary adaptation." The exact nature of this environment is unspecified but is generally assumed to have been something akin to the African savanna during the Pleistocene.

A number of presuppositions form the infrastructure of this view of kinship and marriage. First, there is the notion that reproductive strategies of men and women must be fundamentally different due to a biologically based asymmetry in their relative parental investment. Following from this, it is assumed that men and women have different adaptive problems to solve as they seek to maximize their reproductive success. "Females are constrained by the resources that are available for investment in their relatively few offspring. Males, in contrast, are constrained primarily by access to reproductively valuable females" (Buss 1988: 102; see also Buss 1994: 19–72).

Tucked into the idea that males and females have different reproductive constraints and strategies is a third presupposition: that men control economic resources (food, shelter, wealth, etc.), while women control reproductive resources (fertility and sexual fidelity). Since women are assumed to be biologically disadvantaged (due to their differential parental investment) in their ability to gain the means of subsistence, they are thought to be perpetually in a quandary regarding how to secure resources from men to support themselves and their children. By contrast, since men lack any inherent control over the reproductive resources of women, they are forever in a quandary as to how to attract fertile women and—because of the uncertainty of paternity—how to ensure not only women's fidelity but also that their resources will be invested in their "own" genetic children. In the end, evolutionary psychologists assert a fundamental gendered asymmetry: that women are concerned about the productive resources of men, while men are concerned about the reproductive fidelity of women (Buss 1994: 19–72; Wilson and Daly 1992: 292; Daly, Wilson, and Weghorst 1982: 12, 17).

The accounts of gender, kinship, and marriage put forward by evolutionary psychologists entail a particular theory of both mind and culture. Evolutionary psychologists reject the idea that the evolved human brain manifests a generalized capacity to create a wide array of cultural forms and learn a diverse range of behaviors (see Gibson, chapter 1, this volume). They posit, instead, a series of discrete, content-specific psychological mechanisms that solve particular "adaptive problems" (Buss 1991: 461, 464). Thus, men have developed preference mechanisms for characteristics (such as youth, attractiveness, and shapeliness) that are supposedly cues to female reproductive value, while women have developed preference mechanisms for characteristics (status, ambitiousness, and industriousness) that are cues to "male resource potential" (Buss 1988, 1992, 1994; Buss and Schmidt 1993). These preference mechanisms are thought to have evolved through natural selection and to have elicited—through the operation of sexual selection—the evolution of the desired qualities in the opposite sex (Buss 1991, 1992, 1994; Buss and Schmidt 1993). The resulting preference mechanisms and gender qualities are assumed to constitute innate and genetically inherited psychological features (Buss 1991, 1992, 1994; Buss and Schmidt 1993) that have not changed for millennia. Such a theory of mind implies a specific theory of culture. For if there is a genetic "blueprint" (Tooby and Cosmides 1992: 78) for human behavior, then cultural beliefs, values, and practices are epiphenomenal to, dependent upon, and reducible to the "real" genetic determinants of behavior.

Challenging the Genetic Calculus of Kinship

How does Pinker's quip—that kinship is "digital. You're either someone's mother or you aren't" (1997: 430)—hold up in light of the realities of human systems of kinship? His notion assumes that there is a straightforward, unmediated, and therefore self-evident relationship between an underlying biological (read genetic) "reality" and its realization in social categories. What is the evidence that social categories of kinship can be directly read as derivative of a more fundamental biological reality that is clear-cut and self-evident?

In general, evolutionary psychologists simply assert a direct link between kinship categories and biological relatedness, and they choose not to take seriously any evidence to the contrary. However, one study that purports to demonstrate the genetic calculus of kinship is Martin Daly and Margo Wilson's analysis of stepparental relationships. They argue that "the psychology of parental solicitude in any species . . . [is] designed to allocate parental investment discriminatively, in ways that will promote the individual parent's genetic posterity (inclusive fitness). . . . Indiscriminate allocation of parental benefits without regard to cues of actual parentage would be an evolutionary anomaly" (1998: 39). The high rates of violence of stepparents (particularly stepfathers) toward their stepchildren are taken as "the predictable consequences of putting people who had no human [i.e., genetic] reason to love one another into a relationship that was structurally analogous to— and had to serve as a partial substitute for—the most intimate of loving relationships, namely that of parent and child" (Daly and Wilson 1998: 23). The reduction of "human reasons to love" to the calculus of genetic self-maximization not only erases the many other reasons—social, economic, psychological—that step-relations might be difficult but also suggests that reasons to love that are not grounded in genetics are somehow unreal and even maladaptive. When Daly and Wilson consider adoption, they discount its importance as a counterargument to their thesis on the grounds that "parents are eager to adopt" (1998: 45). Yet that is precisely the point. Human desire, love, and nurturance can neither be defined nor confined by genetics. If a genetic logic does not apply to adoption, why should it apply to stepparental relationships?

Such studies are meant to stand as proof of a genetic theory of kinship in the absence of any attempt to survey the large ethnographic record of the cross-cultural varieties and complexities of kinship formations. It is therefore worth considering the wider historical and anthropological record to see how it compares with the understanding of gender, kinship, and marriage provided by the evolutionary psychologists.

A MULTIPLICITY OF MOTHERS

Let us begin with the kinship category—mother—that is generally considered the most "self-evident." Kinship terminology gives us our first hint of the difficulties in determining who counts as a mother. Systems of kinship terminology are important to consider not only because they reveal the differences in the organization of kinship relations cross-culturally but also because they constitute the categorical framework upon which distinct patterns of social behavior—including acts of nurturance, solidarity, and resource allocation—are built.

There are a limited number of systems of kinship terminology among human societies, but who counts as a mother in each of them varies considerably (see Fox 1967; Parkin 1997). In the kinship system used by Anglo-Americans, one's "mother" is clearly distinguished, terminologically, from all other female kin in the same generation—including mother's sisters and father's sisters—who are called "aunts" (a system called "lineal"). In the Anglo-American system, therefore, "mother" does indeed appear to be singular and self-evident. By contrast, in Hawaii and elsewhere, all women of the first ascending generation are called "mother," including all of the above-mentioned aunts (a system called "generational") (Parkin 1997: 68). In still other societies, mother's sisters are included in the designation of "mother," but father's sisters are not (a system called "bifurcate merging") (Parkin 1997: 68). All of this is, of course, compounded if we ascend the generations, since, for instance, mother's mother's sisters' daughters will also be "mothers," and so on. To complicate matters further, there is the system that anthropologists call "Omaha," in which one's "mothers" include one's mother, mother's sisters, mother's brothers' daughters, and mother's brothers' sons' daughters (Fox 1967: 255–56; Parkin 1997: 111). And none of this includes those systems—found in Africa, Polynesia, and elsewhere—in which one's mother's brother is referred to as a "male mother" (Radcliffe-Brown 1952: 19; Middleton 2000). Thus, even a simple perusal of systems of kinship terminology demonstrates that there is no single straight line between any underlying biological "reality" (either genetic or gendered) and the social categories of motherhood. Those who count as mothers in one system are aunts (or even uncles) in another.

But what happens when what we understand as a biologically based genealogical grid gets complicated by ideas of reincarnation—that is, when the idea of "procreation is not the addition of new persons to the inventory of the universe, but rather the substitution of one for another" (Fienup-Riordan 1983: 153)? Among the Yup'ik Eskimos of Alaska, children are named after deceased grandparents or others in the grandparental generation. Upon taking the grandparent's name, the child then assumes the kinship relations that were appropriate to that grandparent and is addressed and addresses others from that position. Thus, a female child is addressed as "mother" by her parents, whom she addresses as her "children" (Fienup-Ri-ordan 1983: 157).

There are, moreover, other ways of accruing mothers than those calcu-lated along a genealogical grid. Consider, for instance, how the institution of the distinction between legal wife and concubine—and ritual duties of mourning accorded to each—complicated the picture of motherhood in Chinese patrilineal households during the Ming and Ch'ing dynasties.

> The mourning charts describe eight different kinds of mother. . . . The terms are *yang mu* (a mother who has adopted you), *ti mu* (father's legal wife), *chi mu* (a father's legal wife married after the death or, more rarely, the divorce of the first legal wife . . .), *tz'u mu* (a father's concubine who is not your own birth mother who cares for you after the death of your birth mother), *chia mu* (a mother who has remarried after the death of your fa-ther), *ch'u mu* (a mother who has been divorced by your father), *shu mu* (father's concubine who may or may not be your birth mother) and *ju mu* (a father's concubine who has breast-fed you). Note that birth mother (for which there is a perfectly good Ming Chinese term, *sheng mu*) is not one of the eight legal and ritual categories. (Waltner 1996: 71–72)

In this case, the assessment of who counts as a mother follows not from bi-ology but from rank and marital status. In such households, all children were considered—both legally and ritually—the children of the father's principal wife. It was said that a "concubine has no children and a concu-bine's children have no mother" (Waltner 1996: 72). Here, there is nothing "self-evident" about motherhood, or really "real" about biology. What is "real" is a hierarchical system of rank and marriage, and the legal and ritual system through which kinship is created and realized.

Or consider how kinship relations get created out of the behavior that is deemed to be appropriate to kinship relations. In the Tanimbar Islands of eastern Indonesia, men from high- and low-ranking houses may be in a relationship that is called "elder-younger brothers [who] treat each other well" (*ya'an iwarin simaklivur*) (McKinnon 1991: 100–101, 269–70). Be-cause these father's brothers are also one's fathers, the wives of these men are therefore one's mothers. The fact of "treating one another well" says it all: the relationship is created and maintained by acts of nurturance and solici-tude that constitute the very definition of kinship.

Even in the United States, where the ideology of biology is so highly priv-ileged, there are a number of situations in which one might have multiple mothers, not all of whom are biologically related. One might have an adop-tive mother and a birth mother. Or one might have two mothers in a family composed of two lesbian parents—one or both of whom could be biologically related to oneself (Lewin 1993; Hayden 1995). Or, in African American communities, one might have a range of "othermothers"—kin, friends, and neighbors who share with "bloodmothers" the responsibility for nurturing each other's children within a community (Collins 1990: 119–23; Stack 1974). Or, through the wonders of the new reproductive technologies, a child might have three mothers: a gestational mother, a genetic mother who donates the egg, and an intentional mother who contracts the other women to produce the child. In custody disputes over children created through the new reproductive technologies, U.S. law tends to side with the intentional mother—whether or not she makes any biological contribution to the process (Dolgin 1997; Thompson 2001). This multiplication of mothers may be further complicated if the egg donor is the daughter of the intentional mother, in which case one would be the sister of one's (genetic) mother and the (genetic) grandchild of one's (intentional) mother (Thompson 2001: 180–95).

Although some Americans may be troubled by the idea of so many mothers—since, according to the middle-class ideal, there is supposed to be only one—in many other cultures people are comfortable with a multiplicity of mothers. This is evident in those societies where there is a high rate of adoption, as in many Eskimo and Polynesian societies (Carroll 1970; Fienup-Riordan 1983; Bodenhorn 2000). In the circumpolar regions of North America, adoption is virtually "the statistical norm. Most adults have either been adopted in or lived in a household where a child has been adopted in or adopted out" (Bodenhorn 2000: 139). These adoptions are by no means always between kin or always carried out for reasons of childlessness. "A much more common reason was [simply] that someone . . . 'wanted to'" (Bodenhorn 2000: 139). Here there are evidently a multitude of other "human reasons to love" and therefore to create a kinship relationship out of that love.

In Hawaii, as throughout Polynesia, various forms of adoption existed. Adults could "make a child" (ho'okama) "as a result of mutual affection and agreement . . . between the child and the older person" (Howard et al. 1970: 22). A child could also be "taken into the household of his makua hanai 'feeding parents' and reared as their offspring. They assumed complete social rights and obligations in raising their kama hanai 'feeding child'" (Howard et al. 1970: 22). The reasons for adoption were various: "the desire to create a bond between" families; "the belief that twins must be reared apart lest one or both of them die"; "the belief in 'uha kapu 'taboo lap,'" whereby "some women were so kapu that they could not raise their own children"; the idea that cross-sex siblings of high chiefly status "might be raised apart in order that they might marry later in life"; the idea that "to refuse a request to *hanai* a child was to risk death or sickness of the child"; and the "desire to have a child learn skills not possessed by his parents" (Howard et al. 1970: 27–28). *Hanai* relationships continue to be recognized in contemporary Hawaii and used to justify legal claims on children (Modell 1998).

In the end, even with a kinship category supposedly so "self-evident" as "mother," it is hard to see any one-to-one correlation between the "reality" of genetics and the social manifestations of kinship. Instead, the categories of kinship everywhere follow specific cultural logics that always exceed and escape the bounds of any supposedly universal calculation of genetic relation. Ideas about procreation and death, biology and conduct, rank and alliance, nurturance and affection, marriage and exchange, law and ritual are all relevant to the definition of what a mother is, and they shape who gets to count as a mother or a child to whom. A theory of kinship based on the assumption that there is a straightforward relationship between genetic "reality" and social categories of kinship is incapable of explaining a multiplicity of other kinship "realities" such as the ones just noted.

Of course, one could always say that everyone knows who their "real" mother or child is and therefore makes the appropriate discriminations in terms of differential nurturance, altruism, and allocation of resources. Indeed, many people do make distinctions between "real" and other forms of kinship, although who counts as real kin in any particular culture is not always—or even often—defined genetically. Even allowing for such a distinction, however, it is clear that the patterns of nurturance, altruism, and allocation of resources follow from specific cultural classifications of kin relations and cultural understandings of appropriate kin behavior that are never simply reflections of genetic relation and self-maximization.

THE CULTURAL MEDIATION OF KINSHIP CATEGORIES AND GROUPS

The fact that kinship is everywhere mediated by cultural understandings—and is not the precipitate of a universal genetic calculus—is evident not only in the categories of kinship relation, such as mother, but also in the categories of social groupings, which lie at the heart of kinship relations. Marshall Sahlins (1976) long ago demonstrated that the logic of kinship groupings—whatever their form—challenges the logic of genetic self-maximization and kin selection. Even if we begin from a descent-based ideology that presupposes a genealogical grid, it is impossible to generate the range of human kinship groupings from a calculation of genetic proximity. Take, for instance, the systems of kinship known as unilineal, in which descent is traced either through the male line to constitute patrilineal groups or through the female line to constitute matrilineal groups. Either way, such a delineation of groups will always entail that some close genetic kin will be in other groups while some more distant genetic kin will be in one's own group.

> Over time, the members of the descent unit comprise a smaller and smaller fraction of the ancestor's total number of genealogical descendants, diminishing by a factor of ½ each generation. Assuming patrilineality, for example, and an equal number of male and female births, half the members in each generation are lost to the lineage, since the children of women will be members of their husband's lineage. . . . by the third generation the group consists of only ¼ the ancestor's genealogical kin, by the fifth generation, only 1⁄16, and so on. And whereas those of the fifth generation in the paternal line may have a coefficient of relationship of 1⁄256, each has relatives in other lineages—sister's children, mother's brothers, mother's sisters—whose r coefficient is as high as ¼. (Sahlins 1976: 30–31)

If we also take into account the distinction of residence, then the disjunction between genetic and social forms of relationship increases. It is residential groups—which include both kin (however defined) and non-kin—that are the effective units of social solidarity, cooperation, and resource sharing (Sahlins 1976: 26–28). Moreover, forms of residence (patrilocal, matrilocal, uxorilocal, virilocal, neolocal) are not always "harmonic" (Lévi-Strauss [1949] 1969: 215) with forms of descent (patrilineal, matrilineal, double unilineal, cognatic), and they may disburse kin from the same descent group across separate residential groupings.

The point is that social arrangements of kinship relations inevitably cut across genetic lines of relationship and sort genetically related people into distinct social and residential groups. Because cooperation and resource sharing are organized in accordance with such social and residential groupings, the logic of social distinctions utterly contravenes that of genetic self-maximization and kin selection—which presumes that one wishes to expend resources on behalf of genetically close kin rather than distant kin or strangers. As Sahlins notes, "the actual systems of kinship and concepts of heredity in human societies, though they never conform to biological coefficients of relationship, are true models of and for social action. These cultural determinations of 'near' and 'distant' kin make up the de facto form taken by shared interests and manifested in behaviors of altruism, antagonism, and the like. They represent the effective structures of sociability in the societies concerned, and accordingly bear directly on reproductive success" (1976: 25).

If the argument that one can move from genetic relations to the social relations of kinship does not work for descent-based (i.e., genealogically based) systems of kinship, it works even less for those systems of kinship groupings that are constituted in terms of other criteria—such as exchange, labor, or feeding. Anthropologists have recently focused on what they call "house societies," which use other criteria in the constitution of kinship groups, either alone or in combination with descent-based criteria (McKinnon 1991; Carsten and Hugh-Jones 1995; Carsten 1997; Joyce and Gillespie 2000). For instance, in the Tanimbar Islands children are allocated to "houses" not by virtue of birth but rather by virtue of exchange. Thus, one house may include a diverse array of people who have—as the result of the complex requirements of exchange—affiliated patrilaterally (to the house of their father) and matrilaterally (to the house of their mother's brother), been adopted as children, or "lifted" into the house as adults (McKinnon 1991). One's "own" genetic children may end up in the house of other kin or non-kin, while one's own house may be populated by people who either are unrelated or are more distant genetic relatives. Janet Carsten has shown how, in Langkawi, Malaysia, the mechanism for creating kinship relates ideas of blood to that of feeding. "[P]eople are both born with blood and acquire it through life in the form of food, which is transformed into blood in the body. . . . Those who eat the same food together in one house also come to have blood in common" (Carsten 2001: 46). In this way, fostered children (25 percent of the children in Langkawi), affines, and strangers become kin with those who feed them. Feeding is the means for making kin out of strangers. Similarly, for the Iñupiat of northern Alaska, kinship is more about "doing" than about any essential biological "being." As in Langkawi, kinship among the Iñupiat is a process.

> [K]inship bonds [must be] renewed and kept viable through a myriad of reciprocities: shared tools, food, labour, political alliance, ceremonial participation, and simply company. . . . Sharing may be both uncalculated and balanced, but among kin it is not dormant. It is this labour—the work of being related—rather than the labor of giving birth or the "fact" of shared substance that marks out the kinship sphere from the potentially infinite universe of relatives who may or may not belong. (Bodenhorn 2000: 143)

As Bodenhorn notes, "whereas both 'biology' and 'acting' are categories Iñupiat use when talking about kin, it is the latter category that renders kinship 'real.' In curious ways, then, 'labour' does for Iñupiaq kinship what 'biology' does for many other systems" (2000: 128).

In the United States, kinship is created out of the tension between substantial (biological, genetic) relations and social (behavioral, code for conduct) relations (Schneider 1972). In general, the biological is privileged over the behavioral as what makes kinship not only "real" but also distinct from other kinds of relationships. However, there are a number of contexts in which the behavioral codes for conduct in kinship relations come to be seen as that which makes the relationship "real." Often when adopted children in the United States seek their "real," biological parents, they discover that the behavioral part—the years of living together, building up a reservoir of common experience and emotional attachment—is missing, and the "reality" of the social aspect of kinship is made evident. The "thinness of a purely biological relationship . . . [becomes] apparent" (Modell 1994: 164), as does the need to work at the relationship to make it "real" kinship (Modell 1994: 166). Weston notes that the same has been true for gays and lesbians, for whom "disclosure became a process destined to uncover the 'truth' of [biological] kinship relations" (1991: 73), and rejection by biological parents made it evident that "choice always enters into the decision to count (or discount) someone as a relative" (1991: 73). Gays' and lesbians' families of choice shifted the logic of relatedness from one that assumed that biological kinship is what lasts and endures to one that asserts that kinship is what lasts and endures (Weston 1995: 101). It is the "doing" of kinship that makes it real.

There are, thus, a range of criteria that humans use to constitute kinship groupings. While some privilege essential qualities of "being" as that which makes kinship real, others privilege the qualities of "doing" and "creating." In either case, what comprises the relevant qualities of being or doing varies from society to society. The essential qualities of "being" may be blood and bone, flesh and spirit, semen and breast milk, or genetics as coded information. The qualities of "doing" or "creating" kinship may include exchange, feeding, labor on the land, or religious sacrifice.

Evolutionary psychologists have reduced a symbolic, culturally mediated system to what they deem to be a natural, culturally unmediated one. Yet the diversity of cultural understandings of kinship and the range of kinship formations cannot be accounted for as a natural system operating by a fixed genetic calculus. The evidence tells us that what counts as kinship is cross-culturally variable, cannot be presupposed, and certainly cannot be read directly from some underlying biological reality. This evidence of cross-cultural diversity makes it clear that evolutionary psychologists have taken a specific cultural understanding of kinship—one that derives from Euro-American understandings of the essential qualities of genes—and attempted to make it into a cross-cultural universal.

Evolutionary psychologists have also reduced kinship—a fundamentally social relationship—to a function of individual self-interest. Kinship relations are taken as the social precipitate of individual desires to perpetuate one's own genetic inheritance, which presupposes that one would be unwilling to "invest" resources in those who are genetically unrelated or more distantly related. However, what we know about kinship relationships is that they are more often created and maintained precisely to establish and multiply networks of social relationships. That is, people happily expend resources on distant kin and unrelated persons precisely to bring them into a network of kin relations. Evolutionary psychologists presuppose a restrictive understanding of kinship (and wealth) that is a reflection of Western upper-class concerns; but for many people in the world, kinship operates in accordance with an expansive logic, as a means of multiplying social, economic, and political relationships. Social prestige follows less from the restriction of kinship relations and accumulation of resources for oneself and one's closest kin than from the expansion of kinship networks and the dispersal of resources across a wide range of social relations.

Challenging the Gendered Calculus of Marriage

In asserting that a set of gendered preference mechanisms were genetically hardwired in response to the conditions of a Pleistocene environment of adaptation, evolutionary psychologists rely on several sources of "evidence." They create analogies between "preference mechanisms" relating to "mate selection" and organic processes such as sweating. They make cross-species analogies that reduce human systems of sexuality and marriage to "mating" and compare human "mating" to that of other species—such as weaver-birds, scorpion flies, gladiator frogs, and elephant seals. They conduct surveys of university undergraduates, who, although hardly representative of Americans, are made to stand for the human species. They refer to a very small number of anthropological accounts of kinship and marriage—generally the ones that are informed by sociobiology or evolutionary psychology and are therefore most sympathetic to their perspective. Finally, they carry out some cross-cultural surveys of their own that presuppose rather than attempt to discover the categories relevant to the formation of relations of kinship and marriage in other cultures.[2]

My approach, here, is not to debate the validity of specific preference mechanisms. Rather, I wish to paint an entirely different picture of human systems of marriage from that envisioned by evolutionary psychologists. I do so by looking at the gendered division of labor, the diverse patterns of marriage between groups, and the ways in which marriage relates to social hierarchy.

RECONSIDERING THE GENDERED DIVISION OF LABOR

One of the central assumptions in the scenario put forward by evolutionary psychologists is that an asymmetry in parental investment results in different reproductive strategies on the part of men and women. As noted earlier, the reproductive success of men is constrained by their ability to access fertile women (and thereby their ability to produce a relatively large number of offspring), while that of women is constrained by their ability to access men with resources to support a small number of offspring. This presupposes that it is men, not women, who control the resources required for subsistence. _ existance

Evolutionary psychologists have carried out studies that purport to establish that women universally "place more value than men on good financial prospects" (Buss 1994: 25) when considering a potential marriage partner. They then create a scenario of evolutionary adaptation that, they assert, would account for this gendered asymmetry in preferences. The argument is that, given their greater and longer-term parental investment in their offspring, women who depended upon either their own ability to secure resources or that of temporary sex partners would be at a disadvantage over those who depended upon the resources—such as food, shelter, defense, socialization—of a committed spouse (Buss 1994: 23). Buss notes:

> Not all potential husbands can confer all of these benefits, but over thousands of generations, when some men were able to provide some of these benefits, women gained a powerful advantage by preferring them as mates.

> So the stage was set for women to evolve a preference for men with resources. (1994: 23)

What is problematic about this scenario is not the proposition that women might prefer to marry men who would make a positive contribution to the social and economic resources of a kinship unit, although it hardly seems necessary to resort to innate mechanisms to account for such preferences. Rather, what is problematic is the assumption that it is women, but not men, who are concerned with the social and economic resources that their spouses might contribute to the kinship unit.

Such a perspective erases the fact that, in all societies, men and women are embedded in a gendered division of labor in which the productive and reproductive tasks are divided between them in specific and complementary ways. While the division of labor among the middle and upper classes in industrial societies in the West has separated the productive labor of males from the reproductive labor of females, in most societies the system through which resources are produced divides the totality of productive tasks between the genders in such a way that each is dependent upon the other for the procurement of the full range of resources necessary to sustain them. As a consequence, men and women are equally disadvantaged unless they are a member of a productive unit that includes both parts of the gendered division of labor. The assumption that parental investment is such that women, but not men, are dependent upon the productive labor and resources of their spouses seriously misconstrues the gendered structure of the division of labor in nonindustrial (and even industrial) societies.[3]

The scenario of evolutionary adaptation proposed by the evolutionary psychologists relies on narratives of early hominid life that stress the primacy of the hunt not only for the provisioning of the family but also for the rise of language and culture. This myth of "man the hunter" has long been debunked (Slocum 1975; Tanner and Zihlman 1976; Zihlman 1978), and evolutionary psychologists are aware that prehistoric women did not simply stay home and take care of the kids but also engaged in productive labor such as gathering plant foods and small game. However, this awareness has not translated into the set of assumptions about gender relations that guides their research on "mate preferences." Whereas they continually stress women's desire to find mates who are industrious, productive, and laden with resources, they never consider the possibility that men might be concerned to find women with similar qualities (Buss 1994: 19–73).[4]

Yet from the very beginning of hominid history, the most reliable and abundant source of food was obtained through gathering rather than hunting. Indeed, Tanner and Zihlman argue that the innovations in the creation of tools and containers that marked transitional hominid adaptations on the African savanna five million years ago derived not from hunting large animals—which at this early stage was not practiced—but rather from "gathering plants, eggs, honey, termites, ants, and probably small burrowing animals" (1976: 601). Instead of presuming that transitional hominid females were burdened by the long dependency of infants and children, Tanner and Zihlman make a convincing case that it was precisely this dependency that motivated not only the invention of tools, containers, and carrying slings that would facilitate gathering with dependents in tow but also early forms of female-centered social organization and sharing (Tanner and Zihlman 1976: 598–605). The toolkit necessary for large-scale hunting was not available in the Middle Pleistocene, and "[h]afted tools and wooden spears, which are part of our conventional image of such a hunting technology, do not appear in the archaeological record before about 100,000 years ago" (Zihlman 1978: 17). It thus becomes evident that, during the Pleistocene, gathering was the primary means of subsistence, and where hunting occurred, it was the reliability of gathering that made possible its otherwise in-efficient expenditure of time and energy. For, "in spite of time-consuming behaviors which frequently yield no food, such as hunting or obtaining raw materials from some distance away, individuals engaged in such activities, probably primarily males, could follow these pursuits because they were as-sured of a share of the food gathered by women with whom they had close social ties" (Zihlman 1978: 18).

The importance of gathering among contemporary hunter-gatherer so-cieties has long been established. "Studies of living people who gather and hunt reveal that throughout the world, except for specialized hunters in the arctic regions, more calories are obtained from plant foods gathered by women for family sharing than from meat obtained by hunting" (Zihlman 1978: 7). For instance, among the !Kung San of the Kalahari, "[w]omen are the primary providers of vegetable food, and they contribute something on the order of 60–80 percent of the daily food intake by weight" (Draper 1975: 82, following Lee 1965). While meat might be a prestige good, it is nei-ther a predictable nor a reliable source of food. Thus, !Kung San women provide both a disproportionate amount of food relative to men and food resources that are highly reliable and predictable. Since !Kung San women retain control over the resources they gather, it is men who are dependent upon the resources of women for daily subsistence rather than the reverse.

The interlocking, interdependent nature of male and female labor is also evident among the Yup'ik Eskimo hunter-gatherers. As Fienup-Riordan notes: "Men and women work together in the capture and preparation of each animal, yet never duplicate effort. Specific work configurations com-plement specific subsistence activities" (1983: 65), and none of these activi-ties could be completed without interdigitated labor of both men and women. Take seals as an example. Men hunt and capture seals, and although they may do the initial processing of larger seals, women do the initial pro-cessing of smaller seals. More significantly, women cut and dry thousands of pounds of meat (at a rate of 100 pounds a day), render oil from fat, and tan skins for shoes and clothing (Fienup-Riordan 1983: 78–85). Thus, men may hunt and capture seals, but their work would be for naught if the women did not process the meat and oil into a form that can be stored and eaten during the winter and did not fashion food containers, tools, and clothing out of various parts of the seal. Under such conditions, it is hard to imagine that Yup'ik men would not seriously consider the industriousness of potential spouses and their ability to supply them with the resources that are critical for subsistence throughout the year.

The importance of a gendered division of labor is by no means specific to hunter-gatherer societies. In the Tanimbar Islands, subsistence activities include both swidden agriculture as well as some hunting, fishing, gathering, domestication of animals, and planting of long-lived trees such as coconuts and mangos. While men hunt pigs, women care for domesticated pigs; while men do deep-sea fishing, both men and women fish and collect shellfish in the reefs; while men cut down and burn trees to establish swidden gardens, women plant, weed, and harvest the gardens; while men carry building materials home from the forests, women carry food supplies home from the gardens and water from the wells; while men thresh the rice, women pound and winnow the rice; while men build houses and boats, women plait baskets and weave textiles (McKinnon 1991: 166). In such a system, specific resources and the types of labor appropriate to them are gendered; and it is the complementary articulation of gender-specific labor and resources that makes subsistence possible for everyone.

Indeed, in Tanimbar and many other societies, it is not just subsistence that requires both male and female resources. Marriage exchanges—which not only create a union between a man and woman but also allocate children to the group of either the mother or the father—also involve goods that are both gendered and the product of gender-specific labor.

> In everyday life and on festive occasions, "female" wife-takers give the products of male activity—meat, fish, and palmwine—to their "male" wife-givers, while the latter reciprocate with the products of female activity—garden produce and betel nut. Similarly, in the more formal prestations, the gifts of female wife-takers consist of male valuables, which include a particular kind of earring, gold breast pendants, elephant tusks, and swords. These are reciprocated by the gifts of the male wife-givers, which consist of female valuables and include another type of earring, bead necklaces, shell armbands, and textiles. (McKinnon 1991: 166)

This is not a world where men have resources and women seek to secure them through their relations with men. Rather, it is a world that is envisioned as the productive interchange of male and female resources, which are, in turn, the product of the labor of men and women.

Even a cursory consideration of the division of labor makes it evident that production of and control over resources do not belong solely to men. The idea that men around the world look for women who are young, beautiful, and shapely but not productive, industrious, or dependable (Buss 1994) fundamentally misrepresents the way subsistence resources are secured, processed, and allocated throughout the world. Surely women are concerned to find industrious men who are willing to contribute resources to the family unit; but men are just as concerned to find women with the same qualities. A hunter who is not attached to a gatherer is a hungry man; a man who catches seals will have a pile of rotten flesh on his hands (and no clothing on his back) if he cannot find a woman who will process his catch; a man who cuts down the forest for a swidden garden has nothing but a patch of burnt ground if there is no woman to plant and harvest the crops; and a man who brings gifts of male labor to a marriage exchange will remain a bachelor unless they are reciprocated by gifts of female labor. Indeed, if men truly chose spouses on the basis of the qualities that evolutionary psychologists purport to be universal male preferences, they would be at a serious disadvantage in terms of their own survival, not to mention that of their progeny. In the end, evolutionary psychologists have imagined a reproductive strategy for men that would be highly unadaptive in most societies and across most of human history, and one that does not accord with or account for the actual patterns of the division of labor found in the world.

SYSTEMS OF MARRIAGE: ALLIANCES BETWEEN GROUPS

In the myths of kinship narrated by evolutionary psychologists, social groups tend to be erased and the individual stands strikingly alone—guided, in the search for a "mate," only by a set of evolved, innate preference mechanisms. Even when specific social forms are acknowledged, they are configured as the precipitates of individual agency and choice. Thus, for Wilson and Daly, "patrilineal affiliation follows from responses to the uncertainty of paternity" (1992: 308), and systems of marriage alliance—with all their social, economic, and political ramifications—must "first and most basically . . . be understood as reproductive" (1992: 309–10) with individual genetic self-maximization as the primary goal. Thus, marriage is reduced to "mating" (that is, the means to reproduction), and in the process, the wide range of social formations within which marriage takes place is erased. But what of the social classifications and groupings within which human marriage (as opposed to the mating of scorpion flies or elephant seals) actually takes place?

In most societies around the world, marriage is governed, in the first instance, by systematic relationships between groups rather than by individual preference. A crucial distinction is whether one is supposed to marry someone within one's own group (endogamy) or outside one's group (exogamy). If, as is sometimes the case, the whole society is divided in half (i.e., into moieties), then, under a rule of exogamy, one must marry a person from the other moiety. Societies that are divided into more than one group—say, a number of unilineal descent groups such as patrilineages or matrilineages—may operate under a rule of either endogamy or exogamy. The distinction between in-marriage and out-marriage applies not only to lineages but also to other kinds of groups, such as those defined by social criteria of religion, race, caste, class, or region. In all of these cases, the first discrimination that is made is classification by group, and individual preference operates within this system of classification.

A more specific classificatory distinction has to do with the marriage of cousins, which remained a popular option in the West until the late nineteenth century, is still legal in many states in the United States (Ottenheimer 1996), and continues to be prevalent in many societies throughout the world. However, not all systems of cousin marriage are the same, as Lévi-Strauss ([1949] 1969) demonstrated long ago. For a man in Bali, Indonesia, or in many cultures in the Middle East, his preferred marriage partner would be his father's brother's daughter (patriparallel cousin) (Boon 1977). In a patrilineal system, this means that he would be marrying within the group, or endogamously. However, if he were in the nominally patrilineal Tanimbar Islands, his preferred marriage partner would be his mother's brother's daughter (matrilateral cross-cousin), which means that he would be marrying outside the group (exogamously) (McKinnon 1991). And if he were in the matrilineal Trobriand Islands—to the northeast of New Guinea—his preferred marriage partner would be the opposite cousin, his father's sister's daughter (patrilateral cross-cousin). Here again, he would be marrying exogamously.

Cousin marriage, then, depends not only upon a distinction between one's own group and others but also upon a social classification of people and a distinction between marriageable and nonmarriageable cousins. The woman whom a Balinese man might marry is explicitly prohibited in places like Tanimbar and the Trobriand Islands, while the cousin that a Trobriand man might marry is absolutely forbidden to a Tanimbarese man and vice versa. Whatever other cultural preferences might be in play, the distinctions that matter first and foremost are categorization by group and, within groups, by social relation. As a consequence, large numbers of people are removed from the pool of potential spouses, since they will be in the wrong group and the wrong category. What is operative here is not a genetic or gendered calculus but rather a system of social classification.

To complicate matters of classification even more, consider the case of Australian section systems—the famously complex systems of group definition and alliance practiced by the Australian aborigines. In a four-section system—such as that of the Kariera in Australia—the entire society is divided into four sections, two in each of two generations.

Generation A:	Burung	Banaka
Generation B:	Karimera	Palyeri

Intermarriage takes place between individuals who are classed as bilateral cross cousins to one another [i.e., a man would marry a woman who is both father's sister's daughter and mother's brother's daughter], and between the two sections in each generation: i.e. members of Burung intermarry only with Banaka, the children of such marriages being in either Karimera or Palyeri, according to the respective groups of their parents, and vice versa. Thus each section unites people of alternate genealogical levels (in opposition to members of adjacent levels) and common descent (in opposition to affines). (Parkin 1997: 176)

In the even more complex section system known as Aranda, eight sections organize the patterns of marriage and the allocation of children to groups. In such marriage systems, we witness social mechanisms that are of an entirely different order than—and that can neither be predicted nor comprehended by—those individual gendered preference mechanisms imagined by evolutionary psychologists.

MARRIAGE AND SOCIAL HIERARCHY

One of the key discriminations people make when choosing a marriage partner is the relative social status of the prospective partners. Indeed, it is virtually impossible to talk about marriage without also talking about social hierarchy. When evolutionary psychologists talk of social status in relation to "mate selection," however, it is from the perspective of female preference mechanisms: "Women desire men who command high position in society because social status is a universal cue to the control of resources" (Buss 1994: 26). It is assumed that "[w]omen worldwide prefer to marry up" (Buss 1994: 27). Thus, social status is read as a sign of economic resources in a world in which marriage is a function only of individual (gendered) choice and preference. Any female can have access to a male of high status, as long as she is young and attractive enough. What is discounted here is the fact that male (or female) social status derives from a person's position in a larger social hierarchy, which entails categories and rules of social relation that make certain choices possible and others impossible.

In general, systems of social hierarchy and the differential valuation of categories of persons give shape to racialized, economic, or religious distinctions between those who are considered marriageable and unmarriageable. For instance, antimiscegenation laws instituted in the United States in the 1920s enforced "racial" endogamy, with the express purpose of protecting the social superiority and purported purity of whites (Lombardo 1988). Similarly, the stigmatization of marriage between Catholics and Protestants or between Hindus and Muslims works to protect each group's sense of distinctness and superiority (Donnan 1990). Such laws and social or religious values have the effect of limiting the pool of marriageable partners to those within the group for the purpose of maintaining status relative to those outside.

There are also systems of marriage in which women may marry up (hypergamy) but not down or may marry down (hypogamy) but not up. Burma (today Myanmar), as described by Edmund Leach ([1954] 1965), gives us an example of each. In the hypergamous Shan princedoms, women marry up: polygynous royal rulers take commoner and noble women in marriage as a strategy to consolidate political relationships with subordinates (Leach [1954] 1965: 216–19). By contrast, women marry down among the nearby Kachin, where the social hierarchy comprises three classes—chiefs, aristocrats, and commoners—and marriage is asymmetric (i.e., the preferred spouse is the mother's brother's daughter). "[A]lthough most marriages take place within the classes, some women pass between them in marriage. As you might expect, lineages from a superior class give women to lineages from an inferior" (Fox 1967: 213; Leach [1954] 1965). Such a system actually contravenes the expectations of evolutionary psychologists. For if women worldwide have innate preferences to marry up and such preferences shape their behavior, it is difficult to understand the existence of hypogamous systems like that of the Kachin.

While most societies have several categories of marriage, not everyone can make marriages in each of these categories: some forms of marriage are reserved for (indeed, mark the status appropriate to) higher- or lower-ranking people. In Bali, possible types of marriage include marriage by capture or elopement, which is motivated by romantic love and individual preference; exogamous marriage alliance between ancestor groups; endogamous marriage within ancestor groups through either first or second patriparallel cousin marriage (Boon 1977: 121–30); and, mythically, both brother-sister marriages (among royalty) and marriages between brother-sister twins (among the gods). Taken together, the various forms of marriage articulate a hierarchical structure. While gods and kings might marry incestuously, those in high-ranking ancestor groups "actually practice nothing closer than first-cousin unions" (Boon 1977: 139), and those in lower-ranking ascendant houses would dare only second-cousin marriage. Here is a system with both endogamy and exogamy, elopement and alliance, hypergamy and incest, as well as two degrees of patriparallel cousin marriage. Together, the different forms of marriage articulate a system of social hierarchy and are the forms through which people negotiate their position within that hierarchy.

Social hierarchy is not a system of "cues" for the actualization of individual "choices" that are otherwise genetically predetermined by gendered psychological preference mechanisms. Hierarchy is a system of social distinctions that differentiates a range of social positions that are articulated, among other ways, through marriage. It is not that there is no choice involved—individual or otherwise. Rather, it is that choices are made always within a system of distinctions that are neither individual nor genetic in origin. What is possible in a hypergamous system is prohibited in a hypogamous system. What is possible for high-ranking people is prohibited for low-ranking people. Nothing in the evolutionary psychologists' account of marriage will be able to account for the complexity or operation of the kinds of marriage systems found the world over. They may carry out cross-cultural studies, but they do not inquire into the kinds of social distinctions—endogamy and exogamy, hypergamy and hypogamy, parallel cousins and cross-cousins, Hindu and Muslim, this caste or class or that, this race or that—that most people in most societies use to choose a spouse for themselves or their children.

Contrasting Theories of Mind and Culture

Underlying the accounts of kinship and marriage offered by evolutionary psychologists is a theory of mind—and therefore a theory of culture—that contrasts sharply with those to which most cultural anthropologists subscribe. The issue here is not whether mental life is, in part, organically based or whether there is a complex developmental and interactive relation between the organism and the environment. Rather, as Benton points out, what is at issue is "how much inherited 'architecture' there is in the human mind" and "whether sociocultural processes are understood as independent or reducible to inherited psychological mechanisms" (2000: 266, 267). Thus, one question is whether the human mind operates through many domain-specific mechanisms that provide intricate content-laden "'blueprints' at the genetic level" (Tooby and Cosmides 1992: 78) for social behavior or through a few domain-general mechanisms that provide the capacity to create and learn different culturally patterned forms of behavior. Following from this is the question of the relation between the genetic infrastructure of the brain (however it is construed) and sociocultural phenomena. Under the first theory of mind, cultural ideas, beliefs, and values are epiphenomenal to, dependent upon, and reducible to the "real" (genetic) determinants of behavior. For if there are innate mechanisms that determine human behavior, cultural patterns are the incidental "dressing" on an otherwise predetermined foundation. Under the second theory of mind, culture is neither epiphenomenal nor reducible to genetic determinants but rather the conceptual framework within and through which people act. For if the mind is a flexible and creative tool capable of creating diverse cultural forms, it is capable of learning both new and different cultural patterns of behavior.

The proof as to whether the human mind operates by reference to a series of "blueprint" specifications for discrete forms of behavior depends upon the establishment of cross-culturally universal forms of behavior. Yet the evidence reviewed in this chapter demonstrates that the gendered preference mechanisms touted by the evolutionary psychologists are neither universal nor even relevant to most systems of kinship and marriage. They simply do not accord with, and are incapable of generating, the forms of gender relation, the division of labor, the categories and forms of kinship and marriage, and the hierarchies of social relations that we see around the world. Moreover, the utilitarian logic of genetic self-maximization that underlies the preference mechanisms of the evolutionary psychologists is unable to account for and is fundamentally contradicted by all forms of kinship and marriage known to humans.

The answer to the first question, then, must be that the human mind operates through a few general mechanisms that give humans the flexibility to create and learn a wide array of behaviors and to shape their behavior by reference to diverse cultural ideas, beliefs, and values (not just a cost-benefit utilitarian logic focused only on reproductive maximization). The answer to the second question follows from this. The evident flexibility of the human brain and its capacity for creating and learning diverse cultural forms suggest that the cultural complexity and variation evident in the forms of kinship and marriage reviewed in this chapter could not be generated from a single universal genetic blueprint.

Evolutionary psychologists skirt the evidence of cultural variation by casting it as a kind of "manifest" or surface structure that is subordinate to an innate or deep structure of genetically determined psychological mechanisms (Tooby and Cosmides 1989: 36; 1992; Symons 1989; Wilson and Daly 1992). While acknowledging cultural complexity and diversity, evolutionary psychologists argue for "the ubiquity of a core mindset, whose operation can be discerned from numerous phenomena which are culturally diverse in their details but monotonously alike in the abstract" (Wilson and Daly 1992: 291). Yet the distinction between deep structure and surface structure—or what Tooby and Cosmides (1989: 36) call "genotype" and "phenotype"—can, in the end, be made to account for absolutely anything. When the "genotype" preference is not expressed, evolutionary psychologists explain the discrepancy by claiming that developmental or situational forces trigger an alternative "phenotypical" form. For instance, in Buss's cross-cultural survey, he claims that innate psychological mechanisms account for women's preference for ambition and industriousness in men in some cultures, but cultural factors account for men's preference for ambition and industriousness in women in others (Buss 1989: 5–9; cf. Rose 2000: 145–47; Fausto-Sterling 2000: 218). Yet evolutionary psychologists never specify when or how cultural or "environmental" factors come into play or what their relationship is to genetically determined psychological mechanisms (Eagly and Wood 1999: 410). It is therefore only by resorting to heterogeneous arguments in an ad hoc manner—innate factors in one case, cultural factors in another—that their account can be supported.

By reducing the variety of human systems of kinship and marriage to a "core mindset" that looks suspiciously Euro-American in its valorization of the individual, of genetics, of utilitarian theories of self-maximization, and of an idealized 1950s version of gender relations, evolutionary psychologists erase what we know about the complexity of kinship and marriage around the world. Moreover, they elevate specifically Euro-American cultural understandings of kinship and marriage to the status of a universal and render other cultural understandings inconsequential. However, the intricacy and diversity of human systems of kinship and marriage should stand as testimony not only to the poverty of the accounts of evolutionary psychologists but also to the creativity of the human mind and the richness of human cultural forms.

Notes

1. Those evolutionary psychologists that focus most closely on issues of kinship, marriage, and gender include David Buss (1988, 1989, 1991, 1992, 1994), Martin Daly and Margo Wilson (1998), Geoffrey Miller (2000), and Robert Wright (1994). Evolutionary psychologists like Steven Pinker (1997), whose focus is on language, nonetheless feel competent to comment on the nature of kinship.

2. The above forms of evidence and argumentation can readily be found in almost all the writings of evolutionary psychologists. See, e.g., Buss 1989, 1992, 1994; Buss et al. 1990; Daly and Wilson 1998, 1999; Pinker 1997; Wilson and Daly 1992; and Wright 1994.

3. Among the many works that have focused on the gendered division of labor, as well as its relation to gender in/equality, see Sacks 1974; Sanday 1974, 1981; Friedl 1975; Schlegel 1977; Eagly and Wood 1999.

4. When Buss encountered such a preference, among Zulu men, in his cross-cultural survey of mate preferences, he discounted it as reflecting the influence of culture (1989: 7).

References

Benton, Ted. 2000. Social Causes and Natural Relations. In *Alas, Poor Darwin: Arguments against Evolutionary Psychology*, ed. Hilary Rose and Steven Rose, pp. 249–72. New York: Harmony Books.

Bodenhorn, Barbara. 2000. "He Used to Be My Relative": Exploring the Bases of Relatedness among Iñupiat of Northern Alaska. In *Cultures of Relatedness: New Approaches to the Study of Kinship*, ed. Janet Carsten, pp. 128–48. Cambridge: Cambridge University Press.

Boon, James A. 1977. *The Anthropological Romance of Bali, 1592–1972*. Cambridge: Cambridge University Press.

Buss, David M. 1988. Love Acts: The Evolutionary Biology of Love. In *The Psychology of Love*, ed. Robert J. Sternberg and Michael L. Barnes, pp. 100–118. New Haven: Yale University Press.

———. 1989. Sex Differences in Human Mate Preferences: Evolutionary Hypotheses Tested in 37 Cultures. *Behavioral and Brain Sciences* 12: 1–49.

———. 1991. Evolutionary Personality Psychology. *Annual Review of Psychology* 42: 459–91.

———. 1992. Mate Preference Mechanisms: Consequences for Partner Choice and Intrasexual Competition. In *The Adapted Mind: Evolutionary Psychology and the Generation of Culture*, ed. Jerome H. Barkow, Leda Cosmides, and John Tooby, pp. 249–66. New York: Oxford University Press.

——— 1994. *The Evolution of Desire: Strategies of Human Mating*. New York: Basic Books.

Buss, David M., and David P. Schmidt. 1993. Sexual Strategies Theory: An Evolutionary Perspective on Human Mating. *Psychological Review* 100(2): 204–32.

Buss, David M., et al. 1990. International Preferences in Selecting Mates: A Study of 37 Cultures. *Journal of Cross-Cultural Psychology* 21(4): 5–47.

Carroll, Vern, ed. 1970. *Adoption in Eastern Oceania*. Honolulu: University of Hawaii Press.

Carsten, Janet. 1997. *The Heat of the Hearth: The Process of Kinship in a Malay Fishing Community*. Oxford: Oxford University Press.

———. 2001. Substantivism, Antisubstantivism, and Anti-antisubstantivism. In *Relative Values: Reconfiguring Kinship Studies*, ed. Sarah Franklin and Susan McKinnon, pp. 29–53. Durham, NC: Duke University Press.

Carsten, Janet, and Stephen Hugh-Jones, eds. 1995. *About the House: Lévi-Strauss and Beyond*. Cambridge: Cambridge University Press.

Collins, Patricia Hill. 1990. *Black Feminist Thought: Knowledge, Consciousness, and the Politics of Empowerment*. New York: Routledge.

Daly, Martin, and Margo Wilson. 1998. *The Truth about Cinderella: A Darwinian View of Parental Love*. New Haven: Yale University Press.

———. 1999. Human Evolutionary Psychology and Animal Behaviour. *Animal Behaviour* 57: 509–19.

Daly, Martin, Margo Wilson, and Suzanne J. Weghorst. 1982. Male Sexual Jealousy. *Ethology and Sociobiology* 3: 11–27.

Dolgin, Janet L. 1997. *Defining the Family: Law, Technology, and Reproduction in an Uneasy Age*. New York: New York University Press.

Donnan, Hastings. 1990. Mixed Marriages in Comparative Perspective: Gender and Power in Northern Ireland and Pakistan. *Journal of Comparative Family Studies* 21(2): 207–25.

Draper, Patricia. 1975. !Kung Women: Contrasts in Sexual Egalitarianism in Foraging and Sedentary Contexts. In *Toward an Anthropology of Women*, ed. Rayna R. Reiter, pp. 77–109. New York: Monthly Review Press.

Eagly, Alice H., and Wende Wood. 1999. The Origins of Sex Differences in Human Behavior: Evolved Dispositions versus Social Roles. *American Psychologist* 54(6): 408–23.

Fausto-Sterling, Anne. 2000. Beyond Difference: Feminism and Evolutionary Psychology. In *Alas, Poor Darwin: Arguments against Evolutionary Psychology*, ed. Hilary Rose and Steven Rose, pp. 209–28. New York: Harmony Books.

Fienup-Riordan, Ann. 1983. *The Nelson Island Eskimo: Social Structure and Ritual Distribution.* Anchorage: Alaska Pacific University Press.

Fox, Robin. 1967. *Kinship and Marriage: An Anthropological Perspective.* Harmondsworth, UK: Penguin Books.

Friedl, Ernestine. 1975. *Women and Men: An Anthropologist's View.* New York: Holt, Rinehart, and Winston.

Hayden, Corinne. 1995. Gender, Genetics, and Generation: Reformulating Biology in Lesbian Kinship. *Cultural Anthropology* 10(1): 41–63.

Howard, Alan, Robert H. Heighton, Jr., Cathie E. Jordan, and Ronald G. Gallimore. 1970. Traditional and Modern Adoption Patterns in Hawaii. In Carroll 1970: 21–51.

Joyce, Rosemary A., and Susan D. Gillespie, eds. 2000. *Beyond Kinship: Social and Material Reproduction in House Societies.* Philadelphia: University of Pennsylvania Press.

Leach, Edmund R. [1954] 1965. *Political Systems of Highland Burma.* Boston: Beacon Press.

Lee, Richard B. 1965. Subsistence Ecology of !Kung Bushmen. PhD dissertation, University of California, Berkeley.

Lévi-Strauss, Claude. [1949] 1969. *The Elementary Structures of Kinship.* Boston: Beacon Press.

Lewin, Ellen. 1993. *Lesbian Mothers: Accounts of Gender in American Culture.* Ithaca, NY: Cornell University Press.

Lombardo, Paul. 1988. Miscegenation, Eugenics, and Racism: Historical Footnotes to *Loving v. Virginia. University of California, Davis, Law Review* 21: 421–52.

McKinnon, Susan. 1991. *From a Shattered Sun: Hierarchy, Gender, and Alliance in the Tanimbar Islands.* Madison: University of Wisconsin Press.

Middleton, Karen. 2000. How Karembola Men Become Mothers. In *Cultures of Relatedness: New Approaches to the Study of Kinship,* ed. Janet Carsten, pp. 104–27. Cambridge: Cambridge University Press.

Miller, Geoffrey. 2000. *The Mating Mind: How Sexual Choice Shaped the Evolution of Human Nature.* New York: Doubleday.

Modell, Judith S. 1994. *Kinship with Strangers: Adoption and Interpretations of Kinship in American Culture.* Berkeley and Los Angeles: University of California Press.

———. 1998. Rights to Children: Foster Care and Social Reproduction in Hawai'i. In *Reproducing Reproduction: Kinship, Power, and Technological Innovation,* ed. Sarah Franklin and Helena Ragoné, pp. 156–72. Philadelphia: University of Pennsylvania Press.

Ottenheimer, Martin. 1996. *Forbidden Relatives: The American Myth of Cousin Marriage.* Urbana: University of Illinois Press.

Parkin, Robert. 1997. *Kinship: An Introduction to Basic Concepts.* Oxford: Blackwell.

Pinker, Steven. 1997. *How the Mind Works.* New York: W. W. Norton.

Radcliffe-Brown, Alfred R. 1952. The Mother's Brother in South Africa. In *Structure and Function in Primitive Society,* ed. Alfred R. Radcliffe-Brown, pp. 15–31. Glencoe, IL: Free Press.

Rose, Hilary. 2000. Colonizing the Social Sciences? In *Alas, Poor Darwin: Arguments against Evolutionary Psychology,* ed. Hilary Rose and Steven Rose, pp. 127–54. New York: Harmony Books.

Sacks, Karen. 1974. Engels Revisited: Women, the Organization of Production, and Private Property. In *Women, Culture, and Society,* ed. Michelle Zimbalist Rosaldo and Louise Lamphere, pp. 207–22. Stanford: Stanford University Press.

Sahlins, Marshall D. 1976. *The Use and Abuse of Biology.* Ann Arbor: University of Michigan Press.

Sanday, Peggy Reeves. 1974. Female Status in the Public Domain. In *Women, Culture, and Society,* ed. Michelle Zimbalist Rosaldo and Louise Lamphere, pp. 189–206. Stanford: Stanford University Press.

——. 1981. *Female Power and Male Dominance: On the Origins of Sexual Inequality.* Cambridge: Cambridge University Press.

Schlegel, Alice, ed. 1977. *Sexual Stratification: A Cross-Cultural View.* New York: Columbia University Press.

Schneider, David M. 1972. *American Kinship: A Cultural Account.* Chicago: University of Chicago Press.

Slocum, Sally. 1975. Woman the Gatherer: Male Bias in Anthropology. In *Toward an Anthropology of Women,* ed. Rayna R. Reiter, pp. 36–50. New York: Monthly Review Press.

Stack, Carol B. 1974. *All Our Kin: Strategies for Survival in a Black Community.* New York: Harper and Row.

Symons, Donald. 1989. The Psychology of Human Mate Preferences (Commentary on Buss 1989). *Behavioral and Brain Sciences* 12: 34–35.

Tanner, Nancy, and Adrienne Zihlman. 1976. Women in Evolution, Part I: Innovation and Selection in Human Origins. *Signs* 4(3): 585–608.

Thompson, Charis. 2001. Strategic Naturalizing: Kinship in an Infertility Clinic. In *Relative Values: Reconfiguring Kinship Studies,* ed. Sarah Franklin and Susan McKinnon, pp. 175–202. Durham, NC: Duke University Press.

Tooby, John, and Leda Cosmides. 1989. The Innate versus the Manifest: How Universal Does Universal Have to Be? (Commentary on Buss 1989). *Behavioral and Brain Sciences* 12: 36–37.

——. 1992. The Psychological Foundations of Culture. In *The Adapted Mind: Evolutionary Psychology and the Generation of Culture,* ed. Jerome H. Barkow, Leda Cosmides, and John Tooby, pp. 19–136. New York: Oxford University Press.

Waltner, Ann. 1996. Kinship between the Lines: The Patriline, the Concubine, and the Adopted Son in Late Imperial China. In *Gender, Kinship, Power: A Comparative and Interdisciplinary History,* ed. Mary Jo Maynes, Ann Waltner, Birgitte Soland, and Ulrike Strasser, pp. 67–78. New York: Routledge.

Weston, Kath. 1991. *Families We Choose: Lesbians, Gays, Kinship.* New York: Columbia University Press.

——. 1995. Forever Is a Long Time: Romancing the Real in Gay Kinship Ideologies. In *Naturalizing Power: Essays in Feminist Cultural Analysis,* ed. Sylvia Yanagisako and Carol Delaney, pp. 87–110. New York: Routledge.

Wilson, Margo, and Martin Daly. 1992. The Man Who Mistook His Wife for a Chattel. In *The Adapted Mind: Evolutionary Psychology and the Generation of Culture,* ed. Jerome H. Barkow, Leda Cosmides, and John Tooby, pp. 289–326. New York: Oxford University Press.

Wright, Robert. 1994. *The Moral Animal: The New Science of Evolutionary Psychology.* New York: Vintage Books.

Zihlman, Adrienne L. 1978. Women in Evolution, Part II: Subsistence and Social Organization among Early Hominids. *Signs* 4(1): 4–20.

CHAPTER 6

Surveying a Cultural "Waistland": Some Biological Poetics and Politics of the Female Body

Mary Orgel, Jacqueline Urla, and Alan Swedlund

A SPECTS OF THE FEMALE BODY have long served as important intellectual and political sites for understanding and managing sexuality and
gender relations. In this chapter, we analyze the female waist as one such
site. In recent years a spate of research has emerged in the fields of sociobiology and evolutionary psychology focusing on the female waist and its role
in mate choice and sexual selection. Our goal is to provide a brief critical review of the literature on what has come to be known as the waist-to-hip ratio (WHR) research, examine its claims and methodologies, and reveal
some of the more problematic assumptions, erasures, and conflations on
which it relies. Our approach draws inspiration from the exemplary works
of several feminist historians and anthropologists of science and gender.[1]
From Donna Haraway we borrow the notion that the production of science
must be understood in relation to a larger cultural field. Scientists, she argues, write "intertextually," sharing the same narrative resources that other
fields like literature and popular media use in representing women (1989:
366). Following in this vein, Emily Martin's now classic study of medical
accounts of fertilization (1991) has more specifically pointed out how scientists import stereotypical understandings of women and men into their
accounts of female and male biology and, in the process, how these understandings become naturalized and fortified as scientific fact. We bring these
insights to bear in our examination of the WHR research by tacking back
and forth between the scientific findings and the broader cultural field of sex
and gender relations in the context of late consumer capitalism in which it
is being produced. Our agenda is to problematize the generalizations that
are all too frequently made regarding the ideal female body and to be alert

to how a dominant notion of "attractiveness" and sexuality is being written back into our most basic biology.

Why the Waist-to-Hip Ratio?

Sociobiology and evolutionary psychology are powerful and popular voices in North America when it comes to explaining gender and sexuality, receiving large research grants and extensive media coverage. The arguments are seductive because they oversimplify a complex reality and dangerous because they take an a priori set of assumptions about gender roles and sexual desires and generalize these as human universals to be found across all cultures and historical periods. In so doing, not only is human diversity devalued but we are also led to believe that we know more about gender and sexuality than we actually do. Therefore, in our view, it is incumbent upon us not to dismiss the work but to examine carefully its logic, to understand how the results are produced, and to think about what it forecloses in terms of both serious investigation and political challenge.

Both sociobiology and evolutionary psychology take as their point of departure that many contemporary characteristics of gender roles, sexual behavior, and physical morphology are, to use a common metaphor, "hardwired." That is, they are the result of adaptations of the species that occurred at the time of the Pleistocene and continue into the present, impervious to the fluctuations and influence of historical context, culture, politics, ideology, or economics. Central to this work is the fundamental premise laid out in E. O. Wilson's 1975 key work, *Sociobiology: The New Synthesis*, that all organisms, including humans, are born with the drive to maximize their genetic material through successful reproduction. Men and women, however, are seen to pursue goals in different ways. Males focus on frequent mating with fertile females, while females—forced to spend considerable time with gestating and nursing—place less emphasis on frequency of mating and more on securing a mate who can provide resources.[2] Those gender roles—and the male and female body types and traits that contribute to these goals—will, so the argument goes, become selected for and generalized in the population while others will naturally diminish or die out. In short, what researchers in these fields do is take a feature *believed* to be widespread—for instance, male dominance or infidelity—and hypothesize about the advantages this feature might have posed for genetic maximization. Hypotheses are thus post hoc and depend on a presumption of the universality (or at least prevalence) of the trait in question. The validity of the argument, therefore, depends upon a demonstration of the universality of particular gender traits.

The presumed importance of the waist-to-hip ratio stems from a basic observation about the anatomical differences between males and females with regard to body fat distribution. The male body exhibits what is called a tubular or android physique where body fat is deposited in the abdominal region, while the female is typically described as conforming to an hourglass or gynoid pattern of proportionately larger hips (and breasts) due to fat distribution around the hips, buttocks, and thighs. In short, women are seen to exhibit a lower WHR than men.[3] The requisites for shape and space in the human birth canal, the need to lactate and nurse infant young, the need to store additional energy in body fat, and other hypotheses have all been proffered as adaptive explanations for patterns in the shape of the human female body (see, e.g., McFarland 1997; Pond 1997). Male WHRs are regarded as less important indicators of male reproductive potential since male reproductive fitness is assumed to be measured less exclusively by body build and to include behavioral traits like the acquisition and control of resources.

Although a reasonable physiological explanation for this adaptation has been offered, many WHR researchers have been inclined to argue that a woman's torso has less to do with its functional role in birthing or child rearing and more to do with its role in signaling reproductive fitness and attracting male suitors. The arguments we will address here are those that claim that the ratio of waist to hip size serves as a genetically encoded or hardwired signal to human males that the female under surveillance is healthy, fertile, and reproductively available. In other words, such arguments posit that the functional characteristics alone are insufficient explanations and that male preference for body shape in mate selection is the prime evolutionary force involved. Bobbi Low (2000: 80) succinctly summarizes the WHR argument in her observation that wide hips signal fecundability, a narrow waist signals health and nonpregnant status, and comparatively large breasts signal good milk production. An important shift in argument accompanies this explanation. The observable contemporary "fact," now presumed to be universal, is not simply the anatomical difference, itself, but rather a psychological preference—an erotic desire in the form of a male preference for a wide-hipped, narrow-waisted woman.

Early Measures of the Female Waist

Before analyzing the particulars of the research on male preferences, however, it is important to pause for a moment to consider what appears to be a straightforward anatomical fact—that men and women have different waist-to-hip ratios. We suggest that the "discovery" of this difference is overdetermined, since the female waist in the twentieth century was already heavily invested with symbolic significance and meaning for scientists concerned with drawing clear boundaries between male and female. Indeed, the waist has been a subject of fascination to anatomists and evolutionists for over 200 years.

Londa Schiebinger's (1986, 1993) study of early comparative anatomy reveals the emergence of a heated controversy in eighteenth-century Germany, France, and Britain over the correct portrayal of the female skeleton that revolves centrally around this difference. Whereas previously the skeleton was believed to be "unsexed" (i.e., fundamentally the same for males and females), by the late eighteenth century, drawings that represented female skeletons with exaggeratedly broader hips and narrower rib cages— and, not incidentally, smaller brain cases—came to be preferred as the ideal over other less differentiated skeletons (Schiebinger 1986). The most famous of these was the D'Arconville skeleton (1759), which was drawn by one of the few woman anatomists of the time and which captured the imagination of medical doctors for more than half a century. This skeleton was remarkable in its proportions, writes Schiebinger: "The skull is drawn extremely small, the ribs extremely narrow, making the pelvis appear excessively large. D'Arconville apparently either intended to emphasize the cultural perception that narrow ribs are a mark of femininity, or she chose as the model for her drawing a woman who had worn a corset throughout her life" (2000: 36). As Schiebinger notes, in the course of the late eighteenth and nineteenth centuries, these skeletal differences, and the broader pelvis in particular, became central points of reference in the debates over the position of women in bourgeois European society.

In the Victorian era the waist assumed heightened salience in the definition of both female beauty and racial health. In this era, the fair-skinned, fine-boned, delicately featured, and typically corseted young woman became the much-touted ideal of Victorian beauty (see fig. 1). As the eugenics movement began taking shape in the United States and northern Europe, it would make the ideal of the "wasp-waisted" woman synonymous with the "W.A.S.P."-waisted woman. Victorian social theorists like Herbert Spencer and Havelock Ellis defined the W.A.S.P./wasp-waisted woman as the highest ideal of feminine beauty using a kind of evolutionary aesthetic explanation. They claimed that although a narrow waist offset by full breast and wide hips was a universal standard for all humans, it was best realized in the Victorian Anglo-Saxon Protestant female.[4]

Concerns on the part of eugenicists with "race suicide" and the decline of white Anglo-Saxon Protestants prompted a flurry of both popular and scientific representations that conjoined race, class, and the narrow waist. Working-class women and especially nonwhite women were less often por-

Figure 1. Vintage representation of healthy wasp-waisted/hourglass-figured woman.

trayed as delicate and wasp-waisted and more often as thicker waisted, sturdier in build, and coarsely featured; they were also more often portrayed as criminals and prostitutes (Gilman 1985; A. Shapiro 1996).

During the early to mid–twentieth century there was considerable interest on the part of social reformers in the fitness of women as mothers. This concern rose to an anxious pitch in the United States between the two wars as nationalism and eugenics provoked a deepening concern about the physical fitness of the American people. Young men and women—many of them college students and army recruits—were obsessively measured to define the "normal" male and female and to ascertain their fitness. Once again the female waist appears to have been a critical focus of concern. A case with which we are most familiar was a project undertaken by Robert Latou Dickenson in the 1940s. Dickenson, a well-known obstetrician/gynecologist, obtained measurements of thousands of young people to produce statues of Norm and Norma, the "normal" American male and female (see figs. 2 and 3). An unsettling discovery reported both in scientific magazines and in the popular press was that Norma was more full-figured, with a larger waist and wider hips, than her "grandmother"—a statue of the "average" female body that had been produced in the 1890s and based on young college women. To

Figure 2. Statue of "Norma" by Abram Belskie, commissioned by R. L. Dickinson and based on his measurements of thousands of individuals. (From H. Shapiro 1945: 248)

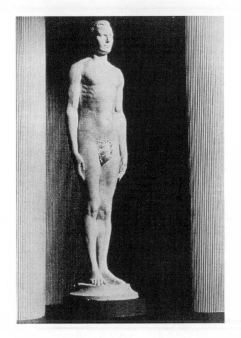

Figure 3. Statue of "Norm" by Abram Belskie, commissioned by R. L. Dickinson and based on his measurements of thousands of individuals. (From H. Shapiro 1945: 252)

Figure 4. 1940s fashion model Rosemary Sankey. (From H. Shapiro 1945: 249)

some commentators, this new Norma had a healthy and voluptuous figure; to others, she was thick-waisted and compared less favorably with the slender Miss Rosemary Sankey (see fig. 4), a fashion model of the 1940s.[5]

A complete history of the scientific interest in the female waist and how it came into tension or coincided with other vested interests like the fashion industry remains to be done. But what these episodes in that history are meant to suggest is that anatomy—in this case the waist—is far from a neutral fact. Certain parts of the body have become encoded with racial, class, and gender meanings while others seemingly have not. That the waist would become a focus of exploration and a key signifier of gender and sex differences among late-twentieth-century Western scientists is inevitably shaped by this past and also by contemporary concerns with sexuality, fat, and gender.

"Vogue" Science: Evolutionary Psychology

We find ourselves today in another moment of heightened popular and scientific scrutiny of this notorious and obviously meaningful region of the female body. In popular culture, the female waist has never been more on display than it is today as bare hyperslender midriffs appear to rule the world of supermodels and pop stars (Bellafante 2003).[6] At the same time, in the realm of evolutionary science, a growing number of researchers are testing the hypothesis that the hourglass figure is universally appealing to males because it is an evolutionary adaptation in the ongoing struggle to find a fit mate.[7] Fashion writer Jody Shields in her 1991 *Vogue* magazine article that heralded the "return of the waist" in fashion has proven to be prescient of a scientific return to it as well. It is not coincidental that the female waist simultaneously became an important icon in both fashion and scientific contexts. The two phenomena are used to reinforce one another in a kind of circular logic: evolutionary psychologists refer to fashion styles to validate their scientific claims about the female waist at the same time that they explain fashion styles in the language of evolutionary adaptation.[8]

The Specifics of the WHR Research

The decade of the 1990s saw the emergence and ultimately widespread acceptance of the pivotal role of the female waist in the evolutionary psychology and sociobiology research on the relationship between physical attractiveness and reproductive mating strategies. Indeed, evolutionary psychology has become predominately identified with its study of sexual selection and sex differences and its claims to show how sexual preferences with regard to mate choice have profoundly influenced human evolution (Jones 1999; Miller 2000).

The WHR stands as one of the more reductive instruments of analysis that evolutionary psychologists use to investigate the relationship between physical attractiveness and reproductive mating strategies—a relationship long assumed in the evolutionary sciences yet difficult to delineate and quantify. Since evolutionary approaches treat reproductive strategies as the fundamental and overriding motive for all of human behavior, the identification of a mathematical index like the WHR is touted as a significant advance in the scientific understanding not only of human mating behaviors but also, by extension, of human social behavior more generally. Our review of the WHR research, however, makes us skeptical of what exactly the WHR does (and does not) measure.

Evolutionary psychologist Devendra Singh (1993, 1994a, 1994b) is one of the most energetic WHR researchers, and his findings, while not uncontested, have been well received within both professional and popular-science circles. The argument about the WHR unfolds in several linked steps. First, the WHR is measured as the waist size divided by the hip circumference. Second, it is assumed that the WHR can be used to measure male attraction to and preference for certain female body types. These pref-

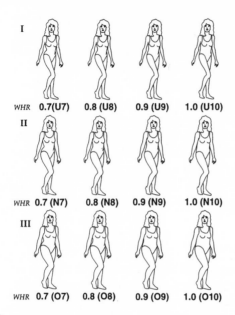

WHR 0.7(U7)   0.8 (U8)   0.9 (U9)   1.0 (U10)

WHR 0.7 (N7)   0.8 (N8)   0.9 (N9)   1.0 (N10)

WHR 0.7 (O7)   0.8 (O8)   0.9 (O9)   1.0 (O10)

Figure 5. Example of the "stimulus figures" used in the research of Devendra Singh representing body size and waist-to-hip ratio (WHR). The letters in parentheses show whether the figure is underweight (U), normal (N), or overweight (O); the numbers show the size of the WHR. (From Singh 1993: 298; copyright © 1993 by the American Psychological Association. Reprinted by permission)

erences are determined from a limited choice of "stimulus figures," which are line drawings of female figures in swimsuits (see fig. 5) that are shown to male research subjects. From his findings, Singh concludes that men prefer, or find most attractive, women with WHRs of 0.7—that is, with a waist measurement that is 70 percent of the hip measurement—whereas ratios of 0.8 and 0.9 indicate a less desirable shape. He writes that the "narrow waist set against full hips" has been "one of the most stable and enduring bodily features [more than breasts, weight, or physique] . . . of female attractiveness" (1993: 296). Third, Singh goes on to argue that this 0.7 WHR is not only an indicator of attractiveness but also a reliable measure of reproductive status (not pregnant), reproductive health (fertile), and good overall health.[9] Finally, he suggests that if a 0.7 WHR measures physical attractiveness, health, and reproductive fitness, the physical attractiveness of this body type has adaptive significance. That is, this female body type has evolved through sexual selection because it morphologically "advertises" (Barber 1995: 396) to men a high-potential female mate choice.

Even though other WHR researchers—such as Kirchengast and Hartmann (1995)—are less explicitly concerned with explaining the evolutionary psychology of physical sexual attractiveness and more focused on the link between body build and fertility, they nevertheless assume more than they explain about female beauty ideals. In their study of Austrian women, Kirchengast and Hartmann (1995) report that smaller women with low

WHRs (whom they defined as more "feminine") were more successful re-producers than taller, thick-waisted women (whom they defined as "mas-culine"). They conclude that in "the majority of societies a feminine body type suggesting higher fertility is a typical ideal of beauty" (1995: 137).

Devendra Singh's and others' attempts to provide a biological explana-tion for the narrow female waist contain several assumptions about what drives human mating behavior. The most significant of these assumptions are that (1) women place more value on a mate's ability to control resources (as signaled through status and behavior) than on body type or appearance and (2) men value appearance most highly and prefer mates who are young and physically attractive.

Evolutionary psychologists like Singh, drawing directly from the work of sociobiologists, claim that since women spend considerable time pre-occupied with gestating and lactating, they seek fewer and more resourceful mates who can provide other child-raising necessities. They claim that since men, by contrast, are biologically exempted from expending much effort on childbirth or child rearing, they seek to maximize their gene transfer by fo-cusing on frequent mating with fertile females. Differential parental invest-ments result in the different and potentially antagonistic mating strategies of males and females. Men, it is argued, prefer relatively higher numbers of mates and more frequent matings (quantity reproduction) and women pre-fer fewer mates and less frequent mating (quality reproduction). Sociobiol-ogists and evolutionary psychologists then go on to argue that men are more energetic and aggressive in mating and, as a result, more responsive to visual cues of fertility, while women are more passive and supposedly respond to cues about male control over resources. It is this assumption or claim that evolutionary psychologists like Singh use in explaining why it is men who are attuned to shorthand cues of female fertility like the WHR when survey-ing the landscape of potential mates.[10]

These hypotheses have been the key ones that the "new" (1990s) science of evolutionary psychology has sought to address (Buss et al. 1990; Buss 1994; Miller 2000). Evolutionary psychologists claim to have provided sci-entific evidence that these mate preferences are nonarbitrary, highly pat-terned, adaptively evolved, and universal. These presumed preferences are treated as evidence that "among cultures and between sexes . . . [there is] a degree of psychological unity or species typicality that transcends geograph-ical, racial, political, ethnic and sexual diversity" (Buss 1994: 249). Evolu-tionary psychologists postulate that since sexually selected body parts—like the WHR—are universal, they evolved during the Pleistocene era in Africa before significant human migration. About ten thousand years ago, at the end of the Pleistocene, "our ancestors were already modern humans, identical to us in bodily appearance, brain structure, and psychology" (Miller 2000: 180).[11] Thus, they conclude it is most likely to have been at this point of our shared humanity that these preferences became firmly established and "hardwired."

For evolutionary psychologists the Pleistocene remains the most relevant context in which to understand human mating practices. They argue that although the current post-Pleistocene era of human history has been "historically crucial" to social and cultural developments that have indeed produced dramatic changes in patterns of human mating, it has nevertheless been too short of a time frame for significant adaptations to have occurred and therefore is an "evolutionarily unimportant" era. As a result, human mating behavior "still reflects our Pleistocene legacy" (Miller 2000: 180).

This focus on the Pleistocene is also the focal point of much of the critique of evolutionary psychology research.[12] Stephen Jay Gould has shown how the primary recourse to the Pleistocene severely limits the scientific testability of evolutionary psychology's claim that human mating practices are evidence of hardwired evolutionary adaptations because there is an insufficient record of this era through which to test the validity of the claim. Since key data regarding "relations of kinship, social structures and sizes of groups, different activities of males and females, the roles of religion, symbolizing, storytelling and a hundred other central aspects of human life . . . cannot be traced in fossils," evolutionary psychologists' claim that the Pleistocene past can explain the present is an untestable and therefore only a speculative one (Gould 2000: 120). It strikes us as paradoxical that, in their attempts to scientifically establish the existence of phenomena like a universal preference for a certain WHR, evolutionary psychologists, on the one hand, focus on an era of human history that is largely scientifically unknowable and, on the other hand, dismiss the last ten thousand years of recorded human history, for which we have at least some reliable knowledge. This seemingly fatal flaw of offering scientific explanations based on speculative scenarios of the primordial past has not, however, hindered the proliferation of a sizable body of research on the evolutionary psychology of human mating practices that has received a wide reading by both popular and academic audiences (Rose and Rose 2000).[13] It is precisely in the face of this absence of any prehistoric evidence that such "measures" as the WHR assume such a crucial role in the attempts of evolutionary psychologists to demonstrate the universality of particular gendered traits. In the sections that follow we discuss the WHR research in light of three major problems: its sampling methodologies and claims to universality; its focus on preferences rather than behavior; and its assumptions about gender and sexuality.

The Assertion of Universality in WHR Research

Because much of the WHR research focuses primarily on contemporary Western society, assumes a white woman as the norm, and relies heavily on the tested preferences of one segment of the American population, we want to argue that it asserts more often than it demonstrates the cross-cultural applicability of its findings. We will first discuss methodological issues and then interpretive issues and problematic assumptions.

One of the more frequent critiques of WHR research is that its sampling techniques are too dependent upon questionnaires and its sample subjects are primarily undergraduate students enrolled in introductory psychology courses in American universities (e.g., Smuts 1991; D. Wilson 1999). Sample size is determined by the number of students within the course population who choose to participate in the study. Therefore much of the WHR research is based upon results obtained from a sample group that is self-selected, overwhelmingly young (eighteen to twenty-one years of age), and predominately white and middle class. The representativeness of this selective population is inadequately addressed with regard not only to American society but also to all other societies and cultures. Some researchers presume to account for cultural diversity (and universality) by comparing the responses of white, Hispanic, African-American, Asian, and other ethnically defined students (e.g., Singh 1994b; Singh and Luis 1995).

The cross-cultural study of international mate preference conducted by David Buss and his colleagues is perhaps the most ambitious attempt to investigate—in thirty-seven cultures in "33 countries located on six continents and five islands"—the characteristics that humans value in mate preference and their cultural variance and invariance (Buss et al. 1990: 7). The authors state at the outset, however, that in spite of their goal to do so, they "fell short of" obtaining diverse and representative samples; as a result, their study mirrors the same lack of representativeness as the North American studies—that is, "rural, less educated and lower levels of socioeconomic status are under-represented" (Buss et al. 1990: 10). The authors also caution that the survey instruments used in the study "carry cultural limitations" since they were translations of American-designed instruments that listed thirty-one mate characteristics that may not include those that are salient to each culture that was surveyed (Buss et al. 1990: 11). With these qualifications in mind the authors conclude that "culture appears to exert substantial effect on mate preferences," and although cultures vary in the ordering of mate preference characteristics, there was an "internationally consistent ordering of mate preferences" in the area of "affective" traits; nearly all samples ranked "mutual-attraction love" as the top characteristic and placed "tremendous value" on "dependability, emotional stability, kindness-understanding, and intelligence" (Buss et al. 1990: 42–43). The authors suggest that since these traits correspond closely with "the most replicable-descriptive model of personality," there may be sexual selection occurring with regard to these personality traits. With this move, "cultural" preferences are reduced to these traits and rendered as invariant. The remaining twenty-five mate preference characteristics (as well as any that might not have been included in the American survey list but may nonetheless matter to other cultures) are deemed insignificant because they do not align with a standardized Western measurement of personality.

Curiously, this study is consistently cited by WHR researchers even though the findings do not seem to underwrite the WHR thesis that posits the universal male preference for wasp-waisted females. The documented preponderant preference for "affective" characteristics appears to argue against a preference for a physical characteristic like a low WHR. However, Buss and his colleagues make another problematic interpretive move with regard to the role of culture, physical attractiveness, and male mate preference that, in our view, facilitates a specious relationship between these research projects. Although they conclude that cultural identity had a strong effect on mate preferences and accounted for the cross-cultural variation in these preferences, they also conclude that sex accounted for a small set of mate characteristics that were "statistically significant within nearly every sample, and appear to be among the most robust sex differences yet documented across cultures" (Buss et al. 1990: 44). Men in the survey preferred female mate characteristics that involved physical attractiveness, while women preferred male mate characteristics that involved earning potential. Because sex-based preference for these characteristics was hypothesized a priori to "signify [respectively] female reproductive value and male capacity for resource provisioning," the authors conclude that these preferences may imply an adaptive function for "species-typical mate preferences" (Buss et al. 1990: 45). In our view they have sought to confirm their working hypothesis rather than proved a universal, species-wide adaptive preference. The link between female physical attractiveness and actual reproductive functioning remains undemonstrated. Interestingly, this is the only a priori hypothesis of the study. Thus, in a strategy that pervades WHR research, with one hand the authors give culture a documented role—albeit a rather constrained one—in accounting for mate preferences and, with the other, immediately undermine the role of culture by fortifying their assertion of specific mate preferences with hypothetical adaptive functions.

Another methodological issue is the mode of representation of the WHR. Devendra Singh's "stimulus figures" (see fig. 5) have become the conventional representation of the female WHR that subjects respond to in their questionnaires. Some critics (e.g., Tassinary and Hansen 1998) have questioned whether respondents can adequately assess body shape from one-dimensional black-and-white stick-figure drawings. We are more troubled by the cultural specificity of the hairdo and the bathing suit. This image bears a striking resemblance to the ubiquitous pinup girl/fashion model used in Western advertising media, where she serves as a "cover" (girl) for a purported link between desire and consumption (e.g., in American beer commercials it is implied that men who drink beer—interestingly represented by a wide range of body types—do so in close proximity to mostly wasp-waisted women who appear sexually available). It is extremely difficult for WHR researchers to control the effects of previous exposure to this image and its associations on the responses of their subject population. Additionally, given the cultural specificity of both the stimulus figure and her garb, it is difficult to know if subjects were reporting their response to a specific female type (i.e., Western women) in culturally specific attire (a bathing suit) or to a purportedly universal WHR, which WHR researchers presume the figure portrays. It is virtually impossible to strip images of the female body of all cultural markers, yet WHR researchers do not appear to be sensitive to the fact that the images they use already bear strong cultural markings for which they are unable to control.

Singh (1993) has attempted to address the issue of universality and cross-cultural invariance by offering some recent (twentieth century) historical evidence for the constancy of the low WHR as well as cross-cultural and ethnic preferences. He has pointed out that Marilyn Monroe, considered fleshy if not even plump by today's beauty standards, nevertheless had a healthy WHR;[14] that Playboy models, in spite of the progressive enlargement of their bust measurements, still maintain consistent and healthy WHRs; that beauty contestants have maintained stable and healthy WHRs; and that today's supermodels, in spite of being superthin, if not anorexic, also maintain "healthy" WHRs (Singh 1993).[15] He has explained cross-cultural and ethnic preferences for what appear to be fleshier if not fatter female body types as variations on the 0.7 WHR preference, where—in spite of higher attractiveness values being placed on heavier female bodies—the WHR remains within the "normal" 0.7 range (Singh 1994a, 1994b). Sociobiologist Bobbi Low has recently stated it this way: "the waist-to-hip ratio reflects many complex relationships, but they all boil down to: Is she fertile? Is she fecundable?" (2000: 80). Concurring with Low, Singh concedes that "socioecological" dynamics can produce diversity within body type preferences but that the WHR—as a doubly endowed signal of beauty and fertility—is most likely a "core cue" and therefore universal (Singh and Young 1995).

In these studies, the diversity of body types is accounted for by positing an underlying sameness—the WHR—that disregards the rest of the body. Historical and cross-cultural variations in female beauty conventions are treated as "non-core" if not tied to the waistline and therefore as less significant. The beauty of the narrow-waisted woman everywhere *is* her fertility. Yet leaving aside for a moment the significance of the rest of the female body (and the female person) to the conduct of human sexual relationships, the low-WHR hypothesis cannot account for all conventionally healthy women even within contemporary American society. For example, we would point out that physically fit young women in the American military have an average waist size of 31 inches and hip circumference of 38.1, resulting in a ratio of 0.813 (Gordon et al. 1989).

In the end, the considerable variation that is manifested normally in women within any population, as well as the variability and complexity of notions of "attractiveness" across cultures and throughout time, is left unattended and virtually erased as a particular socially constructed ideal feminine form is essentialized and rationalized. Also troubling are the reductive behavioral explanations for this body type and the lack of any data—or possibility of gaining any data—on the actual variations in reproductivity of women across the spectrum of their phenotypes.[16] Human interventions and controls on fertility are age-old and culturally mediated and flummox our best efforts to relate phenotype to fertility except at the highest and lowest extremes.

The claim for the universality of the low WHR has received the most sustained criticism within the evolutionary science literature. A number of studies and critiques have argued that the so-called culturally invariant male preference for a curvaceous body is actually a recent Western body ideal, not an evolutionarily longstanding adaptive one. Yu and Shepard have found that the "highly isolated" Matsigenka peoples of southeastern Peru idealize women with "tubular" body builds; the researchers attribute this preference to lack of contact with Western standards of beauty. They suggest that supposedly invariant standards prove to be malleable and that what WHR research perhaps more accurately measures is the "pervasiveness of western media" (Yu and Shepard 1998: 322). Wetsman and Marlowe studied Hadza foragers from Tanzania because—in contrast to the Matsigenka, who are swidden agriculturalists—the Hadza are foragers who, they presume, are "the closest link to the societies in which WHR preferences evolved" (1999: 226). That is, they are presumed to live in Pleistocene-esque conditions, and therefore Hadza men should prefer the low WHR that is considered to have evolved in these conditions. They found instead that Hadza men consider the weight of potential female partners more than the WHR, a finding that challenges, perhaps more robustly than the Matsigenka evidence, the cultural invariance of the WHR. In her cross-cultural comparison of Samoan, "U.S.," and "Arab" body judgments, Brewis finds no "monolithic" pattern of preferences and suggests instead a "more complex socioecology" at work in body judgments (1999: 551).[17]

We conclude this section by citing Anne Becker's (1995) ethnographic study of the ways that Fijians relate body shape to personal identity and social status, a study that has several points of resonance with WHR research. Combining in-depth participant-observation fieldwork with the use of survey instruments that were similar to those used in the WHR research—although more culturally appropriate (e.g., unclothed figure drawings with local Fijian hairstyles)—Becker investigated the Fijian dominant preference for large, corpulent body shapes. She found that the Fijian body shape operates as an index of an individual's social connectedness and the community's level of social cohesion and commitment to care for its members. A fat body signals a well-cared-for and socialized person and a cohesive community; and both measures ensure the vitality and continuity of the local culture. A "thin" person in turn is seen as a sign, not of a sick or failing individual, but rather of an inattentive and fragmented community. Becker's study of Fijian ideal body types helps to reveal the specificity of Western notions of the body. For example, she argues that the Fijian "conflation of body identity with that of the collective reveals our Western notions about the discreteness of the body [that locates and contains a personal self within it] . . . as our own particular cultural metaphor" (1995: 133). The Fijian self is not conceptualized in this way and, as a result, "bodily surfaces and dimensions are not objectified as entities to manipulate"; rather, the body "indexes and records the history and complexity of social relations within the collective" (1995: 133). Becker's study encourages us in our evaluation of the WHR research to look not only at the cross-cultural differences in body type preferences but to develop the methodologies to explore the differences in the conceptualizations and deeper cultural meanings that bodies have in different societies. An appreciation of this variance, we suggest, can help us to begin to consider how our investigations into the waist, the body, and body preferences may be quite unself-consciously rooted in and substantiating our own culturally and historically specific views of the human form.

Preferences versus Behavior in WHR Research

An important distinction that is easily elided in the WHR research is the difference between preference—which is what the research measures—and the occurrence of certain female body types. Evolutionary psychologists routinely assume that the preferences in response to visual cues of female body types are carried through into mating behavior. If preferences are reliable indices of actual behavior—and this is at best a dubious assumption—then the male preference for low-WHR female bodies should manifest not only in preferences but also in female bodies. The human landscape should display, as a result of male mate choice, some visible or measurable density of so-called normal low-WHR women. The WHR never speaks to this point. And what of the non-0.7-WHR women in this "waistland"—how are they to be accounted for? The claim of universality for the low female WHR holds only as a rather circumscribed one that looks at preferences for certain body types rather than their occurrence and discounts other kinds of somatic diversity.

Evolutionary psychologist David Buss (1991), in response to a critique of his elision of the distinction between preference and behavior (Smuts 1991), has provided a helpful clarification of evolutionary psychology's focus on "the psychology of mate preferences" and "psychological mechanisms" rather than "manifest behavior." This underscores the point that what WHR research actually measures is preference for body types and not actual behavioral choice or actual phenotypic occurrence of low-WHR women. Nevertheless, the distinction between preference and behavior is not often explicitly made in WHR studies, and therefore, these two concepts are often conflated. Anne Fausto-Sterling, a critical biologist, has argued that the tendency to conflate preference and behavior in evolutionary psychology research is a more serious issue of failing to meet the basic standards of evolutionary science. That is, WHR research blurs the distinction between the two because it fails to correlate the data obtained from questionnaires with observed or independently documented behaviors (Fausto-Sterling 2000: 217).

It is possible to push the critique of preference still further. While studies that challenge the universal validity of the WHR thesis have pointed out the historical and cultural specificity of the significance of the female WHR, the concern has been not so much with proving mate preference *diversity* but with proving low-WHR *specificity*. That is, the claim that men as a group have a reliably tested preference for a specific body type with regard to a female mate is not subjected to critical examination; the assumption that men everywhere assess women via their waists as a primary strategy of mate choice remains unquestioned. In this way other unquestioned assumptions are also left intact. For example, men remain the privileged arbiters of ideal female bodies, and the physical appearance of the female body remains the primary site for defining what women should be. If the universality, and therefore evolutionary adaptability, of the WHR does not hold, then these assumptions may not either.[18]

Problematic Gender and Sexuality Assumptions of WHR Research

A noteworthy body of critique from feminist biologists, anthropologists, and sociobiologists has pointed to the gender assumptions that inform some of the evolutionary science of the human female. Working within the same scientific frames used in the WHR research, they have nonetheless challenged them in ways that productively destabilize WHR findings and assumptions. This research has provided alternative explanations to the male-dominated narratives of human evolution and new perspectives on such central issues as male and female sexual aggression, the history of patriarchy, the sexual division of labor, and the strategies of motherhood and child care (e.g., Fedigan 1986; Hrdy 1997, 1999; Zihlman 1995). For instance, Sarah Hrdy is well known for her work demonstrating greater female agency in mate selection among primate species than was once suspected. In her research, female primates were anything but the "coy" females represented in classic Darwinian writings (1999: 35–37). Hrdy and others have also pointed out that both female primates and women engage in female-kin-based, child-care-related resource acquisition strategies that are often quite independent of males. In diverse yet convincing ways such researchers have tried to disentangle the power of the intuitive appeal of "facts" like the attractive wasp-waisted woman from the scientific knowledge that claims— through formulas like the WHR—to explain it. So while some evolutionary psychologists may see the shape of the female body as reflecting the importance of male mate choice preference in the course of human evolution, feminist evolutionary scientists argue that this idea reveals instead the dominance of male-centered logic in the science of mate choice and body types.

The gender assumptions that these feminist critiques unsettle within more general models of human evolution compel us to examine further the ways in which the WHR research implicitly and explicitly naturalizes contemporary gender and sexual ideology. Throughout WHR research, for example, we note a pervasive set of assumptions about heterosexual desire and, in particular, about masculine erotics that center on why men seek out and try to "mate" particular women, why they respond to low WHR, and what women must do to "get their man." This is also a crib sheet for explaining and giving a semblance of order to feminine aesthetics at a time in consumer culture when a fashion style seems to last a nanosecond. Underneath all this volatility and artifice, the WHR research tells us, are basic constants: a thin waist, large hips, and big breasts. Reassuring in its simplicity, it goes without saying that this theory requires erasing an enormous number of desires—aesthetic and erotic—that run counter to these prescribed features.[19] In the process it also presupposes and naturalizes the power inequalities that undergird the dynamics of desire and how it is expressed.

The Politics of the Waist

In ways reminiscent of nineteenth-century scientific theories of reproduction, some of the recent sociobiology and evolutionary psychology of the female body provide what Comaroff (1993: 307) has called an "alibi" for prevailing power relations—in this case prevailing gender relations where male dominance and female passivity are biologized. Sociobiology and evolutionary psychology proclaim to discover laws of nature, adaptations of the species that have occurred and explain human behavior or morphology independent of the contingencies of history, politics, or ideology. Feminist critiques of science by Schiebinger (2000), Haraway (1989), Smith-Rosenberg (1985), and Coward (1983), to name only a few, on the whole have resisted this de-historicizing move, prompting us instead to ask questions about how scientific studies are embedded in, and indeed respond to, the historically specific political debates of their time. Scientific knowledge is always produced in conversation with the social conditions in which it is situated. Indeed, it is precisely because they are so embedded in the cultural matrix of their times that scientific arguments about the body have such great intuitive appeal and social resonance.

What does it mean to make a claim for the evolutionary adaptability of the narrow waist at this point in U.S. history? How do these scientific arguments about male preference for low WHR intersect with and respond to the current debates over gender and sexuality? These questions deserve more careful consideration of contemporary cultural politics than we can provide here. We have noted already that the scientific attention to and affirmation of the value of the narrow waist coincide with an emphasis in popular fashion on very trim and very exposed tummies. Singh, we note, has used Barbie dolls—the ultimate narrow-waisted fashion icon—as visual stimuli in his experiments. But, by way of conclusion and provocation for further discussion, we want to signal other kinds of intersections between this research and wider social discourse.

The emergence of evolutionary psychology and especially the spate of articles that we have discussed in this chapter are unfolding in the context of an identifiable "backlash" against the feminist gains within American society. In her book, *Backlash* (1991), Susan Faludi argued that, in both the popular media and the sciences, the women's movement has been misrepresented as being the major cause behind what is seen as a breakdown of the traditional American nuclear-family structure, the establishment of unachievable models of success and happiness for women, and a destabilization of the smooth functioning of conventional democratic society through relentless and excessive demands for gender equality. Public discourses about sexual harassment in popular culture, the workplace, and the courts have been a key area where the sexual nature of men, women, and gender relations has been debated. The WHR research—reported both on television and in such widely read magazines as *National Geographic*—makes no overt argument that women should not or cannot achieve positions of power and authority in society. But it does convey the message that women's appearance has been their primary "strategy" in the struggle for genetic survival, and as we have pointed out in the course of this chapter, it ranks these appearances in a hierarchical way. Whatever the intent of the researchers themselves, the tale science tells of reproductive success is never an innocent story. To the extent that the struggle for maximizing one's genetic contribution functions as a metaphor for the maximization of profit and social success, then this newest episode in evolutionary science seems to be telling women that their best asset has been, and possibly continues to be, a sexy (and reproductive) body.

WHR research, however, does not only speak to women. It also speaks to men. The last decade has witnessed an intensified crisis in the certainties of masculinity and masculine roles. Faludi's latest book, *Stiffed* (1999), is but one of a number of popular books and films, as well as academic treatises, on a dominant, white masculine identity in crisis. WHR research functions as a beacon of certainty in the midst of this ongoing contestation about proper male roles and privilege. It asserts, as did much sociobiology before it, the naturalness of male heterosexual desire. It tells men that what they have "always" wanted is adaptive. But it also inevitably disciplines male desire, legitimating certain forms (desire for the curvaceous female) and erasing other, homosexual, nonnormative erotic inclinations as nonadaptive (read, pathological). The nature of human sexual desire is very much on the table in the late twentieth and early twenty-first centuries. The salience of homosexuality and transgenderism in the public sphere, even if they are routinely demonized, has raised questions about what is normal when it comes to human sexual desire. WHR functions not only as beauty contest predictor but also as a normalizing reassurance of a specific kind of hetero-sexuality. It prescribes much more than it describes about the range of human sexuality.

When we consider the assertions of WHR research, we need to consider not only its scientific validity and methodology but also how it becomes part of these debates about sex and gender. How do the reductive accounts of the hourglass shape seem to reflect gender, class, and racial hierarchies, giving pride of place to an idealized white curvaceous woman? How do the attendant presumptions about mating strategies establish a very narrow range of erotic and aesthetic desires as both natural and universal? As anthropologists we are equipped to do more than prove this science to be flawed. We should also point to the gender and sexual politics it can enable. The growing popular fascination with the science of the female body has extended the currency of concepts like the waist-to-hip ratio, and we should not waste the opportunity that this well-publicized and problematic research provides to point out the crucial work that the female waistline continues to perform in the conduct of our societies and our lives.

Acknowledgments

We would like to thank Susan McKinnon and Sydel Silverman for inviting us to participate in the session "Anthropology United: Challenging Bio-social Reductivisms in the Academy, Popular Media, and Public Policy" and encouraging us to submit our paper for this volume. Special thanks go to Susan McKinnon for her editing assistance on numerous drafts of this chapter. Some of the ideas in this paper were first presented at the 1998 American Anthropological Association panel discussion "Questing for Perfection: The New Eugenics?" in a paper titled "Are You Fit, Norma Gene (Jean)? Gendered Discourses on Fitness in the Old and New Eugenics." We thank Helena Ragoné for her invitation to participate in the panel and for comments on the earlier paper.

Notes

1. Space limitations do not permit a discussion of this literature here. However, as an entry point into some of the key references, we would recommend the following as examples. For discussions of gender in science, see Harding 1986; Haraway 1989; Jordanova 1989; Russett 1989; Schiebinger 1993. For discussions of science and the female body, see, in addition to those above, Martin 1992; Hrdy 1999; Bordo 1993; Terry and Urla 1995; Morbeck, Galloway, and Zihlman 1997; Low 2000; Schiebinger 2000.

2. This theory was first laid out in Robert Trivers's 1972 essay "Parental Investment and Sexual Selection."

3. The WHR is acquired by taking the measurement for the waist size divided by the hip circumference. On average, the difference between women's waist and hip measurements is greater than it is for men.

4. Interestingly, they also argued that it was W.A.S.P. men who—through their selective

mating practices—had beautified, and also civilized, not only W.A.S.P. women but also their "race" more generally (Markowitz 2001).

5. See Urla and Swedlund 1995 for a fuller discussion of these statues and the anthropometric studies on which they are based.

6. The hourglass figure is now sometimes described as a body with "coke bottle curves," a linguistic shift that points to the influence of popular consumer culture in shaping body imagery. It is also an ironic association, given the link between the rise in obesity and the rise of consumption of soft drinks (see Leatherman and Goodman, chapter 8, this volume).

7. The attention this research is getting is illustrated in an article in the January 2000 issue of *National Geographic* entitled "The Enigma of Beauty" by Cathy Newman, which included a discussion of one of the foremost proponents of the WHR research, Devendra Singh.

8. In fact, we first learned of Shields's *Vogue* article through Singh's reference to it (1993: 296).

9. A National Academy of Sciences study (1991) is used by Singh as scientific support for the healthiness category since it reported that ratios of 0.8 and below are more closely associated with reduced health problems and ratios of 0.85 or above with increased risk for health problems.

10. Although Wilson's and Trivers's work are canonical texts for many evolutionary psychologists, evolutionary psychology and sociobiology are two distinct fields of study within the evolutionary sciences and should not be conflated. For more on their distinctions, see D. Wilson 1999 and Zuk 2002.

11. Miller has speculated that "[i]f male hominids have preferred low waist-to-hip ratios for many generations, this may explain why human females have such narrow waists, such broad hips, and such fleshy buttocks" (2000: 248).

12. The focus on the Pleistocene also distinguishes evolutionary psychology from sociobiology, which focuses on contemporary animal behavior rather than human prehistory.

13. As Hilary Rose and Steven Rose put it, evolutionary psychology has found its way into both the "cultural drinking water" and the "syllabuses of university courses" in the United States and the United Kingdom (Rose and Rose 2000: 4, 9). They also note that evolutionary psychology is mostly an Anglo-American subdiscipline.

14. Marilyn Monroe's figure, like her health, was notoriously unstable and, although WHR researchers may well have used a different set of her statistics when they figured her WHR, Marilyn herself is purported to have preferred the measurements of 38−23−36; she once expressed that she wanted her epitaph to read: "Here lies Marilyn Monroe, 38−23−36" (Baty 1995: 144). These figures produce a 0.638 WHR.

15. Although the debate continues over whether or not today's supermodels are anorexic, there is evolutionary psychology research that finds anorexia to be a strategy geared as much to achieving a low WHR as a thin body (Singh 1994a, 1994b). Mealey (2000) has argued that anorexia is neither a strategy to reduce reproductive functioning brought on by stress nor an adaptive behavior gone too far but rather a response to intrasexual competition whereby dominant females manipulate subordinate ones into maladaptive forms of body modification.

16. See Patricia Gowaty's more general critique of the evolutionary science of human mating for a further discussion of the untestability of many of its assumptions (1994).

17. Not surprisingly, this research usually offers the male members of remote, nonindustrialized "tribes" and cultures as counterexamples. In a fashion all too familiar in the Western cultural imaginary, in such studies contemporary non-Westernized subjects are made to represent evolutionarily prior versions of white Euro-Americans rather than distinctive cultural subjects in themselves.

18. Yu and Shepard conclude from their studies of the lack of low-WHR preference among Matsigenka men that, until a "more sophisticated evolutionary analysis" can be done, "the nature of female beauty must remain mysterious, as perhaps it should" (1999: 216). We need to be wary of the elusive and illusive female they conjure here. While she may seem to them to be evading the grasp of science, we worry that she is still in its clutches; her putative elusiveness works to keep her under continual scrutiny and therefore available as a potential explanation for any number of vexing issues of science, sex, and society.

19. Homosexuality does not get explained or explained away as only maladaptive or non-adaptive in evolutionary psychology: it is also treated as instructive. For example, Jones has reasoned that, since homosexuals "are not obliged to compromise with the inclinations of the other sex, [they] display sex differences in sexuality in a particularly pure form" (1999: 568). That is, male homosexuals are more promiscuous than male heterosexuals. For a discussion of how the female homosexual is treated in evolutionary psychology, see Angier 1999.

References

Angier, Natalie. 1999. *Woman: An Intimate Geography*. New York: Houghton Mifflin.

Barber, Nigel. 1995. The Evolutionary Psychology of Physical Attractiveness: Sexual Selection and Human Morphology. *Ethology and Sociobiology* 16(5): 395–424.

Baty, S. Paige. 1995. *American Monroe: The Making of a Body Politic*. Berkeley and Los Angeles: University of California Press.

Becker, Anne. 1995. *Body, Self, and Society: The View from Fiji*. Philadelphia: University of Pennsylvania Press.

Bellafante, Ginia. 2003. At Gender's Last Frontier. *New York Times*, June 8.

Bordo, Susan. 1993. *Unbearable Weight: Feminism, Western Culture, and the Body*. Berkeley and Los Angeles: University of California Press.

Brewis, Alexandra. 1999. The Accuracy of Attractive-Body-Size Judgment. *Current Anthropology* 40(4): 548–53.

Buss, David. 1991. Do Women Have Evolved Mate Preferences for Men with Resources? A Reply to Smuts. *Ethology and Sociobiology* 12(5): 401–8.

———. 1994. The Strategies of Human Mating. *American Scientist* 82(3): 238–49.

Buss, David, et al. 1990. International Preferences in Selecting Mates: A Study of 37 Cultures. *Journal of Cross-Cultural Psychology* 21(1): 5–47.

Comaroff, Jean. 1993. The Diseased Heart of Africa: Medicine, Colonialism, and the Black Body. In *Knowledge, Power, and Practice: The Anthropology of Medicine and Everyday Life*, ed. Shirley Lindenbaum and Margaret Lock, pp. 305–29. Berkeley and Los Angeles: University of California Press.

Coward, Rosalind. 1983. *Patriarchal Precedents: Sexuality and Social Relations*. London: Routledge and Kegan Paul.

Faludi, Susan. 1991. *Backlash: The Undeclared War against American Women*. New York: Crown.

———. 1999. *Stiffed: The Betrayal of the American Man*. New York: William Morrow.

Fausto-Sterling, Anne. 2000. Beyond Difference: Feminism and Evolutionary Psychology. In *Alas, Poor Darwin: Arguments against Evolutionary Psychology*, ed. Hilary Rose and Steven Rose, pp. 209–27. New York: Harmony Books.

Fedigan, Linda. 1986. The Changing Role of Women in Models of Human Evolution. *Annual Review of Anthropology* 15: 25–66.

Gilman, Sander. 1985. Black Bodies, White Bodies: Toward an Iconography of Female Sexuality in Late Nineteenth-Century Art, Medicine, Literature. *Critical Inquiry* 12(1): 204–42.

Gordon, Claire C., Bruce Bradtmiller, Thomas Churchill, Charles E. Clauser, John T. Mc-
Conville, Ilse Tebbetts, and Robert Walker. 1989. *1988 Anthropometric Survey of U.S. Army
Personnel: Methods and Summary Statistics.* Natick, MA: U.S. Army Natick Research, De-
velopment, and Engineering Center.

Gould, Stephen Jay. 2000. More Things in Heaven and Earth. In *Alas, Poor Darwin: Arguments
against Evolutionary Psychology,* ed. Hilary Rose and Steven Rose, pp. 101–25. New York:
Harmony Books.

Gowaty, Patricia. 1994. Review of *Anatomy of Love: The Natural History of Monogamy, Adultery, and Divorce* by Helen Fisher. *Women's Studies International* 17(2–3): 319–20.

Haraway, Donna. 1989. *Primate Visions: Gender, Race, and Nature in the World of Modern Science.* New York: Routledge.

Harding, Sandra. 1986. *The Science Question in Feminism.* Ithaca: Cornell University Press.

Hrdy, Sarah Blaffer. 1997. Raising Darwin's Consciousness: Female Sexuality and the Pre-
hominid Origins of Patriarchy. *Human Nature* 8(1): 1–49.

———. 1999. *Mother Nature: Maternal Instincts and How They Shape the Human Species.* New
York: Ballantine Books.

Jones, Doug. 1999. Evolutionary Psychology. *Annual Review of Anthropology* 28: 553–75.

Jordanova, Ludmilla. 1989. *Sexual Visions: Images of Gender in Science and Medicine between
the Eighteenth and Twentieth Centuries.* Madison: University of Wisconsin Press.

Kirchengast, S., and B. Hartmann. 1995. The Impact of Body Build on the Length of the Reproductive Span in Healthy Women. *Homo* 46(2): 125–40.

Low, Bobbi. 2000. *Why Sex Matters: A Darwinian Look at Human Behavior.* Princeton: Princeton University Press.

Markowitz, Sally. 2001. Pelvic Politics: Sexual Dimorphism and Racial Difference. *Signs* 26(2):
389–414.

Martin, Emily. 1992. *The Woman in the Body: A Cultural Analysis of Reproduction.* 2nd ed. Boston: Beacon Press.

——— 1991. The Egg and the Sperm: How Science Has Constructed a Romance Based on
Stereotypical Male-Female Roles. *Signs* 16(3): 485–501.

McFarland, Robin. 1997. Female Primates: Fat or Fit? In Morbeck, Galloway, and Zihlman
1997: 163–75.

Mealey, Linda. 2000. Anorexia: A "Losing" Strategy? *Human Nature* 11(1): 105–16.

Miller, Geoffrey. 2000. *The Mating Mind: How Sexual Choice Shaped the Evolution of Human
Nature.* New York: Anchor Books.

Morbeck, Mary Ellen, Alison Galloway, Adrienne Zihlman, eds. 1997. *The Evolving Female: A
Life History Perspective.* Princeton: Princeton University Press.

National Academy of Sciences. 1991. *Diet and Health.* Washington, DC.

Newman, Cathy. 2000. The Enigma of Beauty. *National Geographic,* January, pp. 94–121.

Pond, Caroline. 1997. The Biological Origins of Adipose Tissue in Humans. In Morbeck, Galloway, and Zihlman 1997: 147–62.

Rose, Hilary, and Steven Rose. 2000. Introduction to *Alas, Poor Darwin: Arguments against
Evolutionary Psychology,* ed. Hilary Rose and Steven Rose, pp. 1–15. New York: Harmony
Books.

Russett, Cynthia. 1989. *Sexual Science: The Victorian Construction of Womanhood.* Cambridge:
Harvard University Press.

Schiebinger, Londa. 1986. Skeletons in the Closet: The First Illustrations of the Female Skeleton in Eighteenth Century Anatomy. *Representations* 14: 42–82.

———. 1993. *Nature's Body: Gender in the Making of Modern Science.* Boston: Beacon.

Schiebinger, Londa, ed. 2000. *Feminism and the Body.* Oxford: Oxford University Press.

Shapiro, Ann-Louise. 1996. *Breaking the Codes: Female Criminality in Fin-de-Siècle Paris.* Stanford: Stanford University Press.

Shapiro, Harry. 1945. *Americans: Yesterday, Today, Tomorrow.* Man and Nature Publications, Science Guide no. 126. New York: American Museum of Natural History.

Shields, Jody. 1991. The Return of the Waist. *Vogue,* August, pp. 260–62.

Singh, Devendra. 1993. Adaptive Significance of Female Physical Attractiveness: Role of Waist-to-Hip Ratio. *Journal of Personality and Social Psychology* 65: 293–307.

———. 1994a. Ideal Female Body Shape: Role of Body Weight and Waist-to-Hip Ratio. *International Journal of Eating Disorders* 16: 283–88.

———. 1994b. Body Fat Distribution and Perception of Desirable Female Body Shape by Young Black Men and Women. *International Journal of Eating Disorders* 16: 289–94.

Singh, Devendra, and Suwardi Luis. 1995. Ethnic and Gender Consensus for the Effect of Waist-to-Hip Ratio on Judgment of Women's Attractiveness. *Human Nature* 6: 51–65.

Singh, Devendra, and Robert K. Young. 1995. Body Weight, Waist-to-Hip Ratio, Breasts, and Hips: Role in Judgments of Female Attractiveness and Desirability for Relationships. *Ethology and Sociobiology* 16(6): 483–507.

Smith-Rosenberg, Carroll. 1985. *Disorderly Conduct: Visions of Gender in Victorian America.* New York: Oxford University Press.

Smuts, Robert. 1991. The Present Also Explains the Past: A Response to Tooby and Cosmides. *Ethology and Sociobiology* 12(2): 77–82.

Tassinary, Louis, and Kristi Hansen. 1998. A Critical Test of the Waist-to-Hip Ratio Hypothesis of Female Physical Attractiveness. *Psychological Science* 9(2): 150–55.

Terry, Jennifer, and Jacqueline Urla, eds. 1995. *Deviant Bodies: Critical Perspectives on Difference in Science and Popular Culture.* Bloomington: Indiana University Press.

Trivers, Robert. 1972. Parental Investment and Sexual Selection. In *Sexual Selection and the Descent of Man, 1871–1971,* ed. Bernard G. Campbell, pp. 136–79. Chicago: Aldine.

Urla, Jacqueline, and Alan Swedlund. 1995. The Anthropometry of Barbie: Unsettling Ideals of the Feminine Body in Popular Culture. In Terry and Urla 1995: 277–313.

Wetsman, Adam, and Frank Marlowe. 1999. How Universal Are Preferences for Female Waist-to-Hip Ratios? Evidence from the Hadza of Tanzania. *Evolution and Human Behavior* 20: 219–28.

Wilson, David Sloan. 1999. Tasty Slice—But Where Is the Rest of the Pie? *Evolution and Human Behavior* 20(4): 279–87.

Wilson, Edward O. 1975. *Sociobiology: The New Synthesis.* Cambridge: Harvard University Press.

Yu, Douglas, and Glenn Shepard, Jr. 1998. Is Beauty in the Eye of the Beholder? *Nature* 396: 321–22.

———. 1999. Reply. *Nature* 399: 216.

Zihlman, Adrienne L. 1995. Misreading Darwin on Reproduction: Reductionism in Evolutionary Theory. In *Conceiving the New World Order: The Global Politics of Reproduction,* ed. Faye D. Ginsburg and Rayna Rapp, pp. 425–43. Berkeley and Los Angeles: University of California Press.

Zuk, Marlene. 2002. *Sexual Selections: What We Can and Can't Learn about Sex from Animals.* Berkeley and Los Angeles: University of California Press.

CHAPTER 7

Denaturalizing Gender in Prehistory

Lynn Meskell

THE ARCHAEOLOGY OF SEXUALITY and gender has done much to expose the sexual stereotypes that pervade the construction of archaeological narratives. Early studies underscored the "Man the Hunter" model as a key exemplar of an androcentric, or male-centered, paradigm—one that cast human prehistory in the familiar light of our own cultural understandings of sexual difference and inequality. All too often, it has been assumed that gender in the past simply mirrors contemporary terms and agendas and that sexuality exists primarily in a modern Euro-American guise. However, the specificities of the ancient data, when studied contextually, challenge their reduction to our own cultural norms. In fact, anthropology has shown us the inherent pitfalls of that approach, suggesting to those of us who study the past that we too have been guilty of projecting "natural" boundaries and categorizations onto cultural contexts where they are inappropriate. We can neither assume that, in other societies, cultural domains such as gender and sexuality are structured like ours nor expect the same analytic constellations and results.

This chapter explores these issues in relation both to the narratives enmeshed in prehistoric figurines and iconography that have been construed as denoting the presence of an eternal Mother Goddess and to the concomitant myth of matriarchy. Such interpretations have become increasingly prevalent within both popular feminist and New Age circles, even though they capitalize on a long and androcentric tradition. Indeed, they reinforce three pervasive dualisms that feminists have sought to dispel: culture versus nature, mind versus body, and reason versus emotion. Despite many of the positive overtones of the goddess movement, it tends to essentialize the roles of women as well as men in ways that are reductionist. Characterizations of gender and sexuality that derive from our own historically and culturally specific understandings are assumed to be fixed and universal and thus transferable to ancient contexts. The elision of cultural difference results in a picture of the past that may bear little relation to ancient realities. Only through deconstruction of the domains we see as "natural" or given can we truly begin to practice an archaeology that values cultural difference, contextuality, and complexity. Çatalhöyük, currently the goddess site par excellence, occupies a unique place in the contemporary imagination and forms the case study within this chapter.

Plastic Prehistory

Over the past decade gender archaeologists have exposed the androcentric narratives that have underscored accounts of prehistory. Narratives such as "Man the Hunter" have been forcefully critiqued by feminist archaeologists (Conkey and Spector 1984; Conkey and Williams 1991; Hurcomb 1995; Moser 1998), and most scholars would now question all stereotyped accounts of gender in prehistory. However, sexism can work in both directions, as demonstrated in writings about specific Neolithic societies. The most evocative example of this complex problem can be found with the so-called goddess centers of eastern Europe and Anatolia. Archaeologists such as James Mellaart and Marija Gimbutas have been instrumental in constructing a picture of matristic life and worship that has been embraced by popular audiences. Underpinning these interpretations is a set of cultural assumptions about gender roles and experiences in the past that are based on little or no evidence. Many writers have been at pains to set the archaeological record straight (Conkey and Tringham 1995; Eller 1995, 2000; Haaland and Haaland 1995; Meskell 1995, 1998a, 1998b, 1999b; Talalay 1994, 1999). This is a disciplinary reaction to the perceived skewing of archaeological data. Ironically, Gimbutas's followers have claimed that "gender archaeology" has developed because of her groundbreaking research, demonstrating little understanding of the discipline's history (Keller 1997). However, few scholars have highlighted the fact that gynocentric, or female-centered, narratives—as much as androcentric ones—proffer essentialist explanations of subjects in the past. In both kinds of accounts, contemporary gender categories are reified, naturalized, and projected back in time. Such an interpretive move creates the false impression that these categories and characteristics are historically universal, and it thereby validates their normative status in contemporary society.

According to the goddess movement, women of the past are said to have enjoyed supreme status and led powerful, harmonious, and artistic lives. This vision of the past remains unsupported by the evidence. Moreover, it paradoxically relies upon a set of Cartesian dualisms—culture/nature, mind/body, and reason/emotion—that have long been central to patriarchal narratives that have justified the inferiority of women. Through goddess veneration and its reconstruction of the past, women are depicted as more natural, more embodied, and more emotional than their male counterparts. First, the goddess movement asserts women's closeness to nature and the planet, particularly through ecofeminism. Second, it argues that women are more embodied and have an enviable sexuality, which is more sensitive than that of men, and that this is rooted in the matriarchal past. And third, women have a type of intelligence unfamiliar to men, mainly construed as intuitive or emotional knowledge. Each of these three factors reaffirms a Cartesian dualism in which women assume the lesser role. Through the goddess, women are aligned to nature, the body, and emotion, while men become the bearers of culture, mind, and reason. So, in fact, no radical epistemic change has occurred and the whole project of modern goddess veneration is an extension of a patriarchal belief system. This presents an interesting twist for gynocentric feminists. Yet, despite such critiques, gynocracy, or female rule, continues to be a powerful ideology that has mobilized countless people across the globe. The current burgeoning interest in Çatalhöyük is only one example of the connection between gynocentric feminism, archaeology, and politics. As a case study, I attempt to chart the interactions between archaeologists, ecofeminist writers, and goddess groups at the site of Çatalhöyük. This examination will refer to the work of archaeologists Marija Gimbutas and James Mellaart, followed by a discussion of new excavations at the site, under the directorship of Ian Hodder (1996, 1997, 1998, 1999, 2000).

In questioning why archaeology is invoked for such contemporary concerns or why it is deemed such a necessary medium for the message, I would argue that its potential for plasticity and its suggestion of continuity are two major factors. Prehistory is notoriously plastic in its ability to be molded into a myriad of interpretations. Indeed, goddess writers clearly avoid historic cultures where it is evident a specific mother goddess was absent—for instance, in ancient Egypt. In most goddess-based narratives, archaeological material is used to present a singular storyline that is unproblematic, unreflexive, and nonnegotiable. One goddess writer recently declared that "no conscientious person would recommend or condone new distortions of the archaeological record to arrive at alternative models, but fortunately such distortions are not necessary" (Lobell 1997: 378).

Back to Cartesianism

Though contemporary goddess worship is undoubtedly the product of specific cultural conditions, the notion of a matriarchal past has its roots in classic notions of evolutionary social stages, economic inequality, and gender difference. In the mid–nineteenth century, Bachofen proposed that "matriarchy is bound up with matter and a religious stage of development that acknowledges only corporeal life" (Fromm 1997: 23). Bachofen considered prehistory a cruder, less civilized world that was based on the natural productiveness of women and that lacked the institution of marriage, law, principles, or order—all of which were presumed to have been instituted under the sign of patriarchy.

Heavily influenced by Bachofen, renowned psychoanalyst Erich Fromm argued that "patriarchal society" as we know it through the history of the "civilized world" is a phenomenon of relatively recent date. It was preceded by a "state of culture" where the mother was the head of the family, the ruler, and the Great Goddess. Drawing on Bachofen, Fromm extrapolated that "[t]he positive order of matriarchism lies in the sense of equality, universality and unconditional affirmation of life. The negative aspect lies in its bondage to blood and soil, its lack of rationality and progress. The positive aspect of patriarchism lies in its principle of reason, law, science, civilization, spiritual development; its negative aspect in hierarchy, oppression, inequality and inhumanity" (1997: 6–7). The perceived battle of the sexes has been likened to a guerilla war that has been waged for some six thousand years since patriarchy triumphed over women and since society became organized around the principle of male domination.

It is unsurprising, then, that such a bifurcated view of the world played neatly into the patterns of Cartesian dualism that pervaded much of European thought over previous centuries. Such theorizing can be directly traced to Descartes and his essential separation of mind and matter (Grosz 1994: 3). Cartesian dualism does not represent a neutral division but is hierarchized and ranked, thus privileging one term and suppressing and subordinating the other. In such an equation *body* is simply what is not *mind*, what is distinct from, and other than, the privileged term. It is what the mind must expel in order to secure its "integrity." The body is depicted as disruptive and in need of ordered direction. It is merely incidental to the defining characteristics of mind and reason that are privileged within philosophical thought.[1] Thus, blood, soil, equality, and all that is life affirming are construed as female in nature, whereas rationality, progress, reason, law, science, civilization, and, most importantly, "spiritual development" are read as male in Fromm's account.

The image of a more embodied past—a stage where individuals were more in touch with the rhythms of corporeal life—has been popular ever since the works of Bachofen and others. Since women are the primary life givers by virtue of their physical ability to give birth, women have been construed as more natural. Through many contemporary ecofeminist writings, a monolithic female has become synonymous with a global body, often articulated as Gaia theory. Drawing out the analogy, another line of reasoning posits that just as women's bodies have been exploited throughout history by men, the planet has also been exploited and devastated by men and the onset of technology.

These views found resonance in the writings of Marija Gimbutas (1991: xx), who pointed the finger at the Kurgan invasion as the historical turning point for this process. The Kurgans (who all appear to be men) brought metallurgy, horse breeding, agricultural technology, and male deities into a matristic and harmonious Neolithic Europe. As a result of the Kurgan victory, this former environmentally friendly, vegetarian existence was effectively terminated.

Taking this further, the inferred rape and pillage by the Kurgans is likened to modern rape of the landscape. Gimbutas's gynocentric narratives have influenced a whole generation of writers and artists—for instance, Starhawk, Monica Sjöö, Star Goode, Gloria Orenstein, Charlene Spretnak, Joan Marler, and Riane Eisler—who have perpetuated her interpretations and her own mythologies. Later ecofeminists have eschewed feminist theory itself—claiming that it ignores the study of patriarchal origins—and have concentrated rather on the androcentric world (March 1997: 357).

Goddess narratives, inflected with age-old Cartesianisms, relegate women to the position of nature in the nature/culture dichotomy. Women's essentialized roles as "mother" and "nurturer" have been privileged over their other social and corporeal potentials. By an easy extension of this natural self and its associated embodied corporeality, female divinities are understood to assume roles as goddesses of love and sexuality. From this perspective, even mortal women are more embodied than their male counterparts—and always have been. This has been lauded as a positive image and has found some support with older-styled, first-wave feminists, who claim that an intrinsic essence of woman unites us all on the basis of biology. Indeed, the ideology of a female nature or essence has been reappropriated by certain feminists (Eisler 1991, 1995; Getty 1990; Merchant 1995; Mutén 1994) in an effort to revalidate undervalued female attributes, although what constitutes a "female" attribute is informed by an essentialist argument from the outset. In a similar vein, the ecofeminist movement has drawn on ancient pasts to infer that a utopian society, once lived and lost, can be regained yet again. While the desire is basically a positive one, it too relies on assumptions that can be critiqued for the essentialist stereotyping of both men and women (Meskell 1999a).

Third-wave feminists in a host of fields now critique these unitary, essentialist, and reductive positions—arguing that biology alone is no longer destiny (Butler 1993; Gatens 1994, 1996; Lloyd 1993; Meskell 1999a, 1999b). Other factors divide and unite us—including age, sexual orientation, ethnic and racial contexts, religious sentiments, and general life experiences. It is now axiomatic that feminism is a fractured movement, including divergent positions, some of which appear diametrically opposed at times.

This critique is illustrated in the commentary on the Mother Earth concept—which presupposes that the planet represents the female body—a proposition that is central to the Gaia theory. As Joni Seager protests: "The earth is *not* our mother. There is no warm, nurturing, anthropomorphized earth that will take care of us if only we treat her nicely. The complex, emotion-laden, quasi-sexualised, quasi-dependent mother relationship . . . is not an effective metaphor for environmental action" (1994: 219). She argues that this metaphor—the sex-typing of the planet—obfuscates and essentializes gendered power relations. In this form, ecofeminism actually suggests a necessary causal relationship between sexual difference and its expression in the ecologically destructive culture of patriarchy (New 1996). Here ecofeminism lands in what Rosi Braidotti describes as the "double trap": "on the one hand a sociologizing reductivism which, on the binary model of the class struggle, sets the female individual in opposition to the male patriarchal system" and "on the other the utopian model which makes 'women' an entity [on the] outside, foreign to the dominant system and not contaminated by it" (1991: 89). The concept of an abstract masculinity against which all women must struggle is perhaps just as objectionable as blatant androcentrism, and it suggests, ironically, that things have failed to move on.

In considering the narratives of the emergent goddess movement, it is evident that, contrary to developments of academic feminism, several stereotypes place women back from whence they had endeavored to escape. They have been thrust back into the flesh zone: women become the body, they become more natural, more sexual, and more corporeal than their male counterparts (Pollack 1993). Their possibilities for equality, for reason, for mental capacities, for culture, and for individual differences are severely delimited. Women, through goddess-centered explanations of prehistoric society, lose rationality and become more emotional and spiritual in the past and, by extension, in the present. This emotional and spiritual wisdom is understood to defy the "rationalist" interpretations of archaeologists, historians, or anthropologists. In fact, in contrast to the embodied emotive narratives that claim to have an age-old truth at their core, "rationalist" knowledge is often depicted as a form of institutionalized, androcentric reasoning whose subjectivity should be recognized. This tension is best demonstrated by the competing narratives produced for the site of Çatalhöyük, in modern-day Turkey.

Çatalhöyük: The Twin Peaks of the Goddess

Rising from the Konya plain are the two mounds from which the Neolithic site of Çatalhöyük (c. 7400 – 6000 BC) derives its name. Archaeologist James Mellaart discovered the site in 1958 and excavated there from 1961 to 1965. The site has been gaining increasing attention in the last few years for a number of reasons. First, the reopening of the site promises a return of all the sensational imagery witnessed in the 1960s, but further enhanced by improved archaeological technologies. Second, there is considerable interest in the possibilities for undertaking an interpretive excavation and this has already attracted considerable controversy. Third, the site is attracting enormous interest from the Turkish people, Turkish corporations, and an international community of goddess worshipers—all of whom want access to the site and the freedom to create their own interpretations of it (see Hamilakis 1999; Meskell 1998a).

Here it is important to begin by reconsidering the writings of James Mellaart because his vision of Çatalhöyük set the scene for Marija Gimbutas and other writers of goddess archaeology (Meskell 1998a, 1998b). In fact, little rewriting was necessary because Mellaart had already employed the language of magic and paganism. Typical of many excavators in the 1960s, Mellaart emphasized that the site was biggest and best, and the ancient antecedent of Western civilization itself: "Çatal Hüyük shines like a supernova among the rather dim galaxy of contemporary peasant cultures" (1965: 77). Moreover, the lasting effect of the site itself was felt not in the Near East but in Europe, according to Mellaart, since it introduced to the latter agriculture, stockbreeding, and the "cult of the Mother Goddess, the basis of our civilisation" (1965: 77).

From the outset, there was only one goddess at the site. According to Mellaart, she was the "Great Goddess, mistress of life and death, protectress of women, patroness of the arts . . . at this period there can be no doubt that the supreme deity was the Great Goddess" (Mellaart 1964: 49). It seems clear that the initial recording of Çatalhöyük was largely influenced by decidedly Greek notions of ritual and magic, especially that of the Triple Goddess—maiden, mother, and crone. These ideas were common to many at that time but have often been thought to originate with Jane Ellen Harrison, a classical archaeologist and member of the Cambridge Ritualists. Such interpretations were probably inspired by Frazer's *The Golden Bough,* in which he states, on surveying the evidence, that "a great Mother Goddess, the personification of all the reproductive energies of nature, was worshipped under different names but with a substantial similarity of myth and ritual by many peoples of Western Asia" ([1922] 1993: 331). Ronald Hutton (1997) believes these interpretations go back further, to Gerhard in 1849, and were later taken up by classical scholars. These notions of ritual and magic, coupled with the sensational nature of the material, seem to have inspired Mellaart's narrative of Çatalhöyük. This is not commonly recognized within academia, yet his interpretations were eagerly taken up by pagans, goddess worshipers, and feminists.

> When James Mellaart and others excavated a ten-thousand-year-old city near the village of Catal Hüyük, Turkey, they found Goddess statues like pregnant women set atop bread-baking ovens. This strikes us as bizarre, but think: isn't bread and all cooked food a miracle? Various ingredients are mixed together and shaped into a particular form (how wonderful it would be to know the forms Neolithic people chose for bread!). . . . We describe a pregnant woman as having "another bun in the oven." Does this phrase go all the way back to prehistoric Turkey? The idea may seem farfetched, but Gimbutas has shown the value of comparing archaeological remains to country folklore. (Pollack 1993: 102–3)

Mellaart's publications have fueled countless theories of goddess religion and matriarchy at Çatalhöyük. Many such theories purport that Çatalhöyük is the foremost goddess site in a truly global sense, and this is largely due to the later efforts of Gimbutas and her numerous popular publications. They argue that a universal, monolithic Great Goddess was worshiped there. She was the Neolithic "virgin" according to Gimbutas, and her effigies shared characteristics with figurines from the Aegean and Europe. In Çatalhöyük a utopian existence was supposedly enjoyed by all—but mainly women. Life was peaceful, creative, vegetarian, and goddess centered—that is, until men ruined it by bringing increased technology, metallurgy, warfare, and so on.

Mellaart's reports exhibit a progressive simplification of the narrative interpretation of Çatalhöyük, where even the minimal discussion of the multiplicity and complexity of gender relations was subsumed into a more simplistic and monolithic narrative of matriarchy and goddess worship. Mellaart excavated a wide range of materials, but he chose to highlight some materials at the expense of others: the progressive erasure of male, sexless, and zoomorphic figurines is a salient example. He also sought to streamline the interpretation of those materials so that they conformed to his favored theory of the Great Goddess.

This double simplification precluded the possibility of alternative explanations over subsequent decades. Theories of the Great Goddess were vociferously endorsed and promulgated to popular audiences by Gimbutas (1982, 1989, 1991). Her revision of prehistory was, and continues to be, used to explain the suppression of women and the source of women's imposed inequality.[2] Following on from the work of Gimbutas, ecofeminist Riane Eisler claims that Çatalhöyük was essentially free from armed conflict and socially equitable; however, the highest power was bestowed upon female deities. Eisler (1991) tells us that archaeologists, like Mellaart, have proven that sites like Çatalhöyük were peaceful, matrilineal communities where women held high social positions, such as priestesses—despite the fact that Mellaart actually did speak about priests and his reconstruction drawings also predominantly featured men.

Çatalhöyük has inspired many flights of fancy within archaeology that have inevitably filtered down into other disciplines. Recently, renowned social geographer Edward Soja has argued that Çatalhöyük was based on a new form of gender-based, possibly matricentric, division of labor associated with the early stages of urbanization. Such permanent settlement was reliant on women's work (such as baking, weaving, housework, and child care) and on their religious and secular powers through the power of the Mother Goddess, thus enabling them to have a more central role in the formation of culture (Soja 2000: 38). Yet even this optimistic view of women's status in the Neolithic is premised upon the narrow construal of women's roles: they are fundamentally mothers and housewives.

In sum, there is a unified vision of Çatalhöyük, inspired by the original excavators' vivid reconstructions and sanctioned by Gimbutas's universal gynocentric narrative. This vision is still so pervasive that current excavations of the site have to "dig through" Mellaart's prior work, both literally and metaphorically. The site is so steeped in his reconstructions, interpretations, and terminology that it will take some time before a new Çatalhöyük can emerge.

Mirroring Çatalhöyük: Androcentric Reductionism

At the time of excavation, the 1960s, archaeologists typically produced empirical accounts of cultures and belief systems and did not focus on interpretive uncertainty—that is, on the number of plausible interpretations one could construct from the same evidence. Embedded within these narratives, however, were assumptions pertaining to gendered roles and relations that were implicitly predicated upon a contemporary Western social system. As Ruth Tringham (1991) demonstrated over a decade ago, most accounts of prehistory remain unpeopled and thus ungendered. However, when people are present in these accounts, the default gender is always construed as male; and when women are present in them, they are tied to a "domestic sphere" that is both de-privileged and stereotyped. Gender-assigned tasks are extrapolated from "commonsense" understandings of present-day gender roles, or rather gender roles as they were experienced in 1950s America.

Tringham illustrates the interpretive dilemma through the construction of a mock dialogue in which she uses a form of ventriloquism to construct the "voices" and opinions of three other archaeologists: Andrew Sherratt (AS), Marija Gimbutas (MG), and Ian Hodder (IH). Sherratt occupies the position of androcentrist, Gimbutas that of gynocentrist, while Hodder plays the role of structuralist and subversive interlocutor, and Tringham herself embraces an open-ended pluralistic stance:

> INTERVIEWER: *Here is a picture of the ground of House 2 at Opovo* [an archaeological site in the former Yugoslavia]. *What do you think of the "room"?*
> AS: A pathetic attempt to recreate the grandeur of the great households in the aggregated villages of the south.
> MG: A temple to the Goddess.
> IH: A symbolic expression of the richness of the dramatus domesticus, women, domus.
> RT: A separation of domestic labor from surplus production.
>
> INTERVIEWER: *Who built the houses of Opovo?*
> AS: Men while women were hoeing.
> MG: Men under women's (the Goddess's) direction.
> IH: Women under men's direction.
> RT: The coresidential cooperative productive unit.
>
> INTERVIEWER: *What did the women do at Opovo?*
> AS: Hoed.
> MG: Everything.
> IH: Practiced a secret subversive power.
> RT: I don't know; I can't say; I presume they participated in household cooperative action. (Tringham 1991: 113)

Although the conversation is parodied at all levels, it ineluctably reveals the problem of interpreting prehistory. The obvious lack of inscriptions and documentary data—coupled with a shortage of comparative data to determine the function of structures, not to mention the meanings behind objects or images—ensures that interpretation is not explanation. Given that archaeologists cannot easily explain the material residues of prehistory, there are even greater problems with the immaterial elements of social life, such as social and gender relations, ritual action, division of labor, and symbolic expression. One can see how the mock dialogue above is inflected with dualistic models of gendered roles in regard to labor and production: men and women had differentiated tasks, roles, and attitudes.

While our theoretical impasse is considered axiomatic for archaeologists, many outside the discipline who have not witnessed the scholarly wrangling of previous decades have failed to appreciate the complexity of interpretation, especially in prehistoric contexts. When prehistoric archaeology is taken up in public discourse, particularly in the popular media, most choose to simplify archaeological narratives: they smooth over the complexities that result from a lack of data or inconclusive material, and they often fill the evidentiary gaps with narratives shaped by their own cultural presuppositions.

Interpreting the role of women at Çatalhöyük, whether mortal or divine, has been of prime importance since the discovery of the site. Yet these interpretations have swung between androcentric and gynocentric poles, and they have, in some instances, occupied both positions simultaneously. An implicit androcentric bias inheres within early goddess-centered accounts of the site. It is certainly possible to construct androcentric narratives within the totalizing account of a goddess-centered society. Mellaart, for instance, may have premised his interpretations on a pervasive female deity, yet his discussion of male and female activities and objects was entrenched in his own contemporary gender stereotypes. Throughout his reports, women are associated with mirrors and jewelry and men with weapons, although there seems to have been significant overlap in burial treatments. Weapons displaying craftsmanship are described as "prestige objects" (Mellaart 1975: 103; Todd 1976: 69), whereas similarly worked bone tools associated with sewing, clothing, and adornment are not viewed as reflecting prestige. Typically, Mellaart defined hunting and warfare as exclusively male activities, which he assumed conferred power and prestige. Through this association with hunting, men are linked with bulls and the latter are the subject of "cult themes." Bull imagery is deemed male, and therefore structures with a heavy emphasis on such imagery are correspondingly interpreted as male shrines.

Taking this theme further, archaeologist Tim Taylor (1996) has critiqued the goddess-centered explanation of the Çatalhöyük iconography but, in the process, replaced one gender stereotype with another: he finds the horned bulls heads too "virile looking" to be associated with goddess worship. Considering other iconography, Mellaart noted the almost complete lack of reproductive sexual organs in most of the representations. His explanation was that they were painted by women, since only men would be interested in depicting the phallus or the vulva. Similarly, Ian Todd argued that, although most of the paintings depict men, a few women can be identified as "figures who lean back with their legs wide apart in a position for intercourse" (1976: 42). Such interpretations would be widely criticized today, although one should read them as forming an integral part of the complex narrative that is being woven about gender in prehistory. Interpretations of what represented, or was indicative of, males and females have been based upon our own cultural understandings of gender characteristics. This has been the case despite the fact that, as Jonathan Last (1998) has pointed out, the wall paintings at Çatalhöyük have yet to be examined in context—one of the most basic studies undertaken in any excavation!

Interpreters have consciously molded the images of Çatalhöyük into something familiar and desirable, although contemporary viewers (Euro-American or otherwise) can have little real understanding of Neolithic experience—what was feared, celebrated, worshiped, or desired. Many reconstructions of the site look more akin to artistic hippie communes of the 1960s: a utopian refuge for creative, beautiful people to make art and worship the divine female principle. Çatalhöyük ineluctably holds up a mirror to our own culture, and we have seen reflections of our deepest desires: a peaceful, harmonious existence where women are celebrated and the earth with all its bounty is held sacred. It would seem that many people need Çatalhöyük, or rather a specific vision of Çatalhöyük.

Beyond Gender Stereotypes?

The interpretive impasse I have just described is currently being addressed in specific ways by the recent excavations of Çatalhöyük, under the direction of Ian Hodder. As the project develops, it has become clear that the team is both local and international, the excavation strategies are state of the art (Hodder 1996, 2000), the data are being made available to all through the technology of the Internet, and many voices are being encouraged to offer their interpretations.

Although the excavations at Çatalhöyük are in the early stages, new data are emerging to challenge prior assumptions about men, women, and children at the site. Çatalhöyük is famous for its evocative wall paintings and sculptures, often revered as the first "art." Originally, Mellaart thought that the paintings were produced only in a "priestly quarter," presumably populated by high-status men. With further areas of the site currently under excavation, we now know that this interpretation was wrong: paintings have been found in various sectors of the site, suggesting that they were part of everyday life. In the lower/earlier levels, it is impossible to attribute any specific sex to many representations of figures, whereas in the upper/later levels some wall paintings reveal a clear demarcation between men and women (including scenes depicting bearded individuals)—which may reflect a shift over time. In a provocative reinterpretation, Hodder (2001: 111) argues that the iconography suggests that women were depicted as tamers and confronters of wild animals and carnivores—it is this role, rather than the birthing role, that we see so predominantly at Çatalhöyük. Instead of viewing female images as synonymous with a Great Mother, he argues that both male and female imagery suggests a stronger role for sexuality in the Neolithic, although this too seems redolent of our own era's preoccupations with the body and sexuality. More specifically, he has addressed the issue of matriarchy head on: "in my view the evidence that we have gained at Çatalhöyük suggests not an all-powerful Goddess and a priestly elite, but daily domestic rituals and a set of beliefs and myths in which both men and women play a role. . . . I argue that Goddess or other groups sometimes make claims that cannot be supported by any evidence. But I recognize that counter claims can be made" (Hodder 2000: 11).

The concept of a pervasive Mother Goddess at Çatalhöyük is usually supported by reference to representations in the iconography and to figurines of corpulent seated women. However, the new excavations and a reexamination of Mellaart's data have brought to light the numerous sexless and schematic human figures, animals, humans with animals, and so on. Figurines occur in a wide variety of contexts and associations: inside grain bins, baskets, and hearths, on floors, and stuffed into walls. Some figurines have been found in refuse contexts, indicating that the objects themselves may not have been viewed as tacitly sacred. Figurines were used after breakage, as there are examples that have clearly been mended (Hamilton 1996: 219). Others appear to have been purposely burnt in household contexts along with other objects, possibly as a result of ritualized destruction. The vast majority of the figurine corpus (animal, schematic, and human) is fragmented. Some animal figurines, such as those representing boars, evidence intentional stab marks. All these findings complicate any simplistic interpretation, yet since they detract from the goddess theory, they have been deemphasized or erased from goddess-oriented discussions.

From the most recent analysis, several patterns emerge that directly challenge traditional dualistic frameworks. First, the anthropomorphic figurine corpus generally lacks any notable gender patterning: there are very few sexed differences, even if one uses beards, penises, or breasts as indicators. Second, there is no depositional patterning in regard to male or female figurines, thus impelling researchers to move beyond the categories of male and female, which may not, in themselves, have been accorded great importance. Third, even when the figurines can be sexed, as with the few seated females, these come from the later levels of the site, which suggests notable diachronic changes and complements the wall painting data mentioned above. Recent findings from the excavation now suggest that even the most basic data contradict the notion of a clear gender asymmetry.

Another strategy pursued by archaeologists interested in questions of gender difference is to reexamine the older data presented by Mellaart. Paul Wason examined the burial assemblages and other mortuary data from Mellaart's reports and concluded that there are no artifacts at Çatalhöyük that are indisputably status related; rather, they tend to signify degrees of effort and quality. Wason argues (1994: 170) that there is no direct evidence for either social stratification or substantial differences in wealth that would follow from such stratification. One child burial and some infant burials that might be described as high status point to the importance of families and to the possibility of hereditary status (Wason 1994: 178). This may indicate a form of social inequality that is based broadly on kinship but is not evidence for high levels of social stratification or personal aggrandizement. However, Wason correlates high status with strong religious connection, and in this regard, he relies too heavily on Mellaart's older interpretations.

As the new excavations have cogently revealed, the recording system used during Mellaart's excavation was so poor as to preclude any substantive interpretations about gender or status. The scientific sexing of individuals has advanced greatly and much early work has been effectively discredited. Recent excavation under Hodder's direction demonstrates that there are no appreciable gendered differences in burial location, orientation, aspect, or even the goods contained within the burials. Bioanthropological work shows that both male and female heads were removed from their bodies and deposited in the foundations of house posts. In Hodder's view, considering the importance attached to ancestors and to the continuity of the domestic unit, as well as the significant location of the deposits, one might expect to find a gendered pattern of family dominance that conformed to patrilineality or matrilineality. Yet, while the first two skulls discovered were male, another five showed a number of females, so that no gendered pattern was evident.

With the possibilities afforded by new scientific techniques, Hodder's team is able to define social differences as lived and experienced by the occupants of Çatalhöyük. They can, for instance, examine any differentiation in the health or diet of individuals. Isotope analysis has been used to determine whether certain people were eating meat, with the result that there was no clear difference between men and women. In addition, analysis of teeth, specifically types of wear, reveals no gender differences other than, perhaps, some that were related to age. Lastly, neither men nor women generally suffered from the types of long-term stress associated with carrying heavy loads or excessive labor. These findings substantiate other analyses where there are no appreciable gendered demarcations.

These studies are clearly meaningful for modern commentators, but can we be sure that these indices reflect the concerns of Neolithic people? How was difference constituted for the Çatalhöyük community: was gender the axial structuring principle or was it family, age, rank, or skill? In the domestic sphere many of the old gender stereotypes are challenged. For example, preworked obsidian was stored in caches under floors and taken out and knapped in the house when needed. Both caches and production areas were adjacent to the ovens, so if one subscribed to the notion that women cooked and men made tools, the gendering of these activities may have to be rethought. The data remind us that we cannot make any clear-cut statements about gender and task differentiation. Moreover, space and activity areas have to be rethought by casting aside our own categorical thinking.

Social organization at Çatalhöyük tends to involve house-based groupings, so that cooking and storage occurred at the microlevel in this context. Hodder suggests that, in the later Neolithic, more specialized production was required and that this specialization operated at a level of organization above that of the individual household. Nevertheless, more specialization does not entail gender dominance; rather, it simply reflects burgeoning social complexity. At Çatalhöyük we can observe numerous commonalities between men and women and, concomitantly, little evidence for social marking within the domains we find familiar. But there were undoubtedly social rules and patterns that were spatially instantiated, many probably diverse, with individual houses perhaps making up their own rules. Such highly localized societal patterns are invisible to modern observers, and in the absence of interpretive certainty, we have tended to read our own cultural presuppositions into the archaeological data rather than consider the possibilities of cultural difference.

Toward Nonreductive Accounts of Gender in Prehistory

Reductive accounts of gendered relations in prehistory have been created and promoted by archaeologists, feminists, and goddess worshipers alike— whether structured to prioritize women (through matriarchal or goddess-centered accounts) or men (by accruing more prestige to so-called male activities such as hunting or objects such as weapons). For the most part, the veracity of both narratives remains unquestioned and unproblematized. This is true within both academic and public discourses. For instance, when new findings at Çatalhöyük were released to the Turkish press in 2001, the subsequent reports swung like a pendulum between the poles of male power and female power. And thus a pervasive dualistic framework of gender relations remained intact, irrespective of the contrary claims made by archaeologists (Ian Hodder, personal communication). A thin veneer of essentialism and normativity imbues all such accounts with a kind of commonsense explanatory power. As Marilyn Strathern argues, "if one cannot understand the lives of 'women' without also understanding the lives of 'men,' and vice versa, it is also the case that one cannot understand academic feminist practice without appreciating its double relationship to liberation politics on the one hand and to critiques of modernity on the other" (1995: 100).

Ironically, as I am writing this piece in Britain, I am surrounded by the ever popular "reality programs" and "survivor shows" that permeate millennial television. The most intriguing example aims to replicate a prehistoric experience of village life, entitled *Surviving the Iron Age*. Supposedly based on ordinary life in the early Iron Age and set on an archaeological site somewhere in Britain, the program reaffirms the notion that the past is a foreign country (Lowenthal 1985), one that we can visit and relive through techniques of simulation. And even after decades of scholarship, the same old gender stereotypes were affirmed: women were still looking after children, taking care of the cooking, and setting traps (unsuccessfully) for small animals. They were still expected to assume the primary nurturing role. Even the idea of having a female "chief" (a middle-aged woman called Anne) still played into narratives of a matriarchal past. Alternatively, men collected wood, lit fires, forged metal, and crafted goods from wood and metal. By reiterating the specific accounts of prehistory outlined above, proposed by writers as diverse as Bachofen and Mellaart, gender and social stereotypes remain entrenched in the new millennium.

There are, I believe, fundamental problems with many of the precepts underlying goddess narratives and with their use of archaeological evidence and accounts of prehistoric life. These problems rest with the portrayal of women in terms of limiting Cartesian categories and with the representation of men as the sole cause of social malaise and global degradation, to name but two indictments aimed at men. Following Sherry Ortner (1996: 137), I would argue that, in overemphasizing social difference based on gender irrespective of context, archaeologists like Gimbutas have created serious mystifications, blinding themselves to the situations that men and women shared in the past. There are real problems in thinking about women and men purely as political opposites in any context, past or present. Gimbutas not only presupposed gender opposition but also naturalized gendered difference in her desire to foreground matriarchy. Yet, if we have learned anything from the feminist endeavor, it is to create an interpretive space that does not require that women be seen reductively as a "natural" class of being, defined primarily by their bodies and sexuality.

Acknowledgments

My thanks to the volume editors for their incisive comments and to Ian Hodder for information concerning the recent excavations at Çatalhöyük. An earlier version of this chapter appeared in *Archaeological Dialogues* in 1998. I would also like to thank Daniel Puertas for his help in preparing the manuscript.

Notes

1. Many feminists have actively challenged this constitution of the self, specifically its linkage between nature and woman (see Gatens 1996; Grosz 1994; Ortner 1996).

2. Gimbutas's revision of prehistory represents another search for origins, an etiological trope that has been vigorously critiqued by feminists themselves for being an androcentric paradigm (e.g., Brown 1993; Conkey and Tringham 1995).

References

Braidotti, Rosi. 1991. *Patterns of Dissonance: A Study of Women in Contemporary Philosophy*. Cambridge: Polity Press.

Brown, S. 1993. Feminist Research in Archaeology. What Does It Mean? Why Is It Taking So Long? In *Feminist Theory and the Classics*, ed. N. S. Rabinowitz and A. Richlin, pp. 238–71. New York: Routledge.

Butler, Judith. 1993. *Bodies That Matter: On the Discursive Limits of "Sex."* New York: Routledge.

Conkey, Margaret W., and Jane D. Spector. 1984. Archaeology and the Study of Gender. *Advances in Archaeological Method and Theory* 7: 1–38.

Conkey, Margaret W., and Ruth E. Tringham. 1995. Archaeology and the Goddess: Exploring the Contours of Feminist Archaeology. In *Feminisms in the Academy*, ed. Donna C. Stanton and Abigail J. Stewart, pp. 199–247. Ann Arbor: University of Michigan Press.

Conkey, Margaret W., and Sarah H. Williams. 1991. Original Narratives: The Political Economy of Gender in Archaeology. In *Gender at the Crossroads of Knowledge*, ed. Micaela di Leonardo, pp. 102–39. Berkeley and Los Angeles: University of California Press.

Eisler, Riane. 1991. The Goddess of Nature and Spirituality: An Ecomanifesto. In *In All Her Names: Explorations of the Feminine in Divinity*, ed. Joseph Campbell and Charles Musés, pp. 3–23. San Francisco: HarperSanFrancisco.

———. 1995. *Sacred Pleasure: Sex, Myth, and the Politics of the Body*. New York: HarperCollins.

Eller, Cynthia. 1995. *Living in the Lap of the Goddess*. Boston: Beacon Press.

———. 2000. *The Myth of Matriarchal Prehistory*. Boston: Beacon Press.

Frazer, James. [1922] 1993. *The Golden Bough*. Ware: Wordsworth Editions.

Fromm, Erich. 1997. *Love, Sexuality, and Matriarchy: About Gender*. New York: Fromm International.

Gatens, Moira. 1994. The Dangers of a Woman-Centred Philosophy. In *The Polity Reader in Gender Studies*, pp. 93–107. Cambridge: Polity Press.

———. 1996. *The Imaginary Bodies*. London: Routledge.

Getty, Adele. 1990. *Goddess: Mother of Living Nature*. London: Thames and Hudson.

Gimbutas, Marija. 1982. *The Goddesses and Gods of Old Europe*. Berkeley and Los Angeles: University of California Press.

———. 1989. *The Language of the Goddess: Unearthing Hidden Symbols of Western Civilisation*. London: Thames and Hudson.

———. 1991. *The Civilization of the Goddess: The World of Old Europe*. San Francisco: HarperSanFrancisco.

Grosz, Elizabeth. 1994. *Volatile Bodies: Toward a Corporeal Feminism*. Bloomington: Indiana University Press.

Haaland, Gunnar, and Randi Haaland. 1995. Who Speaks the Goddess's Language? Imagination and Method in Archaeological Research. *Norwegian Archaeological Review* 28: 105–21.

Hamilakis, Yannis. 1999. *La trahison des archéologues?* Archaeological Practice as Intellectual Activity in Postmodernity. *Journal of Mediterranean Archaeology* 12: 60–79.

Hamilton, Naomi. 1996. Figurines, Clay Balls, Small Finds and Burials. In Hodder 1996: 215–63.

Hodder, Ian. 1997. Always Momentary, Fluid and Flexible: Towards a Reflexive Excavation Methodology. *Antiquity* 71: 691–700.

———. 1998. The Past and Passion and Play: Çatalhöyük as a Site of Conflict in the Construction of Multiple Pasts. In *Archaeology under Fire: Nationalism, Politics and Heritage in the Eastern Mediterranean and Middle East*, ed. Lynn M. Meskell, pp. 124–39. London: Routledge.

———. 1999. *The Archaeological Process: An Introduction*. Oxford: Blackwell.

———. 2001. Symbolism and the Origins of Agriculture in the Near East. *Cambridge Archaeological Journal* 11: 107–12.

Hodder, Ian, ed. 1996. *On the Surface: Çatalhöyük, 1993–1995*. Cambridge: McDonald Institute for Archaeological Research. 2000. *Towards Reflexive Method in Archaeology: The Example at Çatalhöyük*. Cambridge: McDonald Institute for Archaeological Research.

Hurcomb, L. 1995. Our Own Engendered Species. *Antiquity* 69: 87–100.

Hutton, Ronald. 1997. The Neolithic Great Goddess: A Study in Modern Tradition. *Antiquity* 71: 91–99.

Keller, Mara L. 1997. The Interface of Archaeology and Mythology: A Philosophical Evaluation of the Gimbutas Paradigm. In *From the Realm of the Ancestors: An Anthology in Honor of Marija Gimbutas*, ed. Joan Marler, pp. 381–98. Manchester, CT: Knowledge, Ideas, and Trends.

Last, Jonathan. 1998. A Design for Life: Interpreting the Art of Çatalhöyük. *Journal of Material Culture* 3: 355–78.

Lloyd, Genevieve. 1993. *The Man of Reason: "Male" and "Female" in Western Philosophy*. London: Routledge.

Lobell, Mimi. 1997. Gender-Based Paradigms in Archaeology. In *From the Realm of the Ancestors: An Anthology in Honor of Marija Gimbutas*, ed. Joan Marler, pp. 371–80. Manchester, CT: Knowledge, Ideas, and Trends.

Lowenthal, David. 1985. *The Past Is a Foreign Country*. Cambridge: Cambridge University Press.

March, Artemis. 1997. Old European Ontology: Unlocking the Quantum Systems beneath Our Dead Sociologies. In *From the Realm of the Ancestors: An Anthology in Honor of Marija Gimbutas,* ed. Joan Marler, pp. 356–70. Manchester, CT: Knowledge, Ideas, and Trends.

Mellaart, James. 1964. Excavations at Çatal Hüyük, 1963. *Anatolian Studies* 14: 39–119.

———. 1965. *Earliest Civilizations of the Near East.* London: Thames and Hudson.

———. 1975. *The Neolithic of the Near East.* London: Thames and Hudson.

Merchant, Carol. 1995. *Earthcare: Women and the Environment.* London: Routledge.

Meskell, Lynn M. 1995. Goddesses, Gimbutas and New Age Archaeology. *Antiquity* 69: 74–86.

———. 1998a. Oh My Goddess: Ecofeminism, Sexuality and Archaeology. *Archaeological Dialogues* 5: 126–42.

———. 1998b. Twin Peaks: The Archaeologies of Çatalhöyük. In *Ancient Goddesses: The Myths and Evidence,* ed. Christine Morris and Linda Goodison, pp. 46–62. London: British Museum Press.

———. 1999a. *Archaeologies of Social Life: Age, Sex, Class, etc. in Ancient Egypt.* Oxford: Blackwell.

———. 1999b. Feminism, Paganism, Pluralism. In *Archaeology and Folklore,* ed. Amy Gazin-Schwartz and Cornelius J. Holtorf, pp. 83–90. London: Routledge.

Moser, Stephanie, ed. 1998. *Ancestral Images: The Iconography of Human Origins.* Gloucestershire: Sutton.

Mutén, Bernadette, ed. 1994. *Return of the Great Goddess.* Dublin: Gill and Macmillan.

New, C. 1996. Man Bad, Woman Good? Essentialism and Ecofeminisms. *New Left Review* 216: 79–93.

Ortner, Sherry B. 1996. *Making Gender: The Politics and Erotics of Culture.* Boston: Beacon.

Pollack, Rachel. 1993. The Body of the Goddess. In *Uncoiling the Snake: Ancient Patterns i n Contemporary Women's Lives,* ed. Vicki Noble, pp. 99–117. San Francisco: Harper SanFrancisco.

Seager, Joni. 1994. *Earth Follies.* London: Routledge.

Soja, Edward W. 2000. *Postmetropolis: Critical Studies of Cities and Regions.* Oxford: Blackwell.

Strathern, Marilyn. 1995. Nostalgia and the New Genetics. In *Rhetorics of Self-Making,* ed. Debbora Battaglia, pp. 97–120. Berkeley and Los Angeles: University of California Press.

Talalay, Lauren E. 1994. A Feminist Boomerang: The Great Goddess of Greek Prehistory. *Gender and History* 6: 165–83.

———. 1999. Review of Marija Gimbutas, *The Living Goddesses. Bryn Mawr Classical Review,* October 5, electronic issue.

Taylor, Timothy. 1996. *The Prehistory of Sex: Four Million Years of Human Sexual Culture.* London: 4th Estate.

Todd, Ian A. 1976. *Çatal Hüyük in Perspective.* Menlo Park, CA: Cummings Publishing.

Tringham, Ruth. 1991. Households with Faces: The Challenge of Gender in Prehistoric Architectural Remains. In *Engendering Archaeology: Women and Prehistory,* ed. Joan Gero and Margaret W. Conkey, pp. 93–131. Oxford: Blackwell.

Wason, Paul K. 1994. *The Archaeology of Rank.* Cambridge: Cambridge University Press.

———. 1980. The Straight Mind. *Feminist Issues* 1: 103–10.

PART III

Putting Genes
in Context

CHAPTER 8

Context and Complexity in Human Biological Research

Thomas Leatherman and Alan Goodman

BIOLOGICAL ANTHROPOLOGY takes as its object of study human biological variation in the past and present. It draws on method and theory from reductionist sciences such as evolutionary ecology, molecular biology, and physiology. Yet biological anthropology also has a home in anthropology—a holistic and humanistic discipline that recognizes the diversity and complexity inherent in social and cultural systems—and practices an ethnographic approach that attends to everyday life experiences. As a subdiscipline, biological anthropology thus provides a unique experiment in bridging C. P. Snow's (1959) two cultures: the scientific and the humanistic.

The basic assumption of this chapter is that complex biology/behavior and human/environment interactions cannot be adequately understood using only reductionist approaches that try to explain such interactions as the product of a small number of independent and autonomous factors. A more adequate biocultural approach must also take the "cultural" side of the equation seriously by situating local peoples and environments within global and historical contexts, and by examining social and behavioral variation in relation to structures of power that shape the way people interact with their environments, cultures, and each other.

In this chapter, we first outline basic aspects of reductionism, oversimplification, and determinism in biological anthropology. We then provide two examples to highlight how reductive oversimplifications can limit our understanding of human biology. We argue that attention to the dialectical relationship between people and their environments and to the contexts and dynamics of local-global interactions provides a more integrated, socially contextualized, and ultimately more relevant understanding of human biology.

Reductionisms, Complexities, and Contexts

Reductionist approaches in anthropology attempt to explain biological, be-havioral, and social phenomena by the operation of a few invariant factors and processes. For example, racial affiliation was long thought to predict bi-ological constitution and behavior. Indeed, diseases such as hypertension, osteoporosis, and diabetes are still discussed in direct reference to race. To-day, the genome is metaphorically characterized as the "blueprint" for building the organism,[1] and genetic differences are given primacy as expla-nations for biobehavioral variations. External meteorological conditions such as extreme cold, heat, and high-altitude hypoxia have been proposed as primary determinants of patterns of child growth and adult morphology (understood as adaptations), largely apart from other intervening factors such as nutritional status. The Cartesian model, which metaphorically treats the operation of the body like a machine, and the reductionist methods that follow from it have been highly successful, but they have also tended to ig-nore a range of contexts (hence contributing factors) that we believe need to be included in analyses, and therefore, they have restricted the sorts of ques-tions we ask. It is this restriction of questions, contexts, and analyses that limits the utility of reductionist approaches.

There are three main components of reductionist methodologies with which we take issue. First, the phenomenon in question—for example, the body or the ecosystem—is broken down into its constituent parts, each taken as an independent and autonomous unit. The whole is taken as the sum of the parts, and ideally the whole can be explained by the functional characteristics of one or a few of its most important fundamental units. The operation of the parts then takes on determinative qualities in cause-and-effect relationships. Thus, germs or pathogens cause disease; the carrying capacity of an environment is determined by the least abundant, "limiting factor"; and disease, depression, and even risk taking are explained as a function of genes. In this view, the most elegant explanation is the sim-plest—that is, the one reduced to the smallest, most segregated, and auton-omous units. And an even higher goal of biobehavioral reductionism is the development of deterministic equations and universal laws of causation.

Second, reductionist evolutionary and ecological science separates or "alienates" the organism from its environment. As Smith and Thomas put it: "This is an analysis where the natural environment and organism assume an independent and dependent variable relationship, and where finding out how the parts work is expected to lead us to the dynamics of the whole. Thus, the organism is seen mostly as a passive adjuster to environmental conditions it cannot really control" (1998: 461). This is an alienated view of human-organism interaction and of adaptation in that it assumes that there is a fixed, local, and external world and that individuals simply react to it and are molded by it. It also follows that human-environment interactions can be studied as relatively closed independent systems apart from global and regional connections.

Third, following from the above, a reductive simplification in the representation of complex and differentiated features and processes occurs when categorical constructs are assumed to be relatively homogeneous across broad groups of people. For over half of the twentieth century, a rich array of biological variation was reduced and simplified to a handful of racial categories. Likewise, varying degrees of wealth, poverty, and even social inequality are often categorized in terms of tripartite rankings of socio-economic status (SES). In "modernization" approaches to studying the biological correlates of social change, individuals, households, and communities differentially involved in complex social and economic changes associated with the spread of capitalism into less capitalized areas are categorized as "traditional" versus "modern." Such reductive simplifications are often found in statistical analyses that seek to "control for" a number of environmental and social factors while seeking the influence of a single, independent biological factor. But can we really account for the social environment (and thereby remove it from consideration) by controlling for "occupation," "years of education," or "socioeconomic status" and thereby conclude that intelligence, disease, or infant mortality rates are primarily determined by racial or genetic characters?

The approach we advocate, in contrast, pays attention to both the specifics of local human-environment interactions and to the need for situating people and environments in broader global processes. In dealing with the subject matter of biological anthropology and evolutionary biology, the metaphor of the "triple helix" (Lewontin 2001) is particularly useful. The triple helix calls attention to the dynamic interactions of genes, organisms, and their environment. First, genes provide input, but in no way do they compute organisms; rather, organisms use the information they provide to construct themselves in specific environmental contexts (2001: 17). A great deal of random developmental noise is involved in translating genetic information to body parts and processes, and hence to the entire organism (2001: 36, 38). Second, organisms do not simply react to an autonomous external environment; they interact with nature, selecting relevant resources and modifying the environment as they construct niches (2001: 51). Just as there is no organism without an environmental niche, so there is no niche without an organism. The relationship between organism and environment is a *dialectical* one of codetermination—that is, each is mutually constituted in the other, and both organism and environment are at once subject and object (Levins and Lewontin 1985). This interaction (and the relative survival and reproductive success of individuals), in turn, influences gene frequencies.

A starting point for any biocultural approach is a conceptual understanding of humanity's place in nature. Eric Wolf summarizes such an understanding in rephrasing Marx's concept of mode of production: "The human species is an outgrowth of natural processes; at the same time the species is naturally social. The human species is, however, not merely a passive product of natural processes; it has also in the course of evolution acquired the ability to transform nature to human use" (1982: 73). In transforming nature (through the production process) humans transform themselves—by developing specific modes and relations of production and by building webs of social relationships, institutions, practices, and beliefs. The point is that humans are not only part of nature but also intensely social. To deal adequately with the social dimension, moreover, it is critical to locate it within broad historical contexts.

Thus, a more synthetic biocultural approach must reconnect the parts with the whole and recognize subjects of study as actors in their own history. It must place human biology and its study in historical, economic, cultural, and ideological contexts. It must take culture seriously—attending both to how it structures material reality and people's lived experiences *and* to how it shapes the questions we ask and the interpretations we make. *assumptions*

Using such an approach, we can clarify how genes or pathogens and other insults might best be seen as contributing *agents* as opposed to *causes* of disease (Lewontin 2001; Singer 1989). The cause of disease prevalence in a particular group ultimately lies in the social, biological, and environmental conditions that increase *exposure to* pathogens, as well as unhealthy and unhygienic environments, stress, food insecurity (and malnutrition), and other factors that reduce disease resistance and that limit access to health care and other means of coping with health problems when they arise. Hence, poverty, discrimination, violence, environmental racism, and differential entitlements to land, jobs, and income, as well as other structural inequalities, are certainly as relevant "causes" of disease as the pathogens that invoke biological or psychosocial dysfunction. This is a key message in the metaphor often used by medical anthropologists when they say they need to search "upstream" for the broader causes and contexts of the origins of distress and disease (Goodman and Leatherman 1998; McKinley 1986; Scheper-Hughes 1990; Singer 1989).

In the following sections, we offer an alternative to reductive methodologies. First, taking diabetes as an example, we critique disease etiology that focuses only on a part—racialized genetics—and that fails to situate the growing epidemic of obesity and diabetes within the larger context of increasingly delocalized food systems in which the ~~most affordable~~ foods are high in sugars and fat. We then consider how this epidemic can be better comprehended, in the case of the Yucatec Maya, by attention to the commoditization of food systems, dietary change, and nutrition. We underscore the need to situate local-level analyses of individuals, households, and communities within broader social fields of power, including interregional, national, and global economies—that is, we seek to contextualize human biology.

"Race" and Disease: The Limitations of Genetic Explanations

The idea of race was invented and is constantly being maintained, reinvented, reconfigured, or rejected by scientists in the contexts of specific social and cultural ideologies, technologies, and geographic locations. While most scientists no longer see races as separate and unchanging biological types, race still frequently stands in for genetics, and genetic analyses and explanations currently dominate the study of biological variation (Goodman 1997). As chameleon-like and flexible as the idea of race is, it nonetheless remains a concept that continues to carry analytic force in anthropology and human biology. However defined, race is employed as a categorizing variable in the U.S. census, on birth and death certificates, and on the first line of patients' medical records. The deployment of a "racial discourse" in analyses of diabetes in Native Americans demonstrates the limitations of genetic and "race"-based explanations and points to the importance of considering the cultural and political-economic contexts within which such a disease manifests itself.

Two reductionisms are necessary to accept the idea that "racial" differences in disease patterns are due to genetic differences among "races." The first reductionism involves geneticization: the belief that most biology and behavior is "in the genes." Genes, of course, are often a part of the complex web of disease causality, but they are almost always a minor, unstable, and insufficient cause. The presence of a Gm haplotype that is common in Native Americans, for example, might correlate with increased rates of diabetes in Native Americans (Knowler et al. 1988), but the causal link is unknown.

The second reductionism involves scientific racialism: the belief that races are real and useful constructs. This leap propels one from an explanation of disease variation in terms of genetic variation to one that sees differences in disease frequency as due to genetic variation among "races." To accept this reductive proposition, one must assume not only that races exist but also that most genetic variation occurs among (rather than within) "races." However, we know from the work of Lewontin (1972) and Templeton (1998)—and from the results of the Human Genome Project—that this assumption is false.

The presumption that so-called racial differences in disease are due to genetic differences illustrates the flaws in both these reductionisms. For example, the rise in diabetes among some Native Americans is often thought to be due to a genetic variation that separates Native Americans from European Americans (Weiss, Ferrell, and Hanis 1984). Along with obesity, gallstones, and heart disease, type 2 diabetes is part of what has been called a New World Syndrome (Weiss, Ferrell, and Hanis 1984). The assumption that there is a panracial syndrome helps to reify the idea of race as a bounded and homogeneous entity that is marked by genetically determined features.

In fact, there is enormous variation in diabetes rates among Native North American groups. This variation is almost as great as the variation between European groups and Native Americans. Furthermore, the rise in diabetes rates is a relatively recent phenomenon (Young 1994). Finally, other groups such as Polynesians, West Africans, and poor whites in the United States, who are all experiencing similar shifts in diet and physical activity (from complex carbohydrates to colas, from rigorous exercise to inactivity), have experienced similar increases in the rates of the same diseases that are part of the New World Syndrome. Rather than fatalistically assuming that diabetes is "in our blood," as the Pima have (Kozak 1996), it would be more productive to contextualize the rising incidence of diabetes within a changing political economy that has reverberations in changing diet, activity patterns, ideas about health, and disease rates.

Combined with geneticization, racialization can be deadly in practice—a sort of ideological iatrogenesis, a disease produced by contact with Western medicine. To label the Native American epidemic of diabetes, obesity, heart disease, and related conditions as a *racial syndrome* focuses causality and research dollars on genetics rather than larger cultural and political-economic factors. For those who suffer from these diseases, it encourages both fatalism and the hope that a miracle cure will be found sometime in the future through genetic medicine. But what if we looked at the etiology of these chronic diseases in the interconnections of developing bodies, local conditions, and globalizing processes? What understandings might be produced if we began to call these conditions "diseases of mal-development"?[2]

The "Coca-colonization" of Diets in the Yucatan

The Maya of Mexico's Yucatan Peninsula are one of the populations cited as examples of the epidemic of obesity and diabetes among Native Americans.

Indeed, studies from urban locales such as Merida find a substantial number of men and women—over 50 percent—either clinically overweight or obese (Arroyo et al. 1999; Bastarrachea-Sosa, Laviada-Molina, and Vargas-Ancona 2001; Dickinson et al. 1993). Diabetes has become the fourth leading cause of death in this region (Arroyo et al. 1999). We argue that the etiology of these chronic diseases is best understood not in terms of genetic risk but rather in relation to larger political-economic and cultural forces that shape food systems and dietary change on the local level. Specifically, we situate the changing patterns of diet, nutrition, and health in Mayan communities in the context of the global tourism industry and the ways in which individuals, households, and communities differentially experience tourism-led development.

To be discussing problems of *overnutrition* among the Yucatec Maya is something new: the Maya have frequently and correctly been depicted as economically marginal, impoverished, and *undernourished* (Bastarrachea-Sosa, Laviada-Molina, and Vargas-Ancona 2001). Indeed, studies of Maya child growth—one key indicator of community-level nutrition—have shown severe stunting (low height-for-age), with little change in stature between the 1930s and early 1980s (Daltabuit 1988; Leatherman, Stillman, and Goodman 2000). Increases in both heights and weights occurred in the 1980s and mid-1990s (Leatherman, Stillman, and Goodman 2000; Gurri, Balam, and Moran 2001), yet indications of chronic undernutrition persist—suggesting that the caloric content in diets has increased but dietary quality has not. Moreover, alongside indications of childhood malnutrition there is adult obesity, a situation that Dickinson and coworkers have termed the "double-edged sword of malnutrition" (1993: 315). How has this pattern of "undernutrition" coupled with "overnutrition" emerged in the Yucatan?

A notable aspect of tourism development is the commoditization of food systems, that is, the increased distribution and consumption of commercialized foods, including junk foods. Thus, a proximate answer to the above question would cite a trend toward high fat and sugar consumption typical of Western diets. Yet, to gloss dietary trends as "Westernization" misses the local and regional dynamics of food systems and diets that are the result of processes linked to tourism-based social and economic change.

"Westernization" of the Yucatecan diet is one form of what has been called "dietary delocalization," a process whereby local peoples consume foods produced outside the region (Pelto and Pelto 1983). Since ancient times, trade, internal colonization, and migration have promoted the exchange of foods across regions. After 1492 such exchanges became worldwide as well as regional, and more recently, dietary delocalization has been linked increasingly to global and regional economic development and to the commoditization of food systems and diets (Dewey 1989; Pelto and Pelto 1983). Shifts from locally produced to marketed and commercialized foods have been associated with increased dietary diversity and improved levels of nutrition in industrialized nations (Pelto and Pelto 1983), and at least for some sectors of the population, such shifts have provided a nutritional rationale for economic development. However, growth in the commoditization of foodstuffs typically also means higher market prices that stress the budgets of the poor, thereby resulting in a decreased diversity of foods and nutrients in local diets. Junk foods, including sodas and colas, are highly advertised, widely available, inexpensive, and prominently displayed in local stores. When funds are limited, poor Mayans may reach for these foods, which are high in sugars, calories, and fats, but little else.

Thus, our assessment of changing food systems, nutrition, and health in the context of tourism-based economic and social transformations begins with the identification of contradictions. Child growth has improved somewhat but nutritional deficiencies persist, and at the same time there is an epidemic of obesity and diabetes in adults. Commoditization of food systems can lead to an overall increase in food availability and consumption, but it can also heighten inequalities in access and detrimentally affect nutrition and health. From our perspective, these contradictions reveal how the social, cultural, and health impacts of tourism-led development are distributed unevenly and experienced unequally among Mayan communities, families, and individuals. This variation reflects the way in which communities, households, and individuals articulate with local production systems and with the tourism-based economy.

GLOBAL CONTEXTS AND LOCAL DIETARY CHANGE

Throughout much of the developing world, nations are turning to tourism as a means of attracting foreign capital and generating economic development. Mexico leads this trend in Latin America, and the primary destination for tourists in Mexico is the Caribbean coast of the Yucatan Peninsula. Over the last three decades, this region has experienced a transformation from one of the most economically marginal areas of Mexico into a tourist bonanza. Cancun, the center of this development, grew from a fishing village of 426 inhabitants in the early 1970s to become, by the early 1990s, the state's most important city, numbering over 400,000 people (Daltabuit and Leatherman 1998).

This development has been an unqualified economic success for the Mexican government, and even more so for foreign investors. But such rapid and totalizing development does not come without costs to local populations (Pi-Sunyer and Thomas 1997; Daltabuit and Leatherman 1998). As environmental resources, labor, and food become increasingly commoditized and as symbols of prestige become increasingly Western, substantial disruptions to local patterns of life are inevitable.

Our concern here is with one form of change: the commoditization of food systems and the way it might be linked to the dietary changes and contradictory patterns of nutrition and health that have emerged in the Yucatan. To examine these links, we studied food systems, diet, and nutrition in several Mayan communities that differ in subsistence base and articulation with the tourist industry. One set of communities (Akumal and Ciudad Chemuyil) comprises service villages to a popular resort on the Caribbean coast. The local economy here is based on wage work and small-scale commerce. There are no agricultural lands and little land for home gardens; thus, households are totally dependent on local markets for their food. Coba is an inland farming village with direct local involvement in the tourist economy through archaeotourism. Yalcoba, another inland farming community, has little direct exposure to tourists but experiences substantial out-migration of men to Cancun on a weekly basis, primarily for work in construction.[3]

DIETARY DELOCALIZATION AND FOOD COMMODITIZATION IN CONTEXTS OF CHANGE

While all communities in the Yucatan are increasingly consuming foods from farther and farther away, the nature of changing food systems is markedly different for the coastal and inland communities. In the coastal communities, a fully commercialized system is now in place. Most foods are purchased year-round from local stores and traveling vendors that often specialize in particular foodstuffs from different growing regions. In the two inland communities, products from local slash-and-burn milpa agriculture (primarily corn, beans, and squash) and home gardens are key components of many households' diets, at least for part of the year. By the mid-1980s, however, Daltabuit (1988) had already noted for Yalcoba the decreased consumption of local foods, such as honey, tubers, posole, and wild meat, and an increased consumption of commercial foodstuffs, including rice, pasta, sodas, and snack foods.

This trend was accentuated in the 1990s. Even maize and beans, two key staples, are now imported and purchased from government-subsidized stores or small local variety stores (*tiendas*). Compared to ten years ago, the varieties of food are greater but they come at high prices. As one resident of Coba said, "there are more foods available now, but no money to buy them." The experience of change is thus unequal: many informants in Coba and Yalcoba view the past twenty years as a time of steadily decreasing food availability, while others see it as a time of growth in opportunity and consumption.

Shifts in the local food systems have occurred in the context of a decline in milpa production, a shift toward wage work, and an expansion of local and global markets and of commercialized foods in the regional economy. A common complaint in both inland communities is that the productivity of local communal (*ejido*) lands has decreased markedly in the past several decades. Very few families grow enough corn to last a year, and many of the households more fully engaged in wage work or commercial enterprises no longer plant their fields or else hire someone to plant for them. Mayan youths now prefer to seek their fortune in Cancun rather than in the milpa. Some speak of the drudgery of the *trabajo rudo* (coarse, rough work) of the milpa and hope for a future in the service and construction jobs to be found at tourist centers.

Despite a continued practice of patrilocal residence, some young families supported by wage work have ceased to pool resources and labor or even to share food and meal preparation with their parents and in-laws. The young welcome this social independence, but for their parents it signifies an erosion of the very meaning of family and community. Thus, Pi-Sunyer and Thomas (1997) speak of tourism as a "totalizing" experience that impacts not only the way people produce and consume but also the core fabric of social and cultural life.

The most dramatic aspect of commercialization of food systems in the region is the pervasive presence of Coke, Pepsi, and a variety of chips, cookies, candies, and other snack foods—known locally as *comidas chatarros* (junk foods). Mexico is one of the world's largest consumers of soft drinks, accounting for over 20 percent of Pepsi's and 15 percent of Coke's international sales (Jabbonsky 1993). Indeed, the Mexican market is so important that it is the site of an ongoing "Cola War" between Coke and Pepsi. Company executives see it as a fight over the "stomach share" of the Mexican people. Coke's goal and company slogan is "an arm's length from desire"—to make Coke available at every corner in every town or village in every part of Mexico. Pepsico has waged its version of the Cola War using a strategy of "the Power of One." This entails marketing Pepsi in conjunction with junk foods, and indeed Pepsico's logo is found on most of the chips, cookies, candies, and other processed snack foods prominently displayed in *tiendas*. As this fight for "stomach share" intensifies, we can expect to see an even greater penetration of sodas and snack foods into the diets of the Yucatec Maya.

DIET AND NUTRITION

As shifts in food systems unfold at the intersection of global and local economies, so also do local diets and nutrition. Using a food-frequency questionnaire (see Leatherman and Goodman, in press), we assessed food and nutrient intakes in the coastal and inland communities. We also compared nutrient profiles in households from Yalcoba that have steady employment in the tourist economy with those of households that rely more on subsistence production and irregular wage work to meet basic needs. This comparison sought to further register differential experiences in the local and tourist economies and their impacts on diet and nutrition.

The leading food categories in the diets of the communities we studied were tortillas, fats (oil and lard), sodas, snacks and sugar, beans, meat, and rice or pasta. We found that people in the coastal communities and inland residents with steady wage employment consume half the tortillas and over twice the fruits, meat, dairy, and junk foods of those in the inland communities without steady employment. Although sugar and junk foods accounted for 16 percent of calories in the coastal communities and around 10 percent in the inland communities, these calculations are underestimates because our dietary surveys recorded primarily foods eaten in the household, and most sodas and snacks are consumed away from home. Local sales of soft drinks reflected an average per capita consumption of one soda per day in inland communities and at least 50 percent more in the coastal communities. School-aged children in Yalcoba reported average weekly intakes of over seven soft drinks and ten snack foods (e.g., chips or cookies). During school breaks, it was typical for children to buy a soda and a snack, amounting to about 350 calories, or a fifth of a child's daily caloric requirement (Daltabuit 1988; McGarty 1995). The marketing of chips and sweets in one-peso packages—something everyone can afford—encouraged the choice of these foods.

We found that the diets in all the communities were fairly adequate for macronutrients—carbohydrates, fats, and protein—but exhibited micronutrient deficiencies that can affect both nutrition and growth. The coastal and inland households with steady employment consumed more high-quality animal protein and also exhibited a better micronutrient profile; only the mineral zinc was deficient. In the inland community of Coba we found deficiencies of zinc and vitamins B_2 (riboflavin), B_{12} (cobalamin), and A. In addition, poorer Yalcoba households without steady incomes, reliant on irregular wage work and marginal milpa production, experienced deficiencies in vitamins A and C as well as in the B vitamins and zinc.

These potential micronutrient deficiencies gain importance in the context of diets high in maize and junk foods. Plant-based diets, high in fiber and phytates, are associated with increased requirements and low bioavailability of a number of micronutrients such as zinc, iron, calcium, and vitamin B_{12} (Allen, Backstrand, and Stanek 1992; Calloway et al. 1993). Thus, when the remaining nonmaize calories come from sugar, soft drinks, and snack foods, micronutrient status inexorably worsens.

In sum, food consumption patterns in these communities reflect an increased level of fats, sugars, and other foods with "empty calories" (i.e., with few nutrients) in the diet—the sort of diet often associated with increases in obesity and diabetes. When coupled with poor nutritional quality, such as the micronutrient deficiencies we found, such a diet could contribute to the pattern of stunted but heavy individuals found in studies of adult obesity in the Yucatan (Bastarrachea-Sosa, Laviada-Molina, and Vargas-Ancona 2001; Dickinson et al. 1993).

THE DOUBLE-EDGED SWORD OF MALNUTRITION

Our research bears out Dickinson's description of a "double-edged sword" in the Yucatan, whereby undernourished and stunted children grow up to be obese adults (Dickinson et al. 1993: 315). Children in Yalcoba are growing taller but are still stunted by Mexican and international standards of growth (Leatherman and Goodman, in press). This may well reflect persistent micronutrient deficiencies, since caloric intakes appear to be adequate. An analysis of adult weights collected from clinic records in Yalcoba in the 1990s found that about 40 percent of the men were overweight and 10 percent obese, and that 64 percent of the women were overweight and 20 percent obese (Leatherman and Goodman, in press). While these rates of obesity are not as high as in urban areas of the Yucatan, where obesity and diabetes have reached epidemic proportions (Bastarrachea-Sosa, Laviada-Molina, and Vargas-Ancona 2001), the trends are clearly moving in that direction.

The Yucatan, historically an area of persistent hunger and malnutrition, is now the site of an epidemic of overnutrition—of obesity and diabetes. Diets with limited nutritional quality but high in calorie-dense foods, such as sodas and snack foods, are associated with overweight individuals in urban locales (Bastarrachea-Sosa, Laviada-Molina, and Vargas-Ancona 2001), and this appears increasingly to be the case in the communities we studied as well. The Cola Wars and consumption of junk foods show no sign of slowing, and the emerging pattern of childhood undernutrition and adult overnutrition is a serious threat to well-being. These dietary changes are a product of the commoditization and commercialization of foods linked to a growing tourist economy, and they are differentially experienced—for better and for worse—by communities, households, and individuals depending upon their position within this economy.

To return to the larger themes of reductionism and complexities, our point is that the changing biological realities and lived experiences in the Yucatan are shaped by the intersection of global and local processes of change, and that individuals experience and respond to these changes unequally and in different ways. Perspectives that homogenize global transformations into monolithic entities such as "Westernization" or "modernization"—and that essentialize how the Yucatecan population experiences these transformations—cannot comprehend the contradictions that define the culture, biology, and health of these and similar groups worldwide.

Contexts and Complexities

Biocultural anthropologists today face a set of tensions that are difficult to resolve. To what extent do we follow the simplifying assumptions of a mechanistic and reductionist natural science and so earn our "science" credentials (and funding)? Can we remain true to the founding principles of holism and recognize the diversity and complexity inherent in social and cultural systems? Do we ignore new ideas that are seemingly antithetical to dominant positions in the field, or do we take seriously theoretical developments in anthropology that might open up new lines of inquiry and new avenues of dialogue? These tensions are not limited to biological and biocultural anthropologists, but they are especially challenging for those committed to connecting biology and culture.

The evolutionary and ecological frameworks that have guided biological anthropology over the past three decades provide an incomplete framework for inquiry into many of the factors shaping human biology now and in the future. They may help us detail some of the consequences of global economic change such as increased inequalities in wealth and health, environmental degradation, impaired production, heightened food insecurity, and the growing numbers of displaced peoples and communities ravaged by new and resurgent diseases. But, they will not, in themselves, provide sufficient and satisfying explanations of how such problems arise, why some groups are more vulnerable than others, or how the consequences and responses to such conditions set the stage for future change. We will need to expand our theories, the kinds of questions we ask, and the range of contexts we examine.

In this chapter, we have argued that reductionist approaches to the explanation of biology and behavior restrict possible research questions, oversimplify measurement and analysis, and ignore the broader contexts and social dynamics of human-environment interaction. First, such approaches break down environmental systems into constituent parts for analyses but rarely put them back together so as to obtain a picture of the whole or a description of how the parts relate to the whole. Second, they tend to essentialize variables and processes as autonomous and "natural"—de-historicized and alienated from their interactions with other components of the system. Such naturalized processes are often seen as inevitable and as af-fecting all members of a population in the same way. Rarely, do environ-mental descriptions include extralocal (interregional, national, global) pro-cesses that influence local-level environments or confront the complexities of human-environment interactions. And even when we do attempt to ex-plain biology in terms of social factors such as social inequalities, we fail to ask what created these inequalities and why some people are more vulner-able than others. Third, human-environment interaction is too often viewed as a one-way process whereby autonomous external environments stimulate adaptive responses. In this view, people are often treated as passive agents who adjust and accommodate to environmental variations rather than participate in constructing the environments in which they operate (Leatherman 1996, 1998; Lewontin 1995).

Thus, we advocate for a different approach—one that investigates the dialectics of human-environment interactions. Just as the environment makes humans, so the environment is human made—made by direct phys-ical manipulation and *made relevant* by the cultural meanings humans as-sign it. Resources are not just "out there" but are made relevant as people mobilize them within a framework of cultural meanings and as they become sites of power struggles over who will or will not control them. Global-local interactions need to be part of environmental analyses, and social dimen-sions of biological variation need to be analyzed in terms of relations of power, not taken as natural. Indeed, whatever the unit of analysis may be—individuals, households, communities, populations, or others—this unit is always embedded in webs of relationships, which are directly and indirectly tied to both local and global systems and histories. If we cannot acknowl-edge these broad connections and frame our questions and interpretations within them, how can we hope that our analyses will have relevance in the real world?

Notes

1. Lewontin, however, argues that the current idea that "the development of an individual is the unfolding of a genetic program immanent in the fertilized egg" (2001: 17) is not much different from the eighteenth-century preformationist notions that viewed the organism's de-

velopment as the unfolding and enlarging of the miniature person (called a homunculus) contained in the sperm. He states, "there is no essential difference, but only one of mechanical details, between the view that the organism is already formed in the fertilized egg, and the view that the complete blueprint of the organism and all the information necessary to specify it is contained there, a view that dominates modern studies of development" (2001: 6).

2. Here we refer to the consequences of economic and social development that affect people's diet and activity level (i.e., overnutrition and underactivity). However, by "maldevelopment" we can also refer to problems of physiological growth and development that result from these broader social changes. Recent proposals of a "thrifty phenotype hypothesis" (in contrast to a "thrifty genotype") suggest that the physiological development of a malnourished fetus and infant increases the risk of obesity and non-insulin-dependent diabetes mellitus (NIDDM; type 2) later in life (Hales and Barker 1992).

3. We draw on research begun by Magalí Daltabuit (1988) and continued by us in collaboration with Daltabuit, other colleagues, and students (Leatherman and Goodman, in press).

References

Allen, Lindsay, J. R. Backstrand, and E. J. Stanek. 1992. The Interactive Effects of Dietary Quality on the Growth of Young Mexican Children. *American Journal of Clinical Nutrition* 56: 353–64.

Arroyo, P., J. Pardio, V. Fernandez, L. Vargas-Ancona, G. Canul, and A. Loria. 1999. Obesity and Cultural Environment in the Yucatan Region. *Nutrition Reviews* 57(5): S78–S82.

Bastarrachea-Sosa, Raul, Hugo Laviada-Molina, and Lizardo Vargas-Ancona. 2001. La obesidad y enfermedades relacionadas con la nutricion en Yucatan. *Revista de Endocrinologia y Nutricion* 9(2): 73–76.

Calloway, Doris, S. P. Murphy, G. H. Beaton, and D. Lein. 1993. Estimated Vitamin Intakes of Toddlers: Predicted Prevalence of Inadequacy in Village Populations in Egypt, Kenya, and Mexico. *American Journal of Clinical Nutrition* 58: 376–84.

Daltabuit, Magalí. 1988. Mayan Women: Work, Nutrition and Child Care. PhD dissertation, University of Massachusetts, Amherst.

Daltabuit, Magalí, and Thomas Leatherman. 1998. The Biocultural Impact of Tourism on Mayan Communities. In *Building a New Biocultural Synthesis: Political-Economic Perspectives on Human Biology,* ed. Alan Goodman and Thomas Leatherman, pp. 317–38. Ann Arbor: University of Michigan Press.

Dewey, Katherine. 1989. Nutrition and the Commoditization of Food Systems in Latin America. *Social Science and Medicine* 28: 415–24.

Dickinson, Federico, M. T. Castillo, L. Vales, and L. Uc. 1993. Obesity and Women's Health in Two Socioeconomic Areas of Yucatan, Mexico. *Colloquia Antropologia* 2: 309–17.

Goodman, Alan. 1997. Bred in the Bone? *The Sciences,* March/April, pp. 20–25.

Goodman, Alan, and Thomas Leatherman. 1998. Traversing the Chasm between Biology and Culture: An Introduction. In *Building a New Biocultural Synthesis: Political-Economic Perspectives on Human Biology,* ed. Alan Goodman and Thomas Leatherman, pp. 3–41. Ann Arbor: University of Michigan Press.

Gurri, Francisco D., G. Balam, and Emilio Moran. 2001. Well-Being Changes in Response to 30 Years of Regional Integration in Maya Populations from Yucatan, Mexico. *American Journal of Human Biology* 13: 590–602.

Hales, C. N., and D. J. P. Barker. 1992. Type 2 (Non-Insulin-Dependent) Diabetes Mellitus: The Thrifty Phenotype Hypothesis. *Diabetologia* 35: 595–601.

Jabbonsky, Larry. 1993. The Mexican Resurrection. *Beverage World* 112(1547): 38–40.

Knowler, William C., R. C. Williams, D. J. Pettitt, and A. G. Steinberg. 1988. Gm and Type 2 Diabetes Mellitus: An Association in American Indians with Genetic Admixture. *American Journal of Human Genetics* 43: 520–26.

Kozak, David. Surrendering to Diabetes: An Embodied Response to Perceptions of Diabetes and Death in the Gila Indian Community. *Omega: Journal of Death and Dying* 35(4): 347–59.

Leatherman, Thomas. 1996. A Biocultural Perspective on Health and Household Economy in Southern Peru. *Medical Anthropology Quarterly* 10(4): 476–95.

———. 1998. Illness, Social Relations, and Household Production and Reproduction in the Andes of Southern Peru. In *Building a New Biocultural Synthesis: Political-Economic Perspectives on Human Biology,* ed. Alan Goodman and Thomas Leatherman, pp. 255–67. Ann Arbor: University of Michigan Press.

Leatherman, Thomas, and Alan Goodman. In press. Coca-Colonization of Diets in the Yucatan. *Social Science and Medicine.*

Leatherman, Thomas, J. T. Stillman, and Alan Goodman. 2000. The Effects of Tourism-Led Development on the Nutritional Status of Yucatec Mayan Children. *American Journal of Physical Anthropology* Supplement 30: 207.

Levins, Richard, and Richard C. Lewontin. 1985. *The Dialectical Biologist.* Cambridge: Harvard University Press.

Lewontin, Richard C. 1972. The Apportionment of Human Diversity. *Evolutionary Biology* 6: 381–98.

———. 1995. Genes, Environment, and Organisms. In *Hidden Histories of Science,* ed. Robert B. Silver, pp. 115–38. New York: New York Review of Books.

———. 2001. *The Triple Helix.* Cambridge: Harvard University Press.

McGarty, Catherine A. 1995. Dietary Delocalization in a Yucatecan Resort Community in Quintana Roo, Mexico: Junk Food in Paradise. Honors thesis, School of Nursing, University of Massachusetts, Amherst.

McKinley, John B. 1986. A Case for Refocussing Upstream: The Political Economy of Illness. In *The Sociology of Health and Illness,* ed. P. Conrad and R. Kerr, pp. 613–33. New York: St. Martins Press.

Pelto, Gretel H., and Pertti J. Pelto. 1983. Diet and Delocalization: Dietary Changes since 1750. *Journal of Interdisciplinary History* 14: 507–28.

Pi-Sunyer, Oriole, and R. Brooke Thomas. 1997. Tourism, Environmentalism and Cultural Survival in Quintana Roo, Mexico. In *Life and Death Matters: Human Rights and the Environment at the End of the Millennium,* ed. Barbara Johnston, pp. 187–212. Walnut Creek, CA: Altamira Press.

Scheper-Hughes, Nancy. 1990. Three Propositions for a Critically Applied Medical Anthropology. *Social Science and Medicine* 30(2): 189–97.

Singer, Merrill. 1989. The Limitations of Medical Ecology: The Concept of Adaptation in the Context of Social Stratification and Social Transformation. *Medical Anthropology* 10(4): 218–29.

Smith, Gavin A., and R. Brooke Thomas. 1998. What Could Be: Biological Anthropology for the Next Generation. In *Building a New Biocultural Synthesis: Political-Economic Perspectives on Human Biology,* ed. Alan Goodman and Thomas Leatherman, pp. 451–73. Ann Arbor: University of Michigan Press.

Snow, Charles P. 1959. *The Two Cultures and the Scientific Revolution.* New York: Cambridge University Press.

Templeton, Alan. 1998. Human Races: A Genetic and Evolutionary Perspective. *American Anthropologist* 100: 632–50.

Weiss, Kenneth, R. Ferrell, and C. L. Hanis. 1984. New World Syndrome of Metabolic Diseases with a Genetic and Evolutionary Basis. *Yearbook of Physical Anthropology* 27: 153–78.

Wolf, Eric R. 1982. *Europe and the People without History.* Berkeley and Los Angeles: University of California Press.

Young, T. Kue. 1994. *The Health of Native Americans: Toward a Biocultural Epidemiology.* New York: Oxford University Press.

CHAPTER 9

Alzheimer's Disease: A Tangled Concept

Margaret Lock

IN A RECENT ARTICLE in *The Sciences* entitled "Plundered Memories,"
Zaven Khachaturian, the director of the Ronald and Nancy Reagan Research Institute of the Alzheimer's Association, had this to say:

> Some critics ask whether genetic research is worth the resources it con-
> sumes and the anguish it will bring to those who test positive for a harm-
> ful gene—when a cure still seems so far away. In my view, however, the
> genetic approach is on the right track, and I think the continuing re-
> search on Alzheimer's disease may soon confirm that belief. Those of us
> in the front lines of the fight against Alzheimer's have never been closer
> to unmasking this mysterious thief, the robber of the very thing that
> makes human beings unique. (Khachaturian 1997: 21)

Khachaturian has been associated for years with the National Institute of
Aging, and he has raised millions of dollars for research into Alzheimer's
disease; his mother died of the disease, and he believes that he himself is beginning to suffer from it. He is scornful of those who, like the evolutionary
biologist Richard Lewontin (2000), have suggested that genetic research into
Alzheimer's is a blind alley as far as cures are concerned.

Conflicting viewpoints on causes and cures of diseases can readily be de-
tected throughout the history of European medicine since classical times. A
tension is perennially evident between "internalizing" discourses, which focus on bodily pathologies and their medical management, and "externalizing" discourses, which emphasize contextualization—including the social,
political, and environmental contributions to ill health, as well as the behavior of patients and the narrative accounts given by them (Young 1976).
In the former approach it is above all a physical cure that is desired; in the

latter, knowledge and practices are weighted toward contextualizing findings and toward prevention and societal change, although discerning causal pathways and finding appropriate therapies is also of importance.

The internalizing discourse of today is, of course, thoroughly grounded in the biological sciences and is ceaselessly transformed through technological developments and the production of new knowledge, much of it in molecular biology. The most recent transformation, which some describe as revolutionary, is the development of molecular genetics and its associated technologies (Keller 2000). Genes have become knowable entities, subject to human manipulation. This knowledge is linked closely to a belief held by many that we are now moving well beyond basic mapping of genes to gain substantial control over the last frontier of untamed biology—our own genome. This belief has been associated with a flood of utopian rhetoric about how we will be able to "decipher the mysteries of our own existence" (Keller 1992: 293). What is more, the U.S. Office of Technology Assessment claimed some time ago that genetic information will ensure that each one of us will from now on have "a paramount *right* to be born with a normal, adequate, hereditary endowment" (1988: 86, emphasis added). Daniel Koshland, a molecular biologist and past editor of *Science,* is on record as stating that "no one will profit more from the current research into genetics than the poor." He made it clear that he is suggesting that "weak" and "anti-social" genes will slowly be "sifted out" of the population (Koshland 1989).

Central to this latest round of internalizing discourse is the assumption that genes are in effect independent, self-replicating entities and that when, as inevitably is the case, faulty replication (transcription) takes place, genes essentially become pathogens. However, thanks to an array of technologies including pre-implantation genetic diagnosis, gene therapy, and genetic engineering, we will increasingly be able to create the desired "genetic body," which will not only be freed from disease but will actually be enhanced for "the good life" and greater longevity.

Has this new powerful internalizing discourse won the day? Are we on an irreversible path whereby externalizing discourses are eclipsed, thanks to the clarity brought about by a deterministic molecular genetics? Or will a much more complex picture—one that includes not only interactions among genes and the protein products for which genes code, but also environmental effects on DNA, RNA, cell and system functioning—thoroughly undermine straightforward cause-and-effect arguments?

Knowledgeable commentators suggest that mapping of the human genome is equivalent to having a list of parts for a Boeing 747 but no idea as to how they go together and no awareness of the principles of aeronautics. If this is indeed the case, why are extravagant claims for genetic determinism perpetrated? The media, as is well known, often produce a pared-down deterministic account about genetics and regularly report that we have found *the* gene for a named disease—a claim that frequently has to be retracted at a later date (Conrad and Weinberg 1996; Conrad 2001a).

There is no denying the political power associated with genomics today, nor the hubris that so often accompanies this mega-enterprise, spurred on by the sequencing of virtually the entire human genome (*Time* 2003). Even allowing for hype and misunderstanding on the part of the media, we tend to assume that it is scientists who have generated, or at least are complicit in, the creation and reproduction of these new geneticized accounts. This is indeed often the case. The language associated with both structural and functional genomics[1] is reductionistic in that factors external to the human body that may contribute to the appearance, behavior, and condition of an organism as a whole—the phenotype—are usually marginalized, as the statement cited above by Khachaturian well illustrates.

However, the discourse of genomics is not that of a simple determinism: very few experts argue any longer that organisms—whether microbes or humans—are mere expressions of their genes. Genes are no longer conceptualized as blueprints, and sequencing (mapping) of genes is understood primarily as creating stepping stones toward elucidating an extraordinarily complex picture about which our current understanding is at best crude. Indeed, on the basis of preliminary interviews and observations among geneticists and clinicians in Canada, Great Britain, and the United States, I have found no one who talks an unabashed genetic determinism. None of these scientists makes the assumption that locating the position of genes on the relevant chromosome does more than raise new questions. Nor, they agree, will knowledge about gene location necessarily remove any of the horrendous clinical and familial difficulties associated with the relatively straightforward Mendelian (inherited) diseases,[2] much less the complex multifactorial diseases. Further, they maintain that this knowledge will not inform us as to how gene/gene and gene/environmental issues are inevitably involved in the majority (probably all) disease states.

Given the emerging consensus among geneticists that elucidation of "internal" factors is unlikely to be sufficient to account for disease occurrence, it is important to consider accounts that examine "external" factors. Since the middle of the nineteenth century, efforts to create an externalizing discourse about disease causation have been sustained largely by means of the Galtonian concept of distribution about a norm, by the refinement of measurements of probability, and, more recently, through resort to the language of risk. Today this discourse is peppered with concepts taken from epidemiology and related disciplines, including "social cohesion," "social gradients," and so on. Together with the language of risk, these concepts are used to create an argument for the "social determinants" of health and illness, in which an effort is made to explain why some people get sick and die early deaths, whereas others are much less likely to do so (Evans et al. 1994).

Arguments made by epidemiologists and others in connection with the so-called social determinants of health—even though they draw on the language of probability and therefore do not presume straightforward cause-and-effect connections—are in effect reductionistic because they assume a universal body on which social and political variables are acted out. However, the new genetics has made it abundantly clear that biological variation between and within human populations can no longer be ignored.[3] The objects of analysis in epidemiological research are populations; individuals are subsumed into categories formed on the basis of various social attributes—such as education level, income, sex, age, ethnicity, and race—in order to calculate who in the population at large is vulnerable to becoming diseased. In addition to "black-boxing" the body and consigning its investigation entirely to biologists, the limitations of such an approach are twofold. First, concepts such as ethnicity and race are social constructs, but in the health sciences they are almost without exception applied as unproblematized, "natural" entities. Second, the difficulty of assessing where any one individual falls in relation to distribution curves calculated from population-based probability estimates can never be satisfactorily solved, with the result that estimates of individual risk are notoriously unreliable.

In contrast to basic-science and epidemiological approaches, cultural anthropologists commonly generate ethnographic accounts, created in part from narratives by informants about the subjective experience of illness and disease, which are then contextualized not only in the everyday lives of informants but also in the social, political, economic, and environmental conditions in which they live. In addition, one of the particular contributions of anthropology to the study of illness and disease is a reflexive approach to the production of scientific knowledge, one that explicitly attends to the historical and social construction of the categories used in the health sciences while at the same time insisting that material reality cannot be ignored and that biological variation must be recognized (Lock 1993, 2001).

It is evident that basic-science, epidemiological, and anthropological approaches to the body employ different "styles of reasoning" (Hacking 1996) that are neither commensurate with nor reducible to one another. Yet the knowledge produced by each of these approaches can create lenses that mutually augment one another and, together, generate powerful new insights.

Research in the basic sciences in connection with the normal brain and neuropathologies, including Alzheimer's disease, has advanced exponentially in the past decade, but paradoxically, this new knowledge has made it increasingly evident to scientists that Alzheimer's disease as a clinical entity is historically and socially constructed, thus opening the door for discussion and cooperation across disciplines. The remainder of this chapter will explore the historical and contemporary intersection of internalizing and externalizing discourses concerning Alzheimer's disease that constitute the field within which that discussion and cooperation must take place.

Disease of the Century

Alzheimer's disease (AD) is an example of a complex disorder that has recently been "geneticized"; that is, most experts now believe that it is crucial to recognize the contribution made by genetics to this disorder. To date, however, findings from neither molecular nor population genetics have facilitated any notable advances in preventing this condition or in its management. Indeed, clinicians and advocacy groups seek to dispel any false hopes that may be raised among the public by announcements about genes associated with AD.

Although AD—conventionally described as the most common form of dementia—has been medically recognized for nearly one hundred years, it remains to this day an elusive entity subject to competing professional interpretations. The condition has undeniable bodily effects, both mental and physical, that result in death. Nevertheless, whether AD is actually a disease has been under dispute since its "discovery," because doubts exist as to whether it is a pathological condition affecting a (large) minority of older people or a "natural" effect of aging to which we are all liable if we do not die first of something else. Insights obtained recently—primarily from molecular genetics and brain-imaging technology—have made discourse about AD even more fluid and subject to dispute.

Despite these differing viewpoints, the dominant image of AD today is of a terrible disease whose facticity cannot be doubted. This severe form of dementia manifests itself in characteristic behavioral changes, the end result of pathological transformations in the brain. The atrophy of brain cells, dense plaque formations (likened by some to garbage bags), and neurofibrillary tangles are the consistent, irrefutable evidence of the pathology that has been associated with AD for nearly one hundred years. The behavioral effects of these anatomical changes, usually distinguishable from the effects of other forms of dementia, include a progressive loss of cognitive abilities, most often commencing with memory problems, followed by loss of language and then of visuospatial orientation, and resulting in death within ten to fifteen years after onset. The end point is clear, but there is consensus about little else.

Paradoxically, it is also well recognized that, even though the majority of individuals whose brains show plaques and tangles at autopsy exhibit the behavioral changes associated with AD while alive, this is not always the case (Swartz, Black, and St. George-Hyslop 1999). Some people can apparently "adapt" to these neurological changes, or at least are relatively unaffected by them. Conversely, a few individuals whose brains after death show relatively few anatomical changes exhibit marked behavioral changes while alive. These anomalies immediately raise the question of the ontological status of AD: What is "it" and where exactly does "it" reside? Is it the behavioral changes or the anatomical changes that constitute the disease, or a coproduction of both anatomy and behavior?

Research into AD carries a sense of urgency, given the number of people who are presumed to be candidates as populations age around the globe. AD has been made into a government concern for some time now partly through the efforts of the national Alzheimer's Association in the United States, which was founded in 1982. Its counterparts in Canada, Great Britain, and other countries have been responsible for similar efforts to elevate national concern about the disease. The disquieting metaphors associated with AD—the "silent epidemic," the "disease of the century," a "living nightmare," a "funeral that never ends"—graphically reveal the fear associated with this condition. It is estimated that AD is the fourth biggest killer in the United States, and that a massive sum of $100 billion a year is currently spent on care of four million AD patients. These expenses will multiply as the baby boomers grow older, and by 2030 the number of cases will have tripled unless a "cure" is found.[4]

There is disagreement about the figures, but estimates suggest that people in their thirties have a 1 in 3000 chance of getting the disease, rising to 1 in 1000 by age sixty, to 1 in a 100 for people in their sixties and seventies, and to 1 in 4 (or, according to some estimates, 1 in 2) by age eighty-five. Some scientists and clinicians argue adamantly that the new genetics may rescue us from this very costly fate worse than death. They participate in what Peter Conrad (2001b) has described as "genetic optimism" in that they assume there is more to "discover" and that, once this is accomplished, things will fall "naturally" into place, with new insights about genetics leading to groundbreaking answers in regard to both causation and cure. But even these experts do not deny the contribution made by numerous factors that modify genes and their proteins. Other medical professionals feel marginalized by the hype associated with genetics and are frustrated as funding for improved care of patients with AD is diverted into basic-science research.

Alzheimer's Disease: The History of an Elusive Concept

Virtually no one today would argue that dementia is a myth, and professionals and the public alike approach AD as though it were an undeniable fact. Nevertheless, AD is possibly a fiction or, at the very least, a shifting, unstable target. The history of the scientific research surrounding AD demonstrates just how elusive this concept is.

Paul Rabinow (2000) argues that, from time to time, new forms emerge that bring about a fundamental change in how assemblages of technological knowledge and practices work. I suggest, however, that such changes may not follow hard on the heels of the event. Indeed, the naming of Alzheimer's disease did not bring about an immediate transformation in our understanding or management of dementia, although a trajectory was set in motion that several decades later solidified around the concept of AD.

The conventional story is that Alois Alzheimer reported at a meeting of the South West German Psychiatrists on November 4, 1906, the case of a fifty-one-year-old woman from Frankfurt who presented with progressive cognitive impairment, hallucinations, delusions, and "marked psychosocial incompetence." On postmortem, marked brain atrophy was found, together with "senile plagues" and "neurofibrillary tangles" (Maurer, Volk, and Gerbaldo 1999). In 1910, Emil Kraepelin, a leading psychiatrist of the day, "baptized" this condition as Alzheimer's disease. However, Alzheimer himself insisted that the case should not be thought of as a new disease, and he was much more interested in demonstrating how it related to similar conditions that he had seen repeatedly in older patients. Alzheimer firmly believed that what he had described was simply an atypical form—because the patient was middle-aged—of what at that time was a reasonably well recognized condition known as senile psychosis. Even though Alzheimer and his colleagues were working with large numbers of cases of dementia, in the ensuing years they reported only six cases similar to the one originally reported by Alzheimer. Some of those six had already been reported elsewhere and were, in any case, questioned for their authenticity as indeed constituting examples of the new disease. Because none of the patients was elderly, these cases could not readily be classified as "senile" psychosis; but even so there were serious doubts as to whether they represented anything significantly new taxonomically.

G. E. Berrios has shown that all the clinical and postmortem features of the so-called new disease—including plaques, tangles, and irreversible cognitive decline—were well described before Alzheimer made his particular case public, and the view that dementia was both a clinical and a neuropathological category had been put on a firm footing as early as 1822 (Berrios 1990). The only unusual feature of Alzheimer's case was the age of the patient. Berrios argues that, to this day, it is not clear why Kraepelin heralded Alzheimer's discovery as a new disease. It may have been to create visibility for people working closely with him, or more likely, it was because Kraepelin believed that in some way the disease was indeed distinctly different from the more common late-onset senile dementia.

Kraepelin proclaimed in 1912 that senile dementia should be divided into three distinct pathological entities—"arteriosclerotic dementia," "senile dementia," and Alzheimer's disease (referring to "pre-senile dementia"). Despite its baptism by Kraepelin, Alzheimer's disease lost its way. Not only Alzheimer himself but numerous other scientists and clinicians disagreed with Kraepelin's designation of a new disease, and no systematic follow-up was undertaken to consolidate its recognition. The outbreak of the First World War contributed to this situation by diverting energies from basic laboratory work.

A second reason for the disappearance of Alzheimer's disease for four decades, noted by Lawrence Cohen (1998: 80), was that drug companies became particularly interested in arteriosclerotic dementia associated with strokes; it was assumed that pharmacological agents would soon be found to combat this problem, thus ensuring that medical attention was focused on stroke patients. The more problematic category of senile dementia, closely associated with hallucinations, madness, and moral disapprobation, was hidden in psychiatric hospitals, and the conventional understanding is that AD returned to obscurity almost as soon as it was discovered, to remain so until the 1970s. However, the medical historian Jesse Ballinger has shown that between the 1930s and 1950s psychiatrists in the United States paid a great deal of attention to AD, which they conceived, not as a biologically derived cognitive disorder, but as a mental illness resulting from the "psychodynamic processes taking place between aging individuals and society" (2000: 84). These psychiatrists did not differentiate AD from the aging process as a whole, and links to the emerging field of gerontology were made, opening up a field of old-age psychiatry.

Long before this time, in order to gain recognition for the new discipline of gerontology, its founding father, I. L. Nascher, argued strongly that cell degeneration inevitably accompanies senescence, is a "natural" part of aging, and needs careful medical attention (1914). This theory was supported by later findings of both American and British neuroanatomists, which demonstrated that the brains of virtually all "normal" elderly people at post-mortem dissection show characteristics similar to those of patients who exhibited marked signs of dementia, namely atrophy of the brain accompanied by plagues and tangles (Neumann and Cohn 1953; Tomlinson, Blessed, and Roth 1968). This finding constituted a second "event" in the history of AD, making it highly problematic as to how to distinguish between normal aging and a diseased brain. Explicit arguments for the social construction of senility as disease—similar to those proposed earlier for schizophrenia by the radical psychiatrist Thomas Szasz (1961)—helped to transform senility into an outmoded concept. Moreover, accusations were made that the systematic labeling of elderly people as senile was in fact an expression of the "gerontophobia" characteristic of our society. But these arguments did not dispute that AD—believed at that time to affect 5 percent of the elderly—was a deadly disease (Henig 1981).

The anthropologist Lawrence Cohen—following Gubrium (1987; see also Fox 1999)—has argued that it was families, feeling burdened by care of their senile elderly, who started to push for systematic medicalization of AD in the late 1960s. By the mid-1970s, what had been thought of earlier as a rare brain disorder was clearly on the path to becoming "the disease of the century" (Stafford 1991), with strong support for its recognition from many patients and families.

As of 1976 "pre-senile" and "senile" cases of AD were classed as a single disease, subdivided into early- and late-onset forms (Katzman 1976). The term "senility," now deemed pejorative, was dropped, and the concept of AD as a distinct disease, diagnosable on the basis of systematically assessed behavioral changes, confirmed when necessary by autopsy, was consolidated. In Great Britain, old-age psychiatrists continue to the present time to be much more deeply involved with dementia and AD than they are in North America, where neurologists dominate the medical scene; this results in some significant conceptual differences. But everywhere debates persist about what it is that "protects" those who live to a great age but do not succumb to dementia.

Recent genetic insights have made the fact of AD more convincing. At the same time, this knowledge has raised a flood of new questions that destabilize new insights even as they are produced. It is probably safe to say that just about everyone involved with AD research today recognizes just how provisional—at the level of molecular biology—are the taxonomic categories used for dementia (see Graham 2000 for a critical assessment of the standardization of dementia diagnoses). When a diagnosis of AD is made, it is in practice a residual category, a wastebasket after other forms of dementia have been ruled out. On the other hand, the sensitivity of the AD diagnosis is regarded as high. In other words, following a diagnosis based on psychological testing, by far the majority of patients will proceed over the course of the following years to exhibit increasing evidence of the characteristic irreversible signs of AD. There is wide agreement that the plaques, tangles, and synapse and cell loss assumed to be characteristic of this disease are part of a complex process fundamental to the way in which the normal brain ages and copes with damage. What appears to be distinct in those individuals diagnosed with AD are very dense tangles and abnormal rates of amyloid deposition that lead to a fast buildup of plaques, although as noted above, a poor correlation exists between the concentration and distribution of amyloid depositions in the brain and other parameters of recognized AD pathology, including the degree of dementia and loss of synapses and neurons. Rachael Neve and Nikolaos Robakis conclude that, despite its remarkably uniform pathology, AD is "probably a multifactorial disease that should be approached from many perspectives" and that important aspects of the disorder "remain elusive" (1998: 15).

There is disagreement not only about the status of AD as a pathological entity but also about what factors contribute to its onset. The fact sheet prepared by the Alzheimer's Disease Society of Great Britain (1997) about AD causation states succinctly: "The short answer is we don't know" (Alzheimer's Disease Society 1997). There is general agreement about the variables that place individuals at increased risk: advancing age, a family history of dementia, a history of head injury, and sex. Another widely cited variable is "substandard" education. Among the other factors that have been considered are a history of smoking, aluminum toxicity, and chlamydia infection (not sexually transmitted). Even the "discovery" of a gene associated with increased risk for late-onset Alzheimer's disease has not, as we will see, provided the kind of evidence needed for a deterministic internalized discourse to hold sway. No one thing or event inevitably results in the condition. On the contrary, the provisional, contested internalized explanatory models have become increasingly complex and multidimensional, and internal heterogeneity (Lewontin 2000: 114) must be confronted head on.

In summary, the "fact" of AD has been disputed from the time of its "discovery." Yet, in large part because of a sense of urgency on the part of affected families and most clinicians to have dementias of all forms recognized as bona fide diseases, AD is conceptualized in the clinic and among the public as a distinct, universal, biological entity. Contemporary basic science, however, suggests otherwise.

An Abundance of Genes: Increasing Complexity
in the Internalizing Discourse

As a result of genetic research, AD is now conventionally divided into early- and late-onset forms. Early-onset, "familial" AD has been associated thus far with approximately 170 extended families worldwide. In the past fifteen years, genetic markers for this form of the disease have been found on chromosomes 1, 14, and 21, one variation of which is inevitably present in vulnerable families. These genes are autosomal dominant and are described by most specialists as genetic "determinants," although twin studies have shown that the age of onset of the disease can differ by as much as ten years. This suggests that, although the gene has very high "penetrance" (phenotypic expression of the disease in individuals who have the gene is virtually 100 percent), a simple case of cause and effect is not at work, and other factors, internal and/or external, must be implicated (Tilley, Morgan, and Kalsheker 1998). Onset of this form of AD is almost without exception between the ages of thirty-five and sixty, with one form starting a little later in life and occasionally not making an appearance until age seventy. In all cases of early onset, the condition progresses rapidly to florid dementia and death; it was an early-onset case that Alzheimer first described and interpreted as an anomaly.

Much more common is what is known today as late-onset AD, no cases of which have been associated with the genetic mutations involved with the early-onset disease. Until recently, late-onset AD has been thought of as "sporadic"—that is, as not being linked to one's genetic heritage. However, as a result of findings from molecular genetics, it is now widely believed that certain individuals and, by extension, certain families may be at increased risk for the disease because they have inherited one or more "susceptibility genes." A number of scientists now believe that such genes are implicated in virtually all cases of late-onset AD.

Almost all genes common to humans are "polymorphic"—that is, they occur in a number of variations that are widespread among human populations. Because they are so widely distributed, these allelic variations are not mutations. Although some are associated with an increased risk for disease, such genes are not disease determinants, nor do they indicate that individuals are necessarily predisposed from birth to a specific disease. However, like the effects of smoking addiction or of high cholesterol levels associated with a poor diet, the presence of such alleles in an individual genome (as compared to the population at large) suggests an increased probability of disease occurrence.

A little over a decade ago a third "event" brought about a radical shift in thinking in the Alzheimer world that caused experts to start reassessing received wisdom about late-onset AD. One form of apolipoproteinE (ApoE), found on chromosome 19, was shown by linkage studies to be associated with late-onset AD and also on occasion with the early-onset form of AD (Strittmatter et al. 1993). This finding has now been verified in over one hundred laboratories around the world and is regarded as one of the best-proved "facts" of molecular genetics. Already implicated in heart disease before its association with AD was noted, ApoE is a polymorphic protein with three well-recognized alleles, 2, 3, and 4, that appear to be universally but unequally (clinally) distributed. It has been shown repeatedly in so-called Caucasian populations that the risk for late-onset AD increases and the age of onset decreases by as much as seven to nine years in the presence of the *ApoE ε4* allele. The risk for individuals with one allele is estimated as 3 times greater than in individuals with no *ApoE ε4;* with two alleles, the risk rises to 8–30 times greater. However, a number of studies suggest that once the disease has become established, no difference exists in the rates of cognitive or functional decline even when *ApoE ε4* is present. Moreover, many subjects who are homozygous for *ApoE ε4* never develop the disease, and approximately half the individuals studied who develop AD do not have *ApoE ε4* alleles.

The allele thus *determines* nothing with respect to the incidence of AD. All that can be concluded is that the *ApoE ε4* genotype, under certain circumstances, confers a greater degree of susceptibility. But it is neither necessary nor sufficient to cause the disease. Other genes and/or environmental factors must be implicated (Tilley, Morgan, and Kalsheker 1998).

For those individuals with two *ApoE ε3* alleles (about 60 percent of the population in Europe and North America), lifetime risk is estimated as "average," suggesting that, by age eighty, up to a quarter of such individuals will have AD. Worldwide, relatively few people carry *ApoE ε2.* Those who inherit two copies of this gene are thought to be at very low risk of contracting AD, and the allele appears to be protective.

A new susceptibility locus was recently reported in *Science* on chromosome 10. The paper, authored by 25 scientists participating in an international collaboration, makes the claim that the presence of this locus in individuals modifies negatively their risk for AD independently of the *ApoE* genotype (Myers et al. 2000). A recent study by Andreas Papassotiropoulos and colleagues (2003) reports that a variant of the *CYP46* gene is associated with an increased risk of developing AD. This study has demonstrated a synergistic reaction between *CYP46* and the *ApoE ε4* allele. Other sites currently under investigation are on chromosomes 9, 12, 13, 15, and 19 and at a second locus on 10. In carrying out these investigations researchers are hoping to do much more than pinpoint what is happening at the molecular level once AD has become established. They are attempting to demonstrate increased risk as a result of the presence of specific alleles that can potentially be activated at various points along biological pathways, thus producing a negative effect on normal brain functioning. The excitement around these investigations is palpable, and the molecularization of professional understanding of AD is undeniable.

John Hardy, the chief of the genetics laboratory of the United States National Institute of Aging, stated during a presentation at the 2002 biannual AD conference in Stockholm that "genetics underpins our understanding of this disease AD," [5] and he noted that "findings from genetics are the baseline for research into AD." Toward the end of his talk, he asserted that "genetics have given the 'melody' of AD some form." Although the presentations of Hardy and others who focused on genetics received a great deal of attention in Stockholm, they caused only a limited stir because no findings that derive from knowledge about the genetics of AD—including the *ApoE ε4* discovery ten years earlier—have resulted as yet in clear advances in the prevention or treatment of the disease.

Similarly, genetic knowledge surrounding late-onset AD is of limited predictive value because of the difficulty of converting findings—even those as robust as an *ApoE* genotype—into useful information for clinicians and individuals attempting to relate individual status to future risk of developing the disease. The fact that the molecularized, internalizing discourse has as yet produced no "deliverables" ensures that other types of discourse continue to flourish. Moreover, the heterogeneity of the genetic etiology of AD, when coupled with the heterogeneity of behavioral effects, leaves only the "endophenotype" (Sing, Haviland, and Reilly 1996)—the still poorly understood "final common pathway" that results in dense plaques and thick tangles—as the "fact" of dementia.

The result is that the internalizing discourse presents, not a cause-and-effect chain of events, but rather a complex maze of pathways that may or may not be activated under a specific combination of as yet poorly understood conditions, among which both factors internal and external to the body may well be important. Although molecular geneticists' research is virtually limited to teasing apart the relationship among internalizing factors, they do not deny that social and environmental factors from the time of conception onward may be implicated.

Gene-Environment Interaction: The Problems in Assessing Risk

Research on late-onset AD is amply demonstrating that genes are shape-shifters without peer, the products not only of evolutionary and recent human history but also of toxic environments, the uterine environment, and lifestyle, as well as of serendipitous mutations as a result of faulty replication. Population genetics has been relied upon in attempts to establish the characteristics that place certain populations at an increased risk for disease, including late-onset AD. However, it is impossible to create deterministic arguments because the number of variables under consideration is so large, their individual effect is often small, and most come into play only under certain specific circumstances.

Moreover, there are a number of problems with assessing individual risk from studies of this kind—problems that are, in many ways, no different from the difficulties inherent in the application of large-scale epidemiological information to any specific case. First of all, epidemiology is not "about" individual cases but "about" populations. Along with this basic difficulty, there are several other sources of possible misunderstanding.

Since 1993, many population studies have been published on the *ApoE* gene and its relationship to AD in which the focus has been on so-called Caucasians (Growdon 1998; Korovaitseva et al. 2001; Roses 1998; Saunders 2000; Silverman et al. 2003). Within this literature, inconsistencies about the effects of the *ApoE* gene have the potential for creating confusion. For example, estimates of the number of individuals with AD who carry the ε4 allele range from 30 to 90 percent (Liddell, Lovestone, and Owen 2001; Ritchie and DuPuy 1999), and many studies do not specify whether these numbers refer to those who are hetero- or homozygous,[6] which further confounds the matter.

In addition to retrospective studies of individuals who already have AD, many studies attempt to estimate the number of people with *ApoE* ε4 alleles who will eventually develop AD. There is considerable variation in the estimates presented in these prospective studies. The number of individuals who are heterozygous for the *ApoE* ε4 allele and who are expected to develop AD ranges from 7.6 to 47 percent. The range for homozygous individuals is between 21.4 and 91 percent (Holmes 2002; Farlow 1997).

There is better agreement that individuals with *ApoE* ε4 alleles have an increased relative risk of developing AD. The literature suggests, as noted above, that a person with one ε4 allele has 3 times the chance—and a person with two ε4 alleles has between 8 and 30 times the chance—of developing AD compared to someone with no ε4 alleles (Holmes 2002; Swartz, Black, and St. George-Hyslop 1999). However, the baseline on which this probability is estimated is rarely provided, and without this information, relative-risk estimates are highly misleading.

One of the principal causes of confusion about AD and genetic risk is inherent in the research design. Holmes (2002) and Ritchie and Dupuy (1999) suggest that many studies do not reflect the population at large, since they are based on clinical, rather than population, samples. When general-population samples are used, the relationship between *ApoE ε4* and AD appears to be significantly weaker than is commonly presented.

Moreover, *ApoE ε4* has been shown to work in unexpected ways in certain populations. For instance, among Pygmies and other populations whose subsistence economy was until recently predominantly that of hunting and gathering, possession of an *ApoE ε4* genotype apparently protects against AD. This finding holds when controlled for age (Corbo and Scacchi 1999). Low rates of AD have been reported for parts of Nigeria, and the presence of an *ApoE ε4* allele does not appear to be implicated when it does occur. On the other hand, *ApoE ε4* is significantly associated with AD among African Americans, although less so than in populations of whites (Farrer 2000). It is argued that other risk-reducing factors (in Africa) *and* risk-enhancing factors (in North America) must therefore be implicated, including other genes, their protein products, diet, and environment, but researchers also acknowledge limitations to the research methodologies. To further complicate matters, it has been claimed that *ApoE ε4* apparently becomes a protective factor for people in clinical populations over ninety years of age. Clearly, the specific role of *ApoE ε4* in AD is far from being well understood.

The bottom line is that individual risk assessments for late-onset AD that make use of genetics are at present so vague as to be deemed of little or no use in clinical care by the majority of clinicians and researchers (Farlow 1997; Liddell, Lovestone, and Owen 2001; McConnell et al. 1998; St. George-Hyslop 2000; Tilley, Morgan, and Kalsheker 1998). Although it is acknowledged that this situation may change in the future, official guidelines currently put out by professional and health-policy-making institutions and organizations and by advocacy groups in the United States, Canada, and the United Kingdom state that genetic testing for *ApoE* status should not be carried out routinely. This position is taken because there is no known prevention or treatment for AD that is more than minimally effective.

Even so, a few private companies offer testing (an "Early Alert Alzheimer's Home Screening Test" kit is marketed directly to consumers in their homes; see Kier and Molinari 2003), and a randomized controlled trial approved by the National Institutes of Health is in progress. In this trial, volunteer participants, selected because one or more family members have been diagnosed with late-onset AD, are randomly chosen to be placed in either an experimental or a control group. Those people in the experimental group are informed of their *ApoE* status, and their responses to this information over the following twelve months are then compared with those of individuals in the control group, whose blood is drawn and stored but is not tested (Green et al. 2002). One justification for this research is that testing for susceptibility genes is likely to become increasingly common, especially in the private sector, and therefore knowledge about how people deal with this information is urgently needed. A second justification is that it is patronizing to withhold from people information about their bodies. A third is that in many families where someone has died of AD, some members of the next generation may well believe that they have a virtually 100 percent chance of contracting the disease; if they can learn that, even when homozygous for *ApoE ε4*, their risk for getting AD is never, even in old age, much above 50 percent, then anxiety levels may well be lowered.

The existence of a controlled trial of this type is another sign of a creeping geneticization in connection with AD. But much is left unaccounted for when testing is done: no clear predictions can be made about the future, and no recommendations for preventive care apply that are not relevant to every one of us as we age. Recent research shows that even among families who have direct experience with late-onset AD, the majority of individuals believe that both environment and genetics contribute to the disease, and one can perhaps do something about the environment but nothing about genetics. Moreover, concern about genetics takes a back seat to the pragmatics of living with and caring for an elderly relative afflicted with the "living death" (Lock, Lloyd, and Prest, in press).

Probabilistic knowledge that generates risk estimates works against deterministic accounts among both "experts" and the public. When talking with patients, clinicians do not dissemble about revealing an AD diagnosis, but they usually draw heavily on an externalizing discourse—one that focuses on behaviors that may slow the progression of the disease, the value of support groups, and the like—and studiously avoid discussion of genetics. When these same clinicians discuss laboratory research with their colleagues or the anthropologist, their stance is entirely different—and resolutely internalizing, although not reductionistic.

Clinicians' Perspectives on the Genetics of Alzheimer's Disease

Alzheimer's disease is frequently used in departments of genetics today as a model for teaching genetic complexity and for illustrating gene-environment interaction, but the assumption is that a great deal more remains to be learned about the genetics of AD and that, when these advances are made, we may then be in a position to make some major breakthroughs with respect to medications, perhaps in the form of pharmacogenetics (Hedgecoe, 2004).

However, as noted above, this shift in theoretical perspective has little effect on patient management. The excerpts below were selected from interviews conducted in 2000–2001 with twenty-eight clinicians in Canada, the United Kingdom, and the United States. These preliminary findings are revealing. For one thing, there is a great deal of consistency in the interviews, particularly with respect to how exactly genes are implicated in the etiology of AD.

Two molecular geneticists, who are also clinicians, made the following statements:

> It's very hard now to talk about sporadic—nongenetic—Alzheimer's. Sporadic would be rare—and even then genes are involved—the result of a sudden isolated mutation but not passed on in families. Until recently we thought that no genes were involved in this disease, that it was just aging—but now we know there are: genes are involved with aging and with the pathologies associated with aging. But genes are not causative— it's just that genes increase the risk, or accelerate a process that is already under way. This process would not get expressed as pathology unless genes like *ApoE ε4* are present, so that the "normal" changes of aging are transformed, resulting, for example, in an excess of plaques.

> Genes *for* Alzheimer's are not *for* at all, they simply contribute to one's risk for getting late-onset Alzheimer's. We're talking about common polymorphisms, not mutations, and there's going to be at least four to six of them involved with Alzheimer's—maybe more.

A third clinician, even though he does not dispute the importance of genetics, sounds a cautionary note:

> All we can do is make a judgment of likely cause. Genetics are one influence among many leading to dementia. I'm very skeptical about the whole genetic frenzy—there's so much hype and no money left over for improving nursing homes and home care.

A geriatric epidemiologist openly challenges the idea of AD as a disease:

> As far as I'm concerned, genes are just other variables. They are markers, inherited markers, that have to be put into the pot for analysis along with other variables to see how they look. The great mistake with AD is to assume that because there is one end point there is one cause and one treatment. I don't think AD is a disease.

One clinician, a British psychogeriatrician, gave what appears at first sight to be an outmoded discourse among clinical experts involved with AD but is in fact a common response among doctors who carry out behavioral rather than basic-science research:

You can have Alzheimer's without predisposing genes—the genetics are overblown. Alzheimer's is clearly linked to lifestyle. It all depends on where you work professionally as to what you think about cause, prevention, and best treatment. I think that lifestyle changes are crucial—there is evidence that exercise lowers incidence, and diet is crucial because cholesterol is involved in plaque production.

A language of determinism is not explicitly made use of by these experts. The contribution of genetics is readily acknowledged, but current thinking has it that the complexity of aging ensures that, aside from the inherited mutations associated with early-onset AD, all of us are both protected and vulnerable to some extent, depending on specific events and contexts. Even those individuals who are homozygous for *ApoE ε4* are by no means doomed. Such people are at an increased risk but are not necessarily predisposed to the disease. Not a single clinician interviewed believes that genetic testing for *ApoE ε4* should be used routinely in the clinic.[7]

One clinician stated that in his own mind the category of AD, and even more so that of dementia, is fluid. But he went on to say that using the "construct" of AD as though it were a hard and fast category makes sound political sense. His argument is that the label helps to improve the lives of people suffering from AD because it can be used by advocacy groups and others to raise public awareness and funding. But he added: "in the quiet of the lab it is sensible to be skeptical and make use of these categories in a fluid, provisional way."

At Risk for Alzheimer's Disease: Ambiguities in Externalizing Discourses

In general, data on external variables are consistently relegated to the margins in discussions about AD causation. Although the need for good data on external factors is evident, to date, the externalizing discourse about AD has not been marked by the complexity of the internalizing discourse. It appears, for the most part, oversimplified and occasionally dangerously misleading.

Several external factors, notably age and severe head injury, are regarded as beyond dispute as risk factors for AD and are assumed to be universal in effect. Sex and family history are also recognized as risk factors. Women are apparently more prone to AD than are men, even when age is controlled for, but this difference is not fully accounted for by biology. It has also become clear that late-onset AD is not "sporadic" and occurs much more frequently in some families than in others, presumably because many members of these families have the *ApoE ε4* allele.

One common approach to assessing the contribution of external factors to AD causation focuses on education. Low levels of education have been correlated in many studies with a greater risk for AD, leading to the assertion that "education has proven to be the most important non-biological correlate of cognitive performance" (Anstey and Christensen 2000). The frequently cited "nun's study" is an example of this trend. The statements of 575 nuns about their reasons for entering a nunnery, written when they were novices, were analyzed for use of complex thinking and then compared with their responses to the Mini Mental State Examination (the MMSE is the usual assessment tool for AD and other forms of dementia) carried out when these nuns were in old age. It was found that those women with less education and who exhibited a relatively poor ability for complex thinking when they were young showed a more rapid cognitive decline in old age. However, this difference did not become increasingly magnified with age. The conclusion drawn from this research by the majority of experts is that a good formal education creates numerous synapses in the brain, giving individuals more to fall back on as they age.

A recent article following a similar line of argument suggests that adults with hobbies, who exercise their brains through such activities as reading, doing jigsaws, and playing chess are less likely to have AD than are individuals who spend long hours in front of television sets (*Globe and Mail* 2000). This study adds to the widely held sentiment in the world of AD specialists that the brain, like certain other organs of the body, thrives on regular exercise. A "use it or lose it" slogan is routinely touted to account for what is assumed to be a firm association between levels of education, styles of cognition, and AD incidence. Even the recent, well-publicized death of Iris Murdoch, who suffered from AD, has not dented the assurance with which this argument is made.

Other research that focuses largely on external factors leaves anthropologists with feelings of disquiet, in particular the claims made about race, ethnicity, genetics, and risk for AD. One study found that the greater the "genetic degree" of Cherokee ancestry (as documented in tribal records), the greater the protection against developing AD (Rosenberg et al. 1996). This study was carried out with 26 AD patients aged sixty-five and over and a control group of 26 also selected from the Cherokee community. It was found that the control group had a "higher degree of Cherokee ancestry." This "protective factor" was independent of the *ApoE* allele and was shown to diminish with age. The research, frequently cited, is similar to one involving 192 Cree over age sixty-five in which only 1 case of dementia was found. Such studies are problematic for several reasons. First, far-reaching conclusions are drawn from small samples. Second, tribal identity is confused with something variously labeled as race or ethnicity, which is thought to correlate with specific biological characteristics. And third, "standardized dementia evaluations" in the form of psychological "instruments" designed to "measure" cognitive capabilities were used to assess AD. These instruments were developed originally for use among middle-class urban populations. They are not highly reliable under any circumstances but prove to be considerably less so, and often blatantly misleading, when language differences, education, familiarity with psychological testing, and other factors are not taken into account (see also Lock 1993).

More sophisticated research is being carried out by the 10/66 Dementia Research Group, an international consortium of researchers who argue forcefully that research is urgently needed into dementia and its management in developing countries, where more than two-thirds of the elderly presently live—a number that is increasing year by year. This group argues that studies such as that from Nigeria cited above, with low reporting of AD, may well simply reflect a nonrecognition in many societies of dementia as anything other than "normal" aging, possibly resulting in early deaths for many demented people because their plight is not brought to public attention (Consensus Statement 2000). Ethnographic accounts such as those of Cohen (1998), Herskovits (1995), Ikels (1998), and Leibing (2002) have influenced the way in which this research is being implemented. Recognition of the social construction of aging and dementia, of specific local idioms of distress, and of the moral and political trappings associated with dementia in differing localities is central to this project, making it vastly superior to the much more often cited research noted above.

Some clinicians now recognize the urgent need for an anthropological approach that highlights popular knowledge about AD and attitudes toward the elderly and memory loss, as well as the subjective experience and expectations of that large segment of the public that is directly affected by dementia, whether as patients, potential patients, caregivers, family, or community. For one thing, such an approach may help to explain why many people, even those designated as at risk, do not become demented; and it will be even more necessary as genetic testing becomes routinized. Furthermore, anthropology offers the skill of contextualizing the ways in which emerging basic-science and epidemiological knowledge is applied in specific cultural, political-economic, and environmental milieux. This contextualization is of increasing importance because the diagnosis and management of dementia are rapidly being systematized as part of a globalized endeavor.

The Limits of Genetic Determinism: Inserting Complexity into Accounts of Alzheimer's Disease

In 1992 Abby Lippman coined the term "geneticization" to capture what she perceives as an ever-growing tendency to distinguish people on the basis of genetics. Lippman is concerned above all with the ways in which racism, inequalities, and discrimination are potentially reinforced as a result of a renewed conflation of social realities and biological difference grounded in genetics such as we are apparently seeing in connection with AD research. She believes that we may well be witnessing an incipient neo-eugenics (1998), as do many other contemporary writers (see, e.g., Kitcher 1997).

Adam Hedgecoe takes a slightly different tack. He understands the use of genetic knowledge and technologies as just the latest in a series of attempts to advance our understanding of the body at the molecular level and is less inclined than Lippman to see geneticization as "an opportunistic tactic employed by doctors to gain power over patients" (2001: 877). Hedgecoe argues for recognition of a concept of "enlightened geneticization," by which he means that genetic explanations are prioritized and subtly divert attention away from nongenetic factors, even though the contribution of environmental and other factors is today widely accepted in scientific discourse about disease causation (see also Spallone 1998). He agrees with Lippman that genetic determinism is indeed at work but points out that—like medicalization more generally (Lock and Kaufert 1998)—it has some positive attributes. For example, it is abundantly clear that once a disease is medically recognized, particularly when behavioral changes are involved, then social stigma and allocation of individual and family responsibility for the occurrence of such conditions are reduced (McGuffin, Riley, and Plomin 2001). What is more, many families apparently get comfort from being told that a disabling condition is the result of faulty genetics and therefore has nothing to do with moral shortcomings (Turney and Turner 2002).

Still, in the case of AD, and no doubt other multifactorial conditions, even when a susceptibility gene is incontrovertibly identified, it does not follow that geneticization will become the dominant mode of conceptualizing the condition wherever it is being investigated, treated, and managed. Although geneticism is apparent in most professional discourse in connection with AD, there is dissent and disagreement and, above all, differences in emphasis among the various groups of involved specialists: basic scientists, neurologists, clinical geneticists, clinical psychologists, psychiatrists, and others. Nor is a focus on genetics steadfastly embraced by the media when discussing complex diseases; it is usually emphasized that multiple risk factors are at play. Advocacy-group literature minimizes the contribution of genetics, as do the majority of patients and their families as they face the massive burden of dealing with a disease as devastating as AD (Lock, Lloyd, and Prest, in press).

If the new genetics is indeed bringing about a revolution, it is unlikely to be one in which a doctrine of genetic determinism will dominate the scene. Although, in the space of a few years, advances in genomics and proteomics have been phenomenal, it is, above all, complexity and unpredictability that have been documented to date. Even in connection with the Mendelian conditions such as Tay-Sachs disease, Huntington's disease, and cystic fibrosis, the assumption that we can move ahead rapidly with genetic testing and programs for screening populations (after dealing with the inevitable ethical matters) has proved to be problematic. It is now known that, even in the presence of autosomal dominant and recessive genes, the fit between genotype and phenotype is far from perfect, considerable variation is evident, and estimations of risk have had to be revised downward. Most of the findings that are derived from the new genetics—both molecular and population genetics—have resulted in many more questions than they have answered.

Many basic scientists and clinicians are alert as to how provisional the AD category is, at least when using the perspective of an internalizing discourse. Social scientists, historians, and physicians are beginning to work together to map the fuzzy boundaries between the reality of dementia, the subjective experience of this condition, and the dynamics of classification over time. It is possible that one key concept, that of mind, missing from virtually all medical discussion about AD, with its emphasis on loss of synapse function, may well prove to be essential in creating helpful associations between internalizing and externalizing discourses.

But first it will be necessary to insert complexity into externalizing accounts that discuss the so-called social determinants of dementia. The concepts made use of in both molecular and social epidemiology demand interrogation, and ethnographic research that draws on a critical-interpretive approach is called for. Indispensable to this research will be recognition not only of cultural and political differences and of cultural constructions of the natural, but also of the reality of biological variation and of the inseparability of biology and culture. The task at hand is enormous.

We describe people with AD as having minds that are "fogged." Knowledge about AD is also fogged and will remain so unless we come to appreciate that the contributions made by different domains of expertise that draw on several epistemological orientations, externalizing and internalizing, add up to more than the sum of the parts in our battle with this complex, elusive, devastating condition.

Notes

1. Structural genomics consists of the sequencing, or "mapping," of the DNA out of which genes are formed. Increasingly, the whole genomes of many organisms—viruses, parasites, plants, and animals, in addition to the human genome—are being mapped. Both the pharmaceutical industry and agrobusiness are particularly interested in gene sequencing. Functional genomics has to some extent eclipsed structural genomics. The goal of functional genomics is to establish how genes and their protein products function in living organisms.

2. The use of "Mendelian genetics" is currently limited to instances in which a single genetic mutation, if inherited from both parents, results, with only very few exceptions, in the expression of a phenotypic trait of a known disease. Individuals who carry only one such genetic mutation are known as "carriers" for the disease in question.

3. A shift toward a molecular approach in biology began in the 1930s. This shift was associated with a search for what constitutes "life" and was made possible by the development of several new technologies. For two decades molecular biology focused on protein structure and function. After 1953, when the significance of the discovery of DNA was recognized, emphasis switched dramatically to genes, opening up an era that is currently known as the "new genetics," culminating in the Human Genome Project.

4. It is estimated that currently AD costs U.S. businesses more than $33 million in "lost productivity and absenteeism" and that these costs will soar as the baby boomers take time off to care for their elderly relatives (*New York Herald Tribune* 1998).

5. At this same conference, an epidemiologist clarified the way in which genes are believed to be implicated from before birth in connection with what will happen in old age. Genes influence the building of "cognitive capacity," this epidemiologist argued, starting in the intrauterine environment and playing a large role throughout infancy and childhood and into early adult life. The presentation suggested that, when AD experts claim that people with high IQs and with extensive education are at considerably less risk for AD than are others, what is assumed is that genetic predisposition influences the laying down of the neurological networks required for brain functioning. Thus, certain biologically predisposed individuals will end up as adults with fewer synapses and, as a result, are likely to have lower IQs and therefore will complete less schooling. The plaques, tangles, and cell death associated with AD are thought to do proportionally more damage in a short space of time to such people.

6. The term "heterozygous" refers to the case where a person carries only one *ApoE ε4* allele (along with an *ApoE ε2* or *3*, for example). Someone who is homozygous for *ApoE ε4* has two of these alleles.

7. However, it is increasingly customary for patients and their families to be asked to provide blood for various projects that include DNA testing for genes and proteins thought to be associated with AD. If the family agrees to participate in a study, blood is drawn and the sample is then rendered anonymous before it is sent for analysis. The results of such testing are not made available to patients, families, or clinicians, and therefore participation generally has little effect on clinical encounters, but when clinicians are frank about the uses to which the blood will be put, anxiety levels may well be raised.

References

Alzheimer's Disease Society of Great Britain. 1997. *What Is Alzheimer's Disease?* London: Alzheimer's Disease Society of Great Britain.

Anstey, Kaarin, and Helen Christensen. 2000. Education, Activity, Health, Blood Pressure and Apolipoprotein E as Predictors of Cognitive Change in Old Age: A Review. *Gerontology* 46: 163–77.

Ballinger, Jesse F. 2000. Beyond the Characteristic Plaques and Tangles: Mid Twentieth Century U.S. Psychiatry and the Fight against Senility. In *Concepts of Alzheimer's Disease: Biological, Clinical, and Cultural Perspectives,* ed. Peter J. Whitehouse, Konrad Maurer, and Jesse F. Ballinger, pp. 83–103. Baltimore: Johns Hopkins University Press.

Berrios, G. E. 1990. Alzheimer's Disease: A Conceptual History. *International Journal of Geriatric Psychiatry* 5: 355–65.

Cohen, Lawrence. 1998. *No Aging in India: Alzheimer's, the Bad Family, and Other Modern Things.* Berkeley and Los Angeles: University of California Press.

Conrad, Peter. 2001a. Constructing the "Gay Gene": Optimism and Skepticism in the News. *Health* 5: 373–400.

———. 2001b. Genetic Optimism: Framing Genes and Mental Illness in the News. *Culture, Medicine, and Psychiatry* 25: 225–47.

Conrad, Peter, and D. Weinberg. 1996. Has the Gene for Alcoholism Been Discovered Three Times since 1980? A News Media Analysis. *Perspectives on Social Problems* 8: 3–24.

Consensus Statement from the 10/66 Dementia Research Group. 2000. Dementia in Developing Countries. *International Journal of Geriatric Psychiatry* 15: 14–20.

Corbo, R. M., and R. Scacchi. 1999. Apolipoprotein E (APOE) Allele Distribution in the World: Is APOE*4 a "Thrifty" Allele? *Annals of Human Genetics* 63: 301–10.

Evans, Bob, Morris L. Barer, and Theodore R. Marmor, eds. 1994. *Why Are Some People Healthy and Others Not? The Determinants of Health of Populations.* New York: Aldine de Gruyter.

Farlow, Martin R. 1997. Alzheimer's Disease: Clinical Implications of the Apolipoprotein E Genotype. *Neurology* 48: S30–34.

Farrer, Lindsay A. 2000. Familial Risk for Alzheimer Disease in Ethnic Minorities: Nondiscriminating Genes. *Archives of Neurology* 57: 28–29.

Fox, Patrick J. 1999 The Role of the Concept of Alzheimer's Disease in the Development of the Alzheimer's Association in the United States. In *Concepts of Alzheimer's Disease: Biological, Clinical, and Cultural Perspectives,* ed. Peter J. Whitehouse, Konrad Maurer, and Jesse F. Ballinger, pp. 209–33. Baltimore: Johns Hopkins University Press.

Globe and Mail. 2000. Hobbies Reduce Alzheimer's, Study Finds. Tuesday, March 6.

Graham, Janice E. 2000. Differentially Diagnosing Dementia: A Triage of Texts. In *The Diversity of Alzheimer's Disease: Different Approaches and Contexts,* ed. Annette Leibing and Lilian Scheinkman, pp. 95–112. Rio de Janeiro: Edições CUCA-IPUB.

Green, R. C., N. Relkin, P. J. Whitehouse, T. Brown, S. LaRusse, M. Barber, and S. Roberts. 2002. Among Adult Offspring of Persons with Alzheimer's Disease, Who Will Elect to Pursue Risk Assessment and APOE Disclosure? Preliminary Results from the REVEAL Study. *Neurology* 58: A40.

Growdon, John H. 1998. Apolipoprotein E and Alzheimer Disease. *Archives of Neurology* 55(8): 1053–54.

Gubrium, Jaber F. 1987. Structuring and Destructuring the Course of Illness: The Alzheimer's Disease Experience. *Sociology of Health and Illness* 9: 1–24.

Hacking, Ian. 1996. Disunities of Science. In *The Disunity of Science: Boundaries, Contexts, and Power,* ed. Peter L. Galison and David J. Stump, pp. 37–74. Stanford: Stanford University Press.

Hedgecoe, Adam. 2001. Schizophrenia and the Narrative of Enlightened Geneticization. *Social Studies of Science* 31: 875–911.

————. 2004. The Politics of Personalized Medicine: Pharmacogenetics in the Clinic. Cambridge: Cambridge University Press.

Henig, Robin Marantz. 1981. *The Myth of Senility: Misconceptions about the Brain and Aging.* Garden City, NY: Doubleday.

Herskovits, E. 1995. Struggling over Subjectivity: Debates about the "Self" and Alzheimer's Disease. *Medical Anthropology Quarterly* 9: 146–64.

Holmes, Clive. 2002. The Genetics of Alzheimer's Disease. *Journal of the British Menopause Society* 8: 20–23.

Ikels, Charlotte. 1998. The Experience of Dementia in China. *Culture, Medicine, and Psychiatry* 22: 257–83.

Katzman, R. 1976. The Prevalence and Malignancy of Alzheimer's Disease: A Major Killer. *Archives of Neurology* 33: 217–218.

Keller, Evelyn Fox. 1992. Nature, Nurture, and the Human Genome Project. In *The Code of Codes: Scientific and Social Issues in the Human Genome Project,* ed. Daniel J. Kelves and Leroy Hood, pp. 281–99. Cambridge: Harvard University Press.

————. 2000. *The Century of the Gene.* Cambridge: Harvard University Press.

Khachaturian, Zaven S. 1997. Plundered Memories. *The Sciences* 37: 21–25.

Kier, Frederick J., and Victor Molinari. 2003. "Do-It-Yourself" Dementia Testing: Issues Regarding an Alzheimer's Home Screening Test. *The Gerontologist* 43: 295–301.

Kitcher, Philip. 1997. *The Lives to Come: The Genetic Revolution and Human Possibilities.* New York: Simon and Schuster.

Korovaitseva, G. I., T. V. Sherbatich, N. V. Selezneva, S. I. Gavrilova, V. E. Golimbet, N. I. Voskresenskaya, and E. I. Rogaev. 2001. Genetic Association between the Apolipoprotein E (APOE) Gene and Different Forms of Alzheimer's Disease. *Human Genetics* 37: 422–27.

Koshland, Daniel. 1989. Sequences and Consequences of the Human Genome. *Science* 146: 189.

Leibing, Annette. 2002. Flexible Hips? On Alzheimer's Disease and Aging in Brazil. *Journal of Cross Cultural Gerontology* 17: 231–32.

Lewontin, Richard C. 2000. *The Triple Helix: Gene, Organism, and Environment.* Cambridge: Harvard University Press.

Liddell, M. B., S. Lovestone, and M. J. Owen. 2001. Genetic Risk of Alzheimer's Disease: Advising Relatives. *British Journal of Psychiatry* 178: 7–11.

Lippman, Abby. 1998. The Politics of Health: Geneticization versus Health Promotion. In *The Politics of Women's Health,* ed. Susan Sherwin, pp. 64–82. Philadelphia: Temple University Press.

Lock, Margaret. 1993. *Encounters with Aging: Mythologies of Menopause in Japan and North America.* Berkeley and Los Angeles: University of California Press.

————. 2001. The Tempering of Medical Anthropology: Troubling Natural Categories. *Medical Anthropological Quarterly* 15: 478–92.

Lock, Margaret, and Patricia Kaufert, eds. 1998. *Pragmatic Women and Body Politics.* Cambridge: Cambridge University Press.

Lock, Margaret, Stephanie Lloyd, and Janalyn Prest. In press. Genetic Susceptibility and Alzheimer's Disease: The "Penetrance" and Uptake of Genetic Knowledge. In *The Anthropology of Alzheimer's Disease,* ed. Lawrence Cohen and Annette Leibing. New Brunswick, NJ: Rutgers University Press.

Maurer, Konrad, Stephan Volk, and Hector Gerbaldo. 1999. Auguste D: The History of Alois Alzheimer's First Case. In *Concepts of Alzheimer's Disease: Biological, Clinical, and Cultural*

Perspectives, ed. Peter J. Whitehouse, Konrad Maurer, and Jesse F. Ballinger, pp. 5–29. Baltimore: Johns Hopkins University Press.

McConnell, L. M., B. A. Koenig, H. T. Greely, and A. S. Raffin. 1998. Genetic Testing and Alzheimer Disease: Has the Time Come? *Nature Medicine* 4: 757–59.

McGuffin, P., B. Riley, and R. Plomin. 2001. Toward Behavioral Genomics. *Science* 291: 1242–49.

Myers, Amanda, Peter Holmans, Helen Marshall, Jennifer Kwon, David Meyer, Dzanan Ramic, Shantia Shears, et al. 2000. Susceptibility Locus for Alzheimer's Disease on Chromosome 10. *Science* 290: 2304–5.

Nascher, I. L. 1914. *Geriatrics: The Diseases of Old Age and Their Treatment.* Philadelphia: P. Blakiston's.

Neumann, Meta A., and Robert Cohn. 1953. Incidence of Alzheimer's Disease in a Large Mental Hospital. *Archives of Neurology and Psychiatry* 69: 615–36.

Neve, Rachael L., and Nikolaos K. Robakis. 1998. Alzheimer's Disease: A Re-examination of the Amyloid Hypothesis. *Trends in Neuroscience* 21: 15–19.

New York Herald Tribune. 1998. Alzheimer's Disease Costs U.S. Businesses More than $33 Billion. Friday, September 11.

Papassotiropoulos, Andreas, Johannes R. Streffler, Mgdalini Tsolaki, Simon Schmid, Dietmar Thal, Francesca Nicosia, Vassiliki Iakovidou, et al. 2003. Increased Brain β-amyloidal, Phosphoylated Tau, and Risk of Alzheimer Disease Associated with an Intronic CYP46 Polymorphism. *Archives of Neurology* 60: 29–35.

Rabinow, Paul. 2000. Epochs, Presents, Events. In *Living and Working with the New Medical Technologies: Intersections of Inquiry,* ed. Margaret Lock, Allan Young, and Alberto Cambrosio, pp. 31–46. Cambridge: Cambridge University Press.

Ritchie, Karen, and Anne-Marie Dupuy. 1999. Current Status of APO E4 as a Risk Factor for Alzheimer's Disease: An Epidemiological Perspective. *International Journal of Geriatric Psychiatry* 14(9): 695–700.

Rosenberg, Roger N., Ralph W. Richter, Richard C. Risser, Kevin Taubman, Ivette Prado-Farmer, Eleanor Ebalo, JoAnne Posey, et al. 1996. Genetic Factors for the Development of Alzheimer Disease in the Cherokee Indian. *Archives of Neurology* 53: 997–1000.

Roses, Allen D. 1998. Apolipoprotein E and Alzheimer's Disease: The Tip of the Susceptibility Iceberg. *Annals of the New York Academy of Sciences* 855: 738–43.

Saunders, Ann M. 2000. Apolipoprotein E and Alzheimer Disease: An Update on Genetic and Functional Analyses. *Journal of Neuropathology and Experimental Neurology* 59: 751–58.

Silverman, Jeremy M., Christopher J. Smith, Deborah B. Marin, Richard C. Mohs, and Cathi B. Propper. 2003. Familial Patterns of Risk in Very Late-Onset Alzheimer Disease. *Archives of General Psychiatry* 60: 190–97.

Sing, C. F., M. B. Haviland, and S. L. Reilly. 1996. Genetic Architecture of Common Multifactorial Diseases. In *Variation in the Human Genome,* ed. Derek Chadwick and Gail Cardew, pp. 211–32. Chichester, NY: John Wiley.

Spallone, Pat. 1998. The New Biology of Violence: New Geneticisms for Old? *Body and Society* 4: 47–65.

St. George-Hyslop, Peter H. 2000. Molecular Genetics of Alzheimer's Disease. *Biological Psychiatry* 47: 183–99.

Stafford, Philip B. 1991. The Social Construction of Alzheimer's Disease. In *Biosemiotics: The Semiotic Web,* ed. Thomas A. Sebeok and Jean Umiker-Sebeok, pp. 393–406. Berlin: Mouton de Gruyter.

Strittmatter, W. V., A. M. Saunders, D. Schmeckel, M. Pericak-Vance, J. Enghild, G. S. Salvesen, and A. D. Roses. 1993. Apolipoprotein E: High-Avidity Binding to Beta-amyloid and Increased Frequency of Type 4 Allele in Late-Onset Familial Alzheimer Disease. *Proceedings of the National Academy of Sciences* 90: 1977–81.

Swartz, R. H., S. E. Black, and P. St. George-Hyslop. 1999. ApolipoproteinE and Alzheimer's Disease: A Genetic, Molecular and Neuroimaging Review. *Canadian Journal of Neurological Sciences* 26: 77–88.

Szasz, Thomas. 1961. *The Myth of Mental Illness.* New York: Harper and Row.

Time. 2003. Future Visions. February 17, 161: 42.

Tilley, L., K. Morgan, and N. Kalsheker. 1998. Genetic Risk Factors in Alzheimer's Disease. *Journal of Clinical Pathology: Molecular Pathology* 51: 293–304.

Tomlinson, Bernard E., Garry Blessed, and Martin Roth. 1968. Observations on the Brains of Non-demented Old People. *Journal of Neurological Science* 7: 331–56.

Turney, Jon, and Jill Turner. 2002. Predictive Medicine, Genetics, and Schizophrenia. *New Genetics and Society* 19: 5–22.

U.S. Office of Technology Assessment. 1988. *Mapping Our Genes.* U.S. Congress. Washington, DC: Government Printing Office.

Young, Allan. 1976. Some Implications of Medical Beliefs and Practices for Social Anthropology. *American Anthropologist* 78: 5–24.

CHAPTER 10

The Molecular Revolution in Medicine:
Promise, Reality, and Social Organization

Karen-Sue Taussig

> To truly understand genomics, you are going to need
> access to millions of genomes.—*Eugene Chan, founder
> and chairman of U.S. Genomics, 2002*

IN THE LATE 1980s the U.S. government undertook a major scientific initiative known as the Human Genome Project (HGP), earmarking three billion dollars for an attempt to delineate the billions of base pairs of nucleotides making up the genetic material in human beings. The HGP was founded on the promise that this knowledge would result in new opportunities to improve human health through medical interventions at the molecular level. Since then the nearly constant popular and professional media barrage of genetic findings points not only to the rapid proliferation of genetic knowledge but also to a public discourse in which genetic causality is increasingly used to explain human diversity and affliction.

Public attention is constantly called to the discovery of genes "for" particular conditions and the promise of genetic interventions in medicine. Indeed, one of the persistent promises made by the HGP's proponents is that there will be a revolution in medicine, including the ability to treat and/or cure a wide range of human afflictions. In talking about new genetic knowledge and its potential application in genetic medicine, physicians and others make claims for its transformative powers, likening its emergence, for example, to the advent of the ability to understand, harness, and produce electricity.

At the same time, every thoughtful researcher (and, in fact, many nonscientists) understands that genes are only a part of any story about embodied conditions (Lewontin 2000). Most scientists agree that genes interact with the environments in which they exist. But when dealing with genetic material, what exactly counts as environment? The nucleus, the cell, the body, ecology, and social contexts each constitute an environment in which genes exist. Each of these environments offers a different way to contextualize genetic material. As diverse constituencies—clinicians, members of families bearing genetic conditions, researchers, policy makers concerned about escalating health care costs and the burden of caring for people with disabling or chronic conditions—work to contextualize genes in diverse and sometimes conflicting ways, they are shaping the ways in which genetic knowledge is being translated into new medical interventions.

To date, there have been few significant successful clinical interventions developed from knowledge created through this publicly funded project (Lewontin 2002).[1] This irony is exemplified by the June 2000 announcement of the completion of a "rough draft" of the human genome that came nearly simultaneously with media coverage of the death of Jesse Gelsinger, a teenager participating in a gene therapy trial at the University of Pennsylvania (Stolberg 1999, 2000). In the immediate aftermath of Gelsinger's death, public attention was also called to the fact that virtually every attempt at gene therapy had failed (Lewontin 2002). Human-genome researchers predicted such a gap between new knowledge of molecular structure and clinical utility early in the genome project (Kevles and Hood 1992). With the completion of a human-genome map, scientists have shifted their attention to efforts aimed at closing that gap. This has meant focusing less on structural genomics with its mapping and more on functional genomics—the function of genes in specific environments—with a goal of developing clinically relevant interventions into human health.

It is in this space between the promise and the reality of contemporary genetic medicine that the events explored in this chapter are playing out. Numerous scholars and other social observers have suggested that we are now experiencing a profound moment of social transformation (Appadurai 1996; Fraser 1997; Harvey 1989; Silver 1997). Social theorists from such diverse orientations as Jürgen Habermas (2001) and Francis Fukuyama (2002) are turning their attention to the implications of new molecular knowledge and its associated current and potential technologies. At the same time, we see the constant reiteration of utopic and dystopic visions of what future these phenomena might bring, the appearance of art inspired by genetics (Guidotti 1998; Madoff 2002; Nelkin and Anker 2003), and the rise of the gene as "cultural icon" (Nelkin and Lindee 1995). The proliferation of these kinds of phenomena clearly link developments in molecular genetics and its associated biotechnologies to the current transformative moment.

In contemporary struggles over genetic material and knowledge we see the emergence of a new site for talking about larger social issues having to do with the organization, interpretation, and control of the new knowledge and resources that will undergird future understandings of what makes an acceptable human being. These struggles also help us understand that contemporary genetic practices have both reductive and antireductive aspects, and the tension between them constantly shapes and reshapes people's understandings of and engagement with genetics.

Previous anthropological inquiries into science point to the complex ways medical and scientific practices are shaped in relation to one another (e.g., Fujimura 1988, 1992; Oudshoorn 1994). Monica Casper and Marc Berg argue that studies of the relationships between scientific and medical knowledge and practice have the potential "to reveal how power structures are mediated in and through scientific medical knowledge" (1995: 397). They suggest that understanding the relationship between these different sets of knowledge and practice offers an opportunity to further our understanding of their politics (1995: 403). Contemporary efforts to translate new genetic knowledge into scientific medical practices offer an opportunity to see these processes in action. As Casper and Berg stress, "medical work is a crucial site of *control over* bodies and lives. . . . In the practice of medicine, patients' bodies, lives, and subjectivities become entrenched within networks of technologies, medical personnel, and institutional arrangements" (1995: 402, emphasis in the original).

This chapter is based on two years of ethnographic fieldwork in the United States that tracked developments in genetic medicine and the engagement of a wide array of ordinary people in what I have come to understand as genetic thinking and practices. The social processes I have observed exist at the intersections of people's bodies, corporate interests, medical activism, and medical/scientific research agendas, where, on the one hand, bodies and their molecules provide the material means to develop genetic medicine and, on the other hand, physicians serve as the potential consumers and distributors of clinically relevant knowledge and biotech corporate products. These processes provide a window through which to view the work of transforming molecular knowledge into medical practice. This work plays a significant role in shaping the social relations upon which any new molecular medicine could be built. In every case, those involved in these efforts are actively engaged in future building, imagining and working toward a future in which hopeful visions of scientific progress and human improvement loom large. As people struggle over issues having to do with the source, contextualization, and meaning of DNA, as well as privacy, participation, and control, a range of possible options come into view. The different kinds of social arrangements through which this new medicine is emerging matter very much both for the people involved and for the kind of future that will get built.

In this chapter, I first focus on the tension between the promise and the current reality of genetic knowledge to illustrate the problems geneticists now face because of reductive thinking about genetics, and I highlight current moves to contextualize genes. Contextualizing genes, however, means moving outside the lab and clinic and linking genetic data to the persons, families, medical records, social relationships, and various environments of the people who are the source of genetic material. In this process of contextualization, different models have been produced for how to develop the necessary flows of materials and knowledge into, out of, and between the clinic and laboratory. In these models, we see struggles over ideas about how genetic material should be used and contextualized and how issues of privacy and control should be handled. The remainder of the chapter examines these struggles as I have observed them in my fieldwork.

Wagering on the Genome

Francis Collins, the director of the Human Genome Project, has been clear that the project needs to deliver on its promises of clinically relevant interventions. He has appointed a medical geneticist (a physician with a specialty in genetics) as his clinical adviser, whose job it is to facilitate work toward clinical applications of the new knowledge the HGP is producing. Both large multinational pharmaceutical companies and individuals have invested enormous amounts of capital into a complex multilayered biotechnology industry that does everything from harvest and store DNA to carry out research focused on developing marketable knowledge (e.g., potentially clinically relevant mutations or polymorphisms) and products (e.g., Affymetrix high-throughput chip; prenatal diagnostic kits). Despite all these efforts, it is well known among genome scientists and informed medical practitioners that there are, thus far, few clinically relevant findings from the HGP. Nevertheless, a wide array of media sources repeatedly report that genetics is the future of medicine, offering utopian visions of a medical future in which physicians are able to treat an extensive number of now debilitating and/or fatal conditions.[2]

The fact that knowledge of the human genome has not yet been translated into clinical intervention ironically challenges the certitude and reductivism of science. In her exploration of twentieth-century genetic research, Evelyn Fox Keller points out that, "contrary to all expectations, instead of lending support to the familiar notions of genetic determinism that have acquired so powerful a grip on the popular imagination, these successes [of the HGP] pose critical challenges to such notions" (Keller 2000: 5).

In the early days of the HGP, the Harvard-based Nobel Prize–winning molecular biologist Walter Gilbert was famous for his presentations on the academic talk circuit, when he would pull out a CD-ROM during his descriptions of the likely outcome of the project and tell his audience "this is you" (Nelkin and Lindee 1995; see also Gilbert 1992). Reducing individual people to the sequence of their DNA, which could then be encoded on a CD-ROM, reflected a powerful belief that learning this DNA sequence would give scientists and others the essential information about both individual human beings and the human species as a whole.

The certainty with which scientists such as Gilbert made claims about the value, power, and utility of results of the HGP suggests some of the ways that biological scientists were able to transform their authority and prestige (Bourdieu 1984, [1975] 1998) into a massive commitment from the U.S. Congress to fund the mapping of the human genome.[3] From the inception of the project, scientists estimated that its completion would reveal that the human genome was made up of three billion base pairs, including approximately 100,000 genes (Kevles and Hood 1992). They made grand pronouncements about how this knowledge would result in treatments not only for the rare single-gene conditions long recognized as having a genetic basis but also for the many widespread common conditions such as heart disease, diabetes, and cancer that are believed to have a genetic component (Kevles and Hood 1992).

In the period leading up to the announcement of completion of the rough draft of the human genome, this kind of talk became quite muted. Experimental genetic interventions at the clinical level were failing. Furthermore, it seemed that the closer scientists came to completing the HGP, the more they realized that what they thought they knew was not in fact what they were finding; understanding both the structure and the function of DNA was more complicated than many elite genome scientists had predicted. Humorously highlighting this phenomenon, in May 2000, just a month before the announcement of the completion of the draft, it was reported around the world that scientists at Cold Spring Harbor Laboratories had established a sweepstakes for placing bets on the number of genes that would ultimately be found in the genome (Ahuja 2000; *Daily Yomiuri* 2000; Wade 2000). Scientists of no less stature than Francis Collins himself were reported to have gotten "into the spirit of things" (Abate 2000).

At the sweepstakes' inception, estimates ranged from 27,462 to 200,000 (Ahuja 2000), and, in interviews with the media, participants expressed divergent views about the meanings one might read into numbers. One was quoted as stating that "the value of human life cannot be measured by the number of genes, so the total will not be large," while another said that "it would be illogical if the total number of genes is smaller than that of animals of lower evolutionary rank, such as flies" (*Daily Yomiuri* 2000). The serious nature of this issue is underscored, however, by the fact that *Nature Genetics* had published several articles on the topic just prior to the establishment of the sweepstakes, with estimates ranging from 28,000 to 120,000 (Aparicio 2000; *Nature Genetics* 2000). Later that month at the White House announcement of the completion of a rough draft of the genome, scientists informed the world that the draft indicated that the human genome contained approximately 30,000 genes. This was reported as perhaps one of the most significant findings of the rough draft.

Scientists immediately exclaimed that the existence of so few genes in so complex an organism as humans meant that genes, by themselves, could not explain human biology. Consequently, the concept of proteomics—the study of the proteins produced by DNA sequences and their complex interactions—and an emphasis on gene function rapidly came into the frame of genetic research and its representation in science, in science policy, and in popular-science reporting.[4]

Keller suggests that, rather than finding the "secret of life" at the level of the genome, what has been found is life's enormous complexity (Keller 2000: 7–8). While many scientists and others—including the policy makers and venture capitalists who have supported genetic research—seemed to believe that the delineation of the base pairs making up the human genome would rapidly lead to treatments, the completion of a rough draft and the failure to develop clinical interventions have led researchers to a realization of a more complex relationship between structure and function. This recognition prompted one molecular geneticist to quip, "With regard to understanding the A's, T's, G's, and C's of genomic sequence, by and large, we are functional illiterates" (cited in Keller 2000: 6).

Achieving literacy in functional genomics, however, does not merely require refocusing research activities within laboratories. On the pathway from structure to expression, DNA interacts with its environment at multiple levels, and it is this interaction that must be comprehended if the function of genetic material is to be understood. If one wants to understand why one person with the *BRCA1* gene linked to breast cancer is diagnosed with cancer at age thirty while another never gets the disease, then an examination of the multiple potentially relevant environmental contexts—nuclear, cellular, somatic, familial, social, ecological, etc.—is necessary for understanding gene function.

From Knowledge to Intervention

Enormous resources are now being devoted to translating new genetic knowledge into clinical interventions, thus intensifying efforts aimed at understanding gene function. In seeking to address these problems, geneticists, policy makers, and biotech interests are working not only to develop a clinical landscape in which physicians are receptive to and capable of incorporating new genetic knowledge into clinical practice but also to build the kinds of social relations with people outside laboratories that will facilitate the contextualization of genetic material.

The current lack of understanding and of clinical utility is in tension with a powerful belief among many researchers, physicians, and their institutional administrators that genetic knowledge will take center stage in medical practice in the near future. Calls for revising medical school curricula and attention to studies showing that physicians have little understanding of when to order and how to interpret genetic tests (ASHG 1995; Childs 1993; Collins 1997; Hager 1999) have been followed by conferences focusing on how to integrate genetics into contemporary medical school curricula. At least two medical schools in the United States have reorganized or are in the process of reorganizing their medical school curricula around the teaching of genetics (Taussig, Rapp, and Heath 1999). Health scientists and clinicians in these contexts describe a medical practice oriented toward genetics that reaches far beyond the rare genetic conditions that have been the traditional purview of medical geneticists. Rather, they see an approach to medicine in which it is understood that genetics plays a role in every aspect of human biology, including the many widespread common conditions such as heart disease, diabetes, and cancer. The vision for this new molecular medicine has shifted from a focus on gene therapy to other potential interventions such as cell therapy, drug therapy, and pharmacogenomics.[5] The ability to develop molecular medicine in this direction has implications for the place and value of genetics and geneticists within science (in terms of findings and prestige) and medicine (where it may become a part of every future interaction between patient and physician) and also for the commercial viability of the biotechnology industry.

The powerful belief in this future medicine and its imbrication with the political economy of the biotechnology industry were particularly visible at an elite invited conference at Harvard Medical School that I attended during the summer of 2001. Titled "Conference on Teaching Genetics to Medical Students," attendees included physicians, researchers, and deans from a range of U.S. medical schools, including Harvard, Columbia, University of Vermont, University of Washington, Yale, Johns Hopkins, Howard, University of Michigan, and Duke, and from the National Human Genome Research Institute. Also attending were two representatives from the Applera Charitable Foundation, the group sponsoring the proceedings, and, for a time, Tony White, the chief executive officer of the Applera Corporation. The Applera Corporation is the parent company of two biotechnology companies: Applied Biosystems and Celera. The Applera Charitable Foundation, created in 1999, serves "as the primary vehicle for the philanthropic giving of Applera Corporation. . . . [which] focuses its giving in genomics education. This focus allows the Foundation to use its resources to help educate individuals regarding new genomics and related technologies and their implications for society." [6]

In what one dean described as highly unusual even for an industry-sponsored conference, Tony White, the CEO of the Applera Corporation, was provided time to address participants during the conference. He explained that Applera has focused all of its capital to "move the science of genetics and its pathways along so it will change medicine." Stating that Applera is "going to change the world [and] transform medicine," he said that "we are trying to move science along as fast as possible" and "to move markets along [as well] so there is a market for [their] products." He explained that there are "loads of money moving around" in this area of the market but that "science is moving faster than medical schools can absorb it." The company's charitable foundation is focused on enhancing education in genetics because the company wants to "come up with medically relevant genetic markers or better treatment but we want to be sure you are prepared to use it." He concluded by stating that humans are the "greatest resource on the face of the earth and it's renewable." Here, in emphasizing the need to educate physicians to be appropriate consumers of genetic corporate products, White offers a particularly vivid illustration of people being cast as containers of DNA that need to be mined in order to develop genetic knowledge that could be turned into clinically valuable and commercially profitable molecular genetic interventions into human health. He also outlines a direct path through which medical knowledge and prestige can literally be capitalized upon.

The conference was suffused with enthusiasm about the potential of genetic medicine—with certainty that this was the future of medicine and with concern about how to integrate genetics into medical education. Early in the conference, one physician stated that medicine is at an "inevitable" moment of transition to genetic medicine, arguing that genetics "is comprehensive, all inclusive, the most basic of basic medicine." Grand comparisons and claims about genetics flowed throughout the conference. One physician stated that the "history of the population is a history of the allele; people move and take their genomes with them." Another described the HGP as "a biological and medical watershed." One claimed that "there is going to be tremendous progress going on and the point of today . . . is how to harness this progress for medical education." Another, arguing that medical schools should make genetics a premed requirement, stated that "genetics is fundamental [to medicine] . . . I see the steamroller coming down the pike";

while another compared the scope of changes that genetic medicine will engender to the harnessing of electricity. One participant described the nineteenth century as the "century of steam," the twentieth century as the "century of information," and the twenty-first century as the "century of DNA." Yet another claimed that "it will not be possible to be an educated person in the twenty-first century without understanding something about genetics. . . . it will influence all of life."

At least in their public discussions at this conference, these physicians did not see genetic medicine as reductive. At one point there was a discussion cautioning those present not to use the language of "a gene for" any particular disease. Such language, they pointed out, is "sloppy" and inaccurate in that—save for the small number of rare conditions widely recognized as genetic—most of the conditions with which genetic medicine is now concerned are those caused by mutations that do not necessarily lead to a particular disease but, rather, change an individual's level of risk or susceptibility to that disease.

A number of participants also seemed particularly concerned to understand genetic medicine as an opportunity to think of patients not as their genes but as persons who are embedded in social relationships. One physician explained that "genetic information has implications for the self and for the family that [are] far more than biology. People are embedded in a web of family relationships." Another insisted that it is important to "teach students that there are people living with these [genetic] conditions who are waiting, sometimes quite anxiously, for advances in genetics" and that students should see genetics as "not a clinical but a human experience."

Thus, while there was widespread commitment to the idea that DNA has an enormous impact on human health and disease, participants were also quite clear that people should not be reduced to their genes but that genes create risks and susceptibilities within particular environments in people who are part of families. In this sense, they clearly recognized that genes, in themselves, do not say enough about a person and that, in order to understand genes, it is essential to locate them in the context of people's lives and social relationships.

In tension with their enthusiasm for the promise and potential of genetic medicine was recognition that, thus far, few clinically relevant applications have developed out of knowledge of the human genome. One participant discussed genetic medicine as having the potential to lead to a "new systems physiology" but then said, "we're a hell of a long way from that right now. Clinical application does not leap out of that map [of the human genome]!" Another, describing himself as "a believer, I see the steamroller coming down the path," raised the problem of the fact that there are very few examples of genetic medicine with which to teach. And one presentation emphasized the need to ensure that physicians learn the range of contexts in which a genetic test might or might not be appropriate. This particular paper stressed the need to understand the clinical "utility" of genetic testing. Using the case of the condition known as venous thrombosis, this paper argued that testing for a genetic predisposition for this condition was of virtually no clinical utility because the results would not change what one would do in terms of clinical intervention. Thus, of the few genetic examples that are now useful for teaching physicians, the lesson of this one is that a genetic test is not clinically relevant.

Physicians concerned to integrate genetics more fully into medical practice are well aware that their ability to be successful will rest in part upon their ability to demonstrate the utility of genetic medicine. As one participant at the conference explained, medical institutions "don't want phenotyping or metabolic clinics" (the traditional purview of medical genetics); rather, "it's the promise of genetics and its integration into common disorders that is going to sell genetics. We have to take that promise and turn it into reality, which so far hasn't really materialized. I think it will; it's still early in the day."

Reductive thinking about genetics may have led to the rapid development of a rough draft of a human genome, but as the above examples illustrate, few of the promises for a revolution in medicine have been fulfilled thus far. Nevertheless, there remains widespread belief among many researchers, clinicians, administrators, and ordinary people that genetic knowledge will transform medicine and, thus, human health. The intellectual, institutional, and political-economic processes essential for initiating any possible genetic revolution in molecular medicine are now under way. But such a revolution will depend upon the ability of researchers to translate genetic knowledge into clinical utility. As researchers work to achieve this translation, many of the same scientists who so clearly articulated a reductive position regarding the power of genes have now realized they need to understand genes in a broader context.

Contextualizing Genes: Organizing Access to Data

Today a wide array of social activities are being undertaken that aim to develop the kind of molecular medicine so clearly desired by some scientists and physicians, the biotechnology industry, and many of those living with genetic conditions. Those engaged in these activities recognize that it will always remain "early in the day" unless genes are contextualized in various ways. For those researchers interested in translating genetic knowledge into clinical intervention this contextualization involves not only gaining access to genes but also linking those genes to persons, families, and medical records. It increasingly involves, moreover, developing genetic epidemiological knowledge that aims to understand genes in relation to various environments. Contextualizing genes in these ways has the potential to develop knowledge about the relationship between structure and function by increasing researchers' understandings of gene penetrance,[7] interactions among genes and their protein products, and the relationship between genes and environments.

Developing clinically relevant genetic knowledge about the widespread common conditions geneticists desire to treat requires not only access to human bodily materials that contain DNA but also to the various materials and information necessary for contextualizing that DNA, including the medical records, biological relationships, and ecological and social settings with which those bodily materials interact. It is exactly this realization that provides the theoretical underpinnings for the Icelandic company DeCode Genetics, which has turned virtually every Icelandic citizen (a category of persons defined, in part, by an ideology of homogeneity) into a research subject (Specter 1999).

Gaining access to blood for research purposes in a society such as the United States is a daunting proposition. The United States has a well-documented history of medical and scientific abuses; it is organized around a legal system and ideological regimes based on individualism, individual rights, and privacy; it has no national health care system; and it has a maze of Internal Review Board (IRB) and informed-consent processes that are widely recognized as inadequate. When it comes to the rare obviously genetic conditions, however, gaining access to the material means of knowledge production is a relatively simple matter. Desperate families with sick children are far more concerned to enroll clinicians and researchers in their search for treatment than they are about almost anything else. As genetic activists Sharon and Pat Terry pointed out to me, putting an informed-consent form in front of a family with a genetic condition is "like throwing them a rope. Of course they're going to grab on."

Recruiting the large number of participants required for research on the more widespread common conditions now viewed as having a genetic component is much more complicated. When it comes to research on common conditions, people appear far less willing to participate. For example, in one of my field sites, a woman confided that, although her family history indicated she was at high risk for genetic susceptibility to colon cancer, she had declined to participate in a research protocol at an Ivy League institution that would have provided her with genetic information regarding her indi-

vidual susceptibility to this condition. She explained that she opted out because she understood the physicians involved in the research protocol to
be telling her they could not guarantee her anonymity. She was concerned
about the implications of her participation in this research protocol for her
grown children, who, depending on the outcome of the tests, might also be
considered at high risk for colon cancer.

It has become clear that the project translating new genetic knowledge
into molecular medical treatments requires a second translation. That is, researchers have to translate their research programs into terms that are understandable by and meaningful for the individuals they seek to enroll in
those projects. Without such translation, access to neither genetic materials
nor family records will be feasible. The types of social relations that either do
or do not facilitate that access are therefore central to the project of genetic
medicine.[8]

Three Models for the Social Relations of DNA Access

Contemporary efforts to gain access to bodies for DNA are quite diverse.
Some stem from the desires of individuals and families bearing compro-
mising genetic conditions to further research agendas that may lead to valuable treatments. Others originate with powerful medical institutions seeking
to enroll a wide array of individuals in medical/scientific research. The various efforts I have observed each frame and inform genetic knowledge and
practice in different ways. They each construct complex and contested identities that variously enable or constrain the agency and voice of those people
they seek to engage in genetic knowledge and practice. These are also sites
where diverse individuals articulate and rework notions of health and illness, abled and disabled, normal and deviant. Exploring the range of ways
the material basis of human molecular research is being created throws into
relief the challenges to the development of clinically relevant genetic knowledge as individuals concerned about health, privacy, access to care, and experimentation make choices about becoming research subjects. It also highlights the refiguring of relationships among ordinary people, medicine, and
the biotech industry. Finally, it points to emerging conceptions of what
makes an acceptable human being at the turn of the twenty-first century.
Each of these efforts works increasingly, at some level, to weave genetics into
everyday life. Thus, the stakes are high for which kinds of efforts achieve
acceptance.

In his work on science and democracy the philosopher Philip Kitcher
(2001) tries to outline what science in a democratic society would look like.
He criticizes scientists for promising outcomes that do not accurately reflect

the purpose of their research projects. He also takes scientists and policy makers to task, specifically focusing on the genome project and its Ethical, Legal, and Social Implications (ELSI) program, for denying the politics of their efforts. In what follows I highlight these politics and their more and less democratic impulses in discussing three quite distinct efforts to gain access to DNA. The first is a top-down model that structures access to DNA through institutional policies. The second involves community leaders in translating genetic knowledge and research protocols in order to broker access to DNA in ways that are perceived as "culturally" appropriate. The final model controls researchers' access to bodies, knowledge, and DNA as a means of both controlling and participating in the research process itself.

TOP-DOWN RELATIONS: MANAGED ACCESS TO DNA

One site where contemporary issues associated with access to bodies for genetic research—including those associated with informed consent, privacy, and control—are of particular concern is the ELSI program of the Human Genome Project.[9] An assessment of the work of ELSI was the subject of a conference in January 2001 entitled "A Decade of ELSI Research: A Celebration of the First Ten Years of the Ethical, Legal, and Social Implications (ELSI) Program."[10] There were approximately 145 papers presented on topics ranging from teaching Stanford MBA students about the ethical issues they might confront in the biotech industry (Eaton, Brady, and Koenig 2001) and an initiative to educate American judges about genetics (Zweig 2001) to those focusing on regulating genetic enhancement (Juengst 2001) and clinical practice and policy (Press and Burke 2001; Geller et al. 2001; Zick et al. 2001; Burke 2001). Several papers highlighted both the intense desire to gain access to human biological materials and the activities now under way to facilitate such access.

At least eight papers at the ELSI conference discussed issues about informed consent that have proven persistently thorny with regard to genetic research, including the fact that some genetic tests result in information about people other than those who consented to participate in genetic research. One of these papers addressed researchers' desire for access to stored tissues and medical records such as those associated with the Nurses' Health Studies.[11] Since the specimens associated with these studies were collected "many years before the genetic revolution" (Lehman and Hohmann 2001), the forms nurses signed providing "general consent to participate in research" (Lehman and Hohmann 2001) do not say anything about genetic research. This raised questions about whether it is ethical to pursue such studies on these tissue samples. Although the consent forms signed as part of participation in these research programs did not include consent for genetic research, arguments are now being made that these samples should be made available for molecular research without a reconsent process. The argument for this goes along these lines (and I am paraphrasing here): "These are people who want to participate in research. Genetic research wasn't planned when they enrolled in the research project, so it isn't on the consent form. If there had been genetic research, it would have been on the consent forms, and these participants still would have been willing to sign" (Lehman 2001). Nevertheless, when I asked one physician involved in this effort why, if that was the case, they didn't simply go ahead with the reconsent, she admitted, in what seems a fundamental inconsistency, that "a statistically significant number might opt out" and that could damage the utility of these tissue banks.

The ELSI conference also offered examples of attempts to collect large numbers of new tissue samples. One presentation (Clayton 2001) described such an effort at the medical centers at Vanderbilt University and Meharry Medical College, one of the four historically black medical colleges and one with which Vanderbilt has a joint operating agreement. In order to facilitate molecular research at these institutions, their administrators have decided to request a blood sample from every single individual coming through either institution for any reason. The samples will be attached to their medical records and drawn, if possible, by their regular physicians at a time patients are already giving blood for something else, and participants will be asked to sign a blanket consent for future research.

Recognizing that informed consent for this set of practices might be complicated, the institution has committed to conducting community education on genetics. Reporting on these endeavors at the ELSI conference, Ellen Clayton, a physician-lawyer involved in the project, explained that they had conducted focus groups in order "to try to understand some of the barriers that [the researchers] might experience in undergoing this process." She stated that one important thing they learned from the focus groups is that at "best a third of the people who come to our institutions might be willing to allow us to collect DNA and to allow access to medical records for purposes of research." The focus groups also indicated that, while people very much want what molecular medicine promises, "there is a deep and fundamental confusion in the population about why on earth we need DNA and medical records to do medical research." Clayton went on to explain that "one of the things we found people saying was, 'If you've got my DNA, that's all there is. And so why do you need my medical records? The DNA's gonna tell you everything you need to know.' Well, we know that anonymous [DNA] can't tell you everything you need to know. . . . this is an area [where] we are really going to have to overcome public perception."

One way the Vanderbilt-Meharry endeavor intends to go about overcoming these public perceptions is through education. Vanderbilt-Meharry wants "this to be an exemplary process" in that they are attempting to "go about very seriously seeking consent and doing this in the most ethically appropriate manner." At the ELSI conference Clayton explained that in order to "get these messages out" about "what genetic research is about and why, in fact, we need to connect DNA with medical records, and why that matters," those working at Vanderbilt-Meharry will be turning "not only to the media but also to specific community events, going . . . not only to churches but also to local barbecues and other venues like that in order to talk with the population about why one wants to do this." In this way Vanderbilt-Meharry hopes to educate people so that they will be willing to participate in genetic research and also so that they will be more able to give informed consent to that participation.

The Vanderbilt-Meharry example makes clear that many people have a lot of concerns about participating in genetic research. The problem for the hospitals is that many people care deeply about precisely the kinds of issues the ELSI program is intended to address. Nevertheless, in her presentation, Clayton suggests that, although the hospitals are aware of widespread public concerns about participating in genetic research, they believe that community education will facilitate public participation. The underlying assumption here is that, if only people know what we know, they would be more willing to participate. Implicit in this assumption is the idea that concerns about participating are, by definition, the product of ignorance or confusion.

The Vanderbilt-Meharry effort runs into the effects of scientists' own prior essentialism. Having heard scientists and policy makers promoting genetic research speak of genes in determinative essential terms for some time now, people do not understand why researchers need more than genetic material to further their research. Furthermore, this kind of top-down effort raises concerns related to cultural values of privacy and consent as well as fears of exploitation. The implications of community resistance to participating in genetic research are complex and multilayered. In the first instance, community resistance is certainly perceived by researchers as having the potential to hold back their efforts at translating genetic knowledge into medical interventions. At the same time, what appear to be well-intentioned efforts to educate people so that they will understand and be willing to participate in genetic research turn out, in such a top-down model, to provoke anxieties about medical exploitation. It is just such concerns about exploitation to which I now turn.

COMMUNITY ORGANIZATIONS:
EDUCATION FOR "ACTIVE" INFORMED CONSENT

COMMUNITY ORGANIZATIONS: EDUCATION FOR "ACTIVE" INFORMED CONSENT

In contrast to the Vanderbilt model—where education is viewed as a model to overcome concerns about genetic research—a separate project presented at the ELSI conference offered a model of education intended to enhance subjects' ability to articulate such concerns. This project, Genetic Education for Native Americans (Burhansstipanov et al. 2001), is being implemented by Native American Cancer Research, an Indian-owned and -operated non-profit organization, and is funded by the National Human Genome Research Institute and the National Institutes of Health. Here, the desire to educate people about genetics came about in reaction to requests from researchers for body tissue from Native Americans. The project aims to "provide culturally competent education about genetic research and genetic testing to Native American college and university students" (Burhansstipanov et al. 2001). In a telephone conversation, the director of the program explained to me that the goal was to provide individuals in their communities with "enough information that they can ask smart questions . . . so they don't get tricked."

The concern to provide people with this kind of knowledge is not simply due to a generalized distrust of the dominant society or its medical institutions. Native American Cancer Research has maintained a long-running network of breast cancer survivors' groups. When they began conducting intertribal focus groups about genetics, they learned that some members of their survivors' groups were regularly solicited for tissue samples for research and that some had been given genetic test results without any other information or genetic counseling. Such practices fly in the face of standard ethical practice in genetics today. This group deals with ethical issues by attending to the specific concerns people in Native American communities might have about participating in genetic research. As the director of the project explained, "for some tribes some studies will be acceptable that for others will never be acceptable." The purpose of training Native American college and university students in both cultural issues and genetics is to facilitate "active, not passive, informed consent" to participation in genetic research in their communities.[12]

This model points to conflicting desires regarding genetic research. It recognizes the desire of researchers to gain access to specific types of DNA, as well as the legitimacy of the fact that those whose bodies contain that DNA may or may not desire to donate it. In translating genetic knowledge and research protocols for Native communities, the organization works to promote the desires and rights of Native Americans regardless of the desires and demands of scientific researchers. Depending on the cultural acceptability of a particular research protocol, this model has the potential either to facilitate or to prevent its development. And although this effort would seem to have the potential to influence research protocols, unlike the model to which I will now turn, it is not intended to actively structure the work of laboratory scientists.

COLLABORATIVE RELATIONS: THE WORK OF GENETIC ACTIVISTS

Sharon and Patrick Terry's story and work as genetic activists offers yet another model of crafting genetic social relations. In 2000 Sharon Terry was a coauthor of two back-to-back articles in *Nature Genetics* announcing the discovery of the gene for pseudoxanthoma elasticum (PXE) (Bergen et al. 2000; Le Saux et al. 2000), and Pat Terry joined Randy Scott—the founder and former CEO of Incyte, a major biotechnology company—and three others in securing seventy million dollars in venture capital to establish Genomic Health, a new biotechnology firm.

Their story begins, however, several years earlier. Pat Terry, a technical high school graduate with two years of study at a community college, was managing a construction company, and Sharon Terry, who has a master's degree in religious studies, was home-schooling their son and daughter when the children were diagnosed with PXE in 1994. Following their children's diagnosis, the Terrys beat a path to the University of Massachusetts medical school library, forty miles from their home. There they copied over four hundred articles on PXE and began educating themselves on the state of knowledge about the condition. Realizing how little was known about the condition, the Terrys resolved to facilitate research for the benefit of their children. They learned about a physician studying the condition and contacted him. Describing that encounter in an interview with me, Sharon Terry explains that the physician told them:

> "PXE's a rat-hole. Nobody cares. No one will ever care about this disease. I gave my life to it. You only have me." And we kept saying, "Well, we think we could interest other people if we could get enough people's blood samples"—you know, that sort of thing? And he kept saying, "No, you can't." . . . But . . . that same night he introduced us to a researcher here [at Harvard], a fellow who was working on PXE, looking for the gene. So we said to the fellow, "We'll wash test tubes for you, just to accelerate your research. What do you want done?" This same group had taken our blood and tissue—our blood samples—the day after my kids

were diagnosed, without an informed consent from us. We didn't know at the time that you're supposed to have one. We were grateful that somebody wanted our blood.

The Terrys began volunteering in the laboratory of this Harvard researcher, frequently working through the middle of the night.

At the same time, committed to enrolling additional researchers in order to speed up results and develop a treatment, the Terrys founded PXE International. One role of the organization is to bank patients' tissue, develop pedigrees, and maintain an international registry of affected individuals and families. These materials provide just the kind of contextualization geneticists seek in order to understand the relationship between genetic structure and function. A comprehensive tissue bank linked to medical records, family pedigrees, and similar information provides a unique picture of what a specific condition actually looks like, thus facilitating researchers' ability to understand the complex pathways from gene to expression. The Terrys frame their mission this way: "What is it that researchers need to do their job? Blood, tissue, pedigrees, family studies. And how do we solve this problem? . . . We hold the key and the gold. We hold 900 blood samples, 200 pedigrees, and 1400 affected individuals and they have to come to us for them. And we know that that is real power." Thus, by maintaining control over the material means of scientific knowledge production, the Terrys and their organization are participating in and shaping the basic research process itself. At the same time, they are also shaping the researchers' understandings of what it means to live with this condition.

The Terrys' efforts led to rapid development of contemporary scientific capital: the development of new knowledge involving the discovery and naming of a new gene. At the same time, they responded to the concerns of patients about privacy and control. In this case people were willing to participate in research not only because they had a rare genetic condition (which they had always had) but also because they trusted the Terrys to maintain control over their materials, to protect their privacy, and to push for the interests of people with PXE.

In June 2000, the same week that President Clinton, Francis Collins, and Craig Venter announced the completion of the rough draft of the human genome, PXE International held a celebratory dinner dance at Boston's Park Plaza Hotel to commemorate the recent discovery of the gene for PXE (Bergen et al. 2000; Kolata 2000; Le Saux et al. 2000; Ringpfeil et al. 2000). One speaker at the gathering described PXE International as a model for other lay advocacy groups. In particular, she noted PXE International's role in engaging basic researchers and helping maintain research momentum at the same time that they protected the interests and anonymity of those affected by PXE.

While the Terrys' story is unusual (and not unproblematic for the researchers with whom they work), the model they developed is becoming exemplary for other groups as they, in turn, also seek to play a role in controlling genetic research. Pat Terry told me that he was going to speak at a conference of First Peoples in Vancouver, British Columbia, during the summer of 2002 in order to describe the "PXE model," so that they, too, could adopt a proactive model of regulating scientists' access to the material products—blood, tissue, pedigrees, family studies, and gene patents—necessary for conducting their research. Here we see a dramatic example of a particular model of social relations that supports patient participation in the production of scientific knowledge born out of a deep desire to facilitate knowledge production on a rare genetic condition. This model highlights ordinary people not just as containers of DNA but also as producers and managers of genetic knowledge, as well as potential consumers of the products that knowledge may lead to.

Like genome scientists, the Terrys are seeking a solution to a genetic condition in their family at the molecular level. At the same time, they recognize that in order to understand what is going on at the molecular level genetic material must be contextualized. Their personal abilities to grasp the science and to collect and contextualize genetic material have allowed them to collaborate with researchers in pursuing their mutual desires: scientific knowledge production and a treatment for a genetic condition. And while this is a case of a rare genetic condition, the Terrys see their work as not just a model for democratic participation in science but as a model upon which to build the contextualizations necessary for understanding the complex pathways from structure to function.

The Future of Molecular Medicine

The molecular differences that make us sick can only be fully understood through access to the material means of knowledge production that, in the case of human genetics, reside in people's bodies. The examples I have elaborated bring into view the complex preconditions to developing a fully elaborated molecular medical clinic. This is a future in which we are all implicated. The more researchers have learned about the human genome, the less tenable a reductive view of genetics has become. Researchers and clinicians working in this area increasingly have come to recognize that understanding genes can only proceed if those genes are contextualized. I have elaborated several models of social relations that seek to facilitate this contextualization. These models each frame and inform genetic knowledge and practice as people work to realize fully the promise of molecular medicine. They also construct complex and contested identities that variously enable or constrain the agency and voice of the subjects of human genetic research.

The practices and interpretations I have examined exist at the intersections of people's bodies, medical/scientific research agendas, and the market where bodies and their molecules provide the material means to develop knowledge, products, and practice. As such, these sites play a significant role in shaping the social relations upon which any new molecular medical clinic will be built. While these practices are diverse and have diverse aims, all of them serve increasingly to weave genetics into daily life, and many of them seek fundamentally to transform the relationship between ordinary healthy people and science. Struggles over genetic material and knowledge are emerging as new sites for talking about larger social issues having to do with the organization, interpretation, and control of the new knowledge and resources that will undergird future understandings of what makes an acceptable human being. As such, the kinds of social arrangements through which this new medicine is emerging matter both for the people involved and for the kind of future that gets built.

Acknowledgments

I thank Vinay Gidwany, Jennifer Gunn, Karen Ho, Jonathan Kahn, Susan Lindee, Susan McKinnon, Sydel Silverman, Charles Weiner, and participants in the social-cultural workshop in the anthropology department at the University of Minnesota. Their thoughtful comments on various versions of this paper improved it enormously.

Notes

1. Here I am making a distinction between a diagnostic intervention—using genetic tests for diagnosis of a particular condition or predisposition—and a clinical intervention, by which I mean a genetic intervention that would treat a particular condition. In contrast to the dearth of clinical interventions, there has been a steady expansion of diagnostic interventions. It is now possible to diagnose or predict Huntington's disease through a genetic test, but there remains no cure for the condition, and neither genetic knowledge nor diagnostic results have changed what palliative interventions are possible.

2. These utopian visions exist side by side with dystopian scenarios in which dramatic reproductive technologies (including cloning and genomic enhancement) are de rigueur, individuals and families have no privacy, and corporate entities own various components of the human body.

3. There always were scientists who challenged the reductive stance and what we might now call the irrational exuberance of HGP proponents (Hubbard and Wald 1993; Lewontin 1993).

4. In 2002 the completion of a draft of the rice genome indicated that rice has approxi-

mately 40,000 genes. This finding prompted bemused reactions from scientists mystified by the comment this number made on how exactly to interpret the evolutionary complexity of organisms (Flatow 2002; Harris 2002; Wade 2002).

5. Two types of gene therapy have been discussed since the inception of the HGP: somatic gene therapy and germ-line gene therapy. Both involve intervening at the level of the genome, theoretically by snipping out or adding a piece of DNA. Somatic gene therapy takes place in the somatic cells of a particular individual, while germ-line therapy would alter the genetic material in the germ cells—eggs and sperm—with the aim of changing the genome of generations to come. Cell therapy, rather than intervening at the level of the genome, attempts to intervene in the functioning of particular cells. Drug therapy aims to use particular drugs to intervene in biological processes, while pharmacogenomics seeks to tailor drug therapies to the specifics of a particular individual's genetic makeup.

6. Quoted from the Applera Corporation Web site: http: //www.applera.com /corpinfo/ foundation.html, accessed July 19, 2001.

7. That is, the extent to which the gene "penetrates" the body. For example, some genes, like the mutation for Huntington's disease, are recognized as being 100 percent, or fully, penetrant. If the person carrying that mutation lives long enough, he or she will definitely develop disease. Other genes are seen as less fully penetrant: the BRCA genes linked to breast cancer are generally described as about 80 percent penetrant because approximately 20 percent of those who carry the gene do not develop breast cancer.

8. Lack of access to bodies has created a crisis for medicine in the past. When knowledge of anatomy became an essential component of medical knowledge over the course of the eighteenth and nineteenth centuries, access to bodies for dissection was hampered by widespread concerns about dignity and disfigurement linked to beliefs about the need to maintain the integrity of the body to ensure its passage to the Hereafter (Richardson 1988; Ludmerer 1999).

9. In establishing the HGP, its first director, James Watson, committed to devoting a certain portion of the project's budget to studying the "ethical, legal, and social implications" of this new scientific endeavor. Thus was born ELSI—an endeavor that has had its own controversies, having to do with, among other things, who gets to control what kinds of questions get asked about this scientific endeavor and whether this is a serious effort by the HGP or a public-relations move aimed at undermining serious critique of the project (Andrews 1999; Rapp, Heath, and Taussig 2001).

10. The conference, hosted by the National Institutes of Health on its campus in Bethesda, Maryland, was sponsored by the National Human Genome Research Institute, the National Institutes of Health, and the Department of Energy (which, along with the NIH, is the other government agency responsible for overseeing the HGP).

11. There exist, in various storage facilities around the United States, stores of tissue samples containing DNA that have been collected as part of various longitudinal health studies. These include, for example, the tissue samples stored as part of the Nurses' Health Study and the Nurses' Health Study II, which are among the largest prospective investigations into the risk factors for major chronic diseases in women. These tissue samples, which are associated with medical records as well as extensive survey information regularly filled out as part of ongoing participation in the studies, are considered a potential gold mine for molecular genetic research. The Nurses' Health Study was established in 1976, and the Nurses' Health Study II in 1989. Located at the Channing Laboratory at Harvard, the studies collaborate with investigators and consultants at Harvard Medical School, Harvard School of Public Health, and a number of the Harvard-affiliated hospitals, including Brigham and Women's Hospital, Dana Farber Cancer Institute, Boston Children's Hospital, and Beth Israel Hospital.

12. There also are those who resist participating in these emerging social relations alto-

gether. The Indigenous People's Council on Biocolonialism offers an interesting example of this stance. In speaking engagements, Debra Harry, the council's director, points out that the questions asked by genetic researchers are not organic to indigenous communities and do not articulate well with the interests of those communities. The council argues in its mission statement that genetic research is a new kind of colonization, that indigenous people, their blood, and their body tissues are highly desired as the objects of scientific curiosity, and that current research protections fail to recognize group rights and the rights of groups to collective control over their "collective intellectual and cultural knowledge, and genetic resources" (http: // www.ipcb.org/purpose.htm). The organization conducts its own genetic research and is engaged in a range of educational activities. For more on issues related to group rights and biotechnology see Kahn 2000.

References

Abate, Tom. 2000. Microbiologists Each Toss a Dollar into the Human Genome. *San Francisco Chronicle,* May 22, p. E1.

Ahuja, Anjana. 2000. Counting on the Genome. *London Times,* June 1.

Andrews, Lori. 1999. *The Clone Age.* New York: Owl Books/Henry Holt.

Aparicio, Samuel A. J. R. 2000. How to Count . . . Human Genes. *Nature Genetics* 25(2): 129–30.

Appadurai, Arjun. 1996. *Modernity at Large: Cultural Dimensions of Globalization.* Minneapolis: University of Minnesota Press.

ASHG Information and Education Committee. 1995. Report from the ASHG Information and Education Committee: Medical School Core Curriculum in Genetics. *American Journal of Human Genetics* 56: 535–37.

Bergen, A., A. Plomp, E. Schuurman, S. Terry, M. Breuning, H. Dauwerse, J. Swart, et al. 2000. Mutations in ABCC6 Cause Pseudoxanthoma Elasticum. *Nature Genetics* 25 (June): 228–31.

Bourdieu, Pierre. [1975] 1998. The Specificity of the Scientific Field and the Social Conditions of the Progress of Reason. In *The Science Studies Reader,* ed. M. Biagioli, pp. 31–50. New York: Routledge.

———. 1984. *Distinction: A Social Critique of the Judgment of Taste.* Translated by Richard Nice. Cambridge: Harvard University Press.

Burhansstipanov, Linda, L. Bemis, M. Bignan, C. Poodry, and F. Romero. 2001. Genetic Education for Native Americans: An Update and Preliminary Evaluation Data. Paper presented at "A Decade of ELSI Research: A Celebration of the First Ten Years of the Ethical, Legal, and Social Implications (ELSI) Program," Bethesda, MD, January 17.

Burke, Wylie. 2001. Categorizing Genetic Tests to Identify Ethical, Legal, and Social Implications. Paper presented at "A Decade of ELSI Research: A Celebration of the First Ten Years of the Ethical, Legal, and Social Implications (ELSI) Program," Bethesda, MD, January 16.

Casper, Monica J., and Marc Berg. 1995. Introduction. *Science, Technology, and Human Values* 20(4): 395–407.

Childs, Barton. 1993. Genetics in Medical Education. *American Journal of Human Genetics* 52: 225–27.

Clayton, Ellen. 2001. Creating a Process to Collect Human Biological Materials and Medical Records for Research from Patients in Teaching Hospitals. Paper presented at "A Decade of ELSI Research: A Celebration of the First Ten Years of the Ethical, Legal, and Social Implications (ELSI) Program," Bethesda, MD, January 16.

Collins, Francis. 1997. Preparing Health Professionals for the Genetic Revolution. *Journal of the American Medical Association* 199: 1285–86.

Daily Yomiuri. 2000. Bets Laid on Number of Human Genes. May 30, p. 2.

Eaton, Margaret, David Brady, and Barbara Koenig. 2001. Developing a Case-Based Ethics Curriculum for the Biotechnology Industry. Paper presented at "A Decade of ELSI Research: A Celebration of the First Ten Years of the Ethical, Legal, and Social Implications (ELSI) Program," Bethesda, MD, January 16.

Flatow, Ira. 2002. Rice Genome. *Talk of the Nation/Science Friday,* National Public Radio, April 5.

Fraser, Nancy. 1997. *Justice Interruptus: Critical Reflections on the "Postsocialist" Condition.* New York: Routledge.

Fujimura, Joan. 1988. The Molecular Biological Bandwagon in Cancer Research: Where Social Worlds Meet. *Social Problems* 35: 261–83.

———. 1992. Crafting Science: Standardized Packages, Boundary Objects, and Translation. In *Science as Practice and Culture,* ed. Andrew Pickering, 168–211. Chicago: University of Chicago Press.

Fukuyama, Francis. 2002. *Our Posthuman Future: Consequences of the Biotechnology Revolution.* New York: Farrar, Straus, and Giroux.

Geller, Gail, Barbara Bernhardt, Neil Holtzman, Teresa Doksum, and Ellen Tambor. 2001. The Meaning of Autonomy in Genetic Testing: Lessons from Qualitative Research about the Role of Partnership in Decision-Making. Paper presented at "A Decade of ELSI Research: A Celebration of the First Ten Years of the Ethical, Legal, and Social Implications (ELSI) Program," Bethesda, MD, January 16.

Gilbert, Walter. 1992. Vision of the Grail. In Kevles and Hood 1992: 83–97.

Guidotti, Rick. 1998. Redefining Beauty. *Life,* June, pp. 65–69.

Habermas, Jürgen. 2001. On the Way to Liberal Eugenics? The Dispute over the Ethical Self-Understanding of the Species. Paper presented at the "Colloquium on Law, Philosophy, and Political Theory," New York University School of Law, October 25 and November 1.

Hager, M., ed. 1999. *The Implications of Genetics for Health Professional Education.* New York: Josiah Macy, Jr. Foundation.

Harris, Richard. 2002. Two Independent Studies Release Rough Drafts on the Rice Genome. *All Things Considered,* National Public Radio, April 4.

Harvey, David. 1989. *The Condition of Postmodernity: An Enquiry into the Conditions of Social Change.* Oxford and Cambridge, MA: Blackwell.

Hubbard, Ruth, and Elijah Wald. 1993. *Exploding the Gene Myth.* Boston: Beacon.

Juengst, Eric. 2001. The Conceptual Challenges of Regulating Genetic Enhancement. Paper presented at "A Decade of ELSI Research: A Celebration of the First Ten Years of the Ethical, Legal, and Social Implications (ELSI) Program," Bethesda, MD, January 17.

Kahn, Jonathan. 2000. Biotechnology and the Legal Constitution of the Self: Managing Identity in Science, the Market, and Society. *Hastings Law Journal* 51: 909–52.

Keller, Evelyn Fox. 2000. *The Century of the Gene.* Cambridge: Harvard University Press.

Kevles, Daniel J., and Leroy Hood, eds. 1992. *The Code of Codes: Scientific and Social Issues in the Human Genome Project.* Cambridge: Harvard University Press.

Kitcher, Philip. 2001. *Science, Truth, and Democracy.* New York: Oxford University Press.

Kolata, Gina. 2000. A Family's Goal Is Met and a Gene Is Found. *New York Times,* May 23, p. D2.

Lehman, Lisa. 2001. Informed Consent for Genetic Epidemiological Research. Paper presented at the Pettus-Crowe Seminar, Harvard Medical School, Division of Medical Ethics, Boston, April 27.

Lehman, Lisa, and Elizabeth Hohmann. 2001. Informed Consent for Genetic Research in Epidemiological Studies. Paper presented at "A Decade of ELSI Research: A Celebration of the First Ten Years of the Ethical, Legal, and Social Implications (ELSI) Program," Bethesda, MD, January 17.

Le Saux, O., Z. Urban, C. Tschuch, K. Csiszar, B. Bacchelli, D. Quaglino, I. Pasquali-Ronchetti, et al. 2000. Mutations in a Gene Encoding an ABC Transporter Cause Pseudoxanthoma Elasticum. *Nature Genetics* 25: 223–27.

Lewontin, Richard C. 1993. *Biology as Ideology.* London: Penguin.

———. 2000. *The Triple Helix: Gene, Organism, and Environment.* Cambridge: Harvard University Press.

———. 2002. The Politics of Science. *New York Review of Books* 49(8): 28–31.

Ludmerer, Kenneth. 1999. *Time to Heal: American Medical Education from the Turn of the Century to the Era of Managed Care.* Oxford: Oxford University Press.

Madoff, Steven. 2002. The Wonders of Genetics Breed a New Art. *New York Times,* May 26, p. B1.

Nature Genetics. 2000. Editorial: The Nature of the Number. 25(2): 127–28.

Nelkin, Dorothy, and Suzanne Anker. 2003. *The Molecular Gaze: Art in the Genetic Age.* Woodbury, NY: Cold Spring Harbor Laboratory Press.

Nelkin, Dorothy, and M. Susan Lindee. 1995. *The DNA Mystique: The Gene as Cultural Icon.* New York: Freeman.

Oudshoorn, Nellie. 1994. *Beyond the Natural Body: An Archeology of Sex Hormones.* London: Routledge.

Press, Nancy, and Wylie Burke. 2001. Genetic Exceptionalism and the Paradigm of Risk in U.S. Biomedicine. Paper presented at "A Decade of ELSI Research: A Celebration of the First Ten Years of the Ethical, Legal, and Social Implications (ELSI) Program," Bethesda, MD, January 16.

Rapp, Rayna, Deborah Heath, and Karen-Sue Taussig. 2001. Genealogical Dis-Ease: Where Hereditary Abnormality, Biomedical Explanation, and Family Responsibility Meet. In *Relative Values: Reconfiguring Kinship Studies,* ed. Sarah Franklin and Susan McKinnon, pp. 384–409. Durham, NC: Duke University Press.

Richardson, Ruth. 1988. *Death, Dissection, and the Destitute.* New York: Routledge and Kegan Paul.

Ringpfeil, F., M. Lebwohl, A. Chritiano, and J. Uitto. 2000. Pseudoxanthoma Elasticum: Mutations in the *MRP6* Gene Encoding a Transmembrane ATP-Binding Cassette (ABC) Transporter. *Proceedings of the National Academy of Science* 97(11): 6001–6.

Riordan, Teresa. 2002. Patents: An Obsession with DNA and the Human Genome Leads to Development of a Technology. *New York Times,* March 18, p. C2.

Silver, Lee. 1997. *Remaking Eden: Cloning and Beyond in a Brave New World.* New York: Avon.

Specter, Michael. 1999. Decoding Iceland. *New Yorker,* January 18, pp. 40–51.

Stolberg, Sheryl. 1999. The Biotech Death of Jesse Gelsinger. *New York Times Magazine,* November 28, p. 137.

———. 2000. Teenager's Death Is Shaking up Field of Human Gene-Therapy Experiments. *New York Times,* January 27, p. 20.

Taussig, Karen-Sue, Rayna Rapp, and Deborah Heath. 1999. Translating Genetics: Crafting Medical Literacies in the Age of the New Genetics. Paper presented at the Annual Meetings of the American Anthropological Association, Chicago, November 21.

Wade, Nicholas. 2000. Scientists Cast Bets on Human Genes: A Winner Will Be Picked in 2003. *New York Times,* May 23, p. F5.

————. 2002. Experts Say They Have Key to Rice Genes. *New York Times,* April 5, p. A21.

Zick, Cathleen D., Ken R. Smith, Robert N. Mayer, and Jeffery R. Botkin. 2001. BRCA1 Testing and Insurance Issues: Survey Evidence from Tested and Non-tested Individuals. Paper presented at "A Decade of ELSI Research: A Celebration of the First Ten Years of the Ethical, Legal, and Social Implications (ELSI) Program," Bethesda, MD, January 16.

Zweig, Franklin. 2001. The Einstein Institute for Science, Health, and the Courts. Paper presented at "A Decade of ELSI Research: A Celebration of the First Ten Years of the Ethical, Legal, and Social Implications (ELSI) Program," Bethesda, MD, January 17.

PART IV

---

*The Politics
of Reductionism*

CHAPTER 11

Barbarism, Old and New:
Denaturalizing the Rhetoric of Warfare

Mary H. Moran

THE PERIOD FROM the 1990s until September 11, 2001, was generally considered a time of peace and prosperity for most Americans. With the conclusion of the first Gulf War, the American military participated only in "humanitarian" interventions in Somalia and the Balkans and intervened in "other people's wars" on a very limited basis and with sometimes mixed results. Indeed, warfare had become something that only happened to "other people," which perhaps accounts for some of the shock and disbelief accompanying the September 11 attacks on the World Trade Center and the Pentagon.

Of course, the rest of the world did not have the luxury of a peaceful decade at the end of the twentieth century. In many places, the nineties were characterized by widespread violence, destruction, and the collapse of state institutions charged with guaranteeing civilian security. This was especially the case in Africa, the part of the world that I know best and where I have done research as an anthropologist.

In this chapter, I argue that many Americans, aided by journalists and foreign-policy makers, have developed a coherent yet simplistic way of thinking about distant wars fought by unknown combatants for obscure reasons. Rather than being encouraged to look to local histories and underlying tensions in an area for an understanding of what fuels conflict abroad, Americans have been offered reductionist explanations that resonate with "commonsense" notions in our society. Exemplifying such explanations is what anthropologist Paul Richards has dubbed "the New Barbarism hypothesis." This argument seems to make sense of "terrorist" warfare both at home and abroad, and it provides a satisfying depiction of the fundamental difference between the deployment of U.S. military might and the "senseless violence" perpetrated by others. But it rests on both faulty logic and false information and, as a guide for foreign and military policy, it can lead only to disaster. What it does, in fact, is to use naturalizing, evolutionary rationales as a kind of scapegoat for situations engendered by political forces, including the actions of colonial and industrial powers in pursuit of their own interests.

In what follows, I will lay out the New Barbarism hypothesis and show why, in spite of its seductive power, it has been challenged by anthropologists. I will then offer alternative accounts from an anthropological perspective. Such alternatives, I suggest, can help us critically appraise American foreign policy and some of the assumptions on which it is based.

The New Barbarism Hypothesis

According to Richards (1996: xiv–xvii), the central tenets of the New Barbarism thesis are best represented by journalist Robert Kaplan in his influential article in *Atlantic Monthly* in 1994, "The Coming Anarchy," later expanded into a book by the same name (2000). This article was considered so important by policy makers that it was faxed by the U.S. State Department to every American embassy around the world and sparked a confidential meeting by top officials at the United Nations (Richards 1996: xiv; Ellis 1999: 19–20). Kaplan's thesis, which was based on his rather impressionistic observations during brief visits to various war zones around the world, was read and cited by President Clinton, members of Congress, and academic political scientists. The three basic ideas of what Kaplan has called his "paradigm for the Post–Cold War era" (2000: xiii) are familiar to most Americans; one might say that Kaplan has articulated widely held assumptions with which Americans today view events around the world.

First, cultural identity, either "ethnic" or "tribal," is presumed to be stable, enduring, and almost unchangeable. Cultural differences between human populations are seen as leading inevitably to conflict (Richards 1996: xiv). This idea was also elaborated by the political theorist Samuel Huntington in his famous article "The Clash of Civilizations" in *Foreign Affairs* in 1993 and his 1996 book with the same title, which have enjoyed wide acceptance in political science and policy studies. Anna Simons (1999) notes that the military analyst R. Peters, writing for a defense and state department audience in the journal *Parameters,* took up these ideas and reworked them for policy makers. Peters believes that certain societies, which seem to be coterminous with nation-states, are "rooted in culture." The countries so identified restrict the free flow of information, subjugate women, do not assign responsibility for individual and collective failure, have the clan or family as the basic unit of social organization, are dominated by a restrictive religion, and place little value on either education or work (Peters 1998, cited in Simons 1999). Peters believes that these "types" of societies are in a constant state of struggle against the more "rational" polities of the West but are doomed to failure by their inefficiency; they are simply culturally inferior to the West (Simons 1999: 93; see also Huntington 1996).

One can easily recognize in this laundry list of traits the features attributed to Iraq under Saddam Hussein or Afghanistan under the Taliban. Today's enemies of freedom and democracy are trapped in their outmoded and irrational cultures, just as the communist demons earlier in the century were trapped by their unworkable socialist ideology. The whole construction, therefore, divides the world neatly into two sides or, in Huntington's terms, "civilizations." One represents the rational modernity of the West, while the other consists of less evolved "cultures" still dominated by religion, kinship, and "tradition." I will later discuss how the anthropological concept of culture has been appropriated and even perverted in this account, but for now it is important to point out the evolutionary assumptions on which the argument rests. The West is presumed to have progressed "beyond culture" as a cause of conflict and violence; if and when we go to war, it is in the interest of "democratic principles" or to "make the world safe from terrorism" or to secure strategic resources like oil or uranium. The United States conducts rational "policy debates," holds hearings, and considers opinion polls before making the reasoned judgment to go to war. The unfortunate "backward" regions of the world, in contrast, seem to be subject to outbreaks of "spontaneous" warfare, which erupts, rather like a volcano, from time to time.

The second tenet of the New Barbarism thesis is that the post–Cold War context of globalization has thrown into question the monopoly of the nation-state over the means of violence. Weapons are cheaply made and easily transported; they are small and light and can be operated even by children. Sovereign states can no longer contain the ambitions of ethnic nationalists, warlords, criminals, or disaffected teenagers (Richards 1996: xiv). Since postcolonial states in the Third World and in Eastern Europe are no longer needed as buffers and proxies by two competing superpowers, there is no one to step in and clean up the mess when such states "fail" or "implode."

Driving all of the above, the third tenet holds, is overpopulation in the poorer parts of the world, which leads to inevitable environmental degradation, causing competition for resources and, as a result, local conflicts. With no "big brother" to intervene, these local conflicts become regional or national ones. Since some civilizations or cultures are simply more barbaric than others, and since these nations are multiethnic—and different ethnic groups will naturally want to fight each other—such conflicts consist of assaults on civilians, bizarre masquerades, acts of unspeakable cruelty, and outright genocide, as in Bosnia and Rwanda.

Kaplan's argument, which appears to wrap up a range of variables in one satisfying explanation, has been systematically and effectively dismantled by a number of scholars (Richards 1996; Besteman 1996, 1999; and others). These critiques have not limited its influence, however, in both popular understandings and policy responses to foreign wars. One reason is that it picks up widespread, almost unconscious evolutionary assumptions about how cultural difference can be understood. It should be noted that, in this chapter, I refer to evolutionary theory in the sense that it has been applied to the interpretation of societies and cultures, not to the biological evolution of our species.

In many years of teaching undergraduate anthropology courses, I have come to realize that my students categorize cultural difference as a function of time. The more divergent something is from their own experience, the more they take it to represent an earlier stage of human development (see also Fabian 1983, 1991, for a discussion of the use of time in categorizing human societies). My students share with Kaplan and Huntington the idea that some unfortunate people have made it into the twenty-first century with social and cultural institutions that are more appropriate to an earlier era. They are often astonished that practices such as polygamy, belief in witchcraft, and veneration of ancestors "still" exist in modern times. In this, they are occasionally abetted by anthropology textbooks, some of which continue to present accounts of unilinear progress from "bands" through "tribes," "chiefdoms," and "states." Successful bands can and do "become" tribes, tribes become chiefdoms, and chiefdoms, states; tribes that "still" exist in the present can thus be understood as anachronistic failures. When reading newspaper accounts of "tribal" conflicts in Afghanistan, Rwanda, Liberia, or Sudan, my students imagine premodern, irrational violence that can only be understood in terms of its deep historical and "traditional" roots. Such conflicts are therefore seen as fundamentally different from Western politics, which is grounded in the state and takes place in the realm of rational choices and regulated competition for strategic resources. Kaplan and Huntington make the same assumptions.

Refuting "Ancient Tribal Hatreds"

Many anthropologists have rejected grand theories invoking "tribes," "cultures," and "civilizations," arguing that they depend on "catchall terms . . . to explain phenomena that have local roots" (Simons 1999: 92). Archaeologists have demonstrated that "tribal warfare," rather than being a relic of the past, is actually a *consequence* of the rise of states (Ferguson and Whitehead 1992: 27–28). Indeed, there is striking evidence that so-called ancient tribal hatreds can be manufactured and mobilized with great speed. I offer a case in point from my own field site of Liberia, one of the countries Kaplan used in constructing his New Barbarism thesis.

The Liberian state was founded in the early nineteenth century by a white benevolent organization, the American Colonization Society, as a haven for "free people of color" from the United States. The small, underequipped state, which became an independent republic in 1847, was controlled by the descendants of the American settlers, who were in a constant struggle for existence with the indigenous majority. This indigenous population consisted of people who spoke at least sixteen different languages and who, for at least two centuries, had been deeply involved in highly elaborated trading relations with Europeans and with other Africans along the West African coast. None of these groups of language speakers, nor any other segment of the population, could be said to constitute a unified, bounded tribe; the larger chiefdoms were all multiethnic and multilingual, and local warfare, which was endemic, usually occurred *within* rather than *between* named groups. As one ethnographer noted in the 1960s, intermarriage and extensive travel for trade produced individuals who could claim: "No one can say that I am not a real Gola, but also no one can say that I am not Mandingo, De, or even Vai. I learned to be a leader for many kinds of people, and I was able to show them that I could turn my face to each of them and be one of them" (d'Azevedo 1970: 11). Although the central government attempted to impose a series of tribal categories on this fluid situation, the best they could accomplish was a rough approximation between large administrative units and ethnolinguistic groups. Thus, Maryland County, where I did fieldwork, was represented as the "home of the Grebo tribe," even though everyone recognized that the "Grebo tribe" did not really exist. Rather, there were literally hundreds of named localities whose occupants spoke often mutually unintelligible dialects of languages which have been designated "Grebo," "Kru," and "Krahn." Only in cities like Monrovia, the capital, did anything resembling a situational Grebo identity emerge, and this was undermined by the continuing importance of migrant organizations identified with specific towns in the home region.

Although there was a significant exchange of both culture and personnel between the American settler community and the indigenous peoples, the former—who never numbered more than 3 percent of the population—remained in control of national-level political and economic institutions until the military coup of 1980. Since there was no color bar between the colonizers and the colonized, educated people of indigenous background could "pass" into the elite, especially if one parent belonged to the settler group. Such upward mobility, however, came at the cost of "tribal" affiliation, which was denied or hidden by elite Liberians until the 1960s and 1970s, when it became fashionable, especially for the young, to have had a "Vai grandmother." In general, indigenous people confronted the state not as members of individual tribes but as an undifferentiated mass of "natives" or "country people" as opposed to "Americo-Liberians," until the overthrow of the First Republic in April of 1980.

The military coup of 1980 brought to power a group of young, minimally educated men of indigenous background. One of them, Samuel K. Doe, emerged as the chair of the "People's Redemption Council," which initially included both those who had organized the coup and progressive civilian leaders who joined them. This ruling council was thoroughly multiethnic, even including some prominent Americo-Liberians who had been critics of the former government. As Doe faced more and more coup attempts from other ambitious young master sergeants like himself, he began to surround himself with people he felt he could trust, friends and kin from his hometown of Tuzon in Grand Gedeh County. Under the previous administrative structure, this region had been identified as the home of the "Krahn tribe," and before long Liberians were grumbling about the new "Krahn people's government." After Doe declared himself the winner of obviously rigged elections in 1985, a coup attempt by a former military associate almost succeeded in removing him. For the first time, Doe retaliated not only against his rival but also against the rival's rural homeland, hundreds of miles from the site of the coup attempt in Monrovia. The army, now composed mostly of recruits from Grand Gedeh, was sent into this region, which was identified with the "Gio" people, and went on a rampage of killing, raping, looting, and destroying towns and farms. At the same time, Doe purged the army and the civil service of Gio speakers, and well-known Gio citizens in Monrovia began to mysteriously "disappear." In all, it is estimated that four to five hundred people were killed.

Four years later, another aspirant to unseat Doe, Charles Taylor, brought a small force of Libyan-trained mercenaries into the country through this same area, apparently deliberately. Doe, predictably, sent the army back to the towns and villages they had so recently ravaged. The people responded to Taylor's invitation to join his uprising, swelling his forces from two hundred to over twenty thousand in a few months. Since Taylor's troops were now mostly "Gio" and Doe's army had been made solidly "Krahn," the conflict was represented in the American press as an ethnic war grounded in, as the *New York Times* reported it, "ancient tribal hatreds." Yet, as is clear from the above account, the "antiquity" of those "tribal hatreds" amounted to less than a decade.

The story of how the Liberian conflict became a "tribal war" was not unique in the 1990s, especially as events in Africa have been reported. Catherine Besteman has documented the same process at work in the reporting on Somalia, in which rivalrous "clans" took the place of "tribes" in that conflict (1996: 121). "The crisis in Somalia has been caused by intense clan rivalries, a problem common in Africa, but here carried out with such violence, there is nothing left of civil society, only anarchy and the rule of the gun" (CNN 1992, quoted in Besteman 1996: 121–22). Besteman points out that, far from being a homogeneous, egalitarian, kinship-based society, Somalia was in fact deeply divided by class and race (defined not by skin color but as the difference between northern Somalis and those of southern "Bantu" or slave origins). Economic stratification and a growing gap between rural and urban populations led, ironically, to increasing identification with "clans," which had formerly been just one among many status positions that Somalis could assert. During the 1980s, as external development aid poured into Somalia and "the state became a primary source of wealth and resources, competition among the new urban elite who gained prominence . . . often played out along bloodlines. This urban-based elite struggle for personal enrichment through acquiring state resources is what came to be known as tribalism or clanism, although it bore little, if any resemblance to traditional lineage mediated interactions" (Besteman 1996: 126–27). Just as in Liberia, the cleavages of contemporary warfare are not relics of the past; rather, they are new constructions, employed for specific purposes in contexts that are the result of changes often initiated from abroad.

Likewise, the horrific genocide in Rwanda, represented as the outcome of "age-old" struggles between Tutsi and Hutu, has been analyzed differently by Christopher Taylor, who demonstrates how European colonial powers created this animosity beginning in the late 1880s. According to the so-called Hamitic hypothesis that the Europeans imported, the tall, "Caucasian-featured" Tutsi were the biblical lost sons of Ham and so were the natural rulers of the shorter, more "African" Hutu (Taylor 1999: 55–97). The fact that these supposedly separate groups speak the same language and have intermarried for generations made little difference in the colonial policies of the region. This same hypothesis was later used by competing political factions as justification for the wave of massacres that began in April 1994. The willingness of international bodies like the United Nations to believe that the killings were "tribal" and therefore somehow unavoidable led to the withdrawal of peacekeeping troops and the escalation of the violence.

All three of these examples from Africa demonstrate the fallacy on which the first tenet of the New Barbarism hypothesis is based: that archaic cultural identities are essentially stable, historically unchangeable, and the source of conflict in the present day. Why do we find it so satisfying to believe that other people are "rooted in culture" while we ourselves have somehow evolved beyond tribalism to rational politics? One answer is that this makes complex events easier to understand. "Tribal violence" functions as both a description and an explanation; once something has been designated as tribal, we no longer feel we need additional information. Besteman suggests another way in which this view responds to anxieties closer to home: "Viewing Somalis as caught in a destructive spiral of 'tradition' allows us to imagine them as very different kinds of human beings, to pity them, and feel safe" (1996: 130). We feel safe, she argues, because as long as we are so different from those "others," the horrors they experience could never happen to us. More significantly, displacing the source of conflict away from issues of race and class and onto tribes and clans "allows us to ignore the legitimacy of these categories and our growing inability to manage their 'dangerous' mix within our own societies, borders, and world" (Besteman 1996: 130). In other words, as national borders become more permeable and "others" take to living as our neighbors, it becomes harder to ignore the inequalities and injustices of our own society. Understanding violent conflict as an outcome of primordial hatreds rather than as a product of income disparities is comforting under these circumstances.

Recently, the "othering" of supposedly traditional cultures has become even more pronounced as the United States settles into an extended "war on terrorism." In seeking to understand the motivation behind the suicide bombings of September 11, the notion that the perpetrators were products of "cultures of terror" was given wide currency. During the brief military intervention in Afghanistan, anti-Taliban Afghans were represented as unreliable allies due to their "tribalism" and the fact that "Pashtuns have always hated Uzbeks." Even long-term alliances have come under recent scrutiny as fears of "Islamic culture" grow. In an editorial on August 9, 2002, entitled "Saudis Pose a Threat to U.S.," the syndicated columnist Cal Thomas describes a briefing commissioned by the Pentagon from the Rand Corporation. The report characterizes Saudi Arabia as "a regime that oppresses women, denies human rights and favors a privileged few at the top over the mostly poor and illiterate at the vast bottom." While this may in fact be an accurate portrayal of the Saudi state, the same conditions held ten years before, when the Saudis were American allies in the Gulf War against Iraq. What was tolerated then as merely a "different" form of government has taken on sinister connotations in the new "cultural war." The columnist concludes, "The United States is being invaded by the immigration of such

people." The implication, of course, is that "such people," already dangerous by virtue of their ancient cultural commitments, are violating both
spatial and temporal boundaries through immigration ("invasion"). As
transnationalism becomes a way of life and economic globalization demands the constant shifting of labor and capital, the barriers separating "us"
and "them" dissolve in both time and space.

To anthropologists, the idea that some people "have culture" while others have moved on to some superior rationality is absurd. Anthropologists
understand "culture" to be our species' means of adapting to the physical
world and creating systems of meaning through which experience can be interpreted; *all human beings,* by definition, are rooted in culture. As Clifford
Geertz noted, cultureless humans (if such were possible) would not be tal-
ented apes, but they "would be unworkable monstrosities with very few useful instincts, fewer recognizable sentiments, and no intellect: mental basket
cases. As our central nervous system . . . grew up in great part in interaction
with culture, it is incapable of directing our behavior or organizing our experience without the guidance provided by systems of significant symbols"
(1973: 48). Yet, New Barbarism theorists suggest that we in the West have
somehow transcended or evolved beyond this most human of capacities,
leaving others to stagnate. Until those others are also able to leave behind
their warlike, mystical, and irrational cultures, they will be unable to participate fully in the modern world of the West, forced to occupy a kind of half
life as unreliable allies if not outright threats.

The appropriation and misrepresentation of the anthropological concept of culture by policy analysts who use it in this static, reductionist way
must be challenged. The examples from Liberia, Somalia, and Rwanda
make clear that culture is a dynamic process of making meaning from ongoing events, not a fixed position on an evolutionary scale. After all, what is
the New Barbarism thesis itself if not a cultural product of our own assumptions about the world and our place in it, one that conveniently dis-
guises the role of major powers like the United States in violent conflict elsewhere in the world?

The Paradox of Cold War Peace

I now turn to the second tenet of the hypothesis: the argument that Cold
War policies in the post–World War II period served the purpose of keeping local conflicts "under control." All classic social-science definitions of
the state include the observation that under this form of political organization, the central government (rather than the kin group or the local community) reserves to itself the legitimate use of violence. In other words, if I

kill someone for my own purposes, the act constitutes murder and is defined as a crime, but if I do so while in a police or army uniform pursuing my official duties, the same act may be defined as heroism. From the point of view of the victim, of course, there is no difference, but from the perspective of the state one killing is legitimate and the other is not. One of the defining features of the "failed" states of the 1990s—from Bosnia to Somalia to Liberia—was the states' loss of control over the means of violence and their usurpation by "nonlegitimate" others, defined as militias, warlords, or criminals.

It has been asserted that the Cold War era superpower competition kept such tendencies in check during the post–World War II period (Kaplan 2000). Using the world as a giant chessboard, the United States and the Soviet Union distributed financial aid and military equipment to a carefully balanced assortment of client states, clearly identified as "ours" or "theirs." While admittedly some of the leaders of "our" clients were rather unsavory characters (Mobutu of Zaire comes to mind), at least they provided stability if not democracy and kept tribal and other factional tendencies in check. In this sense, the Cold War was seen as having brought benefits to countries in Africa and Eastern Europe, giving them a much needed break from their own "natural" cycles of internal tribal conflict. The emergence of wars in these regions after the demise of the Soviet Union, on the other hand, was viewed as an unfortunate consequence of what was "good" for those in the developed world: the triumph of the United States as the sole remaining superpower and of capitalism as the uncontested, dominant form of economic organization on the planet. The fact that the former Soviet Union is no longer capable of supporting client states and the United States no longer needs them is the regrettable cause of the "descent into anarchy" experienced by these now expendable societies.

Such a formulation, like the assertion of cultural difference in the first tenet of the hypothesis, sounds reasonable, but it ignores several alternative understandings of the Cold War period and the question of who bears responsibility for the wars of the 1990s. In the first place, the model ignores the fact that both Cold War antagonists attempted to destabilize each other's clients. Superpower competition *generated* rather than prevented warfare in Angola, Mozambique, and Ethiopia, among other countries. Development aid, often granted with no mechanisms for accountability, rewarded cooperative clients but exacerbated the kind of class stratification that Besteman noted was key to the outbreak of conflict in Somalia (1996: 126). Moreover, the tremendous influx of weapons, all manufactured in the developed world, saturated African countries with the means of violence while profits accrued to those at a safe distance. During the height of Cold War tensions in the first Reagan administration (1980–84), tiny Liberia, with a population of two and a half million people and an area the size of the state of Ohio, was the "beneficiary" of the second largest package of U.S. military aid in the world (after Israel). This was presumably to keep Liberia safe from the "communist threat," but these were the same weapons that Samuel Doe turned against his own civilian population in 1986. With the breakup of the former Soviet Union, arms manufacturers in Ukraine and other newly independent republics, as well as in the United States, have depended on demand from the African market to maintain domestic employment in their aging industrial plants (Ellis 1999: 90, 180; Reno 1993: 181). The militarization of Africa was a deliberate Cold War strategy and continues to benefit its principal architects, long after the Cold War itself has been declared over.

A second problem with the "Cold War peace" formulation is that the tendency to view warfare in the non-Western world as simple "anarchy" obscures the very "rational" economic incentives that fuel long-term conflicts. Charles Taylor quickly learned that he did not need the legitimacy of the Liberian state in order to profit from the country's natural resources. With control over roughly three-fourths of the country, including significant timber and diamond reserves, Taylor was able to build his personal wealth over the seven years of the Liberian civil war, even though an international peace-keeping force occupied Monrovia and a series of helpless interim governments struggled to bring him to the "peace table." The logic of global capitalism dictated that international firms were more than willing to buy the products Taylor had to offer, whether or not he had the "legitimate" right to sell them (for an extended analysis, see Reno 1993, 1998). In fact, the rationality of pricing made Taylor an even more attractive trading partner to countries like France and China, since as a "warlord," he was not bound by any cumbersome environmental or labor restrictions. A similar economic rationality supported the flow of "blood diamonds" from Sierra Leone and petroleum from Angola while both countries were trapped in seemingly endless wars. Rather than mindless anarchy, the post–Cold War conflicts of Africa are the logical outgrowth of the triumph of capitalism and economic globalization, achievements celebrated by the same authors who decry the barbarism of their victims.

Refuting Neo-Malthusianism

The final element of the New Barbarism thesis would appear to be the most "natural": that overpopulation and natural-resource depletion are driving the world's poor into a desperate struggle for existence. Richards has dubbed this aspect of the model "Malthus-with-guns." Kaplan dwells at length on the frightening metaphor of the developed world as a luxury limousine, with its few occupants temporarily insulated from the teeming hoards just beyond the tinted windows (1994: 62). Kaplan attributes the population explosion in Africa to "loose family structures" and polygamy, which he sees as "largely responsible for the world's highest birth rates and the explosion of the HIV virus on the continent" (1994: 46). The pressure of this burgeoning population on a fragile and already depleted environment, Kaplan argues, will ultimately overwhelm the continent and the comfortable lives of those in the developed world as the violent, the diseased, and the dispossessed overflow out of Africa to engulf the planet.

I am not a demographer, and so will leave it to others to dissect Kaplan's Malthusian argument. I note, however, several fallacies in its logic. One is that in making Sierra Leone and Liberia his prime examples of the corrosive relationship between overpopulation and anarchic violence, Kaplan chose two countries that have among the *lowest* population densities in sub-Saharan Africa (this point has been made by Richards [1996: xvi]). Rather than driving up population, polygamy is generally considered by demographers to have, if anything, the effect of *decreasing* average fertility per woman. While multiple wives may increase the number of children claimed by a *man,* some men will have no wives at all, and women in polygamous unions are likely to have fewer children than in monogamous marriages. At its root, Kaplan's analysis seems to rest on the old racist trope of the oversexed African, unable to control his animal impulses.

With regard to the supposition that population pressure and resource depletion, especially deforestation, drive young people to violent behavior, it is once again unfortunate for Kaplan's thesis that he chose to base it on Liberia and Sierra Leone. New research by Fairhead and Leach on this region of West Africa has suggest that "the extent of forest loss in the twentieth century has been vastly exaggerated . . . calling into question the commonplace view of population growth and deforestation as linked one-way processes" (1998: xiv). While there may be environmental crises elsewhere in Africa, they are not coterminous with the wars that Kaplan attributes to them.

On all of his major points, therefore, Kaplan is rehashing old, disqualified ideas and assuming that the events he witnessed during his brief visits were the outcome of age-old structures and processes. His observations have much in common with the travel writing of the Victorian era in that he generalizes widely from single examples and assumes in advance that he is witnessing a "clash of civilizations." His "master stroke" and the secret of his ability to "touch a chord with Western policy makers," according to Ellis, was his suggestion that barbaric wars driven by overpopulation and environmental mismanagement "would soon be breaking out in other parts of the world too, and that West Africa was ahead of the trend" (1999: 19). Yet, as we have seen in the case of Liberia, neither environmental factors nor the end of the Cold War nor "ancient tribal hatreds" can fully explain why 200,000 people lost their lives and over half the population was displaced during a seven-year war. Sadly, none of these explanations reassure us that "it could never happen here."

Anthropological Alternatives

Faced with an integrated, seemingly logical construction like the New Barbarism thesis, what critical tools can anthropology provide to create an alternative? The United States is currently the only global superpower, capable of destroying entire nations and regions as well as enforcing peace agreements in those contexts where we choose to intervene. Such immense power confers responsibility not only on our political leaders but on all citizens. The ability to cut through the mythology of the "cultural other" is crucial to understanding and evaluating what we are told about the deployment (or decision not to deploy) American military power abroad. I believe that anthropological analyses can serve to bring to light naturalizing assumptions about violence and war.

Richards notes that the "New Barbarism pays scant regard to the insurgents' own claims concerning the purposes of their movement (that they took up arms to fight for multi-party democracy and against state corruption)" (1996: xvi). Rather, Kaplan talked almost exclusively to elites in the African countries he visited, elites who have their own reasons for defining young fighters as out-of-control criminals. In contrast, anthropologists attempting to understand the violence and disruption bearing down on the people they work with and care about use ethnographic methods of long-term participant observation in specific local situations, spending a year or more "on the ground" and often returning to the same place to build a deeper understanding of communities through time.

In recent years, many anthropological studies have explored the impact of warfare and violence on local communities, both historical and contemporary. Michael Taussig (1987), building on Foucault (1979, 1983), documented the deliberate construction of "cultures of terror" and the ways that local populations respond by drawing on existing traditions and creative innovations. Kay Warren examined the revitalization of older religious practices among Mayan populations in Guatemala—including the idea of multiple "selves" capable of operating independently and taking on supernatural qualities—as a way of answering the question: "Whom can I trust in a world in which I may be betrayed by my neighbors?" (1993: 12). Likewise, Carolyn Nordstrom emphasized the resilience and creativity of Mozambicans in constructing alternatives to the terror and violence of a seemingly endless war (1997).

Although the "ethnic" character of the Guatemalan violence is commonly highlighted (indigenous Maya against Hispanicized ladinos), Warren showed that local people recognized that the troops of the government's counterinsurgency force were also Mayan—in actuality, their own neighbors (1993: 26–27). Similarly, Valentine Daniel, in decoding the Tamil/Sinhala (also often framed as Buddhist/Hindu) conflict in Sri Lanka, wrote that "many Sri Lankans have either forgotten or do not know that there was a time in Sri Lanka when where one lived mattered more than what language one spoke or what one's religion was" (1996: 16). Historicizing and denaturalizing ethnicity have been central to anthropologists' alternatives to the New Barbarism accounts.

Other ethnographers have refuted the notion that Third World wars are anarchic and inscrutable forms of violence, as opposed to the technologically "clean" or "surgical" havoc wreaked by Western militaries. The effort to make conflicts understandable by placing them within a local cultural context is a key theme of this literature. For example, Christopher Taylor explained some of the peculiar mutilations and tortures employed in Rwanda in terms of broadly shared understandings of movement, impediment, fluidity, and blockage employed in folk medicine and in ideas of how the health of land, cattle, and people are maintained (1999: 99–149). I felt compelled to respond to demeaning and frankly racist stories in supposedly serious magazines like *Atlantic Monthly* and *Esquire* that ridiculed Liberian fighters who dressed in women's wigs and dresses. The authors of these pieces could not resist referencing Conrad's *Heart of Darkness,* and they assumed that the bizarre attire of the fighters either was due to ignorance of Western clothing (and hence was evidence that the fighters were unsophisticated tribesmen) or was motivated by "juju" or other magical beliefs. I argued, rather, that far from displaying primitive ignorance, these fighters were asserting the gender ambiguity of the traditional warrior through intentional transvestism, in ways that I had observed numerous times in funeral dances before the war (Moran 1995).

The work of these and other anthropologists undermines the New Barbarism hypothesis by exposing the fallacies on which it rests. First, it underlines the incorrectness of any evolutionary assumption that "progress" is linear and unidirectional, with all human societies moving inexorably toward something resembling contemporary Western life. No society or people can evolve "beyond culture" to a universal rationality, because all hu-

man products (including the belief that one is rational) are cultural by definition. The combatants in African and Middle Eastern wars are behaving ra-
tionally according to their own understandings of the world. They may also
have very real grievances against the West that our own cultural frameworks
do not recognize or acknowledge. By positing archaic "culture" as the cause
of violence in the developing world, this framework blinds us to the tensions
and antagonisms of race, class, and inequality existing in our own communities—a far more dangerous situation than that presented by "invading"
immigrants (Besteman 1996: 130). The New Barbarism thesis also imposes
historical blinders, as when ethnic or tribal identities are projected into the
primordial past rather than understood as products of colonial and postcolonial power struggles.

Finally, the New Barbarism falls back on a reductionism that attributes
violence, in the final analysis, to "natural" causes, both those seen as endemic in humans and those, like population growth and resource competition, that have to do with human interactions with the environment. This
view leads to the inescapable conclusion that nothing can be done; "those
people" will continue to kill each other, and we had best not get involved beyond erecting barriers that will prevent their conflicts from spilling into our
territory. Anthropologists insist on returning local histories of conflict, and
their relationship with global political and economic forces, back to the center of the analysis.

The events of September 11 may have reinforced the sense that many
Americans have of themselves as the end point of a progressive evolutionary
process, waiting as the rest of the world—jealous and resentful—tries to
catch up. The New Barbarism hypothesis fits neatly into this understanding
of self and other, but it is based on a systematic misunderstanding of both
culture and history. A critically aware citizenry, able to see through the essentialism and reductionism of such notions, is our best hope that we will
be able to find a peaceful future. The archaeologist Philip Walker has argued
that the message of the deep historical record is one of equality and universality; no people, in any time or place, have been immune from war and,
conversely, none have held a monopoly on it (2001: 590). Whenever we hear
people described as "naturally warlike" or "barbaric," we should consider
whose interests are served by that description.

Acknowledgments

This chapter was originally written for a session at the 67th Annual Meeting of the Society
for American Archaeology at the invitation of Patricia Crown and Deborah Nichols. I thank
them and my husband, Jordan Kerber, for encouraging me to initially frame these ideas for an

audience of archaeologists. I also thank the University of Pennsylvania Press for permission to reprint parts of this chapter from my forthcoming book with them. I am grateful to Susan McKinnon and Sydel Silverman for their invitation to contribute to this volume and for giving the paper several rigorous readings and providing many helpful and constructive comments. Finally, Kira Stevens and Philippe Uninsky generously provided extra child-free time, without which this final version would not have been possible.

References

Besteman, Catherine. 1996. Representing Violence and "Othering" Somalia. *Cultural Anthropology* 11: 120–33.

———. 1999. *Unraveling Somalia: Race, Violence, and the Legacy of Slavery.* Philadelphia: University of Pennsylvania Press.

Daniel, E. Valentine. 1996. *Charred Lullabies: Chapters in an Anthropology of Violence.* Princeton: Princeton University Press.

d'Azevedo, Warren. 1970. A Tribal Reaction to Nationalism, Part IV. *Liberian Studies Journal* 3(1): 1–19.

Ellis, Stephen. 1999. *The Mask of Anarchy: The Destruction of Liberia and the Religious Dimension of an African Civil War.* New York: New York University Press.

Fabian, Johannes. 1983. *Time and the Other: How Anthropology Makes Its Object.* New York: Columbia University Press

———. 1991. *Time and the Work of Anthropology: Critical Essays, 1971–1991.* Philadelphia: Harwood.

Fairhead, James, and Melissa Leach. 1998. *Reframing Deforestation: Global Analysis and Local Realities, Studies in West Africa.* London: Routledge.

Ferguson, R. Brian, and Neil L. Whitehead, eds. 1992. *War in the Tribal Zone: Expanding States and Indigenous Warfare.* Santa Fe: School of American Research.

Foucault, Michel. 1979. *Discipline and Punish: The Birth of the Prison.* New York: Vintage.

———. 1983. *Power/Knowledge: Selected Interviews and Other Writings, 1972–1977.* New York: Pantheon.

Geertz, Clifford. 1973. *The Interpretation of Cultures.* New York: Basic Books.

Huntington, Samuel P. 1993. The Clash of Civilizations? *Foreign Affairs* 72 (Summer): 22–49.

———. 1996. *The Clash of Civilizations and the Remaking of World Order.* New York: Simon and Schuster.

Kaplan, Robert. 1993. *Balkan Ghosts: A Journey through History.* London: Macmillan.

———. 1994. The Coming Anarchy: How Scarcity, Crime, Overpopulation, and Disease Are Rapidly Destroying the Social Fabric of Our Planet. *Atlantic Monthly,* February, pp. 44–76.

———. 2000. *The Coming Anarchy: Shattering the Dreams of the Post Cold War.* New York: Random House.

Moran, Mary H. 1995. Warriors or Soldiers? Masculinity and Ritual Transvestism in the Liberian Civil War. In *Feminism, Nationalism, and Militarism,* ed. Constance R. Sutton, pp. 73–88. Arlington, VA: American Anthropological Association.

Nordstrom, Carolyn. 1997. *A Different Kind of War Story.* Philadelphia: University of Pennsylvania Press.

Reno, William. 1993. Foreign Firms and the Financing of Charles Taylor's NPFL. *Liberian Studies Journal* 18(2): 175–87.

———. 1998. *Warlord Politics and African States.* Boulder, CO: Lynne Rienner Publishers.

Richards, Paul. 1996. *Fighting for the Rain Forest: War, Youth, and Resources in Sierra Leone.* Portsmouth, NH: Heinemann; Oxford: James Currey.

Simons, Anna. 1999. War: Back to the Future. *Annual Review of Anthropology* 28: 73–108.

Taussig, Michael. 1987. *Shamanism, Colonialism, and the Wild Man: A Study in Terror and Healing.* Chicago: University of Chicago Press.

Taylor, Christopher. 1999. *Sacrifice as Terror: The Rwandan Genocide of 1994.* Oxford: Berg.

Thomas, Cal. 2002. Saudis Pose a Threat to U.S. *Syracuse Post-Standard,* August 9, 2002.

Walker, Phillip. 2001. A Bioarchaeological Perspective on the History of Violence. *Annual Review of Anthropology* 30: 573–96.

Warren, Kay B. 1992. *The Violence Within: Cultural and Political Opposition in Divided Societies.* Boulder, CO: Westview Press.

CHAPTER 12

Language Standardization and the Complexities of Communicative Practice

John J. Gumperz and Jenny Cook-Gumperz

OUR MAIN THEME in this chapter is that the "standard languages" commonly seen as symbolizing national identity are not linguistic entities so much as ideological constructs, the results of politically motivated processes.[1] These processes are reductionist in that they seek to erase the complexity and diversity of language use in a community by conferring legitimacy on selected languages or linguistic practices. We contend, moreover, that ideologies of standardization both draw on and reinforce the claims of those branches of linguistics that treat languages as wholly constituted by grammatical relations, divorced from the social contexts that are, in fact, key to any understanding of how language works in everyday life. Views of language based solely on grammar have led to an idealization of linguistic knowledge and have come to be associated with a conception of language as innate, predetermined by individuals' neural or genetic makeup. Such views have been influential in current debates about education, politics, and legal affairs.

We begin with a brief discussion of the social constructionist approach that underlies our reasoning—namely, the idea that power resides in the ability to create and define the terms and language structures through which we organize our social worlds. We then give a historical sketch that accounts for the relationship among nation building, nationalist ideologies, and linguistic theory. We will propose that the linguistic theories and ideologies that are currently dominant fail to capture the complexities of today's communicative ecologies, and we will point to new work in linguistic anthropology that better comes to grips with those complexities. Finally, we take up some issues that have brought language ideologies into recent policy debates.

Social Construction and Social Diversity

According to social constructionist theory, which has revolutionized our thinking about everyday social life, our social worlds are *constituted* by the same language practices that we use to think and talk about them. It follows from this that the categorizations we rely on in talking about social collectivities are subject to ongoing negotiations of meaning. These categorizations, therefore, are not only cognitive entities but also part of the interactive process through which cultural meanings enter into daily actions.

A socially constructed reality is open to misinterpretation and misuse (Hacking 1999). This is so because the concepts and words with which we talk and think about human collectivities—such as class, gender, race, ethnicity, and nation—are communicative symbols that are themselves contingent phenomena; that is, they undergo shifts in meaning as the circumstances that gave rise to them are transformed. The complexities of cultural reasoning that give power to a symbol can become compacted and encoded in a single term, leaving only the compacted symbol for use in public discourse. Thus, public debates about language and ethnicity, or language and national identity, may proceed without awareness of the very social and linguistic practices that gave rise to these symbols in the first place. Public discussion can then grow circular, keeping in touch with just enough of the historical circumstances behind the symbols to make them seem viable, while the more complex processes that led to their formation are erased from memory. In this way, groups that are distinguished on the basis of one feature—say, a distinct language—may be treated as real ethnic groups and as such may be seen as the actors in interethnic conflicts, even if they are not a unity when other features are considered (Blommaert and Verschüren 1998b: 193). There are dangers in situations where social groups are defined by language and where public discussions rely on such compacted symbols. This situation, we argue, marks many educational and political debates involving the notion of the standard language.

Communication in the contemporary world must be understood in the light of the changes of late capitalism, which have been propelled by economic and political forces such as the shift to post-Fordist modes of production, corporate organizations that transcend national boundaries, and a flexibility of capital deployment that brings about large-scale population movements. Anthropologists studying these processes of globalization have applied the idea of flexibility to the spaces and symbols of belonging—national identity and social boundary—and have begun to concentrate on how globalization also implies a dislocation of experience. Such dislocations present a growing threat to more established community-rooted social practices, as people move back and forth across territorial spaces (Ong 1999; Rosaldo and Inda 2001). Multiculturalism is beginning to be recognized as a permanent condition of life today, and one that brings with it complexities of communication. The effects of these forces on interpersonal relations, and therefore on the communicative practices that constitute them, are now becoming a focus of attention for some linguistic anthropologists, although their work has not, so far, gained a wider audience.

Public debates on language, immigration, and ethnicity tend to rely on folk-linguistic reasoning that separates language as such from the social circumstances on which it depends. The common view is still that human populations come divided into discrete, homogeneous groups, each with its own language or dialect (Blommaert and Verschüren 1998a). Thus, linguistic diversity is seen as an impediment to shared understanding and a threat to national unity. Even advocates of language minority rights who have sought to expose the political biases that underlie public discourse about language accept this view (e.g., Crawford 1992). Although there is much recent research that shows it to be misleading because it fails to account for the observable facts of communication, the debate on multicultural societies remains at the level of political controversy over the dangers of difference (Hill 1998). Specifically, the fear is expressed, in many different ways, that pluralism in a single communicative economy—that is, a multiplicity of languages—will lead to chaos (Gal and Irvine 2000).

We can trace some of these problems to divisions between two contrasting views of language in the discipline of linguistics itself. These divisions have a history that extends well back before the twentieth century, but they were sharpened by the rise of structuralist theory after the publication of Ferdinand de Saussure's *Cours de linguistique générale* in 1916. One tradition, which we refer to as structuralist or idealist, argues that it is necessary to abstract and separate from everyday talk meaningful signs, which then become the raw materials that the linguist uses to formulate general rules of language structure. The other tradition, the empiricist, takes a descriptive approach to uncovering the complexities of spoken languages as systems.

The Search for a Standard

Language standardization has gained prominence in recent decades, but it has its roots in the nineteenth century. Some historical philologists and dialectologists of the time found that by abstracting sound patterns from everyday speech, they were able to devise methods of comparative analysis that could yield community-wide laws of sound change; such analysis could then be used to justify a nation's claim to legitimacy. However, it was in the twentieth century that these views, as well as claims of language superiority and colonial hegemony, were consolidated into a full-fledged ideology of standard language.

In looking for these origins, we must beware of assuming too easily that a single causal chain can be established from historical events and linguistic texts to the subsequent emergence of the idea of a single standard language. To do so would be to underestimate the complexity of the process, in much the same way as mid-twentieth-century language planners arbitrarily chose the standard language for a developing nation, following the simple equation of "one country, one language." When we now talk (in everyday discourse) of standard languages, we are referring to languages—such as Arabic, Chinese, English, Russian, or Swahili—that serve as symbols of nationhood in specific territorially defined political entities. Linguists refer to such languages as standard varieties, "codified form[s] of a language accepted by, and serving as a model to, a larger speech community" (Mathiot and Garvin, quoted in Garvin 1964: 522). As the official media of communication and education, they are widely recognized throughout a nation and its territory. Yet, as the definition implies, they are not the only forms used by members of a speech community. In the course of their daily lives, individuals rely on a wide array of distinct modes of speaking to express what they intend to convey—regional or social dialect, professional or technical idioms, formal or familiar styles—shifting among them as the situation requires.

Historical linguists have concentrated on three aspects of language in their search for the origin of the standard: dialect differences and their influence, written textual practices, and the notion of an "educated accent or speech" (Wright 2000). It has become clear, in the course of this work, that the concept of a "standard" as a guide to correct practice has multiple meanings and derivations. Shirley Brice Heath, who notes the confusion that marks American speakers' views of "standard English," aptly describes how these ideas are played out in the United States today. Standards, she points out, are most often defined by what they are not, and definitions contain a large element of prescriptive moral opinion.

What does it mean to be a speaker of "good English," "proper English," or "standard English" (SE) in the United States? Both those who speak SE and those who don't, recognize it when they hear it, can readily give examples of what it is *not*, and are able to identify places where it is spoken as well as places where it is not likely to be used. When they try to define SE, however, we are reminded of the blind men trying to describe an elephant by identifying its individual parts. Some tell us SE is the absence of accent; some say it is "correct grammar"; and others say it is characterized by Latinate words and sophisticated sentence structures. Some say SE is reinforced by schoolteachers and dictionaries. Some tell us that most printed English is standard, but only some spoken English is.

Some or all of these views on SE are held by most of the population in the United States. But we still don't know what SE is or what it means to speak it. We only know that SE is something that is "clean," "good," and recognizable; it involves pronunciation, vocabulary, and syntax; and it is tied to specific contexts in writing and speaking, especially in school. It is an ideal by which some of us monitor our own speaking and writing and by which we are judged by others. (Heath 1980: 4)

We can see in this description that contemporary lay notions of Standard English contain recognizable traces of the history of its origins.

But the language planners had a different view of the languages they constructed as standard. The very idea of a "codified language" that serves as "a model to a larger community" reflects the awareness that speech communities are intrinsically diverse, and thus for any political community to function there must be a unifying semiotic that enables communication. This awareness was at the core of the process of language planning, which saw language as a key factor in creating a sense of a national identity. A unifying language provided a "conscious integration . . . [as] heretofore local languages . . . become elevated to national, unifying symbols . . . and are related to national heroes, national values, national missions and ultimately to the sacredness of the state and of the moral order" (Fishman 1968: 6–7).

The planners believed that a national language does not just emerge over time; rather, a standard must be chosen and institutionally maintained, even protected from change. Whereas vernacular varieties develop naturally (they are usually learned at home and in friendship circles and then are passed on from generation to generation), the standard language is a variety that speakers must acquire through conscious instruction, such as through state-sponsored choices of the languages of primary education (Whiteley 1971). Early sociolinguists focused on the history of their own societies and looked at the development of their own national languages as models for language choice and language planning in emerging nations (Fishman, Ferguson, and Das Gupta 1968).

Historical linguists, however, pursued a different line of inquiry. Their argument was that standards develop from preexisting supralocal vernaculars, spoken in urban centers and propagated as symbols of national identity. More recently, some have suggested that these languages legitimated the aspirations of a rising urban middle class, which came to stand for the new supralocal polity responsible for managing civil society. Over time these language varieties were regularized and generalized into a single educated standard, which was said to represent the nation-state and its geographic area and which became the medium of official communication (Watts and Bex 2000). In her study of the rise of accent as an essential social discriminator in nineteenth- and twentieth-century Britain, Lynda Mugglestone (1995) argues that the choice of language is guided by prescriptive, as well as normative, principles, which set forth what is considered correct or educated usage. Asif Agha (1993) has explored the semiotic processes by which notions of cultural value become attached to accent, making language use a denominator of prestige or social-class position. Such views are closer to the everyday notions of Standard English described by Heath than to the language planners' definition of a "codified variety."

Thus, we are faced with two distinct senses of "standard language." In one sense, the standard is a moral good achieved only by those who are deemed worthy; in the other, the standard is the outcome of a regularizing process, "standardization," which is presumably available to all within a region or political domain. Yet some sociolinguists have argued, on the basis of their empirical research on everyday talk in English, that there is no such thing as a single standard. Jim Milroy, for example, points out that Standard English did not originate in any one collectivity of speakers or in any particular geographic region. Hence, "the standard language will not be treated as a definable variety of a language on a par with other varieties. The standard is not seen as part of the speech community in precisely the same sense that vernaculars can be said to exist in communities." He concludes "that standard 'varieties' appear as idealizations . . . [that] do not conform exactly to the usage of any particular speaker" (Milroy 2000: 11). Milroy raises an issue for every linguist: if the standard language is an ideal, then how can this ideal be integrated with the assumption that linguistic analyses must build on the perceptible features of everyday talk?

Michael Silverstein suggests a solution to this dilemma. He differentiates between a speech community, defined (in the established way) as "sharing a set of norms or regularities for interaction by means of language," and what he terms a linguistic community, "a group of people who, in their implicit sense of the regularities of linguistic usage, are united in adherence to the idea that there exists a functionally differentiated norm for using their 'language' denotationally (to represent and describe things), the inclusive range of which the best language users are believed to have mastered in the appropriate way" (1996: 285). Silverstein's distinction enables him to speak of a culture of standardization, that is, an array of ideological principles that leads speakers to evaluate talk as if there were a standard. He goes on to argue that although there may not be any one historical individual who in fact has mastery of such an ideal standard, it is allegiance to the concept of a "functionally differentiated norm" of usage that defines the best speakers of the language and that marks membership in a specific linguistic group and produces a sense of community with others in it (1996: 286). Thus, a standard is not a language variety. Standards become ideological objects whose existence cannot be established by the commonly accepted means of linguistic or grammatical analysis. Rather, analysis must focus on metapragmatic processes—that is, how we talk about language use and how this talk affects what we say and do.

Silverstein's argument is representative of the new approach in linguistic anthropology, which focuses on discourse and looks at language not as an abstract system but as communicative practice. In this view, communication is not a matter of referential meaning alone, but reference (or denotation) combines with other communicative signs to yield interpretations in everyday discourse. Silverstein is addressing some of the problems raised earlier in this chapter: how can a standard that is defined only in its absence be considered relevant to the communicative practices of real-life communities; and how can the analyst avoid the pitfall of using the ideal as a model when looking at actual practice?

The Origins of Standard-Language Ideology

How did ideologies of language arise? Current perspectives on language are rooted in the social and ideological concerns of eighteenth- and early-nineteenth-century Europe. Benedict Anderson (1983) attributes the phenomenon of "imagined communities," based in part on standard national languages, to Protestantism, "print-capitalism," and advances in technology. But more was involved than such impersonal forces. The eighteenth century was a time when, with the diminution of monarchic power, scholars and writers, as members of the rising urban bourgeoisie, were pressing for the replacement of classical languages in public discourse and education by the new urban vernaculars. A novel form of discourse arose in what Jürgen Habermas (1989) called the public sphere. Here citizens "met and conversed, exercising their rationality and judgment. Its institutions were the coffee houses, the periodicals and journals" (Crowley 1996: 55). But not everyone could enter this sphere. Tony Crowley cites Jonathan Swift's complaint "that our Language is extremely imperfect; that its daily Improvements are by no means in proportion to its daily Corruptions; that the Pretenders to polish and refine it have chiefly multiplied Abuses and Absurdities; and that in many Instances, it offends against every part of Grammar" (1996: 55–56). In other words, only those who proved themselves worthy by speaking "correctly" could be considered potential participants in the public sphere. Much of the century was taken up with efforts to reform and refine the new language, and in the process the English language came to be seen as a moral good and an embodiment of rising nationalist sentiments. The new idea of a single national language to replace the prevailing heteroglossia carried with it a sense of the moral value of a purified idiom, one that could both unify the nation and civilize its speakers. These changes led to heated public debates. As Crowley notes, "Eighteenth century Britain was fascinated by language; from Universal Grammarians to elocution masters; from defenders of Latin to upholders of English grammar; from literary practitioners to their aristocratic patrons; from religious zealots to working-class campaigners for suffrage" (1996: 54). Much of the century was marked by "a war for the right to the power of words," and the prize "was the right to say who could enter and speak, who was to be excluded . . . what could be said, and what was forbidden, how things could be spoken, and how not" (Crowley 1996: 56–57).

If the eighteenth century laid the basis for linguistic ideologies, structural linguistics has its roots in the attempts by nineteenth-century historical linguists to document the legitimacy of the newly formed national languages. By the early nineteenth century, nationalist movements had established the idea of national languages throughout much of Western Europe. In France, Condillac's writings on language were the motivation for the early French dialectologists who sought to study local idioms so as to be able to destroy them more effectively and make way for the spread of a national language. In Germany, efforts to contribute to the construction of nation through language can be traced back to Johann Herder and his followers, the German Romantics (Bauman and Briggs 2000; Berlin 1977). Similar developments occurred elsewhere in the world wherever popular demands for a separate nation-state were successful, as in the early twentieth century in eastern Europe. Jacqueline Urla (1987) provides a detailed account of the debates and political strategies that went into the formation of a modern Basque language, which was cultivated and introduced into the Basque-speaking areas of Spain by students trained in the tradition of the French Grandes Ecoles.

In sum, national languages are, in a very real sense, social formations, cultivated by intellectuals in response to the exigencies of nation building. But it is important to emphasize that, contrary to nineteenth-century preconceptions, the languages that came to be seen as standards did not develop naturally from the local vernaculars; thus, attempts to derive any standard modern language from a single source were unlikely to succeed. On the other hand, the social climate that gave rise to the concern with language origin in many ways led to the formation of modern linguistics.

The Beginnings of a Modern Linguistic Science

The emergence of a discipline of linguistics was greatly aided by the discovery of Indo-European by William Jones, the eighteenth-century British jurist and scholar. Jones was one of the first Europeans to learn Sanskrit; he then went on to compare Sanskrit grammar with other classical languages, such as Latin and Greek. He found that the similarities were such that these languages were probably historically related. His observations, when elaborated and systematized, became the basis of Franz Bopp's classical treatise *Analytical Comparison of the Sanskrit, Greek, Latin and Teutonic Languages, Shewing the Original Identity of Their Grammatical Structure* ([1816] 1974). Bopp's study laid the groundwork for a new science of comparative philology, which showed that the structure of one language could be illuminated by comparison with another. The term "structure" is important here, because it reflects the view that grammatical form, not words and their specific meanings, must be the basis for comparisons. Bopp's initial findings were refined some decades later by the German neogrammarians, who constructed groupings of languages into distinct families—each deriving from an ancestor or protolanguage—which were ordered in family trees. In this way, elements of what in the twentieth century became structuralist linguistic theory were developed in response to a concern with language as a unifying national symbol.

A basic structuralist principle was that, in order to yield valid generalizations, languages must be analyzed in their own terms, as structures. A frequently voiced argument was that values and political attitudes have no place in a systematic analysis. The notion of meaning had to be confined to reference—that is, word-to-word relationships, leaving out personal opinions. The method of comparison specifically ruled out any consideration of political ideology or moral values, which had played such an important role in the initial impetus to study language. In the search for linguistic means with which to validate the nation's roots, "language began to fold in upon itself, to acquire its own particular density, to deploy a history, an objectivity, and laws of its own" (Foucault, quoted in Crowley 1996: 149).

Like comparative anatomists, who cut up bodies in order to study them, the comparative philologists strove to achieve scientific rigor by dissecting words into sounds. The patterning of such sounds became the basis for sound laws that could demonstrate the regularities of change. Comparative linguistic analysis yielded tools with which to excavate the new nation's "origins" and provide empirical justifications for its claims to legitimacy. As a result, linguistics gained a reputation as the most scientific of the humanistic disciplines.

Structuralist theory began to gain adherents in the first decades of the twentieth century. Saussure, its most important theorist, who had achieved fame as an Indo-Europeanist, was the first to attempt to build a science of language. He argued that empirical description of speech sounds, no matter how dense and detailed, cannot yield scientifically valid descriptions; rather, systems of oppositions defined in relation to each other, abstracted from speech, would enable community-wide generalizations to be made. Structuralism, whether in its Saussurian form or as developed later by Edward Sapir and Leonard Bloomfield, provided empirical proof to counter common preconceptions about non-Western languages and, by inference, their speakers. The assumption was that Saussurian methods would yield abstract grammatical structures that are stable over time and reflect what is significant about a language. Language, when seen in these terms, becomes what Saussure referred to as *langue,* abstract structures of denotational signs that are uniform in a speech community (Harris 1987; Saussure and de Mauro 1976).

Such an analytic procedure supports the presumptions that speech communities are dominated by a single major language and that languages are systems of denotationally defined words and rules, divorced from the observable facts of everyday talk as well as from the dispositions acquired through living, communicating, and collaborating with others in one's social environment. If grammatical systems are relatively stable over time and not readily subject to change, then it could be argued that the linguists' abstract grammars are in fact standard-language grammars. In this way, people began to regard linguists' descriptions of a language as the standard language, which was cultivated in language academies and codified in school grammars and dictionaries and became the model of refined and correct speech.

National Language as Standard Language

Some of the nineteenth-century issues of language description recurred in a different form in the nation-building debates of the 1950s and 1960s, as small-scale groupings were absorbed into larger political entities and as ex-colonial societies became separate states. Linguists, along with other social scientists, became concerned with what was then seen as societal development or modernization. Debates revolved around the question of national language: should the new states continue to rely on the colonial language, or should a local variety be chosen as the unifying medium? Joshua Fishman argued that what was taken as a "national language" began as just another speech variety, which through a political process was selected from preexisting vernaculars to become a national standard. He comments: "local languages or languages of restricted populations or functions become elevated to national, unifying symbols" by being "rendered more differentiated from languages or varieties with which they have long been in contact" (Fishman 1968: 6). Paul Garvin's (1964) characterization of a standard language as a "codified" form, the one that could be taken as most representative of the varieties in a repertoire, reflected a more utilitarian view. Although this variety was only one among other available modes of speaking, it occupied a special position as the most widely understood and most authoritative within the repertoire. Therefore, even if it was not necessarily the language spoken by all members of the community, it served as a criterion of evaluation for all other language practices.

Yet these views can now be seen to be repeating the ideological misconceptions of the nineteenth century in a new guise. Susan Gal and Judith Irvine have made this point in commenting on the nineteenth-century linguistic descriptions that created the language boundaries in West Africa. They highlight the role of ideology in the original linguistic descriptions by which the colonial administrators and European linguists understood regional distinctions:

> Each language . . . was represented in an impoverished way to differentiate it from the other and to accord with an ideology about its essence. At the same time, regional varieties that seemed to overlap were ignored. . . . The same notions of language purity that led nineteenth-century linguists to ignore "mixed" varieties, multilingualism, and expressions they could attribute to linguistic borrowing also discouraged research on African regional dialectology. Once a variety had been declared to belong to the "same" language as another already-described variety, there was no reason to investigate it, unless its speakers stubbornly refused to speak anything else. (Gal and Irvine 2000: 56–57)

In short, once the ideological principle emerged that a standard language was spoken by a people living and speaking within a territorial area—which was viewed as a single nation—it became entrenched within Western (colonial) language history.

As we noted above, the early sociolinguists had advanced the notion of linguistic "repertoires" to explain the pervasive plurilingualism that they discovered in their empirical research and to account for the totality of verbal resources available to members of speech communities (Gumperz 1971). Repertoires are systems of functionally differentiated, partially overlapping speech varieties, such as social and geographical dialects, registers and styles, and trade and professional languages, each with its own grammatical characteristics; the assumption is that speakers choose among these. However, as Gal and Irvine suggest, the very concept of speech community reflects the 1960s sociological thinking that highlighted a view of social order as integrative. The notion of repertoire simply subdivides a larger bounded unit into smaller ones, without challenging the thinking on which this division rests; speech communities continue to be seen as bounded, internally integrated units. In this way, any difference can be treated as positive and nonconflictful:

> Despite increasing awareness in recent years of these European ideologies of language and their historical contexts, anthropologists and linguists have not sufficiently explored their implications. Our disciplines' conceptual tools for understanding linguistic differences and relationships still derive from this massive scholarly attempt to create the differentiation of Europe from the rest of the world. . . . linguistic differentiation crucially involves ideologically embedded and socially constructed processes. (Gal and Irvine 2000: 73–74)

Such an ideologically based perspective left no room for consideration of how diversity works in today's rapidly changing communicative ecologies.

The Idealist Position and the Innateness Metaphor

As part of his effort to extract general laws from the piecemeal writings of his predecessors, Saussure ([1916] 1966) argued that we must turn away from an exclusive focus on "etic," empirically perceptible sounds, to construct abstract systems of "emic" (subjectively meaningful) relations. He showed that once we focused on such structural relationships we could discover community-wide regularities that otherwise would escape us, and that these could ultimately lead to universals. In his work, utterances and their syntactic constitution become the building blocks of language. Theory takes precedence over empirical description.

Noam Chomsky extended the Saussurian structuralist perspective, but in the process he shifted the emphasis from language as a social institution based in speech to a focus on syntax as the property of an individual mind. In so doing, he argued that the grammatical principles governing these relationships are ultimately panhuman universals. Chomsky's approach to grammar laid the groundwork for much that has been done in linguistics and in cognitive sciences over the past four decades. His emphasis on linguistic structures as self-contained independent systems, unaffected by

culture or by social phenomena, depended on a view of linguistic competence that is psychologically—and, by implication, biologically—based.
The claims that human grammatical abilities are innate and that in learning
a first language the developing child simply fleshes out a biologically predetermined program have been hotly contested. Chomsky's supporters defend
them by arguing that syntactic complexities are such that they could not
possibly be acquired through adult models as the only source of input
(Pinker 1999). This claim is contradicted by many developmental psychologists—some of them originally trained in Chomskyan generative grammar—on the grounds that it does not account for their own observational
and experimental findings (Tomasello 1999). Chomskyan arguments have
been enormously influential in redirecting linguistics from its behaviorist,
empiricist roots toward cognition and universals, and they still dominate
linguistic theorizing and language policy.

We have argued that the view of grammar as a separable system is both
empirically untenable and theoretically flawed, in that it builds on an impoverished database. This essentialized notion of language developed out of
a historical process that led linguists to disregard the inherent variability of
real-life speech communities in order to derive internally consistent rules of
syntax. These efforts provided historical justification for national claims to
legitimacy, because the grammar of the language, defined by abstract Saussurian rules, was taken to be representative of a community as a whole. The
structuralist view of grammar, which focuses on the competence of ideal
speakers living in hypothetical, uniform communities, was later joined by
some of its proponents to an innatist conception of language abilities. When
these notions are applied to today's communicative ecologies, they are unable to account for the practices that speakers employ in pursuit of their
day-to-day communicative goals. Feeding into monoglot ideologies of language standardization, they may also lead to unrealistic, self-defeating, and
potentially oppressive language and educational policies.

The Complexities of Communicative Practice

In contrast to the structuralist/idealist perspective, an alternative position
has been developed by linguists and anthropologists that centers on the
practices of speakers and audiences engaged in context-bound, collabora-
tive speech activities. While Saussurian and Chomskyan grammars treat
languages as self-contained systems independent of the social worlds in
which talk occurs, contemporary linguistic anthropology over the past two
decades has provided new, integrated ways of looking at communicative
practice. Such an approach to language sees communicative understanding

as depending upon shared common ground and as constructed in the interpretive process.

We have asked: How representative are standard languages of what people do in everyday life? The answer that emerges is that language practices in real-life communities are far more complex than the identification of a single standard allows for. Such a standard was always more an ideal than an actuality, and the idea of standardization itself was always ideologically charged (Woolard 1998).

Recent empirical studies have demonstrated that despite the prevailing ideology of standardization, actual verbal practices show speech communities of all kinds to be inherently diverse. That is, whenever we communicate we shift among different modes of speaking, depending on what we want to convey and how we want to convey it. As we noted, sociolinguists initially assumed that, given this inherent heteroglossia in contemporary life, language usage at the community level was best described in terms of a linguistic repertoire—that is, an array of socially or functionally distributed dialects or styles. However, it later became clear that the notion of repertoire as made up of distinct varieties was both theoretically and practically untenable, especially in light of the transformations of late modernity. Therefore, in order to understand the complexities of everyday talk and the shifts in styles and genres that it involves, recent work has turned to a broader view of communicative practice (Hanks 1996a, 1996b; Lucy 1993; Silverstein and Urban 1996). As William Hanks comments, "The idea of objectivist rules is replaced by schemes and strategies, leading one to view genre as a set of focal and prototypical elements, which actors use variously and which never become fixed in a unitary structure" (1987: 691). Thus, it is necessary to draw together linguistic form, discursive activity, and ideology if we are to understand current communicative practice and its implications for contemporary life.

While structuralist analysis focuses on isolated sentences abstracted from talk, analyses of communicative practice look at everyday discourse as an interactive enterprise that involves two or more speakers collaborating in a process of interpretation, as they act in pursuit of their goals and aspirations. Speaking is not just a matter of individuals encoding and decoding messages; the speakers engage in ongoing negotiation, inferring what others intend to convey and encoding their own contributions and monitoring how they are received. Speaking, therefore, is basically a social act in which grammatical knowledge, background knowledge, and cultural assumptions of various kinds all enter into interpretation. Discourse-level interpretation is highly contingent; that is, it depends upon context, topic of discussion, participants' background, and other factors. For the analyst, discourse-level variability is a source of important information about the speakers' often unspoken assumptions, which underlie their interpretations. Diversity, when seen in this perspective, is a communicative resource, providing information about other participants that enriches and refines the interpretive process.

The analysis of communicative practice involves minimally a set of three moves: an initiation, a response, and a follow-up that confirms or disconfirms what is said. Interpretation in such exchanges involves two sets of signaling mechanisms: symbolic signs that communicate by grammatical and lexical rules; and indexical signs that communicate by virtue of conventionalized associations between signs and context, associations that have been established through previous communicative experience. In this way, context is intrinsically involved in the interpretive process.

A small example will illustrate how communicative practice works:

> While driving to the office some time ago, my radio was tuned to a classical music station. At the end of the program the announcer, a replacement for the regular host who was returning the next day, signed off with the following words: "I've enjoyed being with YOU these last two weeks." I had not been listening very carefully but the strong accent on "you" in a syntactic position where I would have expected an unaccented pronoun caught my attention. It sounded as if the speaker were producing the first part of a formulaic exchange of compliments. Yet, since there was no one else with him on the program, I inferred that by the way he contextualized his talk the announcer was indirectly—without putting it "on record"—implicating the second part: "I hope you enjoyed listening to [i.e., being with] me." (Gumperz 1996: 382)

Note that to understand what was going on it was necessary for me to retrieve background knowledge that could provide a reasonable explanation of what the announcer intended. The accent on "you" here acted as an indexical cue.

Linguistic anthropologists working along similar lines have shown that indexicality is an integral part of all verbal communication. We rely on indexicality to orient ourselves in an interaction; in fact, culture is in large part conveyed by indexical means. The unspoken character of many indexical signs means that thorough ethnographic knowledge obtained through lengthy fieldwork is often necessary to identify them. Studies by Hanks (1996b) on village discussions among Yucatec Maya and by Elinor Ochs (1996) on children's language socialization highlight the crucial role of indexicality in communicative practice.

Some critics have argued that detailed analyses of communicative practice are relevant only for local, face-to-face interactions. We argue, on the contrary, that the broader issues of power and ideology in public discourse touched on in this chapter can also be addressed by such analyses. A few examples from recent work support this claim. Using detailed analyses of talk, Jane Hill and Ophelia Zapeda (1993) reveal how ethnic stereotyping is produced in private discourse, and they show how complex an issue such stereotyping is. In a later paper, Hill (1998) goes on to examine the rhetoric of media talk to demonstrate how ethnic stereotypes are created in public discourse. She argues that the speech of minorities is subject to intense scrutiny: "The speech of racialized populations such as Chicanos and Latinos and African Americans [is closely monitored] for signs of linguistic disorder," while "the invisibility of almost identical signs in the speech of Whites, where language mixing, required for the expression of a highly valued type of colloquial persona," goes unnoticed and so "indexes whiteness as an unmarked normative order" (Hill 1998: 680). In other words, our ideologies of standardization lead to different interpretations of similar verbal signs, which reinforce existing stereotypes.

In his studies on the construction of power and identity in Venezuela, Charles Briggs (2000) documents in detail how an oppressive social system works to affect people's lives by the way public discourse about an issue is shaped. For example, he shows how during a series of cholera epidemics health officials were able to get the courts to construe culturally conventional practices of health as dangerous, and as therefore constituting criminal violence against persons. In this way, the poor were made criminally negligent for their own deaths. He argues from analyses of other trials in the capital that "as globalization forces some 80% of Venezuelans into poverty, these widely publicized trials turned stereotypes of poor citizens as impoverished, immoral, and criminal into arguments that legitimate the repressive functions of the nation state" (Briggs 2000: 300). Thus, Briggs integrates linguistic forms, discursive activity, and ideology into a unified analytical framework that can speak to large societal issues.

The Politics of Standardization and the Language Wars

The ideology of language standardization has entered the public arena in several areas. We focus on two related issues: bilingual education and the "English-only" movement. Educational policy in the United States has responded to the needs of a diverse society in contradictory ways: on the one hand, sponsoring bilingual education and, on the other hand, mandating English-only policies that challenge existing positive views of language minorities. Louis-Jean Calvet has described "language wars" in this way:

"Plurilingualism is experienced with reference to the Myth of Babel as a punishment, or even as a curse. Note that the neologism "Babelization," multiplication of languages in a given territory, is the linguistic equivalent of the term "balkanization" for nation-states: in both cases this multiplicity is regarded as a bad thing" (1987: 35, our translation). Calvet was summarizing arguments in the history of language wars in France, but he captures sentiments that underlie much public discourse on language diversity.

The rhetoric of the current struggle over English-only legislation in the United States is an example of such language wars that has major implications for politics, law, and education. Political responses to language use in public education seem to reflect the subconscious fear that Calvet alludes to. Thus, the former secretary of education William Bennett, speaking in the late 1980s, echoes these sentiments while at the same time stressing the importance of a single unifying language: "To be a citizen is to share in something common—common principles, common memories, and a common language in which to discuss our common affairs. Our common language is, of course, English. And our common task is to ensure that our non-English-speaking children learn this common language" (Bennett 1992: 358). By his biblical-style repetitions and dramatic use of the term "common," Bennett strongly implies that any disapproval of this position not only would be morally reprehensible but would set oneself up as not a "common man" and so not on the side of God and country.

To express educational matters with such emotional overtones is to take the issues of language and education out of the sphere of academic or policy talk and into the domain of political rhetoric. This is what happened in the debate over bilingualism, "English-plus," and English-only (Cazden and Snow 1990). Academic experts repeatedly offered—in position papers and committee testimony—evidence from research bearing on the debate. Yet their offerings were ignored, especially their attempts to show how recent findings explain the way bilingualism works in communicative practice (Secada 1990). The debate proceeded as if any challenge to English as the national language was unacceptable. In many states the course of public education was changed, from endorsing diversity in early language instruction and supporting bilingualism through various curricular mixtures into an English-only policy. This policy reiterated reliance on Standard English as the acceptable legal standard of the language spoken by the majority.

Rosina Lippi-Green (1996), reviewing arguments about diversity and language, cites the legal statute proposed for the state of Hawaii in 1987, called the Standard English and Oral Communication Act: "Standard English [shall] be the mode of oral communication for students and staff in the classroom setting and all other school related settings except when the objectives cover native Hawaiian or foreign language instruction and practice" (quoted in Sato 1991, cited in Lippi-Green 1996: 118). She points out that this proposal went beyond simply mandating English as the language of instruction; it sought to ban all school talk and public discourse in educational settings that did not conform to an undefined—and, as we have argued, undefinable—Standard English.

Lippi-Green refers to the history of the Hawaiian situation, observing that although the reintroduced original Oleo Hawai'i language (the "native" language in the statute) was protected by legislation and could not be banned, there were no first-language speakers left. However, not only do the people of Hawaii speak many Asian, Indonesian, and Pacific Island languages, but a sizable number speak the language now known as Hawaiian Creole English (HCE), which developed as a response to years of colonial English-language domination. HCE, which emerged in reaction to previous attempts to outlaw the original native language, was now itself being outlawed, even though about half of the 1.3 million Hawaiian inhabitants speak some form of HCE (Sato 1991). As is well known, language changes that result from enforced adoption of colonial languages usually mean that a new variant of the dominant language develops. The Hawaiian education statute placed Standard English in opposition to the home-grown language variety, using the ideology of the standard to reinforce once again the stigmatization of HCE. The same phenomenon has occurred in the case of Native Americans in the mainland United States, where a number of distinctive languages have disappeared through enforced English-only education. A new and distinct pan–North American style, containing idiomatic constructions patterned on those of the Native languages, has been created, which sets off the Indian community from the surrounding White community (Sarris 1993; Collins 1998, 1999).

A decade after the Hawaiian experience, the English-only movement was successful in California, after an extensive, well-financed media campaign in support of legislation to make English the only language of school instruction. This referendum followed the defeat of a proposition that would have excluded nondocumented immigrants and their children from education in California. Proposition 227, entitled "English Language Education for Children in Public Schools," was regarded by many as a renewed attempt by the anti-immigration lobby to discourage immigration by making education less accessible. The proposition mandated that "all children in California public schools shall be taught English by being taught in English" (Unz and Tuchmann, cited in Crawford 1999). The rhetoric of the campaign was seen as successful, as many immigrants themselves seemed to be in favor of it, and finally the proposition was passed with a higher-than-expected margin, thus making English-only the official language policy in California.

These various political and policy debates have one startling feature in common: whenever findings based on established methods of linguistic analysis are introduced in an attempt to reveal the linguistic bases of the issue, the findings tend to be overwhelmed by the ideologies of standardization. Those ideologies are so powerful that language research that challenges them is not only discounted but often suppressed. Yet it is precisely this kind of research that can give us nonreductive understandings of the nature of language and lead to more informed public policy.

Notes

1. This chapter was completed before we had an opportunity to read Richard Bauman and Charles L. Briggs, *Voices of Modernity: Language Ideologies and the Politics of Inequality* (2003), and therefore we were not able to take account of their contribution.

References

Agha, Asif. 1993. Grammatical and Indexical Conventions in Honorific Discourse. *Journal of Linguistic Anthropology* 3(2): 131–63.

Anderson, Benedict. 1983. *Imagined Communities: Reflections on the Origin and Spread of Nationalism.* London: Verso.

Bauman, Richard, and Charles Briggs. 2000. Language Philosophy as Language Ideology: John Locke and Johan Gottfried Herder. In *Regimes of Language: Ideologies, Polities, and Identities,* ed. Paul V. Kroskrity, pp. 139–204. Santa Fe, NM: School of American Research Press.

———. 2003. *Voices of Modernity: Language Ideologies and the Politics of Inequality.* Cambridge: Cambridge University Press.

Bennett, William J. 1992. The Bilingual Education Act: A Failed Path. In Crawford 1992: 358–63.

Berlin, Isaiah. 1977. *Herder and Vico: Two Studies in the History of Ideas.* New York: Vintage Books.

Blommaert, Jan, and Jef Verschüren. 1998a. *Debating Diversity: Analysing the Discourse of Tolerance.* London: Routledge.

———. 1998b. The Role of Language in European Nationalist Ideologies. In *Language Ideologies: Practice and Theory,* ed. Bambi B. Schiefflin, Kathryn A. Woolard, and Paul V. Kroskrity, pp. 189–210. New York: Oxford University Press.

Bopp, Franz. [1816] 1974. *Analytical Comparison of the Sanskrit, Greek, Latin and Teutonic Languages, Shewing the Original Identity of Their Grammatical Structure.* Edited by E. F. K. Koerner. Amsterdam: Benjamins.

Briggs, Charles. 2000. "Bad Mothers" and the Threat to Civil Society: Race, Cultural Reasoning, and the Institutionalization of Social Inequality in a Venezuelan Infanticide Trial. *Law and Social Inquiry* 25(2): 299–354.

Calvet, Louis-Jean. 1987. *La guerre des langue.* Paris: Payot.

Cazden, Courtney, and Catherine Snow, eds. 1990. *English Plus: Issues in Bilingual Education.*

Annals of the American Academy of Political and Social Sciences, vol. 508. Newbury Park, CA: Sage.

Collins, James. 1998. Our Ideology and Theirs. In *Language Ideologies: Practice and Theory,* ed. Bambi B. Schiefflin, Kathryn A. Woolard, and Paul V. Kroskrity, pp. 256–70. New York: Oxford University Press.

———. 1999. The Cultural Wars and Shifts in Linguistic Capital. *International Journal of Qualitative Studies in Education* 12(3): 269–86.

Crawford, James. 1992. *Language Loyalties: A Source Book on the Official English Controversy.* Chicago: University of Chicago Press.

———. 1999. *Bilingual Education: History, Politics, Theory, and Practice.* 4th ed. Trenton: Crane Publishing.

Crowley, Tony. 1996. *Language in History: Theories and Texts.* London and Boston: Routledge.

Fishman, Joshua A. 1968. Sociolinguistics and the Language Problems of Developing Countries. In Fishman, Ferguson, and Das Gupta 1968: 3–16.

Fishman, Joshua A., Charles Ferguson, and Jyotirindra Das Gupta, eds. 1968. *Language Problems of Developing Nations.* New York: John Wiley.

Gal, Susan, and Judith T. Irvine. 2000. Language Ideology and Linguistic Differentiation. In *Regimes of Language: Ideologies, Polities, and Identities,* ed. Paul V. Kroskrity, pp. 35–83. Santa Fe, NM: School of American Research Press.

Garvin, Paul L. 1964. The Standard Language Problem: Concepts and Methods. In *Language in Culture and Society: A Reader in Linguistics and Anthropology,* ed. Dell H. Hymes, pp. 521–26. New York: John Wiley.

Gumperz, John J. 1971. The Speech Community. In *Language in Social Groups,* selected and introduced by A. Dill, pp. 114–28. Stanford, CA: Stanford University Press.

———. 1996. The Linguistic and Cultural Relativity of Inference. In *Rethinking Linguistic Relativity,* ed. John J. Gumperz and Stephen C. Levinson, pp. 374–406. Cambridge: Cambridge University Press.

Habermas, Jürgen. 1989. *The Structural Transformation of the Public Sphere.* Cambridge: Polity Press.

Hacking, Ian. 1999. *The Social Construction of What?* Cambridge: Harvard University Press.

Hanks, William F. 1987. Discourse Genres in a Theory of Practice. *American Ethnologist* 14(4): 688–92.

———. 1996a. *Language and Communicative Practices.* Boulder, CO: Westview Press.

———. 1996b. Language Form and Communicative Practice. In *Rethinking Linguistic Relativity,* ed. John J. Gumperz and Stephen C. Levinson, pp. 232–70. Cambridge: Cambridge University Press.

Harris, Roy. 1987. *Reading Saussure.* London: Duckworth.

Heath, Shirley Brice. 1980. Standard English: A Biography of a Symbol. In *Standards and Dialects of English,* ed. Timothy Schopen and Joseph M. Williams, pp. 3–32. Cambridge, MA: Winthrop.

Hill, Jane H. 1998. Language, Race, and White Public Space. *American Anthropologist* 100(3): 680–89.

Hill, Jane H., and Ophelia Zapeda. 1993. Mrs. Patricio's Trouble: The Distribution of Responsibility in an Account of Personal Experience. In *Responsibility and Evidence in Oral Discourse,* ed. Jane H. Hill and Judith T. Irvine, pp. 197–225. Cambridge: Cambridge University Press.

Lippi-Green, Rosina. 1996. *English with an Accent: Language, Ideology, and Discrimination in the United States.* London: Routledge.

Lucy, John, ed. 1993. *Reflexive Language: Reported Speech and Metapragmatics.* Cambridge: Cambridge University Press.

Milroy, Jim. 2000. Historical Description and the Ideology of Standard Language. In Wright 2000: 11–28.

Mugglestone, Lynda. 1995. *Speaking Proper: The Rise of Accent as a Social Symbol.* Oxford: Clarendon Books.

Ochs, Elinor. 1996. Linguistic Resources for Socializing Humanity. In *Rethinking Linguistic Relativity,* ed. John J. Gumperz and Stephen C. Levinson, pp. 407–37. Cambridge: Cambridge University Press.

Ong, Aihwa. 1999. *Flexible Citizenship: The Cultural Logics of Transnationality.* Durham, NC: Duke University Press.

Pinker, Stephen. 1999. *Words and Rules: The Ingredients of Language.* New York: Basic Books.

Rosaldo, Renato, and Jonathan X. Inda. 2001. *The Anthropology of Globalization.* Oxford: Blackwell.

Sarris, Greg. 1993. Keeping Slug Woman Alive: The Challenge of Reading in a Reservation Classroom. In *The Ethnography of Reading,* ed. Jonathan Boyarin, pp. 239–69. Berkeley and Los Angeles: University of California Press.

Sato, Charlene. 1991. Sociolinguistic Variation and Language Attitudes in Hawaii. In *English around the World: Sociolinguistic Perspectives,* ed. Jenny Cheshire, pp. 640–63. Cambridge: Cambridge University Press.

Saussure, Ferdinand de. [1916] 1966. *Course in General Linguistics,* ed. Charles Bally and Albert Sechehaye. Translated by Wade Baskin. New York: McGraw Hill.

Saussure, Ferdinand de, and Tulio de Mauro
———. 1976. *Cours de linguistique générale.* Paris: Payot.

Secada, Walter. 1990. Research, Politics and Bilingual Education. In Cazden and Snow 1990: 81–106.

Silverstein, Michael. 1996. Monoglot "Standard" in America: Standardization and Metaphors of Linguistic Hegemony. In *The Matrix of Language: Contemporary Linguistic Anthropology,* ed. Donald Brennis and Ronald K. S. Macaulay, pp. 284–306. Boulder, CO: Westview Press.

Silverstein, Michael, and Greg Urban, eds. 1996. *The Natural Histories of Discourse.* Chicago: University of Chicago Press.

Tomasello, Michael. 1999. *The Social Origins of Human Cognition.* Cambridge: Harvard University Press.

Urla, Jacqueline. 1987. Being Basque, Speaking Basque: The Politics of Language and Identity in the Basque Country. PhD dissertation, Department of Anthropology, University of California, Berkeley.

Watts, Richard J., and Anthony Bex, eds. 2000. *Standard English: The Continuing Debate.* London: Routledge.

Whiteley, Wilfred H., ed. 1971. *Language Use and Social Change: Problems of Multilingualism with Special Reference to East Africa.* London: Oxford University Press.

Woolard, Kathryn A. 1998. Introduction: Language Ideology as a Field of Enquiry. In *Language Ideologies: Practice and Theory,* ed. Bambi B. Schiefflin, Kathryn A. Woolard, and Paul V. Kroskrity, pp. 3–47. New York: Oxford University Press.

Wright, Laura, ed. 2000. *The Development of Standard English, 1300–1800: Theories, Descriptions, Conflicts.* Cambridge: Cambridge University Press.

CHAPTER 13

Blood and Belonging: Long-Distance Nationalism and the World Beyond

Nina Glick Schiller

"**B**LOOD, IT'S BLOOD that makes you a Haitian." The power of these words struck me as I sat in a yard in Haiti, interviewing a woman whose face showed the rigors and deprivations of her life. I was in the midst of a study to ascertain whether those who stayed in their homeland believed that people who had migrated, settled abroad, and become U.S. citizens were still a part of Haiti. Most people said they were, and I repeatedly heard people speak of Haitian blood. On this particular day, the use of the concept of blood to claim political connections between a dispersed population suddenly led me to a new set of questions about the continuation of national identities and their use by disempowered people. I knew that references to blood and descent were utilized by Nazi Germany to justify the mass murder of millions of people. Why was I hearing metaphors of blood from poor people who wanted to insist that the Haitian diaspora had obligations to Haiti?

Currently, around the world, we are witnessing a revitalization of biological metaphors to mark belonging—that is, claims that people share a common history or political destiny because of "blood ties." Metaphors of blood in particular are being used to create political identity in the midst of globalization. They legitimate a biological reductionism; that is, they constitute an ideology that explains human behavior and passions on the basis of inherited physical traits. As in other forms of reductionism, claim makers explain complex phenomena by reference to underlying components. Those who deploy biological metaphors of belonging assume that identities and loyalties are inherent and inherited and therefore able to persist across generations and despite changes in culture and language. This form of reductionism envisions the world as divided into unchanging and inherently different peoples, each with its own culture and ethos derived from a distinct biological nature. Economic and social conditions that shape social action, beliefs, and identities have no place in this view of the world. Nor are there possibilities for struggle, change, political movements, or states based on new forms of social and political identities and goals.

From the end of the nineteenth century to World War II, social and biological scientists endorsed a view that linked the concepts of race and nation. Political leaders created public policies and laws based on these beliefs until these beliefs were discredited after the Holocaust. However, concepts of blood remained embedded within citizenship laws. A wide variety of states—from Germany to the Dominican Republic—never fully abandoned the practice of allocating citizenship on the basis of blood ties, a practice called in legal terminology *jus sanguinis* (the law of blood).

Today the link between blood and nation is once again being deployed within a wide range of nationalist struggles, although references to race are less frequent. Many of these campaigns, such as those that followed the breakup of Yugoslavia and the Soviet Union, are supported, and to a certain extent financed, from afar. Members of immigrant groups, identifying themselves as "diasporas" and sometimes building on biblical images of dispersal and return, utilize radio, television, newspapers, books, and the Internet in a passionate effort to maintain their identification with a distant territory they continue to call home. When identification takes the form of transnational political projects to build a state, I call such an ideology, and the actions it motivates, long-distance nationalism (Anderson 1992, 1993; Fuglerud 1999; Skrbiš 1999; Glick Schiller and Fouron 2001b). Long-distance nationalism binds together migrants, their descendants, dispersed minority populations, and people who continue to live within the territory claimed as the homeland into a single trans-border citizenry. As in other versions of nationalism, the concept of a territorial homeland governed by an independent state that represents the nation remains salient, but the notion of a biological belonging rather than the confines of national borders defines the limits of membership in the nation.[1] Long-distance nationalism does not exist only in the domain of the imagination and sentiment. It leads to specific action. These actions link a dispersed population to a specific homeland and its political system.[2]

I begin this chapter with an exploration of the genesis of the tendency to equate concepts of race and nation, the emergence of metaphors of blood to signal identity with a specific nation and its history, and the discrediting of this mode of thinking about belonging. I then describe the various sets of actors who have revived metaphors of blood during the current era of globalization. Reflecting on the renewed salience of long-distance nationalism, I conclude on a cautionary note. Ideologies of belonging and collective identification that invoke biology and metaphors of blood can justify genocidal actions against others who are judged not to belong. However, the same metaphors may serve to unite people desperately struggling to obtain social justice against those with much greater power and to legitimate and popularize their claims to land, resources, or life itself.

Written in Blood: The Previous Union of Race and Nation

External physical differences of skin color, hair type, or facial features, which we casually refer to as "races," do not in any way correlate with other genetically based differences between populations (Brace 1964; Goodman 1995; Marks 1995; Montagu 1964). Nonetheless, precisely because governments, medical data, the media, and people around the world continue the practice of categorizing people in terms of external appearances that they call race, these categories continue to shape our lives. Therefore, although race is a socially constructed, rather than biologically meaningful, category, race matters (Harrison 1995; Hartigan 2000; Mukhopadhyay and Moses 1997; Sheriff 2001). Ideas about race continue to be used to justify, maintain, or impose inequalities of power and resources. And it is this continuity of placing people into racial categories, a process that anthropologists and sociologists call "racialization," that gives continuing life to the intersection of ideas about biology and national identity (Barot and Bird 2001).

The scholarly analysis of racialization is often undertaken without reference to the contemporary analysis of nationalism and the continuing significance of national identities in the midst of current globalization. Too frequently scholars who deplore the violence done to people through direct racist attacks, as well as the destructive effects of the imposition of racial categories, fail to link the processes of racialization to past and present-day nation-building projects.[3] Even authors such as Barot and Bird (2001), who acknowledge the overlap of meanings of race and nation in the past, do not explore the contemporary revival of references to blood and descent as the basis of national identity. When rhetorics of blood and nation are addressed, they are usually in relationship to Germany or to the rise of neo-Nazi movements in Europe or the United States, without a careful exploration of the way in which Nazi politics and science drew from and contributed to globally disseminated ideas about biologically based belonging that remain with us (see, e.g., Linke 1997).[4]

The term "nation" in many of the languages of Europe has a common origin and a similar historical transformation of meaning and usage. There was no connotation of government or state in early meanings of the term, which employed variations of the Latin word *natio* to mean "origin," "birth," "descent group," or "local descent group" (Hobsbawm 1992: 15).[5] In the eighteenth and nineteenth centuries, intellectuals and sectors of political elites in Europe and the Americas, seeking a basis for political sovereignty other than monarchical claims of divine right or colonial assertions of civilizational or religious superiority, popularized a discourse about the nation. For example, in 1789 the French National Assembly, in taking the path of revolution, asserted in their "Declaration of the Rights of Man and of the Citizen": "The principle of all sovereignty resides essentially in the nation" (National Assembly of France 1789). But what was "the nation"?

At the end of the eighteenth century, the nation was not yet clearly delimited by shared language, culture, or descent but was understood to reside in nature—that is, as an aspect of the natural regularities that could be studied by enlightened reason. The observations of nature made by the philosophers of the Enlightenment were configured by the context in which they wrote: the expansion of Europe and the development of capitalism through the conquest and colonization of the Americas and of Asia, and the enslavement of indigenous and African peoples. It was in this framework of exploitation that authors such as Hume, writing in 1748, avowed, "There never was a civilized nation of any other complexion than white" (cited in Gates 1986: 10). Hume popularized a concept of whiteness, which he believed differentiated civilized nations and "all other species of men (for there are four or five different kinds)" (cited in Gates 1986: 10). In this usage, the concept of "species of men" is not directly equated with nation; rather, nation is equated with polity and nations are ranked according to the physical inherited traits of their inhabitants. In the course of the nineteenth century, as political writers searched for a new basis of political legitimization for emerging European statecraft, the word "nation" was transformed and conflated with the concept of race.

The word "race," at the time of the beginning of European expansion in the fifteenth and sixteenth centuries, had been used generally for strains of animals rather than people (Lesser 1999: 7; Smedley 1993). Perhaps the earliest European effort to clearly delineate nations as biologically distinct populations was the political justification used by the English in their colonization of Ireland in the seventeenth century (Smedley 1993; Allen 1995). The English legitimated the oppression of people in Ireland by referring to supposed racial differences that separated them from the Irish; the dynamics of oppression simultaneously created the conceptions of the Irish and English races and linked notions of race and nationality.

The word "race" became widespread as a way of thinking about human difference during the course of the fifteenth- and sixteenth-century European conquests of the Americas and Asia and the accumulation of capital from the African slave trade.[6] In writings from the seventeenth to the mid–nineteenth century, although blackness was linked to physical and mental inferiority and the relationship between appearance and national character was a subject of study, each nation was not yet seen as having a distinctive people.

Early equations of race and nation occurred in the Americas in the eighteenth century, before the nation-state-building projects of Europe were fully articulated (Anderson 1993). There, nation-building elites faced the task of legitimating the establishment of republics that had broken away from European monarchial rule and that lacked established historical traditions and cultures. For example, from Benjamin Franklin's desire to see the new nation as "lovely white" to the first naturalization laws, which allocated the right to become citizens only to whites, U.S. nationalism was built on the idea that out of the many European nationalities would emerge a single white nation (Takaki 1990).

As the nineteenth century advanced, political elites and their allies, who were struggling to obtain or maintain state power, popularized national histories that authenticated and legitimated their dominion over the population living in a particular territory. This nation-state building shaped collective memories (Anderson 1993; Hobsbawm 1992; Gellner 1983). Central to nation-state building were myths about peoplehood. According to these myths, each state contained within it a single nation or people defined by their residence in a common territory, their undivided loyalty to a common government, and their shared origins and destiny.

In many European nations it was not until the end of the nineteenth century that national history came to be seen in terms of particular bloodlines—Anglo-Saxon, Germanic, Slavic, for example (Horsman 1981).[7] Concepts of shared blood that in the feudal political economy of Europe had been used to legitimate differences between nobles and commoners were transformed within an emerging capitalism. Shared blood became a way of imagining the unity of persons within a polity, in counterdistinction to those outside of it, who were seen as of inferior blood, that is, racially different. The shared unity of blood within a nation masked the competing interests of class and the hierarchies of gender.

Scholars of nationalism such as Hobsbawm have emphasized the role of political leaders in creating myths of nationhood by quoting certain nationalist leaders of the nineteenth century. For example, on the occasion of the first meeting of the parliament after Italy had been united, Massimo d'Azeglio remarked, "We have made Italy; now we have to make Italians." Similarly, Colonel Piłudski, the "liberator of Poland," observed, "It is the state which makes the nation and not the nation the state" (Hobsbawm 1992: 44–45). However, in establishing theories of membership in states based on lines of descent, nationalists deployed a political rhetoric that resonated with quotidian practices of family. Nationalists popularized notions of peoplehood that built on references to shared blood found in many localities in the world (Herzfeld 1992, 1997). Neither top-down nor bottom-up, and not separate from what Gilbert Joseph and Daniel Nugent (1994) called "everyday forms of state formation," political theory united with the "common sense" embedded in folk ideologies. The result of this potent mix was the marriage of the concepts of biology and belonging.

As migration increased from Europe, the Middle East, and Asia to the Americas, the concept of a peoplehood united by blood contributed to making salient the home ties of emigrants and incorporating them in transnational nation-state-building projects. Contrary to the post–World War II image of the immigrant as uprooted—popularized through the scholarship of Handlin and U.S. assimilationist ideology—the majority of emigrants at the turn of the twentieth century were transmigrants who lived their lives across borders (Handlin 1973; Glick Schiller 1999a). That is to say, many of the persons who migrated came to obtain capital for family projects back home; they maintained their home ties and, in the case of migrants from such places as Italy, Turkey, Poland, and Hungary, returned home or circulated between Old World and New (Park 1950; Wyman 1993; Cinel 1982, 1991). Often these migrants came with only localized identities, but once faced with racialization in the Americas, discrimination, or segregation, many became engaged in homeland nationalist projects (Glick Schiller 1999a, 1999b). They became long-distance nationalists, espousing ideas about belonging that linked them with people in their homeland and taking action on behalf of their ancestral territory.

By the beginning of the twentieth century, the conflation of race and nation had become part of disparate and often competing political projects (Lebovics 1992). The concept of race simultaneously justified imperial adventures abroad while contributing to the cross-class political unity of the population of the nation-states that were centers of imperialism (Horsman 1981; Takaki 1990). The most powerful states at the time used this ideology as part of the double-sided political projects that not only marked the world of colonizer and colonized but also separated those immigrants who were acceptable for assimilation from the undesirable. In England, for example, beginning with the conquest of Ireland and extending through the Indian Raj, intellectuals and political leaders projected images of colonized racialized others that contributed to the construction of the "British Race" (Miles

1993; Stoler 1989). From the 1880s to the end of the 1920s, U.S. immigration laws, which from the beginning allowed only whites to naturalize, distinguished between the races deemed part of the fundamental American Anglo-Saxon stock and the inferior, undesirable races, such as the Chinese, Italians, Slavs, Serbs, and Jews.

Social scientists in the United States supported such distinctions through their research and writing (Fairchild 1947). Horace Kallen, for example, the philosopher who first popularized the term "cultural pluralism," believed that an immigrant group could never change its identity because "racial quality persists, and is identifiable . . . to the end of generations" (cited in Gleason 1980: 44). Around the world the elites of countries that experienced colonization or a strong Western military presence responded to the dominance of Europe by obtaining educations in Europe or the United States and by accepting and incorporating into their own political projects European ideas about race and nation. They formulated ideologies of biological belonging that reflected both their own experiences of exile, migration, and exclusion and the notion common in Western science and politics of the time that "nations" had distinctive racial genealogies.

Indian elites at the end of the nineteenth century built on European scholarship that canonized Sanskrit texts and that posited a golden age of Hinduism linked to Aryan rule. Ideas about race, religion, and nation contributed to their conceptualization of an Indian nation (van der Veer 1999). Sun Yat-sen, the founder of the Chinese Kuomintang Party, lived for sixteen years in the United States, Japan, and Europe, enmeshed in transnational political efforts to build the Chinese nationalist movement. In his efforts to organize against the Confucian ethos that legitimated the Chinese imperial state, he popularized the notion that national identities have a racial foundation. In his influential statement "Three Principles of the People," which he presented in China in 1923, Sun stated: "The greatest force is common blood. The Chinese belong to the yellow race because they come from the bloodstock of the yellow race. The blood of ancestors is transmitted by heredity down through the race, making blood kinship a powerful force" (cited in Dikötter 1997: 4). Japanese formulations of national identity used a similar language of blood informed by the study of anthropology and the experiences of Japanese elites abroad (Dikötter 1997).

That is not to say that the Third World nationalism that emerged was only a "derivative discourse." Each nation-state built on embedded folk beliefs and indigenous schools of thought about hierarchy, kinship, and identity (Chatterjee 1993). But, beginning in the middle of the nineteenth century, Asian and Latin American reformers and modernizers found legitimation for their political projects in social Darwinism, the scientific racism of nineteenth-century anthropology, and the explicitly racist writings of Joseph de Gobineau (Dikötter 1997; Stepan 1991).

In effect, the conception of the state with which these leaders operated was one of a transnational nation-state in which the population was united by blood rather than residence in a common territory.[8] On the basis of the continuities of blood ties, the Hungarian, Italian, Japanese, and Chinese governments at various times before World War II created special government offices to work with and represent their emigrants settled abroad. Irish leaders seeking independence from England or Korean leaders struggling from 1915 to 1945 against their inclusion in the Japanese empire looked to their emigrants and their descendants for support. They defined these emigrants as members of their national population, united in a struggle for their motherland (Brown 1966; Harrington 1980). Addressing an organization of Germans settled in forty-eight different countries, Rudolf Hess, a builder of the Nazi state, asserted: "The German everywhere is a German—whether he lives in the Reich, or in Japan, in France or in China, or anywhere else in the world. Not countries or continents, not climate or environment, but blood and race determine the world of ideas of the German" (cited in Kamenka 1976: 11). German Nazi ideology was built on an understanding of an indelible link between nation and race that was, by the 1930s, a global ideology.

In the period after World War I, all states began to reinforce their territorial boundaries by requiring passports and monitoring transnational political processes more closely. The United States challenged the transnational loyalties of its European immigrants by launching Americanization and naturalization campaigns. Yet messages about the link between race and nation remained. Such a logic was embedded in the U.S. government internment of the Japanese—including persons who held U.S. citizenship—during World War II, reinforcing the ideology that, at least for persons defined as nonwhite, racial identities were intricately linked to national loyalties to territorially based ancestral states. Moreover, these home ties were not erased even when persons were born outside their ancestral land and were no longer citizens of that state.

It was not until after World War II that a new conception of the relationship between nation-states and populations became hegemonic among political leaders around the world, as well as among emigrating populations. In this new conceptualization, the entire globe was depicted as the domain of discrete nation-states. A government's sovereignty was contained within the territorial borders of its state. Each person belonged to a state, and each person could have only one state. Scholars of immigration ignored or forgot the continuing transnational connections of immigrants and portrayed them as uprooted persons who had abandoned home and family for their new land (Handlin 1973). The institutionalization of the United Nations and the replacement of colonial empires by newly independent states served to popularize this new conception of the human condition.[9] The postwar era and the response to the Nazis' use of the race concept thoroughly discredited the equation of race with nation, and the language of blood and race disappeared from nationalist rhetoric in many locations.

Equations of Race and Nation in the Era of Globalization

Despite the fact that the work we do, the food, clothes, and other commodities we purchase, the music we dance to, and the fads we fancy are increasingly part and parcel of a global system of production and consumption, we currently are witnessing a revitalization of the rhetoric of blood in contemporary political projects. Because racial claims were discredited after World War II, the resurgent European Right generally avoids direct references to racial differences. Instead this revitalization is, in part, fueled by the fact that a significant, vocal, and growing sector of the population of states around the world—including people who have lived their entire lives in the states in which they reside and are citizens of those states—are long-distance nationalists. They claim that their homeland is elsewhere. Such claims, common before World War I, have once again become politicized, vehement, organized, and linked to nation-state-building projects in distant lands. Once again, those who make this type of transnational political connection, which is both personal and organizational, employ biological metaphors of belonging and speak about ties of blood and descent. References to national membership based on blood ties abound in nationalist struggles around the world and resonate with the political aspirations of dispersed populations.

In the past, rhetorics of connection through descent to an ancestral land often were linked to calls to return and "build the land," and certain political movements continue to make this demand. Today, however, members of dispersed populations who speak of blood connections to a nation often do not plan to return to reside permanently in the territory of their homeland. Many of these people want dual citizenship, so that they can belong to two states simultaneously: their state of residence and the distant state they call home. They contribute to a dissident conception of the nation-state, which extends the domain of the state to wherever its members reside.[10] They may use an ideology of long-distance nationalism to gain access to the European Union, as do persons of Portuguese ancestry who heed the declaration by the Portuguese government that it is a global nation that includes those who emigrated to various diasporic locations (Feldman-Bianco 1992, 2001). Or long-distance nationalists may fuel continuing political tensions by forming a base area for the expansionist claims of their homeland, as in the case of Croatian populations in Herzegovina (Skrbiš 1999).

It is important to note that, at the present historical conjuncture, disparate situations seem to stimulate the same type of ideological response. Claims to ancestral identities are being made by diverse sets of actors. These different actors draw on both their life experiences and the growing identity movements that popularize notions of inherited membership in communities based on shared descent.[11] Here I note five sets of actors who currently are employing metaphors of biological belonging as a basis for constructing and maintaining long-distance nationalism. In some situations of transnational nation-state building, such actors—with diverse motivations, class positions, and personal histories—coalesce, strengthening the collective political project and also making it more complex as it becomes imbued with multiple political agendas. In other instances, different social positions are filled by the same actors—for example, when political exiles or members of emigrant diasporas return home to occupy leadership roles in the homeland government while still maintaining their transnational connections with emigrant associations and family abroad. Often there are significant political differences and struggles within a single set of actors, as, for example, among various political factions of Tamil refugees from Sri Lanka (Fuglerud 1999).

In the following listing, I describe various sets of actors who articulate ideologies of biological belonging as if each set performed discrete roles within a single political drama. This delineation must be understood only as a beginning point for identifying the multiple conditions that generate long-distance nationalism.[12]

POLITICAL EXILES

Political exiles are perhaps the most familiar characters in the drama of long-distance nationalism. They play significant roles in developing a political narrative in which all those who have been dispersed are obligated to return and rebuild the homeland. Zlatko Skrbiš (1999) argues that long-distance nationalism develops only if an emigrant population contains a critical mass of political exiles. Beginning in the nineteenth century and continuing into the present, political activists and ideologues who were forced to flee by repressive governments tend to keep alive into future generations a dream of returning to rebuild their "homeland."[13] In the lands to which they have been dispersed they are politically insignificant and often of low social status. Whatever social standing they are able to maintain depends on their building a political constituency abroad and keeping palpable the goal of returning home to political power and social position. As new generations are born who are culturally different from their parents and who are not fluent in their "mother tongue," metaphors of a blood-based peoplehood are often used to link these generations to their "homeland." Skrbiš has described the crucial role of Croatian political exiles in Australia in nurturing the long-distance nationalism of the second generation.[14] In creating their long-distance nationalism, those in the Croatian diaspora "revived the thesis that Croatians are not actually Slavs" but the "descendants of an ancient state Harauhvatis (mentioned by Zarathustra), which existed between 630–553 B.C." (1999: 95).

LAW AND POLICY MAKERS IN THE COUNTRY OF SETTLEMENT

The law and public-policy makers of the country of settlement may contribute, however inadvertently, to the construction of long-distance nationalism and an ideology of biological belonging. Very different kinds of laws of host countries may have similar effects because, in different ways, they serve to treat an entire immigrant population as a uniform whole and, in so doing, give them a public identity and history. Currently, European Union policies make economic immigration very difficult and allow entry to people only for limited purposes such as marriage, certain forms of family reunion, and asylum. In order to win recognition as political refugees, individuals often highlight their identification with dissident political movements in their homelands, encouraging identities that are linked to efforts to build new nation-states. The politicization of Tamil and Eritrean diasporas and the growth of Kurdish identities and its accompanying long-distance nationalism have been fueled by this form of state policy.

In some cases, when laws restrict persons from abroad from obtaining citizenship in their land of settlement, immigrants and their children have little option other than to continue their homeland identities. Until very recently this was the situation that faced the large number of Turks settled in Germany and Koreans settled in Japan. Now German lawmakers finally have allowed Turkish immigrants who can demonstrate full incorporation in Germany and who renounce their Turkish citizenship to become German citizens. In response, Turkey has developed "pink cards" that allow these ex-citizens special privileges in Turkey. However, few Turks in Germany choose this path. They maintain their Turkish citizenship, fearing that, whatever their actual citizenship, they will still be treated as foreigners in Germany and that the pink card will limit their political and economic possibilities in their homeland (Çaglar 2002).

States such as Great Britain and France that wish to limit immigration have resorted to reviving, strengthening, or creating citizenship laws that limit access to the state to those who are defined as sharing common blood. Although such laws are motivated by efforts to restrict access to the country for people of color from former colonies who had previously been given citizenship rights, they are having unintended consequences. For example, the children and grandchildren of emigrants from England and France who now are U.S. citizens have discovered that they can claim citizenship in their ancestors' homeland. This new access to rights encourages an interest in blood and genealogy.

The state of settlement also can fuel the long-distance nationalism of its immigrants and refugees through its foreign-policy goals. This may happen even when, as in the case of the United States, the newcomers are able to become naturalized citizens and there are many assimilative pressures, including an official policy of inculcating political loyalties to the new land in all immigrant populations. Throughout the Cold War, the governments of the United States and Canada fostered the long-distance nationalism of political exiles from what they called the oppressed nations of Eastern Europe and the Soviet Union. Organizations of these oppressed nationalities were made members of the Nationalities Division of the U.S. Democratic Party and of the National Republican Heritage Groups of the Republican Party (Redding 1958; Glick Schiller 1999a, 1999b; Weed 1973). The U.S. government accorded similar treatment to Cuban, Vietnamese, and Cambodian refugees. In fact, emigrants from these countries were classified as political refugees, whatever their personal motivations in migrating. These policies bore fruit at the end of the Cold War, when emigrants with strong roots in the United States or Canada returned to leadership positions in their homeland. Returning from the United States, Valdas Adamkus became the president of Lithuania after it achieved independence in 1990, while Gojko Šašak left Canada to become first the minister of emigration, then minister of defense, of the new state of Croatia. Šašak was instrumental in military efforts to claim Herzegovina as a historic part of Croatia on the basis of the common descent of "Croatians" in Herzegovinian territory (Skrbiš 1999: 8).

POLITICAL LEADERS AND PUBLIC OFFICIALS OF THE HOMELAND

The contemporary situation of Turks in Germany—encouraged by the Turkish government to become German citizens by ensuring that they will maintain some rights and membership in Turkey—points to another set of actors who may forge long-distance nationalism: the political leaders and public officials of the homeland government.

The homeland country may play a significant role in creating or stimulating metaphors of blood ties that foster and maintain long-distance nationalism. Emigrant-sending countries such as Mexico, Colombia, the Dominican Republic, the Philippines, Eritrea, India, Croatia, Ecuador, Brazil, Portugal, and Haiti have recently instituted policies that reach out to their diasporas, seeing them as source of remittances, development capital, and funding for campaigns to maintain national independence or expand the borders of the state (Feldman-Bianco 2001; Graham 1997; Guarnizo 1999; Pessar 1995; A. Smith 1971; Lessinger 1995; Çaglar 2003; Renshon 2001). The "Croatian diaspora" was allocated twelve of the ninety-two seats in Parliament (Skrbiš 1999: 184).[15] The Colombian Constitution now provides for the representation of populations abroad, while Portugal has an official council of Portuguese abroad (Feldman-Bianco 2001; Sanchez 1997).[16] Increasingly, these states see their populations settled in the United States as political lobbies that can defend the homeland. More and more governments are granting dual nationality; others have extended voting rights to emigrants who have become citizens of other countries. Through these changes, as well as the establishment of special ministries responsible for the diasporic populations, the political leaders of these countries signal that emigrants, as well as their children, remain members of the nation of their birth, connected to the homeland on the basis of descent.

KIN "LEFT BEHIND"

The policies and pronouncements of emigrant-sending states may resonate with some of the needs and aspirations of kin left at home, and these kin may become another set of actors who deploy ideologies of biological belonging. Migrants generally leave behind families needing support and persons to whom they are indebted for the money to travel. Rhetorics of blood and nation may be employed by kin in the home country as a way of legitimating and maintaining vital family connections that help them build better housing, send children to school, feed and clothe a wide family network, and improve their social standing. Many Haitians in Haiti—living in an economy dependent on remittances—maintain the belief that those who have emigrated remain Haitian, whatever their legal citizenship, because "their blood remains Haitian."

EMIGRANTS, FIRST AND SECOND GENERATION

Family members abroad may have their own reasons for sustaining narratives of connectedness. Obligations to family left behind depend on communications and transport systems that can send money, information, and goods across international borders and into often remote locations. These needs may make migrants more attuned to homeland politics and issues of development than they were before migration. In the process, they also

learn and embrace the metaphors of blood ties disseminated and legitimated by homeland governments to hold on to their constituencies within
the diaspora. Emigrants, past or present, rarely come from the lowest economic strata of a country because it takes a certain degree of personal or
family resources to migrate. In the contemporary global economy, in which
the gap between rich and poor countries continues to grow, persons from
poor countries who have relatively high levels of education and class standing can earn more by emigrating and performing menial labor in restau-
rants, factories, and service professions abroad than they can in professional
work at home. Often, migrants who experience a loss of social standing
maintain their personal self-esteem by identifying with the homeland, in-
vesting their wages in the social system there, and supporting national narratives that underline their membership in an ancestral homeland, one either already constructed or envisioned (Fuglerud 1999; Goldring 2001).

Migrants settled abroad and their children, even those who have obtained citizenship in their new land, may also articulate an ideology of biological belonging as a response to the racism and negative stereotyping that
they confront in their daily lives. Since 1965, the racialization of Latin American, Caribbean, and Asian migrants in the United States—who tend to be
lumped into broad categories like Hispanic, Asian, and black rather than
distinguished by country of origin—has led many individuals to increase
their identification with their homeland.[17] Their racist treatment in the new
land keeps migrants and their children alive to homeland identities and politics as a source of self-esteem. There are vocal Haitian second-generation
youth, for example, who say "Haiti is me" and "Haiti is my pride," identifying with Haiti not as their cultural roots but as a location to which they belong (Glick Schiller and Fouron 2001a, 2001b). The stereotype of Croatians
in Australia as hotheaded irrational nationalists has contributed to the long-
distance nationalism of second-generation Croatians, some of whom "returned" to Croatia in the 1990s to join the military struggle to build the
Croatian nation-state (Skrbiš 1999).

Whither Long-Distance Nationalism?

How are we to understand the fact that such disparate actors, with different
motivations and goals, share a commitment to the same political ideology
and practices? Why are they all long-distance nationalists? Elsewhere, I have
examined the links between contemporary globalization (defined as the
rapid and worldwide flow of information and goods in the context of the re-
structuring of capitalist relationships) and the long-distance nationalism of
populations in states that are the losers in the global economy (Glick Schiller

and Fouron 1998, 2001b). Current processes of globalization increase economic and political insecurity in these states, fostering migration and the necessity for migrants to support those left behind. Meanwhile, migrants become "helots"—despised but needed labor (Balibar and Wallerstein 1991; Cohen 1987). I have argued that globalization thus fuels territorially based identities and long-distance nationalism from below (see also Smith and Guarnizo 1998). But such an analysis does not encompass the multiple actors and locations from which this ideology is being built, nor does it explain the revitalization of ideologies of biological belonging in the twenty-first century.

If we look more closely at the ideas expressed about diaspora and the persistent ties of blood, we see that in using the same metaphors and the same concepts of peopleness and ancestry, the various actors actually are utilizing a common discourse to express very different, even conflicting, political agendas. People seeking different goals ground their claims in references to the nation because, in our contemporary world, the nation is one of the few forms of identification that has widespread legitimacy (Gellner 1983). People everywhere have been conditioned to think of the world as divided into nation-states and the world's people as divided into nationalities. Consequently, when people come to speak of cross-border connections that they wish to portray as ongoing and imbued with emotion and responsibility, they turn to metaphors of nation and envision long-distance ties as an extension and embodiment of the nation.

Long-distance nationalism can be readily deployed to encompass disparate political agendas because all forms of nationalism serve as "floating signifiers." That is to say, they can hold contradictory meanings, allowing people to pursue diametrically different views of the future, all motivated by a love for their homeland (Glick Schiller and Fouron 2001b). Much of the literature on nationalism distinguishes between good and bad types of nationalism, comparing a democratic or civil type with an authoritarian or ethnic form (Gellner 1983; Kohn 1965). Such distinctions, I believe, miss the point.

All nationalisms draw from a storehouse of biological imagery that can be used for oppressive purposes, beginning with the concept of a "people" in whose interests the government of a particular state acts. Often nationalisms have drawn on reductionist strands of social science to construct or validate such imagery (Hayden 1993). This was the case not only in Germany, with its twentieth-century citizenship laws based on descent, but also in France, which until recently defined its citizens solely in terms of their compliance with republican ideas. The French government celebrated their nation throughout the first half of the twentieth century by exhibitions that distinguished true French nationals from colonials, using the racial categories legitimated by anthropologists of that period (Lebovics 1992). Mexico and an array of Latin American states have continued to uphold *mestizaje* (race mixing) as central to the making of their national identity (C. Smith 1997). Hungary is currently reaching out and claiming citizens in its neighboring states as "kin," in the name of their Hungarian "mother nation" (Stewart 2003).

At the same time, within nationalist movements there can emerge "subaltern forms of autonomous political process and democratic action" (Cockell 2000: 340). James Scott observes that, very often, disempowered people sustain "a sharply dissonant political culture" expressed beyond the intimidating gaze of the powerful. They express their resistance through "a hidden transcript," a "politics of disguise and anonymity that takes place in public view but is designed to have a double meaning" (Scott 1990: 18–19). Nationalist rhetorics also can be used by the poor and disempowered to express their own meanings within a shared public discourse about the nation. In this case, transgressive meanings are attributed to the same rhetoric and symbols.

This process became clear to me when my co-researcher, Georges Fouron, and I listened to the tapes of 104 interviews we conducted in Haiti in 1996 about the relationship between those in Haiti and the Haitian diaspora. Until that point I was puzzled as to why Georges, who supports worldwide struggles against oppression, was a fervent Haitian long-distance nationalist. I myself rejected all contemporary nationalism, including the Zionism of my family, that justified political action on the basis of fixed, biologically based linkages among people and between people and territory.[18] The women and men whom Georges and I interviewed, many of them young and most of them struggling to find their next meal and with little hope for any future, answered our questions about the Haitian state and nation by expressing their love of Haiti and their belief in the enduring connections between Haiti and Haitians abroad. As they did so, they offered glimpses of their aspirations for a different world, in which the state would be responsible to and for the people and in which people could live like human beings.

I do not want to romanticize this form of identity politics. And I want to emphasize that there is certainly no single unified view "from below": neither poor people—whether in rural or urban settings—nor members of a diaspora hold only one perspective and see the world through a single lens. Our informants' love of Haiti is tempered by jealousies and distrust, which exist alongside ongoing family ties and cooperation between neighbors. In multiple ways their narratives reflect the vast divisions among those who identify as Haitian: between rural and urban people, between upper and lower urban social classes, and between those in Haiti and those living abroad. Moreover, there is now a widespread disillusionment with the formal political process and all political leaders. Nonetheless, there is an alternative agenda, and this alternative is embedded within Haitian long-distance nationalism.

The agenda for justice, which links the immediate needs of families to demands for fundamental economic change, appeared as an underlying text in many of our interviews, as impoverished women and men spoke about "the Haitian people" and the need for the state to be responsible to the people. Haitians in the diaspora and in Haiti use an identification with their country to call their leaders to account and to make demands for fundamental change and an end to exploitation in Haiti and around the world.

In the midst of globalization, long-distance nationalism can mobilize people to demand liberation from hunger, poverty, malnutrition, and political oppression. In this sense, oppositional or subaltern long-distance nationalism can contribute to transnational social movements that resist various forms of oppression. As Homi Bhabha has pointed out, "Alternative constituencies of peoples and oppositional analytical capacities" are emerging "within the recesses of national culture" (1990: 3).

Certainly the concept of race continues to be used to excuse and justify ongoing inequalities, as the widespread dissemination of Rushton's *Race, Evolution, and Behavior* (1999) and Herrnstein and Murray's *The Bell Curve* (1994) makes clear. However, it is also clear that the meaning of any word—whether it is "race," "nation," or "anthropology"—is never fixed. As Michael Herzfeld has pointed out, "Any ideology, no matter how consistent its formal expression, may produce radically divergent applications and interpretations" (1992: 14). The concepts of "race" and "nation"—whether these terms are used in narratives of racial purity or in celebrations of hybridity and multiculturalism—are "discursive formations," shared ways of speaking, which have multiple and contradictory meanings that change depending on time, place, and speaker. From this perspective, the debate between biological anthropologists, who continue to use the term "race," replacing its former meaning with a concept of localized populations adapted to specific environments, and the social constructionists, who insist that race is a cultural construct and has no utility in our anthropological vocabulary, misses the point.

It is not sufficient merely to point out, as did Franz Boas, that "racial descent is not the basis of nationality" ([1928] 1962: 90) or even to declare that, whatever its biological status, race matters because notions of race have real effects. Nor is it sufficient to combat reductionism by insisting that race and nationality are social constructions. It is important to combat continually the idea that cultural differences stem from inherited biological differences and to make it clear that neither our natures nor our identities are produced by our genes, or our "blood." However, it also important to understand why disempowered people embrace in their struggles forms of "strategic essentialism," including metaphors of blood (Sturgeon 1999: 257). There are reasons why people struggling against those with much greater control of resources and violent force resort to reductionism.

We must address ideologies of biological belonging by acknowledging that there are multiple meanings and usages contained within the same metaphors, and that there are today multiple actors who continue to construct and articulate nationalism, including long-distance nationalism, on the basis of blood ties. Among those who speak of blood and descent are disempowered people who are responding to the growing inequalities within and between states. Rather than despair about the reduction of identity to biology or dismiss all ideologies that define belonging in biological terms, we need to understand and contest the conditions in the world that promote forms of identification through metaphors of blood and nation—among the oppressed as well as the oppressors.

Notes

1. In offering this definition I mean to distinguish long-distance nationalism from a diasporic consciousness that does not focus on a particular nation-state-building project or homeland.

2. In approaching long-distance nationalism as both words and action—so that nationalism constitutes the state and is constituted by it—I build on Craig Calhoun's statement that "there is nationalism as discourse: the production of cultural understandings and rhetoric which leads people around the world to think and frame their aspirations in terms of the idea of nation and national identity. . . . there is (also) nationalism as project: social movements and state policies by which people attempt to advance the interests of collectivities they understand as nation" (1997: 6).

3. Among those who have reminded us of the historical links between race and nation are Balibar and Wallerstein (1991), Miles (1993), and Williams (1989).

4. For discussions of the link between Nazi science and science elsewhere, see Dikötter 1998.

5. According to *Cassell's Latin Dictionary* the word *natio* means "birth." Cicero used the word in this sense, as in *externae nationes* (those born outside Rome). The Latin word is often translated into English as "tribe," "race," or "people," a translation that loses the original meaning of the word and conveys the false impression that the concept of race and the equation of race with nation dates from Roman times. See also Hannaford 1996.

6. For evidence of this transition, see Blumenbach [1776] 1969; Kant (1775), as cited in Gates 1986: 10.

7. It is interesting to note that the initial classic discussions of nationalism by European in-

tellectuals earlier in the nineteenth century did not equate nation with race. See, e.g., Herder [1784] 2001; Renan [1882] 1994. However, one cannot argue, as Ernst Gellner (1983) did, that the concepts of nation and race remained independent.

8. The fact that persons born in Japan, China, or Korea could not become U.S. citizens reinforced the continuing link that Asian immigrants in the United States had to their home government. However, those home governments also saw themselves as representing the descendants of their emigrants who were born in the United States and were U.S. citizens. The Japanese government used its consuls in the United States to closely monitor Japanese immigrants (Harrington 1980; see also Kwong 1996: 101).

9. In reality, states varied in the degree to which they abandoned dual-citizenship policies and instituted the practices of a territorially restricted nation-state. Although Asian immigrants were accorded citizen rights in the United States after World War II, the governments of both South Korea and the Republic of China continued to regard emigrant populations as parts of their states. They maintained close supervision of their emigrants settled in the United States throughout the Cold War (Kim 1981).

10. In 1994, Linda Basch, Cristina Szanton Blanc, and I called this notion of the nation-state a "deterritorialized nation-state" (Basch, Glick Schiller, and Szanton Blanc 1994). However, this form of state formation continues to be predicated on a territorially based state, the homeland, despite the fact that persons considered to be members of the nation-state may reside throughout the world and can hold citizenship in other states. Therefore, I now call this form of state a transnational nation-state (Glick Schiller 1999a).

11. A whole new academic discipline of diaspora studies has developed to study those who claim a history of connection based on ancestral ties.

12. Rather than using the term "long-distance nationalism," Khachig Tölölyan (2000), referring to the history of what he calls the "Armenian Transnation," employs the term "exilic nationalism" for projects of nation-state building spearheaded by dispersed elites who organize to establish or reestablish a political state. He calls the ideology and practices of belonging that establish dispersed populations as part of a distant homeland, after the establishment of a nation-state, "diasporic transnationalism." This is a useful distinction.

13. Some argue that even before the modern political theory of the nation-state with its concept of a sovereign people, Jewish priests exiled in Babylonia produced historical myths and metaphors of diaspora that have resonated through the millennia (Aberbach 2000; Grosby 1999).

14. Skrbiš, whose ethnographic focus is the second generation, does not explore the Croatian use of metaphors of blood. He does point out that politicians in Australia tend to use a language of ethnic community and in so doing "promote a belief that an ethnic group member . . . recognizes his/her fellow ethnic group members metaphorically as a brother/sister-in-blood" (1999: 61).

15. It is important to note that not every government with a sizable emigrant population welcomes the participation of the diaspora in homeland politics, and even when this participation is legally possible, it may be contested or discouraged. The Republic of Slovenia, another of the new states created by the breakup of Yugoslavia, gave no seats to the diaspora, although citizens living in other countries are allowed to vote (Skrbiš 1999: 184).

16. As Feldman-Bianco (2001) argues, countries that were former colonial powers such as Portugal also are reviving ties and influence with former colonies, a strategy that differs from the transnational politics of countries in Latin America and Asia.

17. These broad and imposed categories of identity have also been politicized and have become labels of self-reference within pan-ethnic movements (Espiritu 1992).

18. Although I had supported national liberation movements that united colonized people to struggle for independence from imperial powers, I was also painfully aware of the ways in which Jewish long-distance nationalism supported an anti-Arab racism in Israel and in the United States.

References

Aberbach, David. 2000. The Roman-Jewish Wars and Hebrew Cultural Nationalism. *Nations and Nationalism* 6(3): 347–62.

Allen, Theodore. 1995. *The Invention of the White Race: Racial Oppression of State Control.* Vol. 1. London: Verso.

Anderson, Benedict. 1992. The New World Disorder. *New Left Review* 193: 2–13.

———. 1993. *Imagined Communities: Reflections on the Origin and Spread of Nationalism.* Rev. ed. London: Verso.

——— 1994. Exodus. *Critical Inquiry* 20: 314–27.

Balibar, Etienne, and Immanuel Wallerstein. 1991. *Race, Nation, Class: Ambiguous Identities.* New York: Verso.

Barot, Rohit, and John Bird. 2001. Racialization: The Genealogy and the Critique. *Ethnic and Racial Studies* 24(4): 601–18.

Basch, Linda, Nina Glick Schiller, and Cristina Szanton Blanc. 1994. *Nations Unbound: Transnational Projects and the Deterritorialized Nation State.* New York: Gordon and Breach.

Bhabha, Homi, ed. 1990. *Nation and Narration.* New York: Routledge.

Blumenbach, Johann. [1776] 1969. *On the Natural Varieties of Mankind.* New York: Bergman Publishers.

Boas, Franz. [1928] 1962. *Anthropology and Modern Life.* New York: W. W. Norton.

Brace, Loring. 1964. A Nonracial Approach towards the Understanding of Human Diversity. In *The Concept of Race,* ed. Ashley Montagu, pp. 103–52. London: Collier Macmillan.

Brown, Thomas. 1966. *Irish-American Nationalism, 1870–1890.* Philadelphia: Greenwood.

Çaglar, Ayshe. 2002. The Discrete Charm of Dual Citizenship: Citizenship Ties, Trust, and the "Pink Card." In *Unraveling Ties: From Social Cohesion to New Practices of Connectedness,* ed. Yehuda Elkana, Ivan Krestev, Elisio Macamo, and Shalini Randeria, pp. 248–62. Frankfurt: Campus Vorlag.

———. 2003. Encountering the State in Migration-Driven Transnational Social Fields: Turkish Immigrants in Europe. Habilitation thesis, Department of Sociology and Anthropology, Free University of Berlin.

Calhoun, Craig. 1997. *Nationalism.* Minneapolis: University of Minnesota Press.

Chatterjee, Partha. 1993. *Nationalist Thought and the Colonial World: A Derivative Discourse?* Princeton: Princeton University Press.

Cinel, Dino. 1982. *From Italy to San Francisco.* Stanford: Stanford University Press.

———. 1991. *The National Integration of Italian Return Migration, 1870–1929.* Cambridge: Cambridge University Press.

Cockell, James. 2000. Ethnic Nationalism and Subaltern Political Process: Exploring Autonomous Democratic Action in Kashmir. *Nations and Nationalism* 6(3): 319–45.

Cohen, Robin. 1987. *The New Helots: Migrants in the International Division of Labour.* Aldershot: Gower.

Dikötter, Frank. 1998. Race Culture: Recent Perspectives on the History of Eugenics. *American Historical Review* 103(2): 467–78.

Dikötter, Frank, ed. 1997. The Construction of Racial Identities in China and Japan: Historical and Contemporary Perspectives. Honolulu: University of Hawai'i Press.

Espiritu, Yen Lee. 1992. *Asian American Panethnicity: Bridging Institutions and Identities.* Philadelphia: Temple University Press.

Fairchild, Henry Pratt. 1947. *Race and Nationality as Factors in American Life.* New York: Ronald Press.

Feldman-Bianco, Bela 1992. Multiple Layers of Time and Space: The Construction of Class, Race, Ethnicity, and Nationalism among Portuguese Immigrants. In *Towards a Transnational Perspective on Migration: Race, Class, Ethnicity, and Nationalism Reconsidered,* ed. Nina Glick Schiller, Linda Basch, and Cristina Blanc Szanton, pp. 145–74. New York: New York Academy of Sciences.

———. 2001. Brazilians in Portugal, Portuguese in Brazil: Constructions of Sameness and Difference. *Identities: Global Studies in Culture and Power* 8(4): 607–50.

Fuglerud, Øivind. 1999. *Life on the Outside: The Tamil Diaspora and Long Distance Nationalism.* London: Pluto Press.

Gates, Henry Lewis, Jr. 1986. Editor's Introduction: Writing "Race" and the Difference It Makes. In *"Race," Writing, and Difference,* ed. Henry Lewis Gates, Jr., pp. 1–20. Chicago: University of Chicago Press.

Gellner, Ernst. 1983. *Nations and Nationalism.* Ithaca: Cornell University Press.

Gleason, Philip. 1980. American Identity and Americanization. In *Harvard Encyclopedia of American Ethnic Groups,* ed. Stephan Thernstrom, pp. 31–58. Cambridge, MA: Belknap Press.

Glick Schiller, Nina. 1999a. Transmigrants and Nation-States: Something Old and Something New in U.S. Immigrant Experience. In *Handbook of International Migration: The American Experience,* ed. Charles Hirschman, Josh DeWind, and Philip Kasinitz, pp. 94–119. New York: Russell Sage.

———. 1999b. Who Are These Guys? A Transnational Perspective on National Identities. In *Identities on the Move: Transnational Processes in North America and the Caribbean Basin,* ed. Liliana Goldin, pp. 15–43. Houston: University of Texas Press.

Glick Schiller, Nina, Linda Basch, and Cristina Blanc Szanton. 1992. Transnationalism: A New Analytical Framework for Understanding Migration. In *Towards a Transnational Perspective on Migration: Race, Class, Ethnicity, and Nationalism Reconsidered,* ed. Nina Glick Schiller, Linda Basch, and Cristina Blanc Szanton, pp. 1–24. New York: New York Academy of Sciences.

Glick Schiller, Nina, and Georges Fouron. 1998. Transnational Lives and National Identities: The Identity Politics of Haitian Immigrants. In *Transnationalism from Below,* ed. Michael Peter Smith and Luis Guarnizo, pp. 130–61. New Brunswick, NJ: Transaction Publishers.

———. 1999. Terrains of Blood and Nation: Haitian Transnational Social Fields. *Ethnic and Racial Studies* 22(2): 340–66.

———. 2001a. The Generation of Identity: Redefining the Second Generation within a Transnational Social Field. In *Migration, Transnationalism, and the Political Economy of New York City,* ed. Hector Cordero-Guzman, Ramon Grosfoguel, and Robert Smith, pp. 58–86. Philadelphia: Temple University Press.

———. 2001b. *Georges Woke Up Laughing: Long Distance Nationalism and the Apparent State.* Durham, NC: Duke University Press.

Goldring, Luin. 2001. The Gender and Geography of Citizenship in Mexico-U.S. Transnational Spaces. *Identities: Global Studies in Culture and Power* 7(4): 501–38.

Goodman, Alan. 1995. The Problematics of "Race." In *Biological Anthropology: The State of the*

Science, ed. Noel Boaz and Linda Wolfe, pp. 215–39. Bend, OR: International Institute for Human Evolutionary Research.

Graham, Pamela. 1997. Reimaging the Nation and Defining the District: Dominican Migration and Transnational Politics. In *Caribbean Circuits: New Directions in the Study of Caribbean Migration,* ed. Patricia Pessar, pp. 91–126. Staten Island, NY: Center for Migration Studies.

Grosby, Steven. 1999. The Chosen People of Ancient Israel and the Occident. *Nations and Nationalism* 5(3): 357–80.

Guarnizo, Luis. 1999. Transnational Migration: A View from Colombia. *Ethnic and Racial Studies* 22(2): 397–421.

Handlin, Oscar. 1973. *The Uprooted.* 2nd ed. Boston: Little, Brown.

Hannaford, Ivan. 1996. *Race: The History of an Idea in the West.* Baltimore, MD: Johns Hopkins University Press.

Harrington, Mona. 1980. Loyalties: Dual and Divided. In *Harvard Encyclopedia of American Ethnic Groups,* ed. Stephan Thernstrom, pp. 678–86. Cambridge, MA: Belknap Press.

Harrison, Faye V. 1995. The Persistent Power of "Race" in the Cultural and Political Economy of Racism. *Annual Reviews in Anthropology* 24: 47–74.

Hartigan, John, Jr. 2000. Whiteness in the Field. Special issue, *Identities: Global Studies in Culture and Power* 7(3): 269–440.

Hayden, Robert. 1992. The Triumph of Chauvinistic Nationalisms in Yugoslavia: Bleak Implications for Anthropology. *Anthropology of East Europe Review* 11(1–2). http://condor.depaul.edu/~rrotenbe/aeer/aeer11_1/hayden.html.

Herder, Johann Gottfried. [1784] 2001. Ideas for a Philosophy of History of Mankind. In *Nations and Identities: Classic Readings,* ed. Vincent Pecora, pp. 87–92. Malden, MA: Blackwell.

Herrnstein, Richard J., and Charles Murray. 1994. *The Bell Curve: Intelligence and Class Structure in American Life.* New York: Free Press.

Herzfeld, Michael. 1992. *The Social Production of Indifference: Exploring the Symbolic Roots of Western Bureaucracy.* Chicago: University of Chicago Press.

———. 1997. *Cultural Intimacy: Social Poetics in the Nation State.* New York: Routledge.

Hobsbawm, Eric. 1992. *Nations and Nationalism since 1780.* 2nd ed. New York: Cambridge University Press.

Horsman, Reginald. 1981. *Race and Manifest Destiny: The Origins of American Racial Anglo-Saxonism.* Cambridge: Harvard University Press.

Joseph, Gilbert M., and Nugent, Daniel, eds. 1994. *Everyday Forms of State Formation: Revolution and the Negotiation of Rule in Modern Mexico.* Durham, NC: Duke University Press.

Kamenka, Eugene. 1976. Political Nationalism—The Evolution of the Idea. In *Nationalism: The Nature and Evolution of an Idea,* ed. Eugene Kamenka, pp. 2–20. New York: St Martins.

Kim, Illsoo. 1981. *New Urban Immigrants: The Korean Community in New York.* Princeton: Princeton University Press.

Kohn, Hans. 1965. *Nationalism, Its Meaning and History.* Princeton: Van Nostrand.

Kwong, Peter. 1996. *The New Chinatown.* Rev. ed. New York: Hill and Wang.

Lebovics, Herman. 1992. *True France: The Wars over Cultural Identity, 1900–1945.* Ithaca: Cornell University Press.

Lesser, Jeffrey. 1999. *Negotiating National Identity: Immigrants, Minorities, and the Struggle for Ethnicity in Brazil.* Durham, NC: Duke University Press.

Lessinger, Johanna. 1995. *From the Ganges to the Hudson: Indian Immigrants in New York City.* Boston: Allyn and Bacon.

Linke, Uli. 1997. Gendered Difference, Violent Imagination: Blood, Race, Nation. *American Anthropologist* 99(3): 559–73.

Marks, Jonathan. 1995. *Human Biodiversity: Genes, Race, and History.* Hawthorne, NY: Aldine de Gruyter.

Miles, Robert. 1993. *Racism after "Race Relations."* New York: Routledge.

Montagu, Ashley. 1964. *Man's Most Dangerous Myth: The Fallacy of Race.* Oxford: Oxford University Press.

Mukhopadhyay, Carol, and Yolanda Moses. 1997. "Race" in Anthropological Discourse. *American Anthropologist* 99(3): 517–33.

National Assembly of France. 1789. Declaration of the Rights of Man and of the Citizen. http://members.aol.com/agentmess/frenchrev/mancitizen.html.

Park, Robert. 1950. *Race and Culture.* New York: Free Press.

Pessar, Patricia. 1995. *A Visa for a Dream.* Boston: Allyn and Bacon.

Redding, Jack. 1958. *Inside the Democratic Party.* Indianapolis, IN: Bobs-Merrill.

Renan, Ernst. [1882] 1994 Qu'est-ce qu'une nation? In *Nationalism,* ed. John Hutchinson and Anthony Smith, pp. 17–18. Oxford: Oxford University Press.

Renshon, Stanley. 2001. Dual Citizenship and American National Identity Center for Immigration Studies. http//: www.cis.org/articles/2001/paper20/renshonmexico.htm.

Rushton, J. Philippe. 1999. *Race, Evolution, and Behavior.* New Brunswick, NJ: Transaction Publishers.

Sanchez, Arturo. 1997. Transnational Political Agency and Identity Formation among Colombian Immigrants. Paper presented at the Conference on Transnational Communities and the Political Economy of New York, New School for Social Research, New York, October 19.

Scott, James. 1990. *Domination and the Arts of Resistance: Hidden Transcripts.* New Haven: Yale University Press.

Sheriff, Robin. 2001. *Dreaming Equality: Color, Race, and Racism in Urban Brazil.* New Brunswick, NJ: Rutgers University Press.

Skrbiš, Zlatko. 1999. *Long Distance Nationalism: Diasporas, Homelands and Identities.* Aldershot, England: Ashgate.

Smedley, Audrey. 1993. *Race in North America: Origin and Evolution of a World View.* Boulder, CO: Westview.

Smith, Anthony. 1971. *Theories of Nationalism.* London: Duckworth.

Smith, Carol. 1997. The Symbolics of Blood: Mesitizaje in the Americas. *Identities: Global Studies in Culture and Power* 4(3): 495–522.

Smith, Michael Peter, and Luis Guarnizo, eds. 1998. *Transnationalism from Below.* New Brunswick, NJ: Transaction Publishers.

Smith, Robert. 1998. Transnational Localities. In Smith and Guarnizo 1998: 196–240.

Stepan, Nancy. 1991. *The Hour of Eugenics: Race, Gender, and Nation in Latin America.* Ithaca: Cornell University Press.

Stewart, Michael. 2003. The Hungarian Status Law: A New European Form of Transnational Politics? *Diaspora* 12(1): 67–102.

Stoler, Ann. 1989. Making Empire Respectable: The Politics of Race and Sexual Morality in the 20th Century Colonial Cultures. *American Ethnologist* 16(4): 643–60.

Sturgeon, Noel. 1999. Ecofeminist Appropriations and Transnational Environmentalisms. *Identities: Global Studies in Culture and Power* 6(2): 255–80.

Takaki, Ronald. 1990. *Iron Cages: Race and Culture in 19th Century America.* New York: Oxford University Press.

Tölölyan, Khachig. 2000. Elites and Institutions in the Armenian Transnation. Paper presented at the Social Science Research Council Conference on Transnational Migration, Princeton, NJ, June 29–30.

van der Veer, Peter. 1999. Hindus: A Superior Race. *Nations and Nationalism* 5(3): 419–30.

Weed, Perry. 1973. *The White Ethnic Movement and Ethnic Politics.* New York: Praeger.

Williams, Brackette. 1989. A Class Act: Anthropology and the Race to Nation across Ethnic Terrain. *Annual Reviews of Anthropology* 18: 401–44.

Wyman, Mark. 1993. *Round-Trip to America: The Immigrants Return to Europe, 1880–1930.* Ithaca: Cornell University Press.

CONTRIBUTORS

JENNY COOK-GUMPERZ is a sociologist and professor of education at the University of California, Santa Barbara. A revised edition of her 1986 edited volume, *The Social Construction of Literacy*, is scheduled to appear in 2005. Recent articles are "Reproducing the Discourse of Mothering" (1996) and "Co-operation, Collaboration and Pleasure in Work: Issues for Intercultural Communication at Work" (2001). Her current research focuses on issues of language socialization, literacy, and life-long learning.

EVE DANZIGER is associate professor in the Department of Anthropology at the University of Virginia. From 1991 to 1997 she was senior research fellow at the Max Planck Institute for Psycholinguistics in the Netherlands. Her research concerns the relationship between language diversity and thought, and is informed by her long-standing interaction with the Mopan Maya–speaking people of Eastern Central America with whom she has been working since 1986. Her publications include *Relatively Speaking: Language, Thought and Kinship in Mopan Maya* (2001) and articles that explore the psychological aspects of cultural particularities in Mopan grammar, vocabulary, and language use.

WILLIAM A. FOLEY is professor of linguistics at the University of Sydney. His research interests include syntax and semantics, language and culture, and the Southeast Asia and Pacific region. He is author of *The Papuan Languages of New Guinea* (1986), *The Yimas Language of New Guinea* (1991), *Anthropological Linguistics: An Introduction* (1997), and many journal articles and book chapters.

AGUSTÍN FUENTES is an associate professor of anthropology at the University of Notre Dame. His research focuses on human and primate behavior, conflict negotiation, and the role of cooperation in human evolution. Recent publications include the coedited volume *Primates Face to Face: Conservation Implications of Human and Nonhuman Primate Interconnections* (2002, with Linda Wolf) and articles on the evolution of pair bonds, social organization, and human-nonhuman primate interconnections.

KATHLEEN R. GIBSON, a biological anthropologist, is professor of neurobiology and anatomy, University of Texas–Houston, Medical School, and professor of orthodontics, University of Texas–Houston, Dental Branch. Her research concerns the evolution and development of primate and human brains and cognition. Her books include *"Language" and Intelligence in Monkeys and Apes: Comparative Developmental Perspectives* (1990, with S. Parker); *Brain Maturation and Cognitive Development: Comparative and Cross-cultural Perspectives* (1991, with A. Petersen); *Tools, Language, and Cognition in Human Evolution* (1993, with T. Ingold); *Modelling the Early Human Mind* (1996, with P. Mellars); *Social Learning in Mammals: Comparative and Ecological Perspectives* (1999, with H. Box); and *Evolutionary Anatomy of the Primate Cerebral Cortex* (2001, with D. Falk).

NINA GLICK SCHILLER is professor of anthropology at the University of New Hampshire and a recurring visiting professor at the Max Planck Institute for Social Anthropology, Germany. She has conducted research in Haiti, Germany, and the United States and has published articles on transnational migration, methodological nationalism, racialization, ethnicity, long-distance nationalism, identity, simultaneous incorporation, and AIDS. The founding editor of the journal *Identities: Global Studies in Culture and Power,* her books include *Towards a Transnational Perspective on Migration* (1992), *Nations Unbound: Transnational Projects, Postcolonial Predicaments, and the Deterritorialized Nation-State* (1994, with Linda Basch and Cristiana Szanton Blanc), and *Georges Woke Up Laughing: Long Distance Nationalism and the Search for Home* (2001, with Georges Fouron).

ALAN H. GOODMAN is president-elect of the American Anthropological Association, professor of biological anthropology, and the former dean of Natural Sciences at Hampshire College, Amherst, Massachusetts. He is the coeditor of *Building a New Biocultural Synthesis: Political-Economic Perspectives on Human Biology* (1998, with Thomas L. Leatherman), *Nutritional Anthropology: Biocultural Perspectives on Food and Nutrition* (2000, with Darna Dufour and Gretel Pelto), and *Genetic Nature/Culture* (2003, with Susan Lindee and Deborah Heath). His research concentrates on the intersections among political-economic processes, culture, ecology, and human biology.

JOHN J. GUMPERZ is emeritus professor of anthropology at the University of California, Berkeley. His current research centers on discourse and understanding in contemporary urban situations. Recent publications include *Rethinking Linguistic Relativity* (1996, coedited with Stephen Levinson) and *Language and Interaction: Conversations with John Gumperz* (2003, edited by Susan L. Eerdmans, et al.).

THOMAS L. LEATHERMAN is professor and chair of the Anthropology Department at the University of South Carolina, Columbia. His publications in medical, nutritional and biocultural anthropology include *Building a New Biocultural Synthesis: Political-Economic Perspectives in Biological Anthropology* (1998, with Alan H. Goodman), and *Medical Pluralism in the Andes* (2002, with Joan Koss-Chioino and Christine Greenway). He has conducted research in Peru, Mexico and the United States on issues such as the nutritional consequences of dietary globalization and the impact of poverty and inequality on human biology and health.

MARGARET LOCK is the Marjorie Bronfman Professor in Social Studies in Medicine and is affiliated with the Department of Social Studies of Medicine and the Department of Anthropology at McGill University. She is a fellow of the Royal Society of Canada and an officier de L'Ordre national du Québec, and has published the following monographs: *East Asian Medicine in Urban Japan* (1980); the prize-winning *Encounters with Aging: Mythologies of Menopause in Japan and North America* (1993), and *Twice Dead: Organ Transplants and the Reinvention of Death* (2002), which has also won awards. She has edited or coedited ten other books and written over 160 scholarly articles. Her current research is concerned with the eclipse of the nature/nurture debate, specifically post-genomic biology and its impact in the clinic, among families, communities, and society at large.

KATHERINE C. MACKINNON is assistant professor of anthropology in the Department of Sociology and Criminal Justice at Saint Louis University. She has conducted field research on various species of monkeys (notably capuchins) in Costa Rica, Panamá, Nicaragua, and Suriname. Her research interests and publications concern primate social behavior and behavioral ecology, primate growth and behavioral development, and primate conservation in Latin America.

SUSAN MCKINNON teaches at the University of Virginia, where she is associate professor of anthropology. Her research on kinship and gender in Eastern Indonesia resulted in a book titled *From a Shattered Sun: Hierarchy, Gender, and Alliance in the Tanbimbar Islands* (1991) and a number of articles that challenge anthropological models of kinship and marriage. She recently coedited (with Sarah Franklin) *Relative Values: Reconfiguring Kinship Studies* (2001), a volume that considers recent developments in the study of kinship.

LYNN MESKELL is associate professor in the Anthropology Department at Columbia University, New York. She is founding editor of the *Journal of Social Archaeology*. Her recent books include *Private Life in New Kingdom Egypt* (2002), *Embodied Lives: Figuring Ancient Maya and Egyptian Experience* (2003, with Rosemary Joyce), and *Object Worlds in Ancient Egypt: Material Biographies Past and Present* (2004).

MARY H. MORAN is an anthropologist in the Department of Sociology and Anthropology at Colgate University. She conducted fieldwork in Liberia in the early 1980s and is currently working with Liberian expatriates in the United States. Her publications include *Civilized Women: Gender and Prestige in Liberia* (1990), *The Violence of Democracy: Paradoxes of Local and National Conflict in Liberia* (forthcoming), and a number of articles on gender, violence, and identity.

MARY ORGEL received her Ph.D. in anthropology from the University of Massachusetts. Her research interests include social movements, the history of anthropology, and the anthropology of Spain.

SYDEL SILVERMAN is president emerita of the Wenner-Gren Foundation for Anthropological Research and professor emerita of anthropology at the City University of New York Graduate Center. A cultural anthropologist who carried out field and historical research in Central Italy, she also has a longstanding interest in the history of anthropology. Her latest books are *The Beast on the Table: Conferencing with Anthropologists* (2002) and *Totems and Teachers: Key Figures in the History of Anthropology* (2004).

ALAN C. SWEDLUND is a professor of anthropology at the University of Massachusetts, Amherst. His primary research interests are in historical epidemiology of the United States, and particularly New England. Recent publications have concentrated on mortality in late nineteenth- and early twentieth-century America, on population dynamics in the precontact and historical American Southwest, and on the discourses of health reformers, eugenicists, and statisticians during the late Victorian and Progressive eras. Most recently, he coedited (with Ann Herring) *Human Biologists in the Archives* (2003).

KAREN-SUE TAUSSIG is an assistant professor in the Department of Anthropology and in the Department of Medicine at the University of Minnesota. She has been studying the cultures of genetics and genetics in culture in the United States and Europe since 1993 and is currently conducting research on contemporary efforts to introduce genetics to a wide array of ordinary Americans. Her book, *Science, Culture, Imagination: Dutch Experiences of Genetic Possibility*, is forthcoming.

JACQUELINE URLA is associate professor of anthropology at the University of Massachusetts, Amherst. She is coeditor (with Jennifer Terry) of *Deviant Bodies: Critical Perspectives on Difference in Science and Popular Culture* (1995) and coauthor (with Alan Swedlund) of "The Anthropometry of Barbie" (1995). Her research interests span the fields of language politics, visual culture, gender and sexuality.

INDEX

accent, 273
Adamkus, Valdas, 300
adaptation, 24–28, 107–8, 180; male aggression as, 88–89; to Pleistocene environment, 23–25, 37–38
adapted mind, 5–6, 24
Adapted Mind, The (Barkow, Cosmides, and Tooby), 24
adoption, 109, 111, 112–13, 116
Afghanistan, 253, 258–59
Africa, 14, 251, 278; New Barbarism hypothesis, 255–57, 262
age-graded respect greeting terms, 69–71
aggression, 89, 93, 98. *See also* male aggression
Agha, Asif, 273
Akhtar, Nameera, 52
all-or-nothing categorization, 65, 67, 68, 76–77
alpha male, 94, 95
Alzheimer, Alois, 202–3
Alzheimer's Association, 196, 201
Alzheimer's disease (AD), 12–13, 30; anatomical changes, 200–201; clinicians' perspectives on genetics of, 211–13; diagnoses, 204–5; externalizing discourses, 12–13, 196, 198–99, 213–15; families and, 204, 216–17; gene-environment interactions, 208–11; genetic determinism and, 200, 206, 216–17; as historically and socially constructed, 200–202; history of, 202–5; internalizing discourses, 12–13, 196–98, 206–8; NIH study, 210–11; race and, 214–15; research design, 209–10; social construction of, 200–202, 204, 217

Alzheimer's Disease Society of Great Britain, 205
American Colonization Society, 255
analogy, 9, 83
Analytical Comparison of the Sanskrit, Greek, Latin and Teutonic Languages (Bopp), 276
ancestor groups, 125
Anderson, Benedict, 274
androcentric reductionism, 157, 165–68
anisogamy argument, 85–86
anorexia, 153n.15
anthropology. *See* archeology; biological anthropology; cultural anthropology; linguistic anthropology; primatology
antimiscegenation laws, 124
antireductionist critique, 98–99
apolipoproteinE (ApoE) gene, 207–10, 213
Applera Charitable Foundation, 229–30
Applera Corporation, 229–30
Applied Biosystems, 230
Aranda section system, 124
archeology, 2; androcentric reductionism, 157, 165–68; of sexuality and gender, 157–58; toward nonreductive accounts of gender, 171–73. *See also* Çatalhöyük; goddess movement
Aristotelian logic, 48–50, 65
arms manufacturers, 260–61
arteriosclerotic dementia, 203
Asian immigrants, 296, 307nn. 8, 9
Australian section systems, 123–24
australopithecine ancestors, 96
Austronesian languages, 56–58
Azeglio, Massimo d', 293